AN OCCASION FOR WAR

Christian quarter in Damascus, destroyed (photograph by Victor Nau de Champlouis courtesy of the Bibliothèque Nationale, Paris).

An OCCASION FOR *War*
~ CIVIL CONFLICT IN LEBANON AND DAMASCUS IN 1860

LEILA TARAZI FAWAZ

University of California Press
BERKELEY   LOS ANGELES

University of California Press
Berkeley and Los Angeles, California

Published by arrangement with I.B.Tauris & Co Ltd

© 1994 by Leila Tarazi Fawaz

Library of Congress Cataloging-in-Publication Data

Fawaz, Leila Tarazi, 1944–
    An occasion for war : Mount Lebanon and Damascus in 1860 / Leila Tarazi Fawaz.
    p.   cm.
    Includes bibliographical references (p.) and index.
    ISBN 0-520-08782-8. — ISBN 0-520-20086-1 (pbk.)
    1. Lebanon—History—Druze-Maronite conflict. 1960.
    2. Christians—Syria—Damascus—History—19th century. 3. Damascus (Syria)—History. 4. Massacres—Syria—Damascus—History—19th century. I. Title.
DS84.F38 1995
956.9204'3—dc20   94-1941
                                                                CIP

Printed in Great Britain

9 8 7 6 5 4 3 2 1

To the memory of Albert Hourani

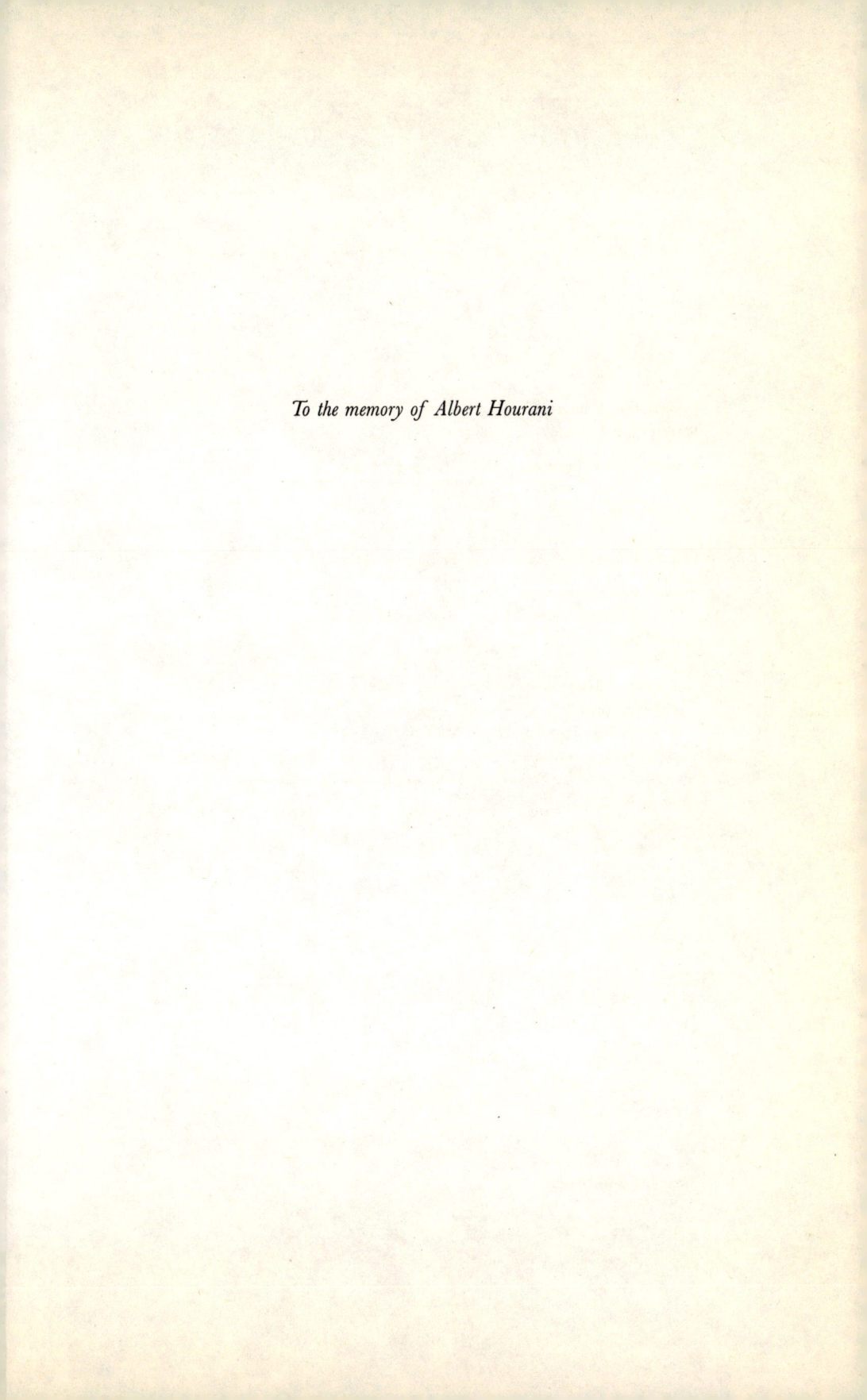

CONTENTS

Note on Transliteration and Exchange Rates · viii
List of Abbreviations · ix
Acknowledgments · x
Preface · xiii

Introduction · 1
1 Changing Worlds · 8
2 Village and Town Life on the Eve of the Civil War · 31
3 Civil War in the Mountain · 47
4 The Damascus "Incident" · 78
5 International Response · 101
6 Retribution and the Restoration of Order in Damascus · 132
7 Reconstruction and the Restoration of Order in Mount Lebanon · 164
8 The Peace Settlement · 193
9 Civil Wars Compared · 218
Appendix: Treaty of Peace between the Christians and the Druses · 229

Notes · 231
Bibliography · 279
Index · 294

Maps: 1 *Traditional Provinces of Mount Lebanon and the Immediate Neighborhood* · xvi
2 *Mount Lebanon: Towns and Villages* · xvii
3 *Damascus in the Second Half of the Nineteenth Century* · 86

NOTE ON TRANSLITERATION AND EXCHANGE RATES

Proper names commonly found in Western literature appear in their familiar latinized form. In the case of people, I have chosen the name most commonly used by the individuals or families themselves. Town and village names have insofar as possible followed common spellings. For transliteration of other Arabic words or names, I have used a simplified system based upon that of the *International Journal of Middle East Studies*, but omitting diacriticals. The prefix "al-" is used the first time a transliterated Arabic name appears in the text, but omitted later (e.g. al-Aqiqi, Aqiqi). Most of the time a roman "s" has been added to make Arabic words plural.

Because of the several different types of currency in circulation in the mid-nineteenth century and the continuously changing nature of relative prices due to debasement and depreciation, it is difficult to determine exact exchange rates. In addition, all sources do not use the same rates of exchange. Therefore, the rates of exchange have been approximated for the purposes of this study. The silver coin introduced around 1688, the *kuruş*, was known to the Europeans as the piastre. While 104 piastres were exchanged for one pound sterling in 1829, 125 piastres were exchanged for a pound sterling for the period 1860–88. The pound sterling approximated 25 French francs, which meant that 5 piastres equaled a French franc. The *kiş, kişe*, or purse, was introduced in the seventeenth century as a unit of account; 500 piastres equaled one purse.

LIST OF ABBREVIATIONS

A.D.A.	Beirut, Lebanon, Archives de la Direction Générale des Antiquités du Liban.
M.P.B.	Bkerke, Lebanon. Archives du Patriarchat Maronite.
M.W.T.	Damascus, Syria. Markaz al-Watha'iq al-Tarikhiyya (Center for Historical Documents).
Hariciye	Amman, Jordan. Markaz al-Watha'iq wa'l-Makhtutat (Center for Documents and Manuscripts). Istanbul, Turkey, Foreign Ministry papers.
A.E., CPC/B	Ministère des Affaires Etrangères, Correspondance Politique des Consuls, Turquie, Beirut.
A.E., CPC/D	Ministère des Affaires Etrangères, Correspondance Politique des Consuls, Turquie, Damas.
A.E., MD/T	Ministère des Affaires Etrangères, Mémoires et Documents, Turquie.
A.E., CP/T	Ministère des Affaires Etrangères, Correspondance Politique, Turquie.
A.E., DPB	Ministère des Affaires Etrangères, Dépêches Politiques de Beyrouth.
V.	Vincennes, France. Archives Militaires du Ministère de la Défense.
F.O.	United Kingdom. Public Record Office, London. Foreign Office.
P.R.O.N.I.	United Kingdom. Public Record Office of Northern Ireland.
U.S.	Washington, DC, National Archives. United States Consuls, Series: Dispatches from the US Consuls in Beirut, 1836–1906.
H.L.	United States. Houghton Library, Harvard University, Cambridge, Mass. Records of the Congregationalist Syrian Mission.

ACKNOWLEDGMENTS

Funding for this book was provided by the Social Science Research Council, the American Philosophical Society, and Tufts University Faculty Awards Committee and the Program in Southwest Asia and Islamic Civilization at the Fletcher School of Law and Diplomacy. I am grateful to the American University of Beirut, especially its History Department and Jafet Library, to the German Oriental Institute, the Museum of National Antiquities, the Maronite Patriarchate in Bkerke, Maronite Patriarch Nasrallah Boutros Sfeir and Father Boulos Sfeir in Lebanon; in Jordan, to the Markaz al-Watha'iq wa'l-Makhtutat at the University of Amman in Jordan and to Adnan Bakhit; in Syria, to the Markaz al-Watha'iq al-Tarikhiyya and its now retired director Da'd Hakim and other private collections, to the Institut Français d'Etudes Arabes, to Asma, Samir, Bashar, and Mazen Kallas, Mona and Bertie Nakhman, Nazim Kallas, and especially Abdul-Karim Rafeq who is one of the most helpful colleagues I have ever had the pleasure of knowing. I am also indebted in England to the staff of the Foreign Office archives of the Public Record Office, the Middle East Centre of St Antony's College, Oxford, and the Centre for Lebanese Studies which provided me with research funds and a friendly and supportive environment; in France to the Archives du Ministère des Affaires Etrangères in Paris, the Archives Militaires du Ministère de la Défense at Vincennes, the Ecole des Hautes Etudes en Sciences Sociales and the Department of History at the University of Provence, especially its division "Histoire Moderne et Contemporaine;" in the United States to Harvard's Center for Middle East Studies and to Widener Library, particularly the excellent staff at the Middle East division, the reference desk and the Document Room.

Chapters 2 and 9 reprint material that first appeared in modified form in two articles, "Understanding Lebanon," *American Scholar*, Vol. 54, no.3 (Summer 1985), pp.377–84, and "Zahle and Dayr al-Qamar: Two Market Towns of Mount Lebanon during the Civil War of 1860," in Nadim Shehadi and Dana Haffar Mills, *Lebanon: A History of Conflict and Consensus* (London: Centre for Lebanese Studies and I.B.Tauris and Co. Ltd., 1988), pp.49–63. I thank the publishers for their permission to reuse these articles here.

I am responsible for the translations from Arabic and French, except for sources that have already been published in English. In such cases, I have consulted the originals but I have quoted from the existing translations. I thank Bedia Ahmed for her translations from modern Turkish.

The Lebanese who endured the ordeals of war between 1975 and 1990 were very much on my mind as I wrote this book. They have shown admirable endurance and courage in the face of a brutal and violent war that no cause can justify.

I am grateful for the support I received on many occasions from members of Tufts University's central administration, especially from its provost Sol Gittleman who both cheered me and provided funds, and from its dean Marilyn Glater for her assistance and encouragement. Jeswald W. Salacuse of the Fletcher School of Law and Diplomacy and, before him, Theodore Elliot supported my travel and several of my projects; Andrew Hess, Richard Shultz, and the rest of the Fletcher faculty have made it pleasant and rewarding to work with them; Natalie Shatz and the rest of the staff at Ginn Library have been unflaggingly helpful. I also have gratitude for the members of the Tufts University History Department; Steven Marrone retrieved a lost chapter from the mysterious depths of my first computer; Pierre Lourent and Daniel Mulholland encouraged me when they served as chairmen of the department, as also did George Marcopoulos; Sugata Bose familiarized me with another continent and introduced me to new historiography; Lynda Shaffer also widened my intellectual horizons. My undergraduate and graduate students remain the most worthy reason for my affiliation with Tufts.

I thank Jamil Aldandany, Monica Eppinger, Anne Marie Johnson, Robert Menzi, Molly Phee, and Elizabeth Voulieris; among Tufts staff I thank Susan Buttrick, Mary Ann Kazanjian, Annette Lazzara, Constance Moynihan, and Gladys Sandmann; in Oxford, Ingrid Hobby, Fida Nasrallah, and Rachel Odams; in London, Giles Egginton and Daphne Trotter. Anna Enayat showed me exceptional kindness and gave me excellent advice; Lynne Withey was remarkably efficient and supportive. Margaret Ševčenko edited my manuscript and gave me the support and encouragement I have come to know is characteristic of her.

I owe a special debt to Kamal Salibi for his work on Lebanon, on which my own depends. I am also grateful to Walid Khalidi, Dominique Chevallier, Fuad Khuri, Michael Gilsenan, and André Raymond for their inspiration; to David Landes for his support and for suggesting the book's title; to Abdul Rahim Abou Hossein, Fuad Debbas, Abdul-Karim Rafeq,

Axel Havemann, Michael Suleiman, Eugene Rogan, Fritz Steppat, and Wheeler Thackston for providing me with copies of rare or unpublished sources; to Roger Owen and Paul Lalor for drawing my attention to the value of the Dufferin papers; to Engin Akarlı and Jean-Paul Pascual for mentioning additional sources; to Fuad Debbas and Nadim Shehadi for providing me with photographs and sources, helping me in many other ways, and welcoming me during my stays in France and England; to Paul Dumont, François Georgeon, Gilles Veinstein, and Robert Ilbert for giving me opportunities to familiarize myself with new research in France; to Makram Alameddin, Feroz and Bedia Ahmed, Tosun Aricanli, John Esposito, Fares I. Fares, Derek Hopwood, Abbas and Madge Kelidar, Boutros Labaki, Seyyed Vali R. Nasr, Carol Nichols, Assem and Vasso Salam, Wadad and Salah Salman, and John Voll for their friendship and help.

Engin Akarlı, Sugata Bose, Edmund Burke III, Cornell Fleischer, Fuad Debbas, Bruce Masters, Jean-Paul Pascual, Abdul-Karim Rafeq, James A. Reilly, and John Spagnolo read the book manuscript with meticulous and judicious attention to details. Their invaluable suggestions saved me many errors. For any left, I remain of course alone responsible.

Nakhle and Randa Tarazi, Hoda, Elie, Joumana, and Dimitri Saddi, Claire Tarazi, Salwa Fawaz, her son Rashid and daughter Leila are pillars of stability and affection in my life, and Karim Fawaz its central source of strength and pleasure.

The book, however, is dedicated to the memory of Albert Hourani who died in 1993 and without whom it would not have been written. He guided me through every stage of my research and writing, read innumerable drafts, encouraged and inspired me. He and Odile Hourani always made me feel welcome, and they became close and dear friends. He was a model of modesty, kindness, and generosity difficult to emulate, and he had an infinite capacity to care which has enriched my life.

Cambridge, Mass.
September 1994

PREFACE

The civil war of 1860 in Mount Lebanon and Damascus is well remembered by the peoples of Lebanon and Syria. Families hand down tales about it from generation to generation. It was the biggest sectarian outburst in the history of Ottoman Syria, crowning decades of social unrest. It was followed by a period of stability and peace that outlasted the Ottoman empire. This book grew out of my earlier work on Beirut in the nineteenth century and of my interest in the relationship between sectarianism and politics in the Middle East as a whole. That earlier book dealt with the growth of the city of Beirut in the nineteenth century and argued that the composition of its immigrant population reflected not only the economic opportunities of a developing port but also the political haven Beirut represented at a time when the rest of the Syrian region was unsettled. I subsequently became very interested in the hinterland of a growing metropolis, the ways in which it absorbs more pervasive socio-economic and political changes into the small scale of village and town life. Partly because of the war in Lebanon between 1975 and 1990, I decided to look into the question of how institutions and people cope with the accumulated pressures of economic, political, and administrative changes at a time of crisis, using the civil war of 1860 as a case in point.

Some excellent studies have dealt with various aspects of this civil war, and some very valuable chronicles and memoirs have been published, but until now it had not been the subject of a monograph. Part of the reason is that it remains a sensitive topic. Like so many other modern nation-states, Lebanon and Syria are made up of a mix of peoples and are consequently particularly vulnerable to references to past civil conflicts. Openly to discuss them is to stir up an unpleasant past and to risk presenting it in a divisive way. To leave them undiscussed is to make them taboos that will haunt us forever.

But caution in writing about a conflict loaded with sectarian overtones is also needed, especially in light of the current tendency to explain so much of Middle Eastern modern history in terms of sectarian issues.

Religious strife and irreconciliable political divisions are always assumed by outsiders to be the source of Lebanon's difficulties. Since 1975, when Lebanon's current troubles began, sectarian conflict and its hopelessly intertwined religion and politics were the most frequently cited reasons for the disaster. The pitfalls of generalizations are often ignored, especially those favored in the 1950s, 1960s, and early 1970s when many of these same people were trumpeting the miracle of Lebanon's harmonious social and religious society. Before 1975, Lebanon was the Switzerland of the Middle East; today "Lebanization" has become a term for a hopeless civil conflict, although Lebanon did not break up despite its long and painful war.

Nonetheless, it is possible to look into the causes of social divisions without either denying or overemphasizing their relevance, as those who have referred to the civil war in their broader histories of Lebanon and of Syria have demonstrated already. This book will try to follow in their footsteps and build on their findings, but it only begins the full investigation of this topic.

I should explain as I have done elsewhere that in the pages that follow the terms "Syria," "Syrian region," "Mount Lebanon," and "Lebanon" are used not in their modern sense but as they were used until the end of the First World War, when "Syria" and "Syrian region" referred to the territory stretching from the Taurus mountains in the north to the Sinai peninsula in the south, and from the Mediterranean on the west to the Syrian desert on the east, that had been under Ottoman rule since 1516. In this book, "Syria" and the "Syrian province" will be used to refer to the territory which today is made of the states of Lebanon, Syria, Jordan, and Israel and the West Bank.

"Lebanon," "Mount Lebanon," and "the Mountain" refer to the old territory of Mount Lebanon and not to the present-day republic. The Mountain included between the late eighteenth century and the end of the First World War both the northern and southern districts of the Lebanon range. Northern Mount Lebanon extended into the areas around the renowned Cedars of Lebanon to the limits of Jabal Akkar and south across Kisrawan; it included the districts of Bsharreh, Kura, Batrun, Jbail, Mnaitra, and Kisrawan (which, before the late eighteenth century, made up the original Mount Lebanon). The southern region covered the area south of Kisrawan and was separated from it by the Beirut–Damascus road. It included the districts often known at that time as "Jabal Druze" (Druze mountain) of Gharb (upper and lower), Jurd, Arqub, and Shuf, and the districts of the Metn, Beqaa, Jezzine, al-Tuffah, al-Kharrub, and Jabal Raihan.[1]

Note

1. For a more complete explanation of the terms "Syria," "Syrian region," "Mount Lebanon," and "Lebanon," consult Albert Hourani, *A History of the Arab Peoples* (Cambridge, Mass.: Harvard University Press, 1991), p.91; *idem, Syria and Lebanon: A Political Essay* (Beirut: Librairie du Liban, 1968), chapters 1 and 2; Kamal S. Salibi, *The Modern History of Lebanon* (London: Weidenfeld and Nicolson, 1965), pp.xi–xii; *idem, A House of Many Mansions: The History of Lebanon Reconsidered* (London: I.B.Tauris, 1988), chapter 3; Leila Tarazi Fawaz, *Merchants and Migrants in Nineteenth-Century Beirut* (Cambridge, Mass.: Harvard University Press, 1983), pp.vii–viii, and chapter 3.

MAP ONE

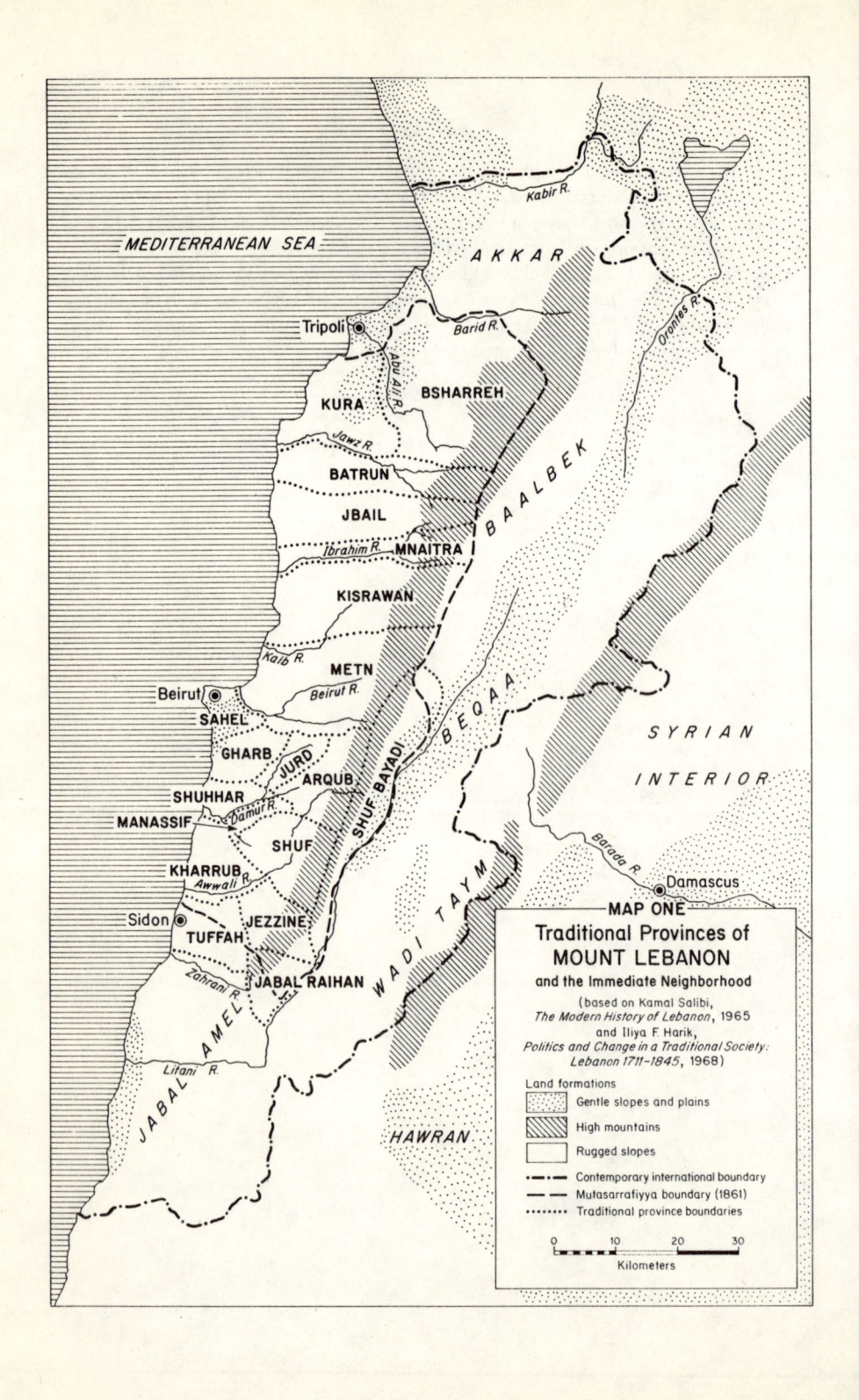

Traditional Provinces of
MOUNT LEBANON
and the Immediate Neighborhood
(based on Kamal Salibi,
The Modern History of Lebanon, 1965
and Iliya F. Harik,
*Politics and Change in a Traditional Society:
Lebanon 1711-1845*, 1968)

Land formations
- Gentle slopes and plains
- High mountains
- Rugged slopes

— · — Contemporary international boundary
— — — Mutasarrafiyya boundary (1861)
· · · · · Traditional province boundaries

0   10   20   30
Kilometers

MAP TWO

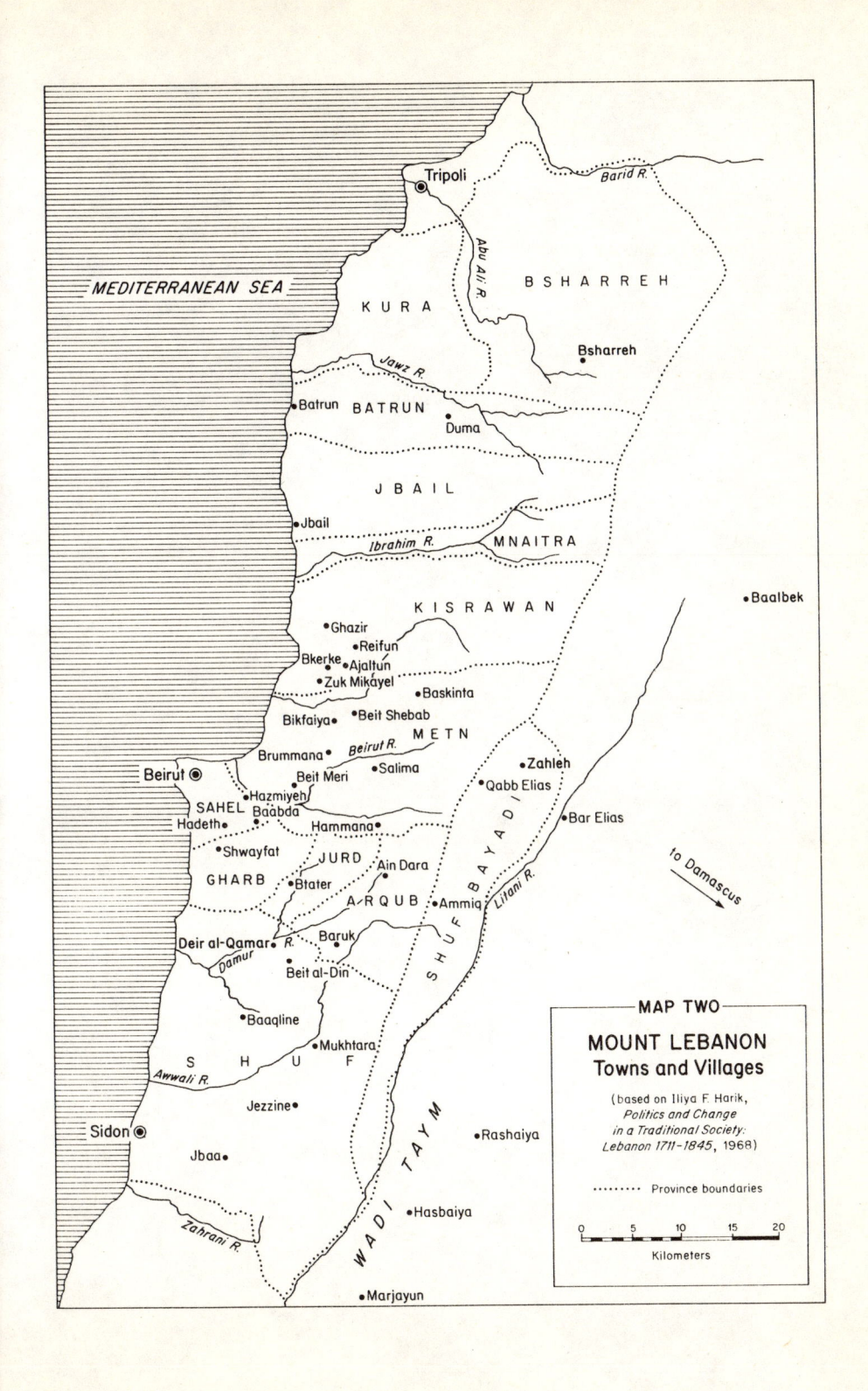

MOUNT LEBANON
Towns and Villages

(based on Iliya F. Harik,
*Politics and Change
in a Traditional Society:
Lebanon 1711–1845*, 1968)

······· Province boundaries

0 5 10 15 20
Kilometers

INTRODUCTION

Despite sporadic attempts by pre-colonial empires and the more systematic projects of European colonial empires and post-colonial nation-states to centralize state structures, the modern nation-state is in serious crisis in many parts of the contemporary world. Social and political dissidents who question central state authority have grown stronger, not weaker, in recent decades. Firm believers in the slow but sure triumph of modernity over traditional identifications had regarded the nation-state as the ultimate institutionalized form that group identity could and should assume. Yet in those parts of the world where modern nation-states have been carved out of areas with populations possessing a diversity of religious, linguistic or "ethnic" identities, such a unilinear drift, if not inexorable teleology, envisaged by the confident votaries of "high modernism" has proved to be a trifle optimistic if not entirely fanciful. Determined to assert or safeguard their distinctiveness, various social groups have clashed with their rulers and competitors alike. In doing so they have rallied around one or more, or a historically changing mix, of their social identities. Far from being an arbitrary and irrational resurgence of primordial ethnicity, the choice of a particular identity has often depended on who they were asserting themselves against, and when and why.

Since very early times most societies have fought a wide array of conflicts, pitting communities against one another or against the established order. These contests, which have sought to bring about change in the state–society nexus, have been diverse, yet one could advance a general proposition that until the twentieth century such movements in the Middle East almost always aimed not at toppling an existing order, but at acquiring a larger share of the status, power, or wealth enjoyed by members of other social groups or by those wielding state power. During the twentieth century insurrections in the Middle East have attempted to bring about radical change in social and state structures. The collective effect of the different strands of these social and political stirrings has been profound and possibly irreversible change.[1]

Although these social and political conflicts have differed in content, scope, and consequences, they have been at the broadest level connected with structural changes associated with the effects of the industrial and technological revolutions in the nineteenth and twentieth centuries. The adoption of modern technologies, the growth of cities and of population, the diffusion of Western culture and the resulting cultural gaps between a Westernized élite and the rest of the population have all become characteristic of modern history in this area, as they have been in other parts of Asia and Africa. The Western presence took various forms, from spheres of influence in the principal power centers of the region, to indirect control, occupation, or annexation in parts of the Ottoman empire and its successor states. In the last four decades the impact of the West has also been associated with regional conflicts, particularly the Arab–Israeli conflict and the Gulf wars. Dissatisfaction with the status quo, appeals to new ideologies, and a search for legitimacy have all become, more than ever, characterized by the inextricable intertwining of domestic, regional, and international issues.

Social harmony in the Middle East as in many other regions of Asia and Africa rested until the era of Western domination on two finely tuned sets of balances – a balance between central state power and regional autonomy and a balance between social groups reflected in economic and political institutions within regions. Recent scholarship has suggested that the Ottoman empire, far from being an "Oriental despotism," aspired for most of its history to a loose and subtle form of suzerainty over far-flung territories. Before the Tanzimat reforms in the middle of the nineteenth century, the Ottomans in common with the Safavids and Mughals could not have achieved or sustained centralized bureaucratic rule as we understand it today, even at the height of their rule during the reign of Sultan Süleyman I (r. 1520–66), and centralization then meant little more than the domination of a major city over others and over the countryside.[2] Intermediary social classes near the imperial center and landed notables in the outlying provinces enjoyed substantial autonomy and were engaged in a constant process of renegotiating the center–region equation. Economic and political understandings cutting across communities were recognized as essential prerequisites of regional stability and prosperity.

The eighteenth century saw the gradual loss of real power from the center to the regions and accelerated processes of social class formation within regions. The weakening of the power of the Ottoman, Safavid, and Mughal courts and armies did not entail, however, a more general social and economic decay. Decentralization rather than decline seems to capture better the broad historical trends of the Middle East and South Asia in that period. Towards the end of the eighteenth century autonomous regions were able to create a measure of economic prosperity and political stability characterized by dynamism in the areas of agriculture, inland trade, and urbanism as well as efficiency in the realms of military organization and revenue collection. The Ottoman provinces in North Africa, including Egypt under Ali Bey al-Kabir (r. 1760–73) and later Muhammad Ali Pasha (r. 1805–49), and the pashalik of Baghdad founded by the Mamluk governor Süleyman Pasha (r. 1780–1802), seem to be comparable in these respects to the Qajar and Zand states that arose in Iran and the Mughal successor states in India. The Syrian province remained more closely tied to the Ottoman center but shared with the other regions a tendency towards the commercialization of political power and the rise of merchants and financiers at the expense of landed and service groups. Mount Lebanon, which had always remained outside the core of the Ottoman empire, enhanced its autonomy while it underwent a broadly analogous process of social class formation. In the early nineteenth century, however, it was denied the stability enjoyed by some of the other successor states when in the 1830s it became contested ground between the Ottoman center and Muhammad Ali's Egypt. But by then most of the territories in the Middle East had become vulnerable to Western economic and political penetration. While the buoyancy of the economies and polities of the eighteenth-century Middle East had attracted European encroachments, some key contradictions and weaknesses within them facilitated the establishment of Western domination by the mid-nineteenth century. The vulnerability stemmed not only from an intercontinental reordering of the world economy in favor of Europe but also from inter-regional imbalances of power and wealth and growing intra-regional disparities between classes and communities.[3]

This book explores the interaction of the intra-regional or local context with the wider regional and international currents in shaping the particular character of social conflicts, insurrectionary movements, and civil wars of modern times. It does so through a close analytical narrative of the civil wars in Mount Lebanon and Damascus in 1860 set against the background of the broader themes of social, economic, and political change in the nineteenth century. The choice of the narrative form in a historical study of the tumultuous events of 1860 needs some justification in the scholarly environment of the 1990s deeply permeated by Edward Said's post-Orientalism as well as several variants of post-modernist and deconstructionist approaches. This first narrative of the Lebanese and Syrian civil wars since the early accounts written in the 1860s has imbibed and absorbed much from Said's critiques of Orientalism in much the same way as "the revival of narrative" in European history in the 1980s was influenced by the far-reaching interventions of Braudel and the Annales school emphasizing deeply embedded and long-term social and economic forces.[4] But it resists the uncritical acceptance of a post-modernist binary dichotomy that asserts there can be no narrative, only irony. Some of the sharper historical insights can be gleaned by recognizing the element of irony *in* narrative and can be conveyed in the form of a textured, and occasionally ironic, narrative. In other words, this narrative shows awareness of the post-modernist critiques of modernist binary fallacies but tries to steer clear of the binary cul-de-sacs that paradoxically have been created by some strands of post-modernist scholarship.

Post-Orientalist scholarly work on the Middle East cannot but be sensitive to the immense potential for mischief of Western colonial knowledge deeply implicated in the project of power. Recent versions of post-Orientalism paint an even more insidious picture of an all-pervasive culture of domination in the field of knowledge characterized by extensive and multiple sites of power.[5] In writing a narrative reconstruction drawing partly on Western sources, one has to be especially careful of the pitfalls of any unquestioning reliance on information as well as knowledge systems tainted and infected with power. One has to be equally circumspect of local sources with sectarian overtones typical of participants and apologists. Without necessarily resorting to the method of "intertextuality" proposed by deconstructionists in literary and cultural studies, this work has sought to balance, cross-check, and verify data and interpretations contained in an array of Arabic and Western sources. It is hoped that this book will encourage other scholars to add a perspective through a study of Ottoman sources on the events and processes narrated and analyzed here. Local and Western sources have been "read against the grain" in presenting this narrative at least in the sense of a healthy, if slightly old-fashioned, skepticism. The resistance to the more technical aspects of the deconstructionist method has stemmed in part from a conviction that it is imperative to tell this story in a form that is of interest to specialists but also intelligible to students and non-specialists. The larger issue here, of course, is the need for communication between the academy and the rest of the world.

Another word of clarification is in order on the question of the "subjecthood" and "agency" of subordinated social groups in the cataclysmic events of 1860 as well as the related question of "society-centered" and "state-centered" approaches to history. The case against the "élitist" bias in historiography and for the restoration of the "subjecthood" of non-élites as historical actors has been strongly argued, among others, by the "subaltern school" of South Asian historiography.[6] This narrative freely acknowledges that the "subaltern" can not only "speak" but also love her/his own kind and kill her/his oppressors or rivals.[7] But it also implicitly says that the "agency" of "subaltern" social groups is played out within the dialectic of domination and resistance that characterizes the élite–subaltern relationship. This narrative would be wide of its mark if it did not recognize the dominating power of élites and the salience of "élite" politics in the historical definition of "sectarian" identities in the nineteenth century. The history of mid-nineteenth-century Syria including Mount Lebanon had a complex authorship which deserves to be reflected in its writing in the late twentieth century.

The narrative presented in this book also deliberately straddles the society–state nexus. An exercise in social history of the sort pioneered by Natalie Zemon Davis in European historiography would not have been wholly appropriate to the subject at hand. The close attention to the context of local society in shaping the culture and consciousness of the actors in the civil wars of 1860 is matched in this book by a depiction of the role of broader processes of state formation linked to supra-local trends in economic and political change.[8]

This work shows how social conflict, including what superficially look like "ethnic" civil wars, cannot be understood or explained without reference to the state at two levels: the center–region dynamic and the communal balance in political institutions within regions. The framework of the state–society nexus is of critical importance in investigating the historical roots and the historically changing basis of sectarianism. Although the divisions in society in the mid-century were due to social and economic imbalances that weakened traditional social classes and made the rise of new ones possible, why did society in times of crisis realign itself principally along sectarian lines? People who had once turned to their traditional networks of protection and identification found that the strength of clan and of local leadership had been undermined and tended to rely now more than ever on their sectarian identity. The book examines the extent to which the weakening of Ottoman central state power in the region and of traditional urban and rural leadership in Damascus and Mount Lebanon in conjunction with changes in economic and institutional life created the political space that was filled by sectarian networks. In Lebanon there seemed to be grounds for hope or perhaps just the modernist illusion that after 1860 sectarian identity was likely to be eroded by the same forces that weakened other forms of traditional identification. But the years of conflict since 1975 have strengthened sectarian ties once again, albeit in an altered framework of state–society relations and changed regional and international contexts.

This book also shows that forces other than sectarian identity were at work in the civil war of 1860, even though that identity had acquired new significance. Identification in terms of region and class also surfaced. People from the same religious community or sect but different regions reacted very differently to the conflict because considerations tied to local traditions and leadership, means of livelihood, and geographical locations were also influential in shaping the nature and articulation of conflicts. People identified strongly with their towns and regions, so that the form and intensity of the clashes varied from place to place.

Observation of the theaters of war reveals undeniably that there was not one but many civil wars of 1860, each made of separate grievances and civil conflicts: the problems caused by the end of one political system and its replacement by another, the frustrations of the peasants, the weakening of the traditional élites, the changing role of the Maronite clergy, the tensions between urban élites and the Ottoman establishment and between rival urban factions in Damascus, the changed status of minorities in the empire at large and of the relative strength of the Ottoman and European powers. Each of these constituted different agendas and different battles; how the conflict was expressed depended again on the particular traditions of a given town, village, and region, on the sources of its livelihood, and on the nature and composition of its population.

In this way, the civil war of 1860 shows the new forces at work in both the Ottoman empire at large and in its Syrian provinces. Changes in the system of control and administration in the Ottoman empire and the growth of European interests and rivalries were tied to a whole series of disturbances in the Arab parts of the empire in the middle years of the nineteenth century, including Mosul, Aleppo, Nablus, and Jedda, and the countryside of Kurdistan.[9] The coming apart of the great Mughal empire and shifting social relations during the colonial transition appear to have fomented urban conflicts in South Asia as well, which often took the form of grain riots but occasionally erupted into Hindu–Muslim and also Shi'i–Sunni antagonisms.[10] When these sorts of conflicts occurred in Lebanon, they took on a distinctive form because of the special nature of that society which made the conflict different from one district to another and which, despite its social and economic origins, tainted it principally with sectarian overtones. What happened in Lebanon precipitated disturbances in Damascus where, again, the particular attitudes of urban groups towards one another and towards the government affected the unfolding of events. The subsequent intervention of the Ottoman and of the European governments reflected their particular interests in the Mediterranean coast at a time of growing Western economic penetration. In the case of Lebanon, the end result after a brief centrally directed Ottoman expedition was a new system of government which was successful in maintaining stability because it took into account Ottoman regional concerns and Lebanese social realities. It was based on measured regional autonomy and a new negotiated balance between communities in the political institutions of the Mutasarrifiyya.

In the narrative that follows, the historical background to the civil war of 1860 is set in Chapters 2 and 3, to give an overview of the changing face of Mount Lebanon and Greater Syria in the first half of the nineteenth century, and then to set the stage of the actual conflict by describing some of the principal theaters of war on its eve. Chapters 4 and 5 describe the eruption of violence, first in Mount Lebanon and then in Damascus. Chapter 6 examines immediate Ottoman and European responses to news of the crisis, the special missions backed by military power which they sent to Syria, and the cooperation and rivalries of their men on the spot. Chapters 7 and 8 describe the immediate measures they took to solve the crisis, and Chapter 9 the more gradual build-up of consensus among Ottoman and European diplomats about the issues of accountability, reparation, and the future administration of Mount Lebanon. In the conclusion, the nature of civil conflict in Lebanon is examined in historical perspective.

CHAPTER I

CHANGING WORLDS

With its highest massifs at Qarnet al-Sauda at 3,083 meters and its second highest Mount Sannin at 2,548 meters, Mount Lebanon constitutes, with Mount Hermon to its south, the highest range of mountains in the territories that stretch from the Taurus mountains to the north, to the Mediterranean in the west, the Sinai and the Hijaz to the south, and northern Mesopotamia and the Syrian desert to the east. Facing it across the Baalbek region, the alluvial valley of the Beqaa and, to its south, the valley of Wadi Taym, is another range, the Anti-Lebanon. South of it is Mount Hermon and, beyond it, the Hawran plateau. The imposing ranges and scenic ravines of the Lebanon and Anti-Lebanon separate the narrow Syrian littoral on the Mediterranean sea from the Syrian interior where Damascus sits southeast of the Anti-Lebanon on the western edge of the Syrian desert.[1]

In the Anti-Lebanon, rainfall is light and crops sparse, but the Lebanon ranges are blessed with heavy rains in the highest elevations, abundant water, and fertile soil that allow intense cultivation on its middle slopes, and this advantage, coupled with the high altitudes, relatively rich vegetation, and pleasant climate, enhances their attractiveness. The Mountain's hundreds of small picturesque villages with their stone houses, interspersed with pine forests and limestone rocks, are covered with the compact terraces made for the cultivation of grapevines and of olive and mulberry trees.

Mount Lebanon was a world unto itself until the first decades of the nineteenth century, but, despite its isolation and inward orientation, it had never been completely self-sufficient either economically or politically. Its restricted territory and limited arable land made it partially dependent on the produce of the rich granaries of the Beqaa, Hawran, and the plains that stretched beyond the Anti-Lebanon toward the Syrian interior. Crop failures could extend this dependence even further, to Egypt. It was also affected by the struggles of power in its midst but also beyond its borders among the emirs of the Mountain, the tribal and other shaykhs of the interior and the Ottoman governors, especially the governor in Damascus where Ottoman power in Syria was centered.

Although Damascus is only 50 miles from the Mediterranean and even nearer than that to Mount Lebanon, before the twentieth century, in geography, history, and culture it was light years away. In the heart of the Syrian interior, its climate is dry, its winters chilly, and its summers hot. Exceptionally for the interior, however, it is abundantly supplied with water, thanks to the subterranean springs and streams which drain the Anti-Lebanon range and make up for often inadequate rainfall. It is situated on the banks of the largest of these rivers, the Barada. The city is surrounded by the Ghuta, its oasis, which is composed of rich agricultural land. It also has easy access to the plains of Homs and Hama to the north, the Beqaa to the west, and the Hawran south and southeast, which benefits Damascus in many ways. Damascus lies at the eastern edge of a series of gorges and lowland passes that offers the best east–west route through the Anti-Lebanon range. Until the mid-nineteenth century it was a "desert port" for the caravan trade of Mesopotamia, Asia Minor, and the regions beyond.[2]

Syria's history has repeatedly accentuated its natural tendency to be compartmentalized geographically and socially. It constituted a crossroad for conquerors coming from various parts of the Mediterranean basin or from the Arabian peninsula, Mesopotamia, or Central Asia. Parts or all of Syria were brought under a succession of ancient and modern empires which included Egyptians, Assyrians, Hittites, Neo-Babylonians, Persians, Macedonians, Romans, and Byzantines. In the seventh century AD through the desert had come the early Arab invaders, converts to Islam who had ridden out of the Arabian peninsula to conquer the rest of the Middle East, Egypt, and North Africa. For more than a century Damascus was the capital for the Umayyad dynasty (661–750) that ruled the first Arab Islamic empire. When Baghdad replaced it as the capital of the Muslim world when the Abbasids (750–1258) came to power, Damascus remained an important center. Baghdad was the more cosmopolitan city as Islam spread to the Persians and Turks, but Damascus remained a purely Arab stronghold and an important stopping-off place for the annual pilgrimage to Mecca. After the mid-ninth century, the decline and later downfall of the Abbasid empire brought new Muslim rulers – the Fatimids (909–1171), the Seljuqs (1058–1157), the Ayyubids (1183–1250), and the Mamluks (1261–1517) – to Syria. The Crusaders controlled its coastal and northern parts between 1098 and 1291. For brief interludes in the thirteenth and fourteen centuries, the Mongols captured Damascus but not the Syrian coast. Finally, in 1516, the Ottomans conquered Syria which they ruled until 1918 when British and French forces occupied it, except for a brief episode between 1831 and 1840 when Syria fell into the hands of the Egyptian ruler Muhammad Ali Pasha (r. 1805-49).

Syria's history under this array of empires guaranteed a diverse population. Christianity spread in the area, and schisms and quarrels over orthodox Christian doctrine, ritual, and discipline established a whole spectrum of Christian denominations. The Eastern Orthodox followed the orthodox Byzantine line that Christians must acknowledge the two natures – human and divine – in the one person of Christ, adopted by the Council of Chalcedon in 451. When the churches of Rome and Constantinople split in 1054, the Eastern Orthodox followed Constantinople and were considered schismatic in the eyes of Rome. In the late seventeenth and early eighteenth centuries, a group of some of these Orthodox accepted the primacy of the pope in Rome, and became one of the "Uniate" churches which in that period acknowledged papal supremacy and in return were allowed to retain their own customs and the Byzantine rite. These Uniates are often known as "Greek Catholics" and the non-Uniates as "Greek Orthodox", but they are Arabs in Arabic-speaking lands who use the Byzantine rite in their liturgy. The term "Melchite" deriving from the Arabic term *malakiyyun*, or royalists, was at one time in use for the Greek Orthodox, but now it is used for the Greek Catholics.[3]

The Nestorians refused to accept the dual nature of Christ adopted by the Council of Chalcedon and chose to keep the distinction between the two natures of Christ in their creed; today they are limited to the Assyrians of Syria and Iraq. In reaction to the Nestorian doctrine, the Monophysites stressed the union between Christ and the man Jesus to the point of believing that Christ has not only one Person but also one Nature. They were considered heterodox Christians by Constantinople and Rome. They include the Copts of Egypt, the Gregorians or Armenian Orthodox, and the Jacobites or Syrian Orthodox of Syria.

An offshoot of Monophysitism was the Monothelete doctrine briefly adopted as a state doctrine in the Byzantine empire in the seventh century, which maintained that Christ possessed both a divine and a human Nature but only one divine Will. In 680 the Council of Constantinople rejected this doctrine as heresy, condemned Monothelites as "One Will" heretics, and declared that Christ not only had two natures but also two energies and two wills. Nonetheless, the Monothelite doctrine seems to have survived among a Christian community of Syria known as the Maronites, after their patron saint Maron (Marun) who, according to one tradition, died in the early fifth century. Although Maronite historians have argued that Maronites had nothing to do with the Monothelite heresy, it is commonly believed by other Christians and by Muslims that the Maronite church was established as Syrian Monothelete in 680, and that it abandoned Monothelism in the twelfth century, when it recognized papal supremacy without giving up its own Syriac liturgy and priesthood. Although some of the Maronite historians have also argued that the Maronites are of non-Arab origin (Mardaites), most probably they are Arabs. The Maronites first lived in the valley of the Orontes and in other parts of northern Syria, including the northern part of Mount Lebanon. They still inhabited all these areas by the middle of the tenth century, but by the end of the eleventh they opted to make Mount Lebanon their haven and central homeland, largely because their relations with the Byzantine church were strained. In Mount Lebanon, they grew as an agricultural community known for its prowess in war and its proclivity for feuding.

Other Uniate groups – the Syrian Catholics, Armenian Catholics, and Chaldean Catholics, along with Roman Catholics of the Latin rite, were also represented in Syria. In the nineteenth century, the various Protestant denominations acquired small numbers of followers, principally as a result of Western missionary activity which, on the whole, was more successful in converting Christians of other sects (principally Greek Orthodox) to Protestantism than it was in converting Muslims to Christianity. Protestants in Syria were generally Presbyterians; in Palestine they were more apt to be Anglicans.

Islam began to spread in Syria, as elsewhere in the Middle East, after the Arab conquest in the seventh century, and as it spread, so did the divisions among Muslims. Sunni ("orthodox") Muslims believe that the leadership of the Islamic community had passed from the Prophet Muhammad to the first four "rightly guided" successors ("caliphs") chosen by acclamation – Abu Bakr, Umar, Uthman, and Ali – and then to the Umayyad caliphs. To them, caliphs are temporal rulers, and the sole source of the faith lies in the Qur'an, the Muslims' holy book, and the Traditions of the Prophet. In the first century of Islam, Shi'is ("partisans") split from them, in a quarrel over the succession to the Prophet. For the Shi'is, the Prophet's successors ("imams") should belong to the family of the Prophet's cousin and son-in-law Ali. Persecuted by the Umayyads and the Abbasids whom they did not recognize as legitimate, they developed a cult of the Prophet's family, particularly of Ali and his successors whom they regard as infallible secular and spiritual leaders who can interpret the law and doctrine.

The majority of Shi'is believe that the line of imams ended with the Twelfth Imam who disappeared in the ninth century and has since remained "hidden;" he will some day reappear as "al-Mahdi" or the divinely guided, to rule the world and give his followers their due. Some of these so-called Twelver Shi'is are found today in Lebanon, mostly in Jabal Amel in the south and in the Beqaa. They are known also as Matawila or Bani Mitwal. A second sect of Shi'is known as Sevener Shi'is, or Isma'ilis, after the name of the eldest son of the Sixth Imam who they believe was the one who went into hiding, are also found in Syria. For them, one of the "hidden" successors of Isma'il was the founder of the Fatimid caliphate.

One of the Fatimid caliphs of Egypt, Hakim (996–1020), presented himself as the final incarnation of God and two of his followers, Hamza and Darazi, spread this doctrine among the rural inhabitants of the Shuf mountains in southern Lebanon, and of Wadi Taym in the Anti-Lebanon, and founded the sect known as the Druze. Within a few decades, the Druzes halted conversion to their sect and, in effect, made it so that henceforth their numbers could only increase by reproduction, not proselytizing. They believe that Hakim is not dead and will return. They also believe, with the Isma'ilis, in emanations of God, in supernatural hierarchies, and in the transmigration of souls. They practice systematic concealment of their beliefs (*taqiyya*), a practice also common among Shi'i sects and meant to protect believers by allowing them to resist pressure and persecution by denying their true faith. Druze beliefs are fully known only to a select class of "initiates" (*'uqqal*) who perform religious duties and lead the majority of the believers or non-initiates (*juhhal*). Druzes share with Maronites the reputation of living in warring rural communities, but unlike the Maronites, Druze solidarity is highly valued; it is nurtured by making the rank-and-file majority follow the counsel of their initiates and of their political leaders; long-standing rivalries among the latter are put aside in times of threat from the outside world: they close ranks in the face of external danger.

Another offshoot of Shi'ism, also limited to Syria, are the Nusyris or Alawis from the Syrian hill country of Latakia. A mountain people like the Druzes, their origins are obscure. Like the Shi'is they venerate Ali. They believe in a divine triad, reincarnation, the transmigration of souls, and in esoteric teaching revealed only to a class of initiates. Much of their ritual is of Christian origin.

Until the late thirteenth century, the majority of Syria's population was still Christian and mainly Eastern Orthodox. Under the Fatimids Shi'ism dominated in the Muslim population, except in some of the districts of Mount Lebanon where, by the end of the eleventh century, it had been replaced in the southern regions of the Shuf and Wadi Taym by Druzes. In the northern districts of Bsharreh, Batrun, and Jbail, Maronites predominated over Muslims. But over time as Sunni dynasties, especially the Mamluks, ruled in Syria the Shi'is lost their majority, holding out only in Kisrawan where they retained a foothold until a steady Maronite migration that began in the sixteenth century had finally displaced them by the end of the eighteenth century. The Shi'is remained in rural communities in the Beqaa and Baalbek, the highlands of upper Galilee or Jabal Amel, and other areas in south Lebanon, but in the coastal towns as in the interior of Syria the Sunnis remained the majority from Mamluk times to the present day mainly, though not exclusively, as an urban population. The Druzes lived in the southern districts of Mount Lebanon. Christians constituted important minorities in Syrian towns and the countryside; Greek Orthodox dominated in the urban centers of the coast, in the rural district of Kura near the coast in the north, and in the interior including Damascus. Maronites grew steadily in Mount Lebanon; from their original areas of settlement in the districts of Bsharreh, Batrun, and Jbail, they spread from the limits of the district of Akkar in the north to those of the Shuf in the south, so that by the end of the eighteenth century, they dominated in the north. They began to infiltrate the south in the sixteenth century; by the eighteenth century, they were an important segment of its population. Greek Catholics and other Christians were found in cities of the coast and the interior, and in Mountain villages. Jews constituted small communities of traders and artisans in the towns of the Syrian coast and the cities of Damascus and Aleppo in the interior.[4]

Under the Ottomans, as under the Arab empires before them, Syria's natural compartmentalization in small geographic and social enclaves was reinforced by administrative organization. When they first conquered Syria, the Ottomans divided it into the three provinces (called *eyalet*s, *vilayet*s, or *pashalik*s) of Aleppo, Damascus, and Tripoli. In 1660, a fourth *vilayet* of Sidon was created, and now and then the *vilayet* of Tripoli was absorbed into one of its bordering *vilayet*s, Damascus or Sidon. The northern region of modern Lebanon formed part of the *vilayet* of Tripoli (which also included parts of the modern republic of Syria). The Beqaa was separated from these two regions and made part of the *vilayet* of Damascus. In the nineteenth century, the Ottomans introduced further administrative changes. In 1840, the *vilayet* of Sidon was enlarged and Beirut made its center. In 1864, a *vilayet* of Syria was formed out of those of Sidon and Damascus and subdivided into five *sanjak*s (subdivisions of a province): Beirut, Acre, Tripoli, Latakia, and Nablus. In 1888, a *vilayet* of Beirut was formed from the *vilayet* of Syria.

Through this administrative apparatus, the Ottomans kept a rather loose rein on Syria for the first three centuries of their rule, concentrating their control in the main cities where their governors and garrisons were located and often leaving the hinterland to itself. On the whole they were more concerned with their European territories than their Arab ones, the exceptions being Cairo, Aleppo, and Damascus, the most prestigious of the Ottomans' thirty or more provinces.[5] In both cases, the source of this importance was that both Damascus and Cairo were starting points for the two chief caravans to the *hajj*, the major pilgrimage to the holy cities of Mecca and Medina which took place during one month of the year (individual visits could be made at any time). Since the early eighteenth century, the governors of Damascus had performed the important religious function of Commander of the Pilgrimage, and pilgrims from all over the northern territories of the empire (including its capital) assembled in the town for the yearly caravan.[6]

Concern for the security of the pilgrimage led the central government to appoint in Damascus a governor of ministerial rank and to station imperial troops in the city. Arms and ammunition were kept in the citadel, where the rulers could also seek refuge in times of trouble, barricading themselves in against the unfriendly mob. The authority of the government of Damascus was based on the janissaries made up of local (*yerli kullari*) and imperial (*kapi kullari*) corps. The governor also had to cope with the tribes in the countryside, and the notables or *a'yan*, the great families who drew their main strength from the city from which they dominated the hinterland.[7]

The notables derived their wealth from trade and land ownership. They included the religious learned élite (*'ulama'*, sg. *'alim*), the heads of the local janissaries and of other military corps (*agahawat*, sg. *agha*), and men or families who derived their power from secular sources and based it on political, military, or economic clout (*umara*, sg. *amir*, *aghawat*, sg. *agha*, and other names that include the word *a'yan* to refer to this subclass in a more restricted use of the same word that also applied to the whole class). The notables competed for power – or collaborated as the situation warranted – in the complex game, dominant in its purest form in Damascus or Aleppo, that Albert Hourani refers to as the "politics of the notables." Their power derived mainly from their role as intermediaries between the Ottomans and the urban population which the notables could speak for and control. They were represented in the governor's council, which made it impossible for a governor to rule without them. They controlled the religious institutions and the mass of the population; they also controlled tax collection especially in the countryside in their capacity as holders of *malikane* or tax farms for life.[8]

By the second half of the eighteenth century Ottoman power had weakened, and the government began to rely more and more on local governors to maintain order and implement Ottoman policies. This gave the notables some power, but they never became totally free of Ottoman authority, for they were held in check by the local governors, and the central government saw to it that local ambitions were contained in the province of Damascus by playing one notable off against the other or even, if necessary, by bringing in the army. The Azms, a family already well established in the early eighteenth century in al-Numan in the province of Aleppo, on the main road between Aleppo and Damascus, rose to power in the province of Damascus and monopolized the governorship of Damascus for about fifty years. They were typical of the combination of local assertion and submission to Ottoman authority that characterized the provincial government.[9]

Ottoman control was hardly felt in Mount Lebanon, where no direct Ottoman authority existed before the nineteenth century. The Ottomans kept an eye on it, but left it alone. In the north, from the mid-seventeenth century, the Maronite districts of Bsharreh, Batrun, and Jbail, together with the Orthodox district of Kura close to the coast, were ruled by the Shi'i Hamada shaykhs from the Baalbek region. In Kisrawan, the control of the district had passed at the beginning of the seventeenth century from Shi'i to Maronite shaykhs of the Khazin family, although the population was still principally Shi'i. In the south local princes or emirs became virtually autonomous. When the Ottomans conquered the Shuf, they first tried to bring the Druzes directly under their control, but then relied on local emirs to do it for them. In theory, these emirs were no more than tax farmers (*multazims*), accountable to the Ottoman governors of Sidon, and their tax-farming estate (*iltizam*) was subject to annual renewal. In practice, the Ottomans were content to collect from them an annual tribute and, in exchange, to leave them to their own devices. Over time, as emirs of leading families succeeded one another, they gave the government of Lebanon some of the characteristics of a dynastic emirate, although technically it never was one.[10]

The leading Druze emirs of the sixteenth and seventeenth centuries were the Ma'n emirs from the Shuf, who had replaced the Druze Buhturids from the Gharb after the Ottoman conquest. The most famous Ma'n emir was Fakhr al-Din II (1590–1635) who extended his territories within and beyond Lebanon and established relations with European powers. After him, the dynasty went into decline, and in 1697 it was replaced by the Shihabs, originally from Wadi Taym, who extended their rule further north and remained in control until 1842. They were Sunni Muslims, but by the late eighteenth century many of them had converted to Maronite Christianity, among them the most famous Shihab ruler, Bashir II (1788–1841).

Although the Ottoman government invested the Ma'n and Shihab princes with some formal power by confirming their seats through its governors in Sidon and Tripoli, their major source of legitimacy and prestige resided in their place at the top of the social hierarchy. Historians often describe the system as "feudal," and it was based on a tenured land system of districts of varying size (the *iqta'* or *muqata'a*) which were acknowledged to be hereditary and were governed by hereditary chiefs or shaykhs (the *muqata'ji*s), who recognized the ruling emir as the supreme authority of the Mountain, were responsible to him for their districts, presented him with a yearly tribute, and were willing, upon request, to contribute armed men for his purposes. In return, the emir acted as arbitrator (*hakam*) among them, as a unifying force among their self-contained smaller fiefs, and as mediator between their interests and those of the Ottoman overlords to whom he forwarded the yearly tribute.[11]

The hereditary land tenure system which already existed in the Druze areas was introduced in the north of Mount Lebanon in the seventeenth century, when the Ma'n emir Fakhr al-Din II extended his control over all the Mountain, and it was maintained by the Shihabs. In Kisrawan, the Khazins, although until then second to the family of the Hubayshes, were the first Maronite family to achieve the status of *muqata'ji*s, and they became the leading Maronite family in the Mountain. Other Maronite families received the same privileges, and they adopted the social customs of the Druzes.

Within their domain, the *muqata'ji*s wielded great power. They were responsible for public order, the safeguard of their lands from any intruders, the upkeep of a unit of cavalry, and the arming and upkeep of their peasant soldiers. They administered justice and could imprison, flog, fine, and impose other penalties, and they implemented the decisions of religious courts. They acted as tax farmers, collecting taxes from their dependents, holding back their share, and sending the rest to the emirs of the Mountain. In addition to a land tax (*miri*), they collected special taxes on specific agricultural and commercial goods, payments and in-kind "gifts" from their dependents on specified holidays or ceremonial occasions (*'idiyya*), or the marriage of a landlord's son, daughter, or sister. Their authority was tied to a lordly style of life, which included keeping an open house, being served by a retinue of servants, and bestowing favors on their dependents.[12]

The *muqata'ji*s' power also meant that the ruling emirs could not interfere in their domains unless invited to do so. The most striking example of this was the town of Deir al-Qamar in the Manasif district of the Abu

Nakad Druze family, the seat of power of the Shihabs (and, before them, the Ma'ns), whose modest palace was in the town until Bashir II around 1811 moved to the adjoining hill of Beit al-Din, where he had built a magnificent palace known by that name. In Deir al-Qamar, the emir's jurisdiction extended only within the confines of his palace; beyond it the town, like the rest of the district, obeyed the *muqata'jis*' rule. Only for imposing the death penalty did they require the emir's permission.[13]

A clear and, on the whole, stable relationship existed among the Lebanese leading families, dictated by their titles – emirs, *muqaddam*s, and shaykhs – although these often offered more in prestige than real power. At the top, by local convention, were the princely families of the emirs. By the nineteenth century there were three of them: the Shihabs, the Abu'l-Lamas, originally the Druze *muqaddam*s of the Metn, raised to the rank of emirs under Haydar Shihab (1707–32), and the Druze Arslans from the Gharb. Next in rank came the families who held the title of *muqaddam*; only one of these, the Druze Muzhirs from Hammana in the Metn, was left after the elevation of the Abu'l-Lamas to the rank of emir. Below them were those families who held the rank of shaykh, the lowest rank of the notable families, and among these a pecking order made some more prestigious than others. Two old families of Druze shaykhs were the Janbalats and the Imads (also called Yazbaks), to which Emir Haydar Shihab added three new families of Druze shaykhs: the Abu Nakads, the Talhuqs, and the Abd al-Maliks. Of about the same rank were the Maronite families of the Khazins, Hubayshes, and Dahdahs. Other leading families in the north included the Shi'i shaykhs of the Hamada family, the Maronite Dahirs, and the Orthodox Azars.

Below the *muqata'ji*s were other landed families of lesser affluence or influence, often of peasant origin, and peasants, either small landowners or landless sharecroppers, who cultivated olive trees, vineyards, and mulberry trees for the silk trade. They also grew some grain, tobacco, and cotton.[14]

Maintaining the autonomy of Mount Lebanon depended on a network of alliances among its leading Druze and Maronite families based on a chain of clan loyalties that cut across sectarian lines and took precedence over loyalty to village, district, or church. The *muqata'ji*s gave their allegiance to the ruling emirs, and the commoners gave theirs to the *muqata'ji*s. Alliances of Druzes and Maronites transcended geographical and religious lines. The Druze Ma'ns and Sunni Shihab emirs of the sixteenth to eighteenth centuries allied themselves with the Maronites and encouraged them to move into the Druze districts, partly in an effort to build political support outside the Druzes of the Shuf, and partly in an effort to meet the needs of the burgeoning silk trade. In the eighteenth century, many of the Shihabs became Maronites without losing the allegiance of their allies and followers. Lebanese politics consisted of fluid alliances where members of the same families could be pitted against one another, in alliance with one another, or changing sides. They also involved clan rivalries among the leading Druze families and their Druze and Christian supporters. An old standing feud of "Qaysi" and "Yemeni" factions cut across religious lines. In 1697, for example, the Qaysi notables elected a Qaysi Sunni Shihab emir to succeed the last Qaysi Druze Ma'n emir. The feud between the two factions ended, however, in 1711 with the defeat of the Yamanis. Subsequently, "Janbalati" and "Yazbaki" feuding pitted the Janbalats and the Khazins against the Imads, Talhuqs, Abd al-Maliks, Hubayshes, and Dahdahs.[15]

In the sixteenth century, the Druzes were the senior partners in that alliance, but by the end of the eighteenth century the Maronites were becoming more powerful. The population explosion of the Maronites in the seventeenth and eighteenth centuries, which spread them into the south, combined with reforms in the church in the eighteenth century which increased its membership, wealth, and political weight and forged a sense of identity and solidarity, helped bring this about.[16]

The reform movement involved ties with Europe going back to the twelfth century which also contributed to defining and strengthening Maronite identity. In the fourteenth and fifteenth centuries, the Franciscans, and after the sixteenth century the Jesuits, served as advisers to the Maronites and as intermediaries between them and the Vatican. Maronite priests were sent to study in Italy, and in 1584 a Maronite college was established in Rome. By the eighteenth century, Catholic missions spread in Syria and, as they did, they made Maronite interests one of their concerns. In the seventeenth and eighteenth centuries, literacy spread slowly among the Christians who used it to rise to positions of scribes, financial controllers, administrators, and agents in the households of the Shihab emirs. Of these the most influential position was that of *mudabbir* or adviser and administrator to the emir himself, a position which came to be filled solely by Maronites. Educated Christians also served as clerks and household managers of leading Druze and Maronite families, and some of them wrote local histories.[17]

The imbalance in numbers between Druzes and Maronites built up slowly and in itself would not necessarily have resulted in sectarian warfare. In fact, the Druzes were very slow to react to it and for long after the Maronites had become preponderant, the Druzes felt confident enough in their political traditions and status to continue to encourage Maronite emigration to the south and to operate on the basis of the traditional intrasectarian alliances.

What turned sectarian imbalance into sectarian hatred was a change in the nature of leadership and governance in Mount Lebanon beginning in the 1820s. Although in many ways Bashir II was the most powerful of the Shihab leaders, he contributed to the weakening and demise of the Lebanese emirate and traditional system of government. During his reign, for reasons which were partly of his own making and partly beyond his control, he took a number of initiatives which effectively changed the relationship of the emirate to its *muqataʻji*s, sapped the strength of the Druze leadership, and eventually also caused the loss of power of the emirate itself. His bid for total power ended by destroying the Druze leadership altogether. He tolerated no rivals of any sect or category and, in some forty years of rule, even undermined members of his own family, not to mention other leading families and the clergy. He weakened the Khazins and other Maronite *muqataʻji*s and cultivated the Maronite clergy instead.

Because the Druze shaykhs constituted the single most important source of power in the Mountain other than himself, Bashir weakened the leadership by taking sides in clan politics, a breach in the practice of maintaining a balance among the clans beneath him. With his help the Janbalats defeated the more numerous Yazbaki faction and emerged as the most powerful clan. Then Bashir II turned against the Janbalats, when that very success made them a threat. In 1825 he had Bashir Janbalat, their leader, imprisoned and strangled in Acre. That act established Bashir II as the unchallenged ruler of Mount Lebanon, but it also weakened the Druze leadership which had been the backbone of the Lebanese political system.

The death of Shaykh Janbalat also introduced sectarianism into Lebanese politics, for although Bashir II himself had nothing but self-serving motives in mind when he had him assassinated, the Druzes believed that he had done it because he was a Christian Shihab enemy bent on destroying the Druzes.[18]

Bashir II also broke another law of the social contract by serving the interests of outsiders against those of his own people. That aspect of his career began when he was appointed by Ahmad al-Jazzar ("the Butcher") Pasha (1775–1804), the tyrannical governor of Sidon who stopped Bonaparte's advance on Acre in 1799. In 1789, the governor ordered Bashir's troops against Yusuf Shihab, Bashir's predecessor who had supported enemies of the governor, lost his position, but still resided in Lebanon. Bashir obeyed; Yusuf was forced out of Lebanon, sought refuge in the

Hawran, and then gave himself up to Jazzar in Acre. The following year, Yusuf regained Jazzar's favors briefly by promising him a huge tribute and he was reinstated as emir of Lebanon. But Bashir then outmaneuvered his cousin and regained his title by offering Jazzar an even bigger tribute. Yusuf was sent to prison in Acre where he was hanged. After that Jazzar continued to fuel partisan politics in Mount Lebanon, and altogether on three occasions he recalled Bashir II from office. Bashir also let himself be drawn into political struggles of Ottoman governors on the Syrian coast and, in doing so, made the Mountain a pawn of regional politics beyond its control.

Jazzar was followed as governor by Süleyman Pasha, and he too collaborated with Bashir II who as a consequence was once again drawn into politics outside the Mountain. He sent troops to defend Damascus against the Wahhabis of Arabia, rigorous Sunnis who had invaded Syria in 1810. Süleyman Pasha died in 1819, and was replaced by Abdallah Pasha who remained in power until the Egyptian occupation. Bashir got involved in his quarrels with the governor of Damascus. For Abdallah Pasha, Bashir also agreed to collect a particularly heavy tribute from the Mountain, but when in 1820 he sent his agents to do so, they met an organized rebellion at Kisrawan and Metn. This became known in Lebanese history as the *'ammiyyah*, or common people's rebellion, the first of a new kind of uprising in which Maronite peasants and clergy stood up against the Druze-dominated political order. Bashir II was unable either to control the rebellion or raise taxes, and he decided to take refuge in the Hawran. Two of his cousins were appointed in his place. After he had gone, however, unrest became so widespread that he was reappointed in 1821 and called back to restore order, and this time he was able to crush the rebels.[19]

In 1831, Ibrahim Pasha conquered Syria in the name of his father Muhammad Ali Pasha, the governor of Egypt, who rose against his Ottoman overlords to challenge them and, for a while, defeat them. The Egyptians proved to be no less exacting than the governors they replaced. At first they had been welcomed, at least by Christian and Jewish minorities, but their expansionist policies led to heavy burdens of conscription, taxation, and forced labor that turned the Syrian populations against them. The Egyptian rulers of the nineteenth century thus learned a lesson their descendants would have to learn all over again in the twentieth: it is one thing to maintain control in Egypt, whose population is relatively homogeneous and centralized by geography, and quite another to control the Syrians, whose diversity and compartmentalized geography make it easy to defy authority and resist conquest.

Under Egyptian rule, Bashir II allowed outsiders to interfere with

Mountain politics. He had been friendly with the Egyptians even before they took over Syria, and he openly sided with them against his Ottoman overlords when they attacked Syria and complied with their requests for tax levies and arms. He provided Druzes to serve in the army, and although he persuaded the Egyptians to halve the number of recruits they demanded from him, the draft was extremely unpopular among the Druzes. He then agreed to their request to disarm the Druzes – allegedly because they had resisted conscription – along with the rest of the Lebanese population. Reluctantly the emir spread the word that Druzes and Christians had to surrender their arms. New conscription orders were also issued, calling for the enlisting of Druzes from the Hawran and Muslims from the interior. In response, a major insurrection broke out in 1838 in the Hawran, supported by the Druzes of Wadi Taym and Lebanon. Bashir II's son and 4,000 Christians under his command helped the governor of Damascus and Ibrahim Pasha to suppress the revolt.[20]

The Christians in Syria had at first welcomed the Egyptians because they appeared to promote Christian equality with the Muslims. The Druzes sided against them, first because they were allies of their enemy Bashir II, and later in protest against their conscription and disarmament policies. In 1831, when the Egyptians were still advancing in Syria, clashes broke out between the two sects in Deir al-Qamar, the Metn, and the Beqaa. Throughout the decade, improvement in the lot of Maronites and other Christians at the expense of the status of the Druzes fed misunderstandings and resentments. When the Druze rebellion broke out in 1838, Bashir II's use of Christian troops to repress it turned resentments into lasting hostility.

For a brief period in 1840, it seemed that the old Maronite–Druze alliances could be revived. The Christians in Lebanon had turned against the Egyptians and they, like the Druzes, rebelled against the government's demands that they give up their arms. Encouraged and armed by British representatives in Syria, the Lebanese openly declared their opposition to the disarmament and, starting in Deir al-Qamar, they broke out in open and widespread revolt which was joined by Shi'is, Sunnis, and Christians from other areas. The Egyptians blockaded Mount Lebanon and, with the support of Bashir II, crushed the revolt. That precipitated the intervention of Britain, Russia, Austria, and Prussia, which were set on preventing a break-up of the Ottoman empire, and the reestablishment of Ottoman rule in Syria.

The cooperation of Maronites and Druzes in that revolt showed that a Maronite–Druze alliance was still possible in 1840; nonetheless, the relations of the two sects had suffered serious damage. Perhaps a return then and there to peace and to a strong but even-handed and autonomous rule in Mount Lebanon could even then have prevented a permanent rupture. But that is not clear because changes in the relations of Maronites and Druzes were tied to broader changes in the relations of the Ottoman empire and the West, one effect of which was to polarize its communities.

The Ottoman government was in the midst of change which had begun to affect sectarian relations among its subject peoples. The change was a response to a general political, military, and economic decline which made it a prey to the ambitions of rival European powers and to the emerging aspirations to autonomy and independence by subject peoples of the empire, attracted to the European-inspired ideology of nationalism. Evidence of Ottoman decline was there for all to see, not least in Syria which the Ottomans could not even keep hold of in the 1830s and reconquered only with the help of Europe. To check Ottoman decline the government launched the Western-inspired reforms known as the *tanzimat*, or orderings, a series of laws promulgated between 1839 and 1876, which were intended to strengthen the Ottoman empire by centralizing its administration, the only effective avenue for change. The Tanzimat introduced a new principle of equality between the empire's Muslim and non-Muslim populations, and the Muslims began to lose ground to outsiders. Christians, who along with Jews and other *dhimmi*s or protected people had been a separate class of citizens (they paid special taxes and did not serve in the army), gained privileges. The Tanzimat provided the legal basis for their growing influence by making all Ottoman subjects, regardless of religion, equal before the law.

European influence and interference were felt both at the heart of the empire and in its provinces. Beirut became the center of a new trade with Europe in which raw silk was the principal export and manufactured goods were imported. Consulates were opened in Beirut to promote economic interests and allow them to play a role in local politics. The Ottoman representatives in Syria, like the Syrian populations themselves, understood that perfectly well.

In Syria, France and England were the most important, although by no means the only, powers to be reckoned with. France had had trading contacts since the seventeenth century with the Syrian coast, where it was established in the important ports. These relations strengthened in the nineteenth century as the importance of the silk trade grew, because France dominated the silk trade and thereby the export trade. England had concentrated on the Indian trade; Syria's importance to England centered on the caravan routes crossing the interior to Iraq and Iran; it also had the largest share of the import trade. Both governments began to look upon local minorities as their clients and protégés.

In the sixteenth century, a system known in the West as "Capitulations," treaties arranged by *capita* or headings, recognized and codified the special status of, first the French, and then all other European subjects in the Ottoman empire. It remained in place until the First World War. At first, these capitulations were concessions to trading communities that provided for commercial and legal privileges within the empire, but their function changed with the growth of European power and influence in the nineteenth century and with commercial conventions, the first of which was the Anglo-Ottoman convention of 1838 when they were extended all over the empire to apply not only to European nationals but to local inhabitants in the service of consuls and foreign merchants. By the early nineteenth century, these European protégés numbered in the thousands, among them Arab Christians who were the main beneficiaries of the growth of European influence in Syria.

The European powers developed special ties with various local sects in Syria, which contributed to their polarization. Russia was a protector of the Orthodox, while the British, after some success in developing an Orthodox, Sunni, and Jewish clientele, came to favor some important families among the Druzes. The European Catholic states turned their attention to their local co-religionists, and none did so more dynamically than the French who put a high premium on their missionaries and their schools. At the time the Capitulations were signed, France was the main Catholic power in Europe, and the self-appointed protector of the Maronites. Close ties between France and the Maronites had continued in subsequent centuries. Members of the Khazin family often served as French consuls in Beirut. Maronites developed the feeling that France was their special protector and friend. By the early 1840s, they depended almost exclusively on the French consulate in Beirut, as the Druzes did on the British.

The Maronites were in an ideal position to garner their share of profits from the silk-centered economy. In some parts of the Shuf, raw silk had been produced for the local production as early as Mamluk times, and from the late sixteenth century onwards it was cultivated for export. By the nineteenth century, it was the main crop in the Mountain. The Ma'n and Shihab emirs had encouraged its cultivation in the Shuf and Kisrawan. Druze shaykhs had encouraged Maronite labor to move to the Shuf, and had donated land to the Maronite church as additional incentive to cultivate silk. Other Christians also came to settle in the Shuf as laborers in the silk cultivation. Maronite peasants, monks, and shaykhs became cultivators of silk or in the cities money-lenders who advanced money on the crop, middlemen between the European wholesaler and the local retailer, brokers between the European merchants and the producers of various crops, partners and owners in trading and landowning ventures, manufacturers of silk and other products. The Druzes, who owned the land on which much of the silk crop was grown, essentially took no part in any of these activities.[21]

The integration of Syria into the world economy through the silk trade promoted a merchant class at the expense of the rest of the population. The Christians who benefited from the trade with the West posed a threat to the traditionally privileged classes, whether Maronite or Druze in Mount Lebanon or Sunni on the Syrian coast and interior. The landlords of the Mountain and the old urban élite began to lose their prominence to these new entrepreneurs in the regional and international markets, ready to exchange goods profitable in trade with the West and in particular to finance the cultivation, production, and export of raw silk. Agriculture began to specialize and to be organized for a regional and even international, rather than a local, market. Some villages and towns turned into centers of trade and artisan production, which brought them prosperity. Grain brought new wealth to villages, and particularly to Zahleh on the eastern flank of Mount Lebanon, the principal center of the rich valley of the Beqaa. Production in silk and cotton cloth, weaving, and spinning brought money to villages such as Zuq Mikayel in Kiswaran and Deir al-Qamar in the Shuf. Deir al-Qamar, which had always enjoyed a special administrative role as a capital of the Ma'n rulers of Lebanon and a center of power, now grew rich on trade as well. For the peasants, especially those in mulberry cultivation, for the first time it was possible to borrow money from someone other than the landlord. The new entrepreneurs from the cities loaned money against the silk crop. Peasants could make sizable profits and become landowners themselves, or they could become wage earners in the fields around Beirut where mulberry tree cultivation had spread or in the new silk mills scattered about the Mountain.

To the extent that the new economy benefited new social classes and not the old privileged ones, whether Maronite or Druze in Mount Lebanon or Sunni elsewhere, sectarian issues could have been overshadowed by class issues. But by the time class issues had surfaced, sectarianism had already polarized local communities, including the landed and traditionally powerful *muqata'ji*s of Mount Lebanon, at odds since the days of Bashir II, and the inhabitants of Aleppo, Damascus, and other Syrian towns.

In the Muslim heartland for centuries the Syrian desert had formed the nexus of the major north–south and east–west caravan routes linking Africa to the Fertile Crescent, Iran, and India. Although caravan trade between Damascus and the Syrian coast existed as well, it was irregular, risky, and expensive compared to trade with regions to the east. In the late eighteenth century, two or three caravans a year traveled between Damascus and Baghdad, its most active trading partner, bearing both staple and luxury goods.[22]

In the course of the nineteenth century, trade with Europe grew at the expense of the ancient caravan routes through Syria, although at least through the 1830s goods arriving from Baghdad and other eastern centers still comprised a fair share of the economy. In 1825 it was half the amount coming in from the coast; by 1833 it had declined to 30 percent, but that was still a significant share, and Damascus had also begun to act as distributor to the east, north, and south of goods imported from Europe. In particular, cotton goods flowed from Beirut to Damascus, Aleppo, and Baghdad. After the mid-century, the caravan trade began to decline as sea trade grew.[23]

At the beginning of the nineteenth century Damascus had been a prosperous city. Among merchants, diversification of trade and business, real estate, and intermarriage with the ulema had led to riches and influence. Unlike the newly rich merchants of Beirut who liked to flaunt their wealth, the merchants of Damascus led what appeared to be austere lives. Their bazaar shops were small; their simple houses gave no hint of the lavish furnishings, the elaborate tiles and woodwork within that testified to the riches they had accumulated.

The decline in trade and the competition from the Christians favored by the Europeans meant that Muslim merchants began to lose ground, replaced by Christians and Jews supported by the European consulates. The small merchants of Damascus were hard hit. A recession in Europe in 1857–8 tightened credit; a poor grain harvest cut the profits of both importers and local producers; and, partly as a result of the hard times, caravans were more and more frequently plundered by nomads on the Damascus–Baghdad road. In need of funds, Damascene merchants turned to Beiruti merchants for bills of exchange on European commercial houses.[24]

Textile workers were also hard hit. Until the late 1830s, the textile industry was the largest employer in Damascus, with some 4,000 silk and cotton looms. In the face of European competition, however, the local textile market went into recession, and by the late 1840s only 1,000 looms were still at work and only one type of textile, a fabric called *'alaja* made from local silk and English cotton thread, was still being produced although under severe strain.[25]

The non-Muslim population – Christian and Jewish – fared much better. They could become European protégés, a status that was more or less closed to Muslims and that protected the holder from commercial restrictions and guaranteed preferential treatment with European businesses. Christians and Jews protected by British, French, Austrian, Prussian, and Russian consuls accumulated wealth, and by mid-century were the main moneylenders to the provincial treasury. When short-term bonds called *serghi*s were issued by the Ottoman governor to raise revenue, the buyers were apt to be either local Christians and Jews or Europeans.

The Ottoman Land Code of 1858 allowed Europeans and their protégés to buy up both urban real estate and agricultural land from the impoverished Muslim Damascene notables.[26] The Muslim notables, hard hit economically as well as politically, deprived Damascus of the strong local leadership it needed in times of social unrest. The loss of the power of the Azms at the end of the eighteenth century was symptomatic of these changes. During the Egyptian occupation, and for a while after 1842 when the Ottomans tried to reestablish a centralized administration and introduce reform to this end, factionalism was momentarily kept at bay through an effectively enforced policy. That same policy, however, produced a whole new set of tensions. Some of the notables for the first time were alienated from the government, and although lack of manpower and money often made Ottoman reforms ineffective in practice, the resentment of the notables towards the Tanzimat sponsors was nonetheless real. Ineffectiveness at imposing reform or centralization also allowed the notables to interfere in Ottoman affairs and regain the ear of government and the loyalty of the populace. However, in the absence of clear leadership either among the notables or in the central government, factionalism further weakened authority and encouraged social unrest.

In Lebanon, the arrival of the Europeans and of the Tanzimat spelled the end of the emirate system. When the Ottomans reconquered Syria, they deposed Bashir II, who had sided with the Egyptian invaders, sent him on a British ship into exile, first to Malta and then to Istanbul where he died in 1851, and replaced him with Bashir III. This Bashir was weak, both because he had been brought to power by foreign intervention and because he lacked the strength of character needed to impose himself as ruler. The Shihabs lost their legitimacy in the eyes of both the Lebanese and the Ottomans, and the power vacuum which followed did away with any remaining constraints on sectarian hatreds. Bashir II had helped create this situation, but he himself had been a strong leader who had managed to keep in check the very divisions he had fostered. The Lebanese, however much they might have disliked control, were awed by power and despised weakness in their rulers; some of their most legendary rulers, Bashir II most of all, were in fact oppressors. His successor, in contrast, failed to gain the cooperation of either Druzes or Maronites and to keep their sectarian tensions under control. In 1841, the first of a series of Druze–Maronite clashes occurred in the Shuf; it then spread to other parts of Lebanon. This gave the Ottomans the excuse they were looking for to end the special status of the Mountain. In January 1842, they deposed Bashir III and declared the end of the Shihab emirate.[27]

After Bashir III had been removed, the Ottomans tried to rule Lebanon directly by appointing as Ottoman governor an official named Umar Pasha, but the unrest in the Mountain did not stop. This unrest was partly anti-Ottoman in inspiration. The new governor tried to generate support for the central government in the Mountain by circulating petitions calling for direct Ottoman rule and by trying to win over the Druzes and Maronites, but he ended up by alienating both. The Druzes at first welcomed him, as they saw in him a means to recover some of the privileges and property they had lost in the last years of the Shihab emirate. They soon turned against him, when they discovered he had no intention of giving back privileges and in fact was bent on imposing Ottoman rule. They mounted a revolt under the leadership of Shibli al-Aryan, who had stood up to the joint Egyptian–Syrian forces in the Hawran in 1838; he once again met with defeat.

The Maronites in the meantime incessantly lobbied for a return of the Shihabs and were at odds with the Druzes over their opposition to them, their initial support of direct Ottoman rule, property disputes dating back to the last years of the Shihab emirate, and over compensation for their losses in the sectarian clashes of 1841. The Maronites had been partly responsible for that outbreak, but they had also been the main loser and hated the Druzes for it. The Druzes resented the disarming of their most noble families, who had then been conscripted, crushed, driven into exile, deprived of their property, and dispersed. The Christians had taken over Druze territory and refused to return it, so there were claims, petitions, and property disputes. The Druzes resented the Maronite clergy for lobbying against the restoration of Druze rights and privileges, and for encouraging their co-religionists not to join the Druzes in an alliance against the Ottomans, despite the fact that the Maronites did not support the Ottomans either.

Consular pressures also defeated Ottoman effort to rule Mount Lebanon directly, and in December 1842 the Ottoman government and the Great Powers introduced a new plan for the government of Mount Lebanon called the Double Qaymaqamate. It took effect in 1843 and, with a revision in 1845, remained in place until 1861. It divided the Mountain into two self-governing districts, each under a district governor (*qaymaqam*): a northern district under a Maronite, and a southern district under a Druze. These *qaymaqam*s were appointed directly by the Ottomans and were accountable to the Ottoman governor in Sidon who, in spite of his title, since 1840 resided in Beirut (the Egyptians had moved the center of administration of the Syrian coast from Acre and Sidon to Beirut, and the Ottomans kept it there when they reconquered the area).

The Ottomans chose Haydar Abu'l-Lama as Christian and Ahmad Arslan as Druze *qaymaqam*s, probably because these shaykhs came from prestigious families without being as politically influential as, say, the Shihabs among the Christians and the Janbalats among the Druzes. This new government represented a compromise between the Ottoman effort to implement its new centralizing reforms and replace the Shihabs with direct Ottoman rule in Mount Lebanon at one end of the spectrum, and the French who had alienated the Ottomans in the 1830s by supporting Muhammad Ali Pasha, and who, after his withdrawal from Syria, lobbied incessantly for a restoration of the Shihab emirate, at the other. In between, ranging from full support to conditional support of the Ottomans, were the remaining Great Powers. The British were opposed to a return of the Shihabs and they favored a consolidation of Ottoman rule in Mount Lebanon, consistent with their more general policy of support for the Ottoman empire. The Russians had no objection to the Ottoman preference for direct rule over Lebanon, until, when the compromise of the Double Qaymaqamate was put in place, they began to demand a third *qaymaqam* for their co-religionists, the Greek Orthodox. The Austrians, represented by Prince von Metternich who was anxious to maintain the status quo, had first supported the restoration of the Shihabs along with the French, and were the originators of the compromise solution.

Although the European powers had created the Double Qaymaqamate, neither they nor the Maronites of Lebanon acted on the assumption that Lebanon had been divided in two.[28] As a result, the new administrative units created more problems than they solved because they did not correspond to the social realities of nineteenth-century Lebanon. The Double Qaymaqamate could only have worked if the populations within the northern Christian and southern Druze qaymaqamates had been homogeneous, which was not the case. Although censuses were made at the time, their reliability varied because young men hid from the census taker to avoid conscription and from everyone else to avoid taxation. Although approximate, however, the numbers do suggest that in reality the populations of the qaymaqamate were mixed in many parts of the Mountain, especially in the south. In most of the Christian qaymaqamate, the Christians were the overwhelming majority, but in the Metn many

Druzes lived among them. In the Druze qaymaqamate, the Christians formed approximately two-thirds of the population; only the Shuf proper had a Druze majority, but even there the Christians were numerous. Deir al-Qamar, in the heart of Druze country, was the leading Christian town of Mount Lebanon.[29]

The powers of the *qaymaqam*s were restricted to their own districts, which created additional problems for the new system. To take care of the scores of Christians in the south, the Ottoman authorities decided to appoint one Christian and one Druze agent or *wakil* to exercise judicial and tax-collecting functions on behalf of the landlords in the mixed south. The *wakil*s were responsible to the *qaymaqam* of the south. In the northern district, no *wakil* was appointed because the population was mainly Christian, and the Ottomans therefore thought it unnecessary. As a result, in the north the Christian *qaymaqam* was free from checks on his power from *wakil*s or anyone else, aside from internal resistance to his rule by his own people. The Maronite shaykhs envied his power and vied for his position, and Shihab supporters lobbied intensively to bring the Shihabs back, with encouragement from the French and Austrian representatives.

In the south the *wakil* system and the constraints in Deir al-Qamar curtailed the Druze *qaymaqam*'s power, but he had the advantage of Druze solidarity behind him. The Druze shaykhs quickly reached a consensus over Shaykh Ahmad Arslan and, unlike their Maronite counterparts, rallied behind their new appointee. He had been in prison for resisting the Ottoman governor when he was appointed, but he had the authority to unite the other Druze shaykhs behind him.

The existence of a *wakil* system in the south and its absence in the north resulted in a difference in the relations of peasants and shaykhs in the two areas. In the north, the absence of *wakil*s left the peasants undefended from abusive landlord exactions, while in the south the *wakil*s were chosen by the people in their district and, because of that, became in effect ombudsmen between peasant and shaykh.[30]

In the Double Qaymaqamate, Deir al-Qamar was given a special status. Although it was in the Manasif district of the Abu Nakad shaykhs, the town was put outside their jurisdiction. No Druze or Christian *qaymaqam* was permitted to reside in the town or to have representatives in it. It had its own Druze and Christian *wakil*s. In addition, the district of Baabda, traditionally Druze controlled, was put under the Christian *qaymaqam*, on the grounds that the population had become almost entirely Christian. In 1845, however, the district was partitioned between the Christian and Druze *qaymaqam*s, restoring some of the Druze rights over it.

The unworkability of this dual government in Lebanon added new problems to the unresolved ones inherited from the last decades of the Shihabi emirate, with disastrous effects. After 1840, the absence of a strong and effective government was coupled with the continued buildup of Druze and Maronite frustrations and ambitions. In 1845, under pressure from the Great Powers, Shakib Efendi, the Ottoman foreign minister, was sent to Beirut and in October 1845, a *Règlement Shakib Effendi* amended the Double Qaymaqamate as rebellions broke out everywhere. In addition to the *wakils*, councils were introduced, officially to assist – in their view to curb the power of – the Druze *qaymaqam*. These councils included a deputy *qaymaqam*, a judge, an adviser for each of the Maronite, Druze, Greek Orthodox, Greek Catholic, Shi'i, and Sunni sects. Although the separate status of the Mountain was upheld, the *qaymaqam*s had been reduced to the status of public officials appointed by the Ottoman governor resident in Beirut.

Although the *iqta'* system was still in place, the power of the *muqata'jis* was severely curtailed by the councils who, along with the *wakils*, appropriated many of the *muqata'jis*' functions. The Maronite and Druze shaykhs had to resist encroachments on their power from rivals within and outside their community or from the government. They spent the following decade reasserting their traditional privileges over their peasants; within each community they vied with one another for its leadership; they defied the government and cultivated Western allies. The hostility that built up between shaykhs and peasants took on a character in the religiously homogeneous north different from that in the religiously mixed south. Tensions increased among shaykhs and clergy in the north and to some extent among shaykhs in the south until, by the 1850s, Sa'id Janbalat – Shaykh Bashir's son and a British protégé – emerged as their unquestioned leader.

In this situation the continued absence of a strong government, coupled with Druze and Maronite frustrated ambitions, was a recipe for disaster. Any social unrest could trigger warfare within communities and between them, and opportunities for generating unrest were clearly not lacking.

CHAPTER 2

VILLAGE AND TOWN LIFE ON THE EVE OF THE CIVIL WAR

Village life in Mount Lebanon in the middle of the nineteenth century was not very different from what it was until very recently. Life was slow and predictable. Cackling hens, crowing roosters, and braying donkeys greeted each new dawn. Housewives fried meat and vegetables in lard taken from the large containers stored near the kitchen, beginning a day of labor at home and in the field that lasted until long after the sun had set. All the women of the household shared the daily work of airing, sweeping, and scrubbing the house. Although water was abundant in the Mountain, it was used sparingly because it had to be brought in clay jars from sometimes distant streams and fountains either on the backs of donkeys or on the women's heads. It was used first for washing, or for the laundry that was hung up to dry on lines strung either in the yard or on the house's flat roof; then it served for scrubbing floors, roofs, and porches.

Bread was baked in the village oven or, more traditionally, on the *tannur*, a grill over a hole dug in the ground within a small windowless ventless cubicle, or in a loaf called *marquq* that was cooked outdoors over an open fire. The women squatted to throw a lump of dough from hand to hand until it formed a large round loaf; then it was flattened onto a convex surface and baked over the fire. In the kitchen of the prosperous peasant, something was always cooking in the pot. Vegetables, meats, fat, or jams were preserved for later use or the daily main meal was cooking there, usually a stew made of vegetables cooked in olive oil with browned onions and garlic, soup bones, and on Sundays and the numerous religious holidays, perhaps small chunks of meat.

Social life was important, and gave the poorer members of a family a chance to keep in touch with their more fortunate relations. Neighbors, relatives, and friends dropped by to drink tiny cups of coffee, eat dried fruit, and, in hot weather, sip lemonade prepared in the tradition of Batrun, with halved lemons left in sugar for days and then squeezed and mixed with water, or juices made from mulberries, grapes, and other fruit. On special occasions, pinenuts were added to the cold drinks.

A death of a family member was an event that brought out most clearly the unity of the family, clan, and village. Funerals and rituals of condolence were a central part of social life, more so than marriages or any other social occasion. Wailing was part of the ritual of expressing grief. For days after a funeral, people visited the bereaved family, presented their condolences, and sat in chairs taken from the stack in the corners of the reception areas. The room was hushed; people conversed in whispers. The women wore black for the occasion; the women of the family remained in mourning black for years.

The birth of a son was an occasion for particular rejoicing. In Christian villages and towns, pregnant women prayed to the Virgin to give them sons, promising in return to dress the baby in monk's clothing for a stretch of time of their choice during his childhood. When a boy was born, word spread quickly and the whole neighborhood rejoiced. Women uttered the cries reserved for the celebration of marriage and other festive occasions. Visitors, however remotely acquainted with the family of the newborn male, brought presents, especially the blue talisman that warded off the evil eye. In well-to-do families, *mughli* – rice flour and sugar mixed with anise, caraway, and other spices and slowly cooked – was served cold, garnished with nuts. If the child was a firstborn son, it was the custom, as it still is all over the Middle East, for the parents to drop their own given names and henceforth style themselves as parents by assuming the name they chose for the child and adding to it Abu, "father of," and Um, "mother of."

The adulation of male children continued throughout their early years and into adulthood. They were doted upon by grandmothers, mothers, aunts, sisters. They were the pride of the family and the old-age security of their parents. They grew up accustomed to being the center of attention. They expected to be served and to be given the choice tidbits at family meals. In return they defended family and community and upheld its honor. For that they were ready to kill and be killed. Even a sibling who shamed the family name – a sister seen with other men, for example – could incur severe punishment at their hands. An outsider who slighted the family honor, however lightly, could expect quick revenge if public apology was not speedily forthcoming. The slightest breach could be interpreted as betrayal.

All villagers were ready to fight to protect their village or town, but few were as protective as the mountaineers. In the villages under *muqata'ji* rule, subservience was expected, but it was increasingly hard to enforce as the transformations of the nineteenth century brought opportunities to the inhabitants of the villages and market towns of the Mountain that made them more independent. These men were not afraid to take risks; when they closed ranks against rival gangs or outsiders, they were quick to violence – *hadduni, hadduni,* "restrain me, restrain me," they would call to their friends lest their strength do unnecessary damage.

They lavished attention on friends and visitors, with no heed to the trouble or sacrifice their generosity might cause the family. They were the *shuyukh al-shabab* ("popular youth chiefs," sg. *shaykh al-shabab*) whose hot blood and sense of honor and justice would end in bloodshed when the opportunity arose. The opportunity came in the mounting unrest of the Qaymaqamate era.[1]

Despite these general traits which were shared by all parts of the Mountain, there were regional differences. The following section illustrates that with examples from some of the areas that affected, or were affected by, the 1860 civil war and where it all began.

Zahleh

Located in a deep and narrow valley carved out by the Berdawni river, on whose banks it stands, and on the eastern flank of the Mountain about 3,000 feet above sea level, Zahleh enjoys a temperate Mediterranean climate modified by the aridity of the steppe to the east. The Berdawni almost never goes dry, though often it is only a few yards wide; it separates the town "like a sharp sword, more limpid than the water of the ocean" into two sections connected by bridges. It is the inspiration of Zahalni poets and songwriters who to this day love to sit on its banks or in coffee houses overlooking its waters, drinking the locally made licorice-flavored arrack and taking turns singing improvised melodic rhythmic poems called *jazal*, with the whole group contributing the refrain to clapping hands. The abundance of water in the town ensures flourishing vegetation and supports many gardens.[2]

In the nineteenth century Zahleh's economy also flourished, so that by mid-century it had become Lebanon's largest commercial center. Trade was a natural outgrowth of its location between the grain-producing areas of the Beqaa and Hawran and the pastures of Mount Lebanon. It was surrounded by vineyards, vegetable gardens and orchards, olive groves, and mulberry trees. Products flourished that needed abundant water: tanning, flour mills (there were 13 of them at the beginning of the nineteenth century), cloth dyeing, and arrack distilleries. It was also a center of transportation and therefore of trade with the grain-producing regions, a natural function of its location on the western edge of the Beqaa valley, which lies between the Lebanon and Anti-Lebanon ranges and the Syrian hinterland.[3]

Zahleh had in fact already assumed all of these functions by the late eighteenth century. When early in the nineteenth the growth of population in the Mountain, coupled with the intensification of silkworm cultivation, had made Metn, Kisrawan, the Shuf, and other districts dependent upon it for grain, it became the major grain and livestock center for the entire region. Its population also grew as its economy expanded, from less than a thousand people at the end of the eighteenth century to probably between 10,000 and 12,000 by the late 1850s. Most of this growth came from emigration from the countryside, peasants and semi-nomads who left the Beqaa, Baalbek, and Hawran. Most were Greek Catholics or Greek Orthodox. The emigration therefore shifted the balance from equal Greek Catholic and Druze populations in the eighteenth century to an overwhelmingly Greek Catholic majority in the nineteenth.[4]

Thanks to prosperity, a goodly portion of this growing population was made up of entrepreneurs who traded with the itinerant merchants plying their trade between the Syrian coast and the interior; exchanged goods with wholesalers and small buyers in other districts; speculated in grain; bought and sold land; and, finally, acted as tax farmers and advisers to the shaykhs of the Beqaa and the governors of Damascus.

Because theirs was an agricultural economy the people of Zahleh never removed themselves completely from the agrarian life. The population continued to include a substantial number of peasants who tilled the land in the valley. The town also sheltered the nomads of the area on their way to or from the Beqaa, the Hawran and regions to the east. The *qabaday*s contributed to the maintenance of this agrarian life with their frontier attitudes of self-reliance, bravery, and a vigilante tradition of law and order. All these strains ensured that, although the town was in fact larger than many of its neighbors, it maintained a rural way of life that other settlements soon lost. As a result the Zahalni were at one and the same time open to strangers and provincial in attitude. Through the caravans they heard of worlds beyond: they knew of the riches of Damascus and the diversity of Beirut's trade. They were aware of the power struggles between Ottoman authorities in Damascus, shaykhs and emirs in the Mount, and Ottoman governors and European consuls on the coast. The European missionaries, especially Jesuits, in their midst opened them up to the influences of European culture, politics, and industry. But though the outside world in this way came to them, they only rarely, if at all, ventured forth into it. They were content to live and work in Zahleh; it answered their needs, and they had no desire to leave it.[5]

This provinciality coupled with the continuous hostility between shaykhs and emirs encouraged the people of Zahleh to maintain their distance from the Mountain; the administrative divisions introduced by the *qaymaqam* system in the 1840s and 1850s added further to their aloofness. Nor did the instability of the Syrian steppe encourage any alliances there: nomad attacks from that direction only served to make them feel more isolated and besieged.

This combination of isolation, vulnerability, and arrogance encouraged the already aggressive behavior of the *qabaday* class. Europeans complained that they were insolent, abusive to strangers, and tyrannical. Charles Henry Churchill, a British colonel who spent most of the 1840s and 1850s in Mount Lebanon and Beirut and wrote extensively about his stay there, tells us that 3,000 of the townsmen bore arms. Even those who admired their bravery accused them of cruelty and highhandedness. Whenever Zahleh was threatened they were eager to throw themselves into the fray. The Zahalni also took pride in their town and boasted endlessly that it was the most beautiful in Mount Lebanon and no doubt the world and its climate the best. They met challenges aggressively, indeed provocatively. They were often divided among themselves; but, easily taking offence, they faced the enemy with determination, and were quick to fight. Adding fuel to the fire, they thrived on the skirmishes, disputes, and conflicts that resulted. They threw themselves in equal measure into alliances and quarrels. Through it all, they increased their reputation for courage, bellicosity, and foolhardiness. They relished a fight and would brawl at the slightest provocation in the name of their town, their leaders, their sect, and their families. These were the limits of their loyalties and concerns. Indeed, they were the ultimate *qabadays*.[6]

Zahleh was the stronghold of Greek Catholic interests in the Mountain, and its enemies were identified primarily in terms of religion. Anyone who was not Greek Catholic – be he Christian, Druze, or Muslim – was the foe, an attitude abetted by their particularly aggressive and powerful clergy, who repeatedly urged their parishioners to take up arms against non-believers. Greek Catholics were a minority in Mount Lebanon, and this too encouraged belligerence. When Christians were attacked by non-Christians they willingly came to the defense of the Church, but when another Christian sect was the aggressor they were just as eager to fight. John Burckhardt, a Swiss-born English-sponsored explorer and traveler, visited Zahleh in 1810 and commented on their bigotry which was "not directed so much against the Mohammedans, as against their Christian brethren, whose creed at all differs from their own."[7] The few Protestants, mainly Presbyterian missionaries, were special targets. The Reverend J.L.

Porter, an Irish Presbyterian missionary who was sent to Syria in 1849 and spent ten years there, and who no doubt had his own set of prejudices, wrote that the Zahalni were "as ignorant a set of priest-ridden bigots as ever polluted a country." In 1844, on orders from the patriarch, the Greek Orthodox of Zahleh had mounted an attack against Protestant converts in Rashaiya to the south.[8]

When the Druzes were targets, their hostility had its political aspect. The Greek Catholics had ended the domination of a Druze family, a move applauded by Bashir II since it could only aid his own campaign against the Druze shaykhs, so that "not one [Druze] would dare raise his head in their presence." They also attacked the Shi'is of the Beqaa and Baalbek regions. According to Iskandar ibn Ya'qub Abkarius, a Christian of Armenian descent, who lived in Beirut and wrote his account of the disturbances in Syria, sometime before 1840 they killed a Shi'i shaykh of the Harfush family of Baalbek and beat up his followers. In retaliation during the Druze–Christian clashes of 1840–41, the Shi'is sided with the Druzes, and were ferociously attacked by the Zahalni in 1844. The Zahalni by "their high-handed manner struck terror in the hearts of all, and the name inspired fear in the Druzes and Mutawalis [i.e., Shi'is], who regarded even their unweaned babies with dread."[9]

They were not always enemies, however. Abkarius tells us that in 1841 the Zahalni appealed to the Harfush emirs and that Shi'i tribesmen from the Baalbek region fought alongside the Zahalni against the Druzes in 1840–41. Ad hoc alliances such as these could override sectarian loyalty, and perhaps explain the contradictory evidence of Zahalni–Shi'i hostility and collaboration. The rich Zahalni who owned land in the villages of the Beqaa and their Muslim, predominantly Shi'i, tenants had ample grounds for argument. A Druze chronicler, Husayn Abu Shaqra, tells us that the Zahalni landowners subjected the Muslim villagers in the Beqaa to "injustice and oppression" and drove them to the side of the Druzes.[10]

Relations between the Zahalni and Druzes deteriorated steadily in the first half of the nineteenth century. In 1840 the Zahalni sent aid to the town of Deir al-Qamar. The Druzes of Rashaiya led by Shibli al-Aryan and "thousands" of supporters (perhaps including Shi'is and Kurds) twice attacked Zahleh in the fall of 1841, killing what Abkarius described as a "great many" Zahalni, but probably in fact no more than 45 people; five houses were burned. Three years later, the Zahalni attacked the Druzes and totally defeated them, a rare occurrence in sectarian clashes of the mid-century.[11]

Peace was imposed in the Mountain after 1845, but the source of tensions had not been resolved. The Zahalni were all excited about the struggle against the Christian *qaymaqam* in the northern districts, and challenged him by electing a *shaykh al-shabab* in 1857. At the same time, distrust among sects grew, and the *qabaday*s of Zahleh, the self-named guardians of Christian rights in the Mountain, were eager for war. At the first opportunity they would show both the Druzes and the government who was stronger.

Deir al-Qamar

Deir al-Qamar had been the administrative and political center of the Manasif district since the seventeenth century, and as such was of importance both to the rulers of the Mountain and to their Ottoman overlords. A small village in the sixteenth century, it began its growth when it became the capital of the Ma'n dynasty. Fakhr al-Din was the first to beautify the town with fountains, marble courts, mansions, and a serai of Italian inspiration. His successors used Deir al-Qamar as a summer headquarters and, at least when the political climate allowed, wintered in Beirut. The Shihab emirs kept it as their capital, and more buildings were constructed, especially under Bashir II who, although he moved his seat of government to the serai at Beit al-Din, kept Deir al-Qamar as a political center. As such it was exempted from taxes. The leading local historian Isa Iskandar al-Ma'luf (himself a native of Zahleh) wrote that Deir al-Qamar had become a "paradise." Its special status had been recognized under the Double Qaymaqamate.[12]

By the nineteenth century, Deir al-Qamar was a prosperous industrial and trade center of the region, thanks in part to its location. In the heart of the southern Mountain, it had functioned since the seventeenth century as a relay between Sidon on the coast, the Mountain, Damascus, and the Syrian interior beyond. One of its major items of trade was raw silk, as it was a collection center from where silk was sold to middlemen working for entrepreneurs in Sidon and Beirut, or to Syrian traders in Damascus, Aleppo, Homs, and Hama. The town was also a center for the local grain and livestock market. "Anyone who prefers regular daily work to the nomadic and uncertain life of the peasant can come and settle within its walls,"[13] so there was a continuous stream of people who came there and traded with the interior, the coast, and beyond.

Through trade and immigration, Deir al-Qamar soon acquired a community of merchants and moneylenders centered in the town's active bazaar, which included an old Jewish community whose peddlars went up and down the villages of the district trading and lending money against the next crop. The merchants of Deir al-Qamar diversified their sources for income and trade. When in 1821 or about, Bashir sought a large loan from bankers in Damascus, a wealthy Christian silk merchant from Deir al-Qamar by the name of Butrus al-Chawish heard about it. He sent a Muslim moneylender to the emir whom he had trusted with more gold than "all the bankers in Damascus" possessed. Another employee of Bashir II was a jovial character who became the emir's emissary to the central government in Istanbul.[14]

Deir al-Qamar was also an administrative center, which created retinues of advisers and followers and generated all sorts of jobs. The town benefited from the emirs and shaykhs who dominated the surrounding area and needed employees. The shaykhs of the region employed in their armies the Druzes from the Aleppo region who sought refuge with Bashir II when his relations with the Druze shaykhs were still cordial. The largest recruiter was Shaykh Bashir Janbalat. Mikha'il Mishaqa (1800–88), whose memoirs are an invaluable source for Mount Lebanon and Syria in this period, tells us that his father Jirjis was recruited by Bashir II to become his scribe. The emir paid him a good salary, took over his debts, saw to it that he was given clothing suitable for his new position, and gave him provisions for his household. From then on the Mishaqas cultivated political and commercial connections and used them to protect their interests and further their business by acting as tax collectors and moneylenders for the emirs, shaykhs, and the peasants who sold them their raw silk. Among those who obtained loans from them were the Shihab emirs and Bashir Janbalat. When the emir's requirements were beyond their means the Mishaqas raised money from others and paid back the loan when the silk came in. They also made money from the production of silk fabrics and trade with Damascus.[15]

Deir al-Qamar had a large population of industrial workers and artisans; it had flour mills, a soap factory, and what was described vaguely by one traveler as "numerous branches of industry," but it was especially known as a center of manufacture for silk cloth. Large numbers of small workshops employing a handful of workers were organized in the mid-nineteenth century, until the textile industry of Deir al-Qamar boasted 120 looms. The town was also a center for cotton weaving and it crafted objects of exceptional quality that were said to rival even those of Damascus. The *'abaya* robes, worn by shaykhs, of cotton or silk woven with gold and silver, were made there. By the middle of the nineteenth century, Deir al-Qamar had established itself as the richest town of Mount Lebanon.[16]

The prosperity of Deir al-Qamar was reflected in its population figures. At the beginning of the nineteenth century it had 4,000 people; by the late 1850s, the population probably reached between 7,000 and 10,000,[17] and the Christian population overtook the Druze. Greek Catholic and mostly Maronite Christians dominated the town in an otherwise Druze part of the country. Colonel Rose, the British consul in Beirut in the 1840s, tells us that this was the result of a deliberate policy by Bashir II so that by 1843 the Christian population was five or six times as large as the Druze. Churchill tells us that the landed property once owned by Druzes in the neighborhood of Deir al-Qamar had passed into Christian hands, and that the few Druzes who still lived in the town had lost all influence. Mishaqa's memoirs corroborate this.[18]

Deir al-Qamar was the most urbane town of Mount Lebanon (though still provincial by Beiruti, not to mention Damascene or Cairene, standards), thanks in part to the involvement in politics and government of the Ma'n and Shihab emirs who lived there, and in part to the trade that brought a continuous stream of people to town.

A few townspeople had relatives in other countries – the Mishaqas in Egypt, for example – with whom they established a lively trade. One of these native sons was the sophisticated and open-minded Mikha'il Mishaqa who was exceptional even by Deir al-Qamari standards: he could not have been produced by Zahleh or north Lebanon as they were then. He learned from his father that a good education was an asset for survival in politics and trade. He went to Egypt for three years to learn about trade and then returned to Deir al-Qamar to go into the silk business. He was an entrepreneur, not a civil servant, a profession in which his father had no interest for his sons. There were few people who knew how to compute and keep books as well as Mikha'il, a skill his father had taught him. He was also interested in astronomy and physics. A rich uncle kept him supplied with books when he came from Egypt to visit. While he was in Egypt, Mikha'il Mishaqa was accused by a man from Acre of being ignorant of music because he was a mountaineer. Mishaqa thought that the people of the Lebanon were "far superior" to the hoi-polloi of Safed in Palestine, and set about learning about music. At the first opportunity he showed off his knowledge and the ignorance of the offender. In such ways, Mishaqa continued to educate himself. He taught himself medicine and became a doctor; in 1859 he was appointed vice-consul of the United States in Damascus.[19]

Unlike the Zahalni frontier mentality, the Deir al-Qamaris favored compromise and conciliation, a wise attitude for a Christian enclave in the Druze heartland, where persuasion and not force was an asset. Compromise had also been encouraged when the Shihabs made the town an asylum for many political refugees. When early in his career Bashir II had allied himself with the Druzes, he offered protection to Druzes from Aleppo who had rebelled against the Ottomans. One of these Druzes was said to have arrived accompanied by 300 men with their horses and mules. The town also took in people from the Syrian coast and beyond. Mishaqa describes how his family came from Corfu to settle in Syria, and then had to seek the protection of Bashir II because of the oppressive rule of al-Jazzar.[20]

Another citizen of Deir al-Qamar was Hanna Baydar who had also been driven away from his native village near Sidon by Jazzar. After he had rescued three young men of Shaykh Abu Nakad's family from the Manasif district whom Jazzar had imprisoned in his fortress at Sidon, the four had fled to the safety of Deir al-Qamar. Baydar remained in the town until his murder by an assassin seeking the reward Jazzar had put up for his capture.[21]

Deir al-Qamar became an asylum from the oppression of the governors of the Syrian coast once again under Abdallah Pasha's harsh and unpopular rule. He executed the Jewish superintendent of the treasury, a trusted man. He conducted reprisals against Christians whom he suspected of aiding the Greeks in their revolt against the Ottoman empire in the 1820s. Some of the great merchants of Acre left for the more secure city of Beirut, and some of them fled to Mount Lebanon and the relative safety of Bashir II's power. Deir al-Qamar also attracted peasants seeking the protection of a government from the skirmishes in the countryside in the 1820s and 1830s.[22]

Among the Deir al-Qamaris some treated the Druzes with regard, however, aware that cooperation between them had always characterized relations in the Mountain, that the custom among clansmen was "to distinguish followers not with regard to sect, but rather with regard to allegiance and loyalty." People all knew stories of how Druzes and Maronites had joined forces to vanquish oppressors who had brutalized them both. Hanna Baydar, the hero who had settled in Deir al-Qamar after rescuing some Druze boys of the Abu Nakad family from Jazzar's prison, was Greek Catholic. His assassin, however, was a Druze. In the 1890s, a Druze shaykh from a nearby village thwarted a Druze plot to attack the Christians by reminding the conspirators that they had chosen to live in the Mountain because it kept them from Muslim interference and that many Christians had defended them and helped them further their fortunes there. "If there had been two like him among the Druze and Christians of our time," wrote Mishaqa, "they could have preserved their land from the calamities which befell them in the Incidents of 1841 and 1860."[23]

Prosperity and a shift in the sectarian balance at a time of growing Christian–Druze tension in Mount Lebanon at the end of Bashir II's reign changed the attitude the Deir al-Qamaris had earlier held toward compromise and conciliation. As they became richer, they began to be complacent, flaunting their wealth in grand houses and elegant clothes, and in their shops and buildings, which were "of a beauty not found in any other locality in the Mount," and in their "fine mansions and houses ... with marble courts and fountains and furnished in costly style." "Their leading citizens amassed riches, they kept horses; their wives and daughters dressed in silk and satin, and blazed with jewelry, gold, and pearls and diamonds." Outsiders found them "wealthy, rude, and arrogant." They began also to maintain a standing armed force, which Rose in 1841 said was 800 or 900 strong; Churchill claimed it was more like 2,000 warriors ready to overrun three times that number of Druzes. Abkarius called them "strong;" Rose found them "warlike." They became more aggressive, involving themselves in the affairs of the districts around them to protect Christian interests against the Druzes. The Druzes in the town itself grew uneasy.[24]

Young thugs not unlike *qabaday*s elsewhere became typical of the new arrogance and lack of restraint. The deeds of one of them displays the kind of mood that had grown there. A young man named Zakkhur al-Sham'uni, known for his temper, was sent to kill a cobbler from Sidon. He armed himself with a pistol and a little axe and set off to fulfill his mission. As he waited for the cobbler to appear, he noticed a guard at the city gate who was humiliating the Mountain people whenever one of them would appear seeking entrance to the city. So Sham'uni decided to get rid of the guard as well. He followed him to a latrine, struck him down, stole his watch, seal, and pistols, and cut off his ears. He killed the cobbler in much the same fashion. When he looked for a place to rest on his way back to Deir al-Qamar, he came upon a Shi'i shaykh he recognized from the Shqif region in Jabal Amel. He was near a bridge saying his prayers. Remembering that he had heard Bashir II complain about the shaykh, he decided to kill him, too, and proceeded to do so as his victim was prostrate in prayer, removing his ears as he had done with the others. Two Shi'i muleteers driving ten laden donkeys saw him do this deed and tried to shoot him. He attacked them with the dead shaykh's sword, cut their ears off, and took their donkeys. He presented Bashir II with his day's work: ten human ears and ten loaded donkeys.[25]

A young Maronite by the name of Ghalib Abi-Ikr from Deir al-Qamar was a servant of Bashir II. He was arrested for no apparent reason near Khan al-Tutun in Damascus, as he was on his way to supper with friends in the Christian quarter. In jail, he learned that the soldiers who had arrested him had been ordered to strangle 17 prisoners that evening and were rounding up men they hoped would do the job for them, since they were not anxious to accomplish it themselves. Each new prisoner was to take on the task for one of the victims. The newly arrested men were loudly objecting to having to take on this chore and were crying like babies. Then Abi-Ikr volunteered to kill all the condemned men and made the soldiers release the rest of the prisoners. He strangled them as gently as he could. When he asked whether there were more victims to finish off, he was astonished that the soldiers cursed him "instead of showing their appreciation."[26]

The young thugs of Deir al-Qamar did not hesitate to provoke the Druzes. Rose, whose sympathy lay with the Christians and who described the Druzes as "semi-barbarians," nonetheless had to admit in 1843 that impartiality compelled him "to say that the Christians were as ready to attack the Druzes, and would assuredly have done so had they been similarly influenced." In 1841, as soon as violence broke out armed men from Deir al-Qamar attacked and killed 17 Druzes from Baaqline, and returned home in triumph. But the following October the Druzes came back to settle scores with them in a surprise attack which lasted for three days until the Ottoman authorities and the British consul intervened. Even then the Druzes continued to blockade the town, and they kept it under siege for over three weeks, at the end of which they attacked Bashir in his palace at Beit al-Din. It took further intervention from the authorities before these clashes ended.[27]

After that the Deir al-Qamaris were somewhat more cautious in their dealings with the Druzes and did not provoke them as the Zahalni regularly did. They had learned the price to be paid for armed conflict. The presence of an Ottoman garrison nearby encouraged them to count on the government, and not only on themselves, for protection. The location of the town in the midst of Druze territory also entailed commercial and financial transactions between the town and the countryside that were vital to their welfare. Anyone who did not want to deal with the Druzes simply left town. After the clashes of 1841, many of the Christians who could afford it sought the protection of European consuls and co-religionists in Beirut, but that was an option open mainly to the merchants and other wealthy townspeople. For the majority, the only choice was to stay. As a result, many of those who could afford to were leaving; those who could not were moving from the surrounding countryside into the comparative safety of Deir al-Qamar itself, the only Christian haven available to them. By choice or by force, or a combination of both, Deir al-Qamar lived in relative peace with its Druze neighbors until 1860.

Kisrawan

Northeast of Beirut on the western slope of the central Lebanon range which overlooks the Mediterranean, between the gorges of the Ibrahim and Dog (Nahr al-Kalb) rivers, Kisrawan presented a landscape of villages made of stone houses and terraced fields in the midst of limestone rocks and pine forests. Clustered in the central, southern, and western zones were the most fertile lands where the majority of the farming population lived.[28]

Much of the land in Kisrawan was controlled by the shaykhs of the Khazin family and their relationship with their peasants was that dictated by the *iqta'* system which bound field workers and the shaykhs who owned the fields into a tightly knit society often unchanged for generations. Loyalty protected the society from the unrest that might otherwise have been generated by inequalities between shaykh and peasant. The holdings of tenant farmers were leased according to their expected yields: for mulberry cultivation, for example, one of the main crops of Kisrawan and the Mountain, rent was expressed in number of leaf loads. Each contract was valid for only a single season, but it was renewable. The lease also defined other peasant responsibilities, including the land tax, and a deposit, most often in cash, at the time of the contract or in kind at the time of the crop. The landlord had the right to dictate what the peasant was to cultivate on his parcel and to exact other forms of corvée not only from him but from his family, for the women could be required to work in the shaykh's household. The peasant had to give presents to the landlord on holidays and numerous other specified occasions, including the weddings of the landlord's sisters and daughters, happy occasions for all but the peasants who were taxed to pay for them.[29]

Nor did the peasant's private life escape the landlord's exactions. He had to pay his lord for permission to marry; he could not associate with people outside his lord's domain. Though the peasants were not serfs and theoretically could move freely, in practice it was difficult.

Bashir II was particularly hard on both shaykh and peasant. The Khazins' power was seriously reduced by their involvement in partisan politics in the Mountain and by the emir's deliberate undermining of their power through appropriation of many of their judicial functions and the cultivation of members of the clergy as an alternate Maronite leadership. The Khazins' power was so reduced that when the *'ammiyyah* revolted they turned for leadership to priests and peasants, rather than to influential Maronite families. In addition, the growth of the money economy and of the new trade with the West bypassed them almost entirely. They began to run into debt and to sell their lands. In their effort to fight off poverty and the diminution of their state they wasted money on luxury imports from Europe, on political bribes, and on arms for their followers. They also wasted their peasants' goodwill by continuing to exact their traditional privileges.[30]

The peasants bore most of the burden of taxes levied by the government, in addition to the land tax. Bashir II also introduced the corvée to construct his many public works, of which a canal that took three years to dig and a bridge over the Dog river north of Beirut were only two examples. During the Egyptian occupation, peasants labored in the coal and iron mines. Although after the Ottomans regained power, the Double Qaymaqamate abandoned the corvée, the hostility it had induced remained. Dependence on landlords diminished with the growth in the number of money-lenders and a market economy, but the peasants were still expected to serve them. Finally in 1845 the Kisrawani peasants were handed a new cause for resentment when they were deprived of the representation the *wakils* gave to the peasants of the south.

Just as the peasants were reaching the limits of their endurance, the Maronite shaykhs and especially the Khazins weakened their position by opposing the Qaymaqamate. Although the Abu'l-Lama had a higher social rank then they did, the Khazins had long wielded more real power, and they bitterly resented the appointment of an Abu'l-Lama as *qaymaqam*. When he died in 1854, his kinsman Bashir Ahmad Abu'l-Lama replaced him and tried to curb their power. Joined by other Maronite shaykhs they waged war against him, encouraging rebellion as far as Zahleh, which was outside Kisrawan, but where the townsmen had chosen a *shaykh al-shabab* and council in defiance of the *qaymaqam*. In 1858, they organized rallies and drew up petitions in various districts. By March the *qaymaqam* was in retreat and the Christian districts in a state of anarchy.

This encouragement of unrest soon backfired, however. In 1857, the town of Ghazir in Kisrawan clashed with supporters of the Hubaysh shaykhs in what had started as a demonstration against the *qaymaqam*. They also elected a *shaykh al-shabab*, after the example set in Zahleh. In the spring of 1858, just as the shaykhs were drumming up opposition against the *qaymaqam*, the peasants of Kisrawan assembled in their villages, elected *shuyukh al-shabab*, and protested their oppression particularly at the hands of the Khazin shaykhs. In the town of Ajaltun, they met with the shaykhs but every effort at reaching an agreement was unsuccessful; they simply took turns being intransigent.[31]

The unnerved *shaykh al-shabab* of Ajaltun resigned, and in January 1859 was replaced by Taniyus Shahin, a popular and ambitious ruffian who was something of a folk hero. Mounting unrest led the Khazins to ask for help from Khurshid Pasha, the governor of Sidon. Then the peasants attacked the Khazins and, while the Ottoman authorities stood by, the Khazins were expelled from the district.

Through it all, the clergy maintained some pretense at neutrality but mainly sympathized with the peasants. In 1854, Boulus Mas'ad, a commoner, was elected patriarch. He had no love for the Khazins, as in 1845 he had been bypassed as patriarch for a Khazin who was less educated but more high born than he.[32] His sympathy for the peasants in their struggle against the *muqata'ji*s and their traditional privileges was symptomatic of the growing role of the church and the diminishing one of the *muqata'ji*s in the life of the people and of the related strengthening of Maronite identity among the latter.

The peasant rebellion in Kisrawan unsettled the rest of Mount Lebanon. In the mixed districts of the south, it revived sectarian tensions, and it was only a matter of time before political, social, and economic grievances were channeled into sectarian fighting and the civil war of 1860.

Beit Meri

On August 30, 1859, a minor incident in the small village of Beit Meri in the Metn district northeast of Beirut gave a first inkling that the social unrest in Kisrawan was spreading to the rest of the Mountain where tensions simmered just below the surface. Two children, one a Maronite and the other a Druze, began to quarrel; although people trace the beginnings of the sectarian war of 1860 to them, afterwards no one was certain what the quarrel was about or even whether children or adults had started it.[33] The parents took their own child's side and, as happens when parents become involved, the quarrel became more serious. One outraged father, the Maronite, backed by three friends, reprimanded the Druze and demanded punishment. Insulted, the Druze father appealed to his relatives who, together with co-religionists from neighboring villages, came back the morning after to demand an apology from the impulsive Maronites.

Tension was beginning to ease when another event triggered fighting. Some Druzes fired off their muskets in the air in a show of bravado, a custom well ingrained among the men of all groups. The Maronites immediately interpreted the gesture as a provocation. They fired back at the Druzes, attacked them, and drove them out of the village. That only fueled the anger of the Druzes who returned to Beit Meri on September 1 when members of the Maronite and Druze communities fought. The Christians were beaten, but the Druzes incurred more losses: Churchill tells us that the Druzes lost 28 more dead than their rivals, Abkarius that 14 Christians and 18 Druzes were killed and 7 Druzes were wounded, and the Druze chronicler Abu Shaqra that 18 Druzes and 11 Christians were killed.[34]

News travels fast in closely knit societies and bad news travels fastest. Throughout the Mountain, the word spread that Maronites and Druzes had clashed in Beit Meri and each side began to take both diplomatic and military precautions. Throughout the fall and winter of 1859–60, against a background of growing agitation in the mixed districts, the Christians began to organize. Their religious leaders condemned the fray in Beit Meri and told their co-religionists to keep calm.[35] At the same time, they appealed to consuls and Beiruti co-religionists for support and for money to purchase arms and ammunition to be distributed to the men in the Mountain. In Beirut, Bishop Tubiyya Awn organized a Maronite Young Men's League.

The Druzes kept a low profile. Like the Maronites, they were concerned that the situation was deteriorating and they prepared for trouble. Unlike the Maronites, however, they did so secretly.[36] They were anxious to maintain a united front and they stayed in communication with one another and with the Ottoman authorities. Perhaps because they were apprehensive about the situation or because they were careful to neutralize the authorities or gain their support, several of the Druze leaders spent the winter of 1859–60 in Beirut, although on the whole they tended to stay away from the city: it then had few Druze residents and was the center of a government which, under ordinary circumstances, they did not seek out. In the spring, they returned to their Mountain.[37]

The leaders of the various religious sects were not alone in taking precautions. To the villagers and town dwellers of Mount Lebanon who wanted no part in any fighting and who had lived through the disturbances at the end of the Shihab emirate and the early years of the Double Qaymaqamate, news of rising tensions in parts of the Mountain were unwelcome. Whole families in the vicinity of Beit Meri took their belongings and came down to Beirut. In the spring of 1860, as war seemed more and more imminent, whole Christian families abandoned their villages for what they believed to be safer towns, such as Deir al-Qamar, Zahleh, and Jezzine.[38] Their departure only made looting and disorder easier for those who turned to it more and more often in those early months of 1860.

CHAPTER 3

CIVIL WAR IN THE MOUNTAIN

Civil war began in the Mountain with a series of skirmishes in the mixed districts of the south in March, April, and early May 1860. In those early months the fighting was random and unpredictable enough to seem more the acts of lawless men than a calculated war against other sects, especially since banditry was in fact always part of the objective. Then the conflict spread, and by the end of May the battles were being led by the acknowledged leaders of the various sectarian groups. But in these early months looters dominated the scene, attacking travelers on the highways and in the local khans or inns, robbing the houses of the rich and looting convents and monasteries.

The crime and vandalism in themselves exacerbated the already increasing hostility. Bands of looters stole linens, shawls, money, jewelry, watches, gold cups, and church treasures – vessels, and on at least one occasion, a jeweled cross with diamonds.[1] When a gang attacked the Catholic monastery of Ammiq near Deir al-Qamar, one of the wealthiest of the Catholic monasteries, sometime in March they murdered the father superior Athanasius Na'um in his bed.[2] Another attacked the convent at Mashmusheh (between Jezzine and Sidon) on June 1 and carted off its treasures; the fathers estimated their losses at £80,000 sterling (10 million piastres).[3] As the violence escalated, so did the amount of plunder. Furniture, merchandise, corn, tons of silk cocoons, the current crops, and farm animals – mules, donkeys, oxen, and cattle – were carted away.[4]

Some idea of the amounts involved can be garnered from the "General Chart of the Losses of the Christians of Deir al-Qamar" drawn up in June 1860.[5] Property destroyed, stolen, or otherwise lost included 447 warehouses and shops, 1,738 "rooms" (*chambres*; no elaboration is given), 711 houses, 111,110 items in miscellaneous goods and tools, for a total estimated value of 9,775,400 piastres; 60,000 pieces of furniture worth 4,905,600 piastres; equipment and commodities at 6,135,500 piastres; jewelry at 2,641,000 piastres; and some unspecified items worth 1,750,000 piastres.[6]

From the beginning looting spread because there were no police to stop it (a police force was not established until after 1860, as part of the reorganization of the Mountain that followed the civil war). Order in the Ottoman empire was maintained by the leaders of the religious communities who were responsible for the good behavior of their communities in a given district, and by Ottoman garrisons established both to defend imperial territory against outsiders and, more often, to quell domestic disturbances. In 1860 local leaders were more apt to invite violence than to stop it, and the Ottoman garrisons were too poorly manned to maintain order once the fighting was out of control.

European consuls and local Christian groups in Beirut and Damascus repeatedly urged the Ottoman representatives to send more troops but apparently without effect. As anarchy spread, the irregular troops there simply joined in the looting. These underpaid military recruits, wages often in arrears, were stationed in regions of the Ottoman empire whose languages they rarely understood. Ignorant and needy, they often could not resist the temptations offered by the breakup of the social order. In the few areas of Mount Lebanon where Ottoman troops were garrisoned during the civil war, looting was common. The troops were seen selling stolen goods in the bazaars of Damascus and were said to have encouraged looting and killing.[7] Their officers were not involved in the traffic, but they were accused of negligence and some even of conspiracy.

As the conflict spread, the Christians and Druzes both began to select specific targets from among the members of rival communities, and as a result, confronted with an unexplained death, they jumped to the conclusion that some member of a rival community was responsible for it — a conclusion that was by no means unlikely. When the father superior of a Catholic monastery was found robbed and murdered in his bed,[8] or when a clergyman known to be stirring up the Maronites of Jezzine against the Druzes was found dead on the highway, the Christians assumed the Druzes had killed them.[9] If a Druze muleteer who spent the night in a khan was found shot and cut to pieces, it was assumed by the Druzes that Maronites had done the job.[10] In March, shortly after the murder of Athanasius Na'um, a Druze from the village of Ainab in the Shuf district reportedly killed a Christian from the village of Abadiyeh. By the end of April "killings began to succeed one another with a speed the more frightening as, in these lands, they are forerunners of war."[11] Two Druzes were killed near Beirut, then three Christians near Sidon. On April 26, some Druzes who had come from Hasbaiya attacked four Christians from Jezzine at Khan Iqlim al-Shumar to its south; two were killed and two wounded.[12] Near Sidon, on the night of April 27, three Druzes killed four

Christians from the village of Katuli who had been farming the land that belonged to Muhammad Ali Shabib, a Shi'i shaykh from Iqlim al-Shumar. On May 11, at noon, three Druzes were attacked near a river, the Nahr al-Assal, by three Christians from the village of Katuli; two were killed and the third seriously wounded. On May 14, two Druzes from the Shuf were killed in the neighborhood of Sidon.[13] And so on, until Christians and Druzes "began to kill everyone they met in a lonely place or on the road, and in course of time this thing took [such proportions] between the [marauding] bands that the roads and paths became quite unsafe and the dangerous and perilous places were many."[14]

In the last two weeks of May, according to the French consul general, every day brought news of more murders. The British consul general reported agitation and unrest throughout May, with occasional outbursts of violence. By May 20, Christians were complaining of attacks in the mixed districts of Arqub, Gharb, and the Beqaa, and European merchants in Beirut reported a succession of incidents presaging civil war. Maronite religious leaders were very concerned that violence had increased and they wrote to one another that it had to be stopped. Tubiyya Awn was pessimistic, however, that it would be.[15]

When exactly the unrest could be said to have turned into civil war is difficult to say. The British consul general identified the turning point as the afternoon of May 29, but consensus places it two days earlier, on May 27, and ends its first phase on June 20 or 21, when the last blood was shed at Deir al-Qamar, though violence continued there sporadically until the end of the month.[16]

The civil war started south of the Maronite district of Kisrawan – where exactly is difficult to determine. Tension was so high everywhere that fighting appeared to erupt in any number of places at once. It seems to have started almost simultaneously in the Metn and Arqub districts. In the French consul general's version the conflict broke out first in al-Sahil (the plain of Beirut) and in Metn. Other sources say that the first full-fledged battles were in the Arqub and the region around Zahleh. In any case, one by one the districts were drawn into the conflict. The villages and the Christian towns of the Shuf region and beyond – Deir al-Qamar, Zahleh, and Jezzine – all suffered. From there the war spread west of the Lebanon range, to the plains of Baalbek and the Beqaa, south and southwest into the Anti-Lebanon range, to Hasbaiya and Rashaiya in Wadi Taym.

Whoever started the war and wherever it began, two Christian groups, the Kisrawanis and the Zahalnis, helped unleash it. In the plain of Beirut and the Metn, hostilities started with the arrival at the end of May of a band of Christians from the Kisrawan, composed, according to the French consul general, of some 250 to 300 men. They had come to Naccashe, a village half-way between Kisrawan and Beirut, to appropriate the silk crop of the Kisrawani shaykhs. "This band, with no direction" advanced on Sunday, May 27, to Baabda in al-Sahil, some one-and-a-half hours' walking distance south of Naccashe, which had once been the winter residence of the Shihab emirs. The band was led by Taniyus Shahin, the *shaykh al-shabab* of Reifun who, in 1859, took over the leadership of the rebellion in Kisrawan. On that occasion they came from Reifun in the north to the small village of Antelias in the plain of Beirut to protect the Shihab emirs who resided in Baabda.

To the Druzes, the presence of the Kisrawanis in the plain of Beirut, so close to the Metn where many Druzes lived among Christians, was a provocation. The Christians, on the other hand, chose to see provocation in the arrival of Ottoman troops they believed had come to help the Druzes. On May 26, Khurshid Pasha, the Ottoman governor general in Beirut, had established a military camp a mile away from Naccashe, at Hazmiyeh on the Beirut–Damascus highway, with the approval of the European consuls, who probably pressured him into sending the 500 troops, 200 irregulars, and four cannons to Hazmiyeh. Whatever the motive, deployment was believed by Christians to be the signal for attack the Druzes had been awaiting.[17]

The Ottomans tried limited action, which the Christians immediately interpreted as support for the Druzes.[18] Cannons were fired from the Ottoman camp. As the French consul general wrote, the firing of the cannon was made "to stop the Druzes and prevent the massacre of Christians, according to the Pasha; to encourage the Druzes and kill the vanquished, according to the [Christians]." The Christians decided that Khurshid Pasha persuaded the Shihabs to make the Kisrawanis withdraw from Baabda with the ulterior motive of preparing the ground for a Druze attack; he had ordered the firing of the cannon to notify the Druzes to start their attack. The pasha, on the other hand, believed that the Christians were the aggressors provoking the Druzes.

When fighting broke out on May 29, each side claimed the other started it. The Druzes of Beit Meri in the Metn appealed to the Druzes of the village of Abadiyeh for help when the Christian band turned up. Some 40 to 50 Christians from the plain of Beirut also went up to Beit Meri to help defend their co-religionists. Each faction burned the houses of the other. Irregular troops led by an officer named Ibrahim Agha helped the Druzes.

Although the Christians blamed the Druzes and often the Ottomans for beginning the war, they sometimes imply that they welcomed it, even if they did not invite it. Abkarius, who believed that there was a compact between the Druzes and the Turks and that Ottoman cannonfire was a prearranged signal to the Druzes that it was time to attack, also admits that at Beit Meri on May 29, "the Christians overcame [the attack] and routed [the Druzes] and set fire to their houses." In Baabda and Sabnay the next day, he continues, "the Christians hastened to meet them in battle, and were well content" to fight. The British consul general's first reports on the outbreak of civil war mention that the Christians in the Metn had attacked mixed villages, but then as war spread and turned against the Christians, he became concerned about their welfare and began to present them as victims.[19]

May 30, the day after the Beit Meri attack, began peacefully enough. The Kisrawanis had tried to enlist the support of the Christians of the plain against the Druzes but, when they failed, they appeared to have obeyed the pasha's injunctions and withdrawn. Then, for some reason, they turned back and advanced toward Beit Meri, a move the Druzes interpreted as a threat. Some 1,800 to 2,000 Druzes met them on the way and, ignoring the presence of the Ottoman garrison at Hazmiyeh, attacked them. The Christians of Baabda, Wadi Shahrur, Hadeth, and other nearby villages on the plain of Beirut, who had thus far stayed out of trouble, were now drawn into the fighting. They suffered few casualties and renewed the attack the next day. Some 150 to 200 of them left the plain of Beirut to unseat the Druzes in Beit Meri, but once again they were beaten back by the Druzes and forced to retreat to the neighboring village of Brummana. The fighting then spread throughout the Metn district, where 35 or 40 mainly Christian villages, were set afire.

The Christian forces sent from Kisrawan were undisciplined and ineffective. The rest were unprepared. When fighting broke out in Baabda, the Druzes from the Gharb district, reportedly led by the shaykhs of the Talhuqs and Abu Nakads, moved to attack the Christians in Baabda and Metn. "The band of Christians wavered and became confused, getting bewildered and stunned, so that they were unable to persevere and swerved from right to left. And they retreated, wishing flight (trying to save themselves) but were routed in the worst of routs." In less than a day, the Druzes were in control, and 600 Christians had been killed.[20]

Fighting also broke out in the Arqub and the region around Zahleh on May 31.[21] True to their hot-headed reputation, the Zahalni rushed to fight the Druzes in retaliation for their attacks on the Christians of Arqub district, but on their way to Zahleh they were ambushed by the Druzes.[22] Their justification, as in so many other acts of war, was that "the Christians of the Lebanon, in self-defense, took up the gauntlet of defiance."[23]

The clashes between the Zahalni and the Druzes were set off by an incident in Dahr al-Baidar, a small Christian village described by the French consul general as Zahleh's "front gate." There fighting broke out between 400 armed villagers and an advancing Druze force of some 200 men led by Ali Imad, son of Khattar Imad, a well-known Druze shaykh and leader. The villagers gained the upper hand and forced the Druzes back to the nearby village of Ain Dara. There the Christians were reinforced by the Zahalni fighters, but they were easily and quickly routed. The number of casualties was apparently not high, even though Churchill implies the defeat of the Christians was total. Antun Dahir al-Aqiqi – a Maronite from Kisrawan who left a partly first-hand account of Mount Lebanon between 1840 and 1860 – says that only four Christians and three Druzes died.[24]

Three days later a second battle of Ain Dara began when Ali Imad died of the wounds received in this first encounter. Ali Imad's father led the Druzes. Hundreds of Christians, many from Zahleh, rushed to battle, but although the Christians outnumbered the Druzes 3,000 to 600 and the Druze casualties outnumbered the Christian 20 to 10, the Druzes still managed to gain the upper hand and drive the Christians back to Zahleh.[25]

From the first, it was obvious that the Christians did not have effective leadership and the Druzes did. The anonymous and probably Christian author of a book entitled *Hasr al-litham 'an nakabat al-Sham* ("Unveiling the Calamities of Damascus") published in 1895 and based on oral and written histories of the civil war, writes that "the Christians were all chiefs" and, consequently, leaderless and disorganized. As Aqiqi put it, the Christians in the Shuf "were arming themselves, but it was of no use, because they lacked a leader and because of their lack of foresight: they were concerned with their worldly wealth, but not with their own dignity."[26] If any area of the Mountain should have provided Christians leadership, it was the north. There the Maronites were in the majority, and a number of local leaders had gained combat experience when Kisrawan had revolted between 1858 and 1860. On several occasions they had also promised to help their co-religionists elsewhere in the Mountain, but the latter had waited in vain for that help to appear. If help arrived at all, it was too late or too little to do any good. Abkarius believed that the divisions among the Kisrawanis were of great help to the Druzes:

> And among the Christians of Kasruan rose discord and dissension after this [their former] concord and good understanding. They disagreed in their counsels and [in their ideas] on the conduct of affairs, and the one who had received commands became commander. And they felt disinclined to war and battle, and refrained from sudden attacks and sallies, and kept quiet, remaining at home after they had drawn their swords in [open] rebellion.

Nor did they occupy themselves with what [the affairs that] occupied the other peoples of the Lebanon. And this change was most fortunate for the Druzes and of the greatest help and assistance to them.[27]

Nor was the Kisrawani division the only one among the Maronites. Until the outbreak of civil war in the Shuf, the Maronites generally were all too willing to side with non-Maronites against other Maronite groups. The Druze Janbalat leaders, for example, owed their success before Bashir II turned against them in part to Maronite support.[28] Under these circumstances, other Christian sects could not be blamed for distrusting the Maronites. During the Kisrawan rebellion between 1858 and 1860, they stood by while the Maronite clergy battled the shaykhs – two sources of leadership weakening each other. That, combined with the peasant alienation from the shaykhs, eliminated the Maronite shaykhs as defenders. The new populist leaders who replaced them failed to act decisively and swiftly when the interests of the rest of the Maronites – let alone other Christians – were threatened.

Nor were the Maronites alone among the Christians in weakening their forces by internal divisions. When the two most important Christian strongholds of the south, Zahleh and Deir al-Qamar, were attacked in turn, discord among their inhabitants played into the hands of their enemies.[29] Divisions kept the Christian sects from closing ranks. The Greek Orthodox Christians had always sided with Druzes rather than Maronites in the power struggles of the Mountain.[30] Now when the Maronite clergy, anticipating war, made a concerted effort to invite other Christians to unite with them,[31] there were no visible results. Everywhere, the Christian forces were quickly defeated. So poor was their military organization that in the first general battle of Ain Dara, they were reported to have fired, not on the enemy, but on each other.[32] In the battle in Baabda, Maronites from Kisrawan came to their aid, but "because they [the Kesrouanis] were strangers in that area and because they found themselves without a leader, when the fighting began they immediately scattered and fled." On yet another occasion, 15,000 Maronites from Kisrawan stood and watched the Druzes attack the Zahalnis. Not one of them went to their defense.[33]

Although the Christians later claimed to be the victims, at the beginning they often started the fight. On May 24, the French consul wrote, "I am assured that as much on the side of the Christians as on the side of the Druzes, each village is preparing its contingent of men to send it to the scene of hostilities."[34] In his dispatches to Yusuf Karam, the shaykh of Ihdin, a chief Maronite town in the northern district of Bsharreh, he repeatedly advised that "no aggressive or provocative move be made" and that he hoped the Christians would be "wiser" in the future. On June 13, he admonished:

> Here are my last words on the subject: peace! peace! peace! ... Those who started [the conflict] will have to account for it before God and mankind. Furthermore, make the Christians understand that France neither can nor wants to protect such acts ... that if [the presence of] French ships puts combative and bellicose ideas in the heads of Christians, I would be obliged to make them leave Beirut: you can tell that to everyone ... truly, I repeat, if you do not want to bring the greatest misfortune on the Christians in all Syria, it must be peace! peace! peace![35]

War raged in the Metn and its vicinity for weeks. The Druzes ravaged the land, but the Christians may have started the fighting and they jumped at every opportunity to keep it up. According to the British consul, on the afternoon of May 29, a group of Christians attacked the mixed Druze and Christian villages of Salima, Qarnayel, and Btekhnai and drove out the Druze inhabitants. The Druzes attacked the village of Beit Meri and set fire to several villages in the Metn and in the plain near Beirut.[36]

The disorganized Christians were never able to take advantage of their numerical superiority. They boasted of 50,000 troops – a number apparently derived from Taniyus Shahin's claim that he could muster up that many. The Druzes had only 12,000,[37] but on only one occasion did they not prevail. The Christians quickly lost confidence and, with it, any chance of victory. In a society where bravery in battle was a source of honor, military defeat meant loss of face and, with it, of moral superiority. Although they were often brave, they were also accused of cowardice.

The enemy in contrast was indomitable. The Druzes did not have the Christians' reassuring record of growing influence, but they did have a "God helps those who help themselves" mentality that made up for their small number. In times of duress, they closed ranks, rallied round their leaders, and threw themselves into battle with an assurance that the indecisive and demoralized Christians could not match.

Their leadership was also superior. The Druze shaykhs and trusted old Druze families, in contrast to their Maronite counterparts, kept the loyalty of their followers. Janbalat in the Shuf, Abu Nakad in the Manasif as well as in the Shahahir of the Gharb, Imad in the Arqub, Talhuq in the upper Gharb, Abd al-Malik in the Jurd, the older Abu'l-Lama in the Metn, and Arslan in the lower Gharb wielded undiminished influence among their people.

The shaykhs had help from their commanders who had fought over the years defending the Druze against Shihabi oppression, Egyptian occupation, and Christians generally. Like its Christian counterpart, this group included both ruffians and honorable men. Though the Christians dreaded them, some grudgingly acknowledged their successes and sometimes even paid tribute to their courage and resolve. The French consul general called them "well commanded."[38] Among them was Isma'il al-Atrash, the Hawran chief and Druze hero of the rebellion of 1838 against Egyptian rule, who was feared and admired by Christians. Some of the Europeans depicted him as "savage" and "bloody," but Abkarius gave him his due:

> Now there lived in the country of Hauran a man of mighty heart and eloquent tongue. Prominent among his equals ... a companion ... of flocks and domestics, servants and attendants, he belonged to the notable Druzes in that region, who had great faith in him. His name was Isma'il al-Atrash and in courage and strength he was like a speckled wolf.[39]

As news of the civil war spread, business came to a standstill. Work on the Beirut–Damascus highway, begun in 1858, came to an abrupt halt as workers dropped their tools and left,[40] either to hide from or to join in the fighting. Though foreign observers had assumed that simple economic self-interest would guarantee peace until the harvest was in, they were wrong. The silk crop lay unharvested. The silk was either destroyed or appropriated.[41] Cities were blockaded, water supplies were cut, mills ground to a halt, and the modest craft and industrial production of the market towns and regional centers of the Mountain was suspended.[42]

If there was time, people collected their valuables and fled. In fact that process had already begun early in the spring, as turmoil in the Mountain slowly grew. When the first battles were fought at the end of May, however, whole villages and towns fled the mixed districts for the safety of calmer regions on the Mountain or along the coast. On the way, many lost their belongings and even their lives when they were attacked by armed bands looking for loot or revenge.

An account of one episode in this period of panic is provided by Henri Harris Jessup, an American Presbyterian missionary who arrived in Syria in 1856 and stayed for 53 years. He was stationed first in Tripoli and then from 1860 in Beirut, but he spent the summers in Abey in the domains of the Abu Nakad shaykhs. He was there on Sunday, May 27, conducting a service for the small congregation of Protestants when the news came that a Christian who had killed a Druze 15 years earlier had now himself been killed. The church emptied in a moment and "the entire male Christian population fled, over walls, terraces, vineyards and through pine groves and the rocky slope, avoiding the roads." The Druze elders tried to reassure the missionaries, but to no avail; not a single Christian male over ten years old was left in the village.[43]

Each of the warring parties searched for allies. Appeals for support were presented by both sides to the Ottoman authorities and to the European consuls. The Christians of the mixed districts had appealed for help to the Kisrawanis under Taniyus Shahin, and the Druzes to their co-religionists in the Anti-Lebanon, particularly Isma'il al-Atrash. As the Kisrawani forces moved into al-Sahil, Metn, and other areas, the Hawrani forces under Isma'il al-Atrash advanced across the Anti-Lebanon into Wadi Taym where they raided Christian villages.[44]

Both the European and the local Ottoman authorities appealed for calm. The European consuls visited Khurshid Pasha to offer their help and press him to put a stop to the conflict. He responded that he was "exerting himself to the utmost to check the war." The pasha blamed it on a group of Maronites known as the "Maronite Young Men's League," commonly referred to as the "Beirut Committee," which had been founded in Beirut sometime before the civil war by Beirut's bishop Tubiyya Awn. He believed it had encouraged Taniyus Shahin to advance on Baabda on May 27, spread the conflict by buying and distributing arms to the Christians in the Mountain and, more generally, was responsible for provoking the Druzes. Khurshid Pasha told the consuls that if they would stop the Beirut Committee from supporting the Christians in the Mountain, he would restrain the Druzes. He had even considered arresting the Beirut Committee, but was dissuaded by the consuls who were afraid it would provoke the Christians in Beirut into taking up arms. But Khurshid Pasha's comments and the consuls' response suggest that, contrary to the rumor that he was encouraging Druze attacks against the Christians, he in fact may well have wanted to stop the conflict, at least at that time. However well-meaning the consuls were in preventing his arrest of the Beirut Committee, they may also have limited his ability to control the Druzes and to stop the war.[45]

While these negotiations were going on between the various local factions and the centers of power, the situation continued to deteriorate. In the last days of May, the ground had been prepared to extend the conflict to the Manasif. Druze forces blockaded the town of Deir al-Qamar toward the end of May. The inhabitants were caught unprepared and, partly because their leaders hesitated and disagreed as to how to proceed, were unable to ward off the blockade. By the beginning of June, both the British and French consuls general in Beirut had been informed that the Deir al-Qamaris were on the point of starvation. The Ottoman authorities promised to send flour and grain, but by June 3 these supplies still had not arrived "allegedly for want of animals and muleteers willing to take them."[46] By then, Deir al-Qamar had been taken and sacked.

The battle for possession of Deir al-Qamar is said to have begun when "the Druzes of the Nakad estates" attacked it, the two sides fought "a little" and suffered some losses, and then the Druzes retreated, but this first Druze offensive may in fact have been more substantial than that. The French consul general claimed that 3,000 Druzes were involved in attacks on June 2 and 3, led by Bashir Nakad and seconded by Janbalati and Imadi forces, but that the townsmen seem to have resisted relatively well. They held on for eight consecutive hours and, uncharacteristically for the civil war, suffered fewer casualties than their attackers. Khurshid Pasha mentions a heavy death toll among the Druzes; the British consul general reported the death of 100 Druzes and 25 Christians, and his French counterpart 70 to 80 Druzes and 17 Christians.

The town's resistance was weakened by divisions among the population within, so the Druze assault need not have been massive. The attackers destroyed the outskirts of town, but the town itself was not damaged appreciably until after its surrender. Then 130 houses were sacked and the town was plundered for three days. However limited the attack, the loss of lives that followed the city's fall and the antagonism generated by its plunder prepared the ground for the violence to come.[47]

Until then, hostilities in the civil war were only partially drawn along sectarian lines. Betrayal by Christians is mentioned by Christian sources as the cause of the surrender of Deir al-Qamar. That this accusation could be made against a town that was more commercially and industrially developed than most towns and villages of the Mountain suggests that commercial interests lay behind the betrayal. Instead of counting on communal solidarity, the townsfolk trusted the Druzes with whom they did business until war taught them otherwise. To explain their lack of preparation against the Druze siege, Churchill mentions their credulous reliance on Druze professions of friendship and Ottoman promises of protection and adds:

> They had even refused to listen to appeals sent to them from different quarters, and especially from the Maronite bishop, Toubyah, to join the common cause, to rise in the general defense. "The brave men of Deir-el-Kamar were the right arm of the Christians; would they consent to stand passive spectators of the slaughter of their co-religionists?" To all these remonstrances they invariably replied that they meant to stand perfectly neutral; that they were in an exceptional position; and that, being under the very eyes, as it were, of the Turkish government, it would be useless, as well as unbecoming in them to draw the sword.[48]

Even after Deir al-Qamar had been attacked, many townsmen hesitated to take sides. That was consistent with their past record of pragmatism and conciliation, as they lived among the Druzes and depended on them for their prosperity. Churchill, however, criticized their caution and would have preferred them to be more impetuous, regardless of the cost. His own motives are questionable when he even accuses them of treason:

> Even of the Christians only one half were engaged – those in the immediate vicinity of the point of attack. The other half refused to join, and even withheld the necessary supplies of ammunition from their comrades. Treason had done its work. Some had already held secret communication with the Abou Nakads, their ancient lords. Many thought, by maintaining a passive attitude, to secure the peculiar favor of the Turks. Thus, even in the extremity of their distress, the Christians were wavering and divided.[49]

In the last days of May, the fighting spread to Wadi Taym in the Anti-Lebanon, already the scene of rivalry between the Druzes and the Sunni Shihab family. This time the battle began with a power struggle between the Shihabs and a Druze by the name of Salim Shams, who had risen in society by marrying Sa'id Janbalat's niece (the daughter of Sa'id's sister Nayifa who was also a relative of Salim Shams). The marriage gave him the backing of the Janbalat family. In Hasbaiya in particular, the Shihab shaykh Sa'ad al-Din had antagonized the Druzes by inviting Ottoman troops to the area to thwart a Druze revolt.[50]

Resentment against the Christians built up among the Druzes as well when the local Christians refused to join them against the Shihabs. That resentment found its first expression toward the end of May. All month long Druze families in Wadi Taym had been clearing out their houses – to defend themselves according to the Druzes, to prepare for war in the opinion of others. At sunset on May 31, Druzes from various villages in Wadi Taym assembled in Hasbaiya and asked the Druzes of the town to join them to fight the Christians in the nearby village of Mimas where a battle had already begun. The Hasbaiya Druzes responded by firing their guns as they crossed the town. The Christian townspeople started shooting back. Then the Ottoman authorities intervened.

The local headquarters of the Ottoman garrison for Wadi Taym was in Hasbaiya. The officer in charge was Lieutenant Colonel Uthman Bey of the first Ottoman regiment. His orders came from Ahmad Pasha in Damascus, as Wadi Taym was under the jurisdiction of the Damascus *vilayet*. When news of the fighting was brought to him, Uthman Bey sent a battalion under an officer named Yusuf Agha to restore order. After a few men on both sides were wounded, he succeeded, one of the few occasions when the Ottomans did manage to regain control. Then news reached Hasbaiya that fighting had broken out in neighboring Shibaa. Uthman Bey went to the village and then to Marj Shwaya, where he remained closeted with the Druzes for several hours. When he returned to Hasbaiya, he told the Christians that he had negotiated with the Druzes, and the fighting would stop.

In that he was wrong, however; the situation in and around Hasbaiya grew more violent. The Druzes burned down a Christian village, and its inhabitants sought refuge in Hasbaiya. Druzes then surrounded and attacked Hasbaiya itself. When the Christians asked Uthman Bey what they should do, he suggested they take refuge in the serai and surrender their arms to him; his troops then would assure their safety. They complied, and their arms were collected and sent on mules with a small escort to Damascus. It is unlikely they ever arrived. Cyril Graham, an English gentleman traveler connected to the British government, sent several reports to the Foreign Office from Syria during the civil war. In one of them he wrote that the Druzes had seized the arms before the mules even left the Hasbaiya valley "as had been intended." The Ottoman soldiers escorting them reportedly did not resist. The French consul general claimed the weapons did not even leave the town; they were simply piled up in the courtyard of the serai so the Druzes could help themselves. The 500 guns not taken by them were then loaded on mules and sent to Rashaiya, but the men who transported them soon returned to report that the Druzes had taken most of them as well, either on the way to Rashaiya or once they had reached the town.[51]

On June 1 the district of Jezzine was brought into the war. Overwhelmingly Maronite, it harbored a number of people eager to stir up the population against the Druzes.[52] The Christians did not expect an attack, however, because Sa'id Janbalat had told them to remain calm and assured them of his protection.[53] Between 1,500 and 2,000 Druzes from the Shuf came into the district of Jezzine. There they divided themselves into two groups. One advanced on Jezzine, the other on Bkassine, another Maronite town, whose defenders were several hundred young men who were the followers of a local chieftain named Abu Samra. When they heard that the Druzes were advancing, they prepared to meet them. The battle was fought at the village of al-Ghabbatieh. Although outnumbered by more than three to one, Abu Samra's men forced their enemies back in a battle that lasted four and a half hours. Though the Druzes were the ones who retreated, they lost only four men.[54]

From the small town of Jezzine 300 young Maronites joined Abu Samra's band. A few of them under the command of a local leader, Yusuf al-

Mubayyad of Dahr al-Sin, crossed to the Shuf and set fire to many villages.[55] In other parts of the district of Jezzine, Maronite forces took on the Druzes – they claimed in self-defense, the Druzes claimed in provocation. Although the Maronites rather quickly lost their taste for fighting in these encounters, they serve to remind us that the civil war began as a conflict between two equally determined opponents. It was only later that the idea was planted that it was a Druze offensive that victimized the Christians.[56]

After their initial rout, the Druzes regrouped and turned the tide. Within hours Bkassine was devastated, Jezzine and several other villages and towns plundered and burned. A force composed of the men of Jezzine and of its environs and the followers of Abu Samra and Yusuf al-Mubayyad who had attacked the Druze villages in the Shuf went out to meet the Druze forces marching on their district, lost their resolve, and were beaten back.[57]

A more violent stage of the civil war was reached when killing and plunder became indiscriminate. In Jezzine 165 people died, 1,500 in the district. Thousands of villagers fled, most of them toward Sidon on the Syrian coast. On their way hundreds of them were attacked. Qasim Imad, according to one source "the confidential agent" of Sa'id Janbalat, attacked them on the road and pursued them to the coast.[58]

Among the refugees was a man fleeing to the village of Jbaa in the Shqif region, because there was a reputed Shi'i shaykh and scholar named Abdallah Ni'ma there, known for his integrity and respected by all. Among the Shi'is he carried more weight "than a patriarch among Christians." Nonetheless the Druzes pursued the Christian refugee into Shaykh Ni'ma's house, killed the Christian before his eyes, and looted his house. At the news, the Shi'i shaykhs from the district of Jbaa and the regions of Shqif, Shumar, and Bsharreh, raced to Jbaa to attack the Druzes, but they were stopped by the Ottomans.[59]

The refugees who went to Sidon were refused admittance and forced to hide as best they could in caves and gardens around the town and along the coast. Many Muslims, both Sunnis (probably for the most part townsmen from Sidon) and what the sources invariably called "Metwalis" – Shi'is from the countryside around Sidon, Tyre, and the southern coast[60] – joined the Druzes in attacking them; they killed 250 to 300. The survivors tried to escape to Tyre, only to be driven back by the Shi'is.

The arrival of refugees outside Sidon had also set off violent demonstrations within its gates that resulted in both wounded and dead. Four thousand local Christians and Europeans took refuge in the French khan in the center of town, where they remained stranded without provisions or arms. But the violence did not continue or spread, perhaps because British ships were anchored off the coast.[61]

On June 3,[62] the Christians in Hasbaiya collected their cattle and belongings and assembled in the serai, a three-story building with high ceilings and spacious rooms and corridors, together with the Sunni Shihab emirs. For eight or nine days they lived in misery. Water and food were scarce; bread sold for up to ten francs (250 piastres) a loaf and its quality declined; people survived on this bread, grape leaves and mulberries. Conditions grew worse when 150 Christians from the village of Qaraaoun near Wadi Taym joined them, escorted by some Druzes to whom they had been entrusted by Ahmad Pasha, the governor of the *vilayet* of Damascus. To their dismay, many of the Druze soldiers then departed and when they tried to find out why, they received only evasive answers.[63]

To ensure their safety, the Christians in the serai collected money and the women handed over jewelry to buy Uthman Bey's good will. Uthman Bey's sympathy, however, was with the Druzes, or so it then began to appear to the Christians. He met with Druze leaders in one of their two best-known sanctuaries, Khalwat al-Baiada, a hill above Hasbaiya (the other was Baaqline in Mount Lebanon near Deir al-Qamar), and for three hours at Marj Shwaya, not far from Hasbaiya. He was also a frequent visitor at the house of Sa'id Janbalat's sister Nayifa, which served as a rallying point for the Druzes of Hasbaiya. He was in touch with virtually all the Druze leaders of the Mountain, including Isma'il al-Atrash, who came to Hasbaiya, other chieftains and Druzes from the Hawran, including Wakid al-Hamdan, Hazim Hanidi, Abu Ali Hannawi, al-Nawafli, al-Kal'ani, and a Shi'i chief, Halil Agha.

It was rumored that it was at the insistence of Nayifa Janbalat that Uthman Bey told the Christians to hand over their arms. Nayifa may have been well intentioned: she advised the Christians not to go to the serai because she expected trouble, and she sheltered some 400 of them in her house.[64] She also may have been acting on the advice of her brother Sa'id. To the Christians, however, there was something sinister about her. Few trusted either Nayifa Janbalat or Uthman Bey and some among them even suspected the latter of disarming them in order to make it easier for the Druzes to attack them.[65]

Not all the Christians in Hasbaiya went to the serai or surrendered their arms. A few hundred – perhaps as many as a thousand – instead preferred to fight. But their eagerness was matched neither by experience nor by organization. Later, the survivors of the massacre claimed they had been encouraged by Uthman Bey to attack the Druzes, but since they also accused him of making them give up their arms, it is difficult to believe he did both.[66]

The Druze forces drawn from nearby areas in the Anti-Lebanon –

Wadi Taym, Majdel Shams (between Wadi Taym and Iqlim al-Ballan), Iqlim al-Ballan, and Hawran, surrounded Hasbaiya on June 3, a strategy they were often to repeat, usually with success. They were led by Ali Bey Hamada, Kenj Ahmad, and Hasan Agha Tawil who had been seen conferring with Uthman Bey.[67]

They far outnumbered the Christians, who were defeated in less than an hour and forced to flee.[68] Abkarius says that at first the Christians had the advantage but instead of following up on their success by pursuing Druzes, turned to burning down Druze houses in the vicinity. He estimates 130 Druze dead and only 26 Christian casualties, a rare occurrence in a war where Christian losses were routinely higher. The day after, however, the tide turned in favor of the Druzes, because, according to Abkarius, the Ottoman troops the Christians had been promised failed to appear.[69]

The Christians still dwelling unarmed in the serai were now prey to the advancing Druzes. After the latter entered the town and set fire to some of its houses, they pursued one of the Christian leaders, an official of the Shihab emir Sa'ad al-Din named Jiryus al-Rayyis, who had hidden in the women's quarters of a friend's house. He was betrayed and had his hands cut off. Emir Sa'ad al-Din himself was cornered on the second or third floor of the serai; his head was cut off and flung down into the courtyard. Altogether 17 Shihabs, it was said, were seized and killed. Their deaths were not the result of random killing motivated by sectarian hatreds, but of calculation, a result of political antagonisms between the Shihabs, and the Druzes of Hasbaiya and the governor of Damascus.[70]

The Druzes then turned their attention to the Christians in the serai. A bloodbath followed, the first on that scale in the civil war and one of its darkest moments. Most women were spared; for the rest, the Druzes "divested themselves of the garment of self-restraint to clothe themselves with the garment of revenge."[71]

> Then [brandishing] their weapons ... [the Druzes] rushed in [for a general attack] like wild beasts of prey and began to butcher the Christians as sheep are butchered. Some cut them up with axes as firewood is cut up, and some lopped off ... limb after limb until they got to the parts which it is not meet to mention among well-bred people. And the men were slaughtered in the embrace of their wives, and the children at the breasts of their mothers. ... Oh, what an hour that was, like an hour of the day of resurrection! Full of awe and destitute of safety because the shouting of the men and the crying of the women and the little children filled the valleys and the mountains.[72]

Altogether something like a thousand people may have perished;[73] perhaps 40 or 50 men escaped.[74] Several were left for dead; others threw themselves under the heap of the corpses until dark. A few reached the coast, their clothes bloody and torn, to tell the tale of the massacre of Hasbaiya, a story that was to be passed down and undoubtedly embellished, for generations. Some of the escapees were caught by the Druzes, or by soldiers who turned them over to the Druzes. Among the victims were children, though women were usually spared, at least by the Druzes. Ottoman soldiers were occasionally accused even of maltreating them.[75]

The most fortunate Christians were those who had placed their trust in Nayifa Janbalat, among them members of the Shihab family. Nayifa Janbalat took them to her brother's headquarters at the family home at Mukhtara. From there, they were sent to Sidon and thence by British warships to Beirut.[76]

After their victory at Hasbaiya, the Druze forces advanced on Rashaiya, reinforced by Druzes from the Hawran led by Isma'il al-Atrash, who had crossed the Anti-Lebanon attacking Christian villages along the way. The two groups met in front of Rashaiya on June 11 or 12, where they found the town's fortress already surrounded by yet another large Druze force. The Druze army now numbered about 5,000 men.

This battle too had begun, as was so often the case, with a minor local quarrel. Ten muleteers from the adjoining village of Dahr al-Ahmar had been carting earthenware to Damascus when a band of Druzes in the vicinity of Kfar Quq and Rahla nearby fired on them, killing two. The rest fled. The relatives of the dead men complained to the Ottoman officer at Rashaiya and to Emir Ali Shihab, the governor of the district. An inquest followed, and two Druzes from Kfar Quq were arrested.

The Druzes of Rashaiya in their turn then clamored for the release of the prisoners. The authorities complied, but the Druzes nonetheless swore to retaliate against the Christians of Dahr al-Ahmar. On Friday, June 8, the Christians sought refuge in Rashaiya, and the next day the local Druzes set fire to their houses. Then for two days, the Druzes attacked other Christian villages in the area, including Hawush, Beit Lahia, and Kfar Mishki.

In asking for protection, the priests and elders of Rashaiya called upon the Aryans, its principal Druze family, one member of which – a man by the name of Shibli – had distinguished himself during the 1838 Druze revolt against the Egyptians. The Aryans agreed to help and called a meeting of the Christians and Druzes in the town and the neighboring villages. Their spokesmen then met Emir Ali Shihab and the Ottoman officer in charge, and the latter issued a proclamation guaranteeing protection.[77]

The Christians in Rashaiya were still apprehensive, however. Their numbers were insignificant compared to the thousands of Druzes at their doorstep. Proclamation or no, some 150 of them sought refuge in the fortress where Ottoman troops were stationed, realizing that the Druzes had their eye on them because of the presence among them of the Shihab family. The news of the massacre in Hasbaiya had already reached them. This time they decided not to rely solely on military protection. They built their own barricades on the gates and roads to the fortress.

The Druzes attacked the town on the very evening the authorities issued the proclamation to reassure the Christians. They set fire to the houses of Christians, killed and pillaged, and drove many Christians into the serai. On Sunday, the Druze chiefs and the Ottoman colonel reportedly met at Ziltatiat, a nearby village. On his return, the colonel instructed the refugees in Rashaiya not to leave the serai.

The following Monday, the Druzes in the area combined forces with the troops of Isma'il al-Atrash and others, and launched an attack. While some of them attacked nearby Aya, the rest entered the serai and killed all the men, even the priests. Houses also were set on fire, churches were sacked and burned down, and about half the Christian inhabitants were killed. Mishaqa tells us that only the Christians who hid from the soldiers and found Druzes to protect them escaped. Among the dead were all but two of the Shihab emirs of Rashaiya. The dead of Hasbaiya, Rashaiya, and the surrounding villages exceeded 1,800.[78]

The Druzes now seemed unbeatable. They swept over the Beqaa valley and Baalbek. Shi'i chieftains of the powerful Harfush clan in the Baalbek region, crowds of Shi'is, and irregulars joined them as they ravaged villages and set them aflame. The Harfushes, with a few hundred followers, paused to attack the town of Baalbek with its small Ottoman garrison; the rest marched to Zahleh.[79]

Zahleh, the most important town of Mount Lebanon, was by then the only remaining Christian stronghold. It had good reason to fear a Druze attack, because bad blood had run between its inhabitants and the Druzes for decades. In the 1820s and 1830s, backed by the ruling Shihab emir Bashir II, they had treated Druzes severely. In 1841 and again in 1844, the Zahalni had fought the Druzes and emerged victorious and more arrogant than ever. The Zahalni also had alienated the Shi'is of the Beqaa plain, forcing them to negotiate political alliances with the Druzes. Under Bashir II, the Zahalni had humiliated members of the Harfush clan and outraged the Shi'is and Druzes by interfering in disputes involving Christians in neighboring Shi'i villages.[80]

More recently, the Druzes and the Zahalni had piled up new causes for resentment. When the civil war broke out, the first encounters between them occurred at the battles of Ain Dara near Zahleh. The return of the defeated Zahalni forces already had stirred up the population when around June 1 the Zahalni men, led by a town leader named Abdallah Abu Khatir, went to Kfar Selwane, a nearby village, to protect the Christians there. Others engaged the Druzes in a series of skirmishes in the plains around Zahleh to protect threatened Zahalni property.[81] Still other Zahalni were busily looking for outside support, appealing to Maronites in the northern districts, where Taniyus Shahin of Reifun, Yusuf Karam of Ihdin, and lesser leaders such as Yusuf al-Shantiri of Metn could muster large forces. Taniyus Shahin, however, had political ambitions and was reluctant to take any steps that might antagonize the Ottoman authorities. Yusuf Karam was equally reluctant to leave Kisrawan, and Yusuf al-Shantiri delayed action until he could figure out what his more powerful counterparts planned to do.

In the end, their support did not materialize, and its promise had weakened the Zahalni by encouraging them to count on outside help. Taniyus Shahin never came to their rescue. Yusuf Karam assembled 4,000 men, supplied them with arms and ammunition obtained from supporters in the Mountain and in Beirut, but went only as far as Bikfaiya in the Metn. Yusuf al-Shantiri pretended to make preparations to leave Metn, but never actually departed. While the Zahalni awaited their arrival, the Druze from the Shuf, Hawran, and Wadi Taym collected nearby.[82]

Both Yusuf Karam and Yusuf al-Shantiri later claimed that the French consul general and the pasha had forbidden them and the rest of the Christian forces in Bikfaiya to move, a claim that was not without foundation. On June 21 the French consul general wrote to Edouard-Antoine Thouvenel, the French foreign minister, that the Zahalni could expect no help from the Christians. "I must add, Mr Minister, that it could not have been otherwise after the agreements of June 16" between the consuls and the pasha of Beirut, one result of which was that the pasha sent 300 soldiers under Colonel Nuri Bey to Zahleh to force the Druzes back home. In exchange, the consuls were to keep any Christian force from going to Zahleh's defense.[83]

The Ottoman troops did not succeed in their mission. They did not even reach Zahleh, but stopped at the village of Makseh some two hours' march away and were still there when the Druzes launched their attack. On Sunday, June 17, Nuri Bey met with Druze leaders. The authorities assumed that the meeting was meant to recommend peace to the Druzes; the French consul general and the local Christians believed, on the contrary, that it took place to plot war. The first is the more likely, however; throughout the authorities tried to avoid conflict and to rely on persuasion rather than force.

In addition to Zahleh's available young men, the town could rely on a number of able-bodied refugees, a small force provided by a member of the partly Druze, partly Christian, family of Shaykh Abu'l-Lama in the Metn, and 400 horsemen from Baskinta. (The sources give numbers ranging from 4,000 to 7,000 but the latter number is rather high since the whole town had no more than some 8,000–10,000 people.)[84] To prepare for battle, they dug a large trench, built a brick wall with small openings along it on the southern edge of town, erected fortifications in the narrow passageways and streets, filled vaults with food and other supplies, and hid away their valuables. They were well equipped with ammunition and horses.[85] What they lacked, however, was good leadership. They acted on impulse rather than calculation.

On June 14, they went forth to confront the enemy at its headquarters at Qabb Elias, a mixed village on the Beirut–Damascus road two hours' walk from Zahleh in the Beqaa plain. "Without discipline and blindly heedless of danger," they spread themselves over the fields, some standing, others lining ditches, and began to shoot. Before long, they had to retreat in disarray and return to town. They tried again over the next few days, but with no success; they fell back to take a defensive position in Zahleh.[86]

From the Druze viewpoint, Zahleh was the most dreaded Christian stronghold in the Mountain. Its soldiers were known for their valor, and that knowledge deepened the esteem the Druzes held for their own effective leaders. Abu Shaqra, the only Druze chronicler of the civil war of 1860, tells us about the care with which Khattar Imad, the Druze shaykh from the district of Arqub who had lost a son in the first battle of Ain Dara, targeted the entrance points into Zahleh, prepared the attack, and organized and encouraged the soldiers. He walked among them, back and forth, "tireless in encouraging his soldiers, strengthening their resolve, appealing to their sense of honor, stimulating their intentions, without his neglecting any matter, be it important or not, or his overlooking a problem, be it noble or negligible."[87]

Under the leadership of Khattar Imad, the Druzes launched another attack on Zahleh on the morning of June 18. Joined by Bedouins and Shi'is, they numbered 3,000 men, perhaps many more. While the townspeople diminished their already poor odds by feuding, the Druzes acted in concert. They directed their assault against the southern, eastern, and western flanks, and left the northern flank to Khattar Imad who planned to conduct there a surprise attack.[88]

It was carried out with cunning and skill. The Druzes knew the Zahalnis expected help from the Christian forces in the north and thus had neglected to fortify the town on the north side. Khattar Imad equipped a force of his best men with Christian flags with crosses taken by Druzes in earlier battles and approached Zahleh from that neglected flank. As he came closer, the Zahalni presumed Yusuf Karam and his Christian forces had arrived and began to rejoice, until fire broke out in the upper quarter of town.[89] This kind of feat won the Druze leaders the admiration and loyalty of their followers. Abu Shaqra tells us that the discipline and organization of the Druze fighters reflected the competence of their shaykhs.

Within hours, the Druzes were in control of the center of town. Abu Shaqra tells us that the first to enter Zahleh were the Druzes of the Shuf, who had opened up the northern flank and set fire to its houses. When the rest of the Druzes saw the flames, Isma'il al-Atrash and his men struck, and Zahleh fell.

The Zahalni fought bravely. Although they were defeated, their bravery saved the tattered reputation of the Christian side, which had few other reasons for pride in the civil war. Division undermined any advantage their fighting spirit might have given them, however. An anonymous Christian Damascene who left us an account of the civil war, entitled *Kitab al-ahzan*, generally criticizes the Christians for their rivalries and divisions, but judged those of Zahleh particularly vicious. Within hours of the Druze onslaught, the townspeople had fled, jumping from windows and off roofs to reach the mountains and find refuge in Kisrawan, Metn, and other districts in the north and along the seacoast. Most of them had to leave all their possessions behind. When the Druzes returned the next day, the town was deserted.[90]

Estimates of casualties range between 40 and just below 900 Christians killed, and 100 to 1,500 Druzes. Much of the town was destroyed. Although most sources attribute the looting to the Druzes, the Druze chronicler Abu Shaqra said:[91]

> As for the booty and gains from Zahleh, the Druzes did not care for them. They agreed among themselves on this matter, because whoever devotes his energy to material gains will lose his courage and be distracted by these gains, at the expense of defending, repelling, thrusting and striking. Do not ask, however, how much the Hawrani Arabs [Bedouins] have plundered and obtained horses, jewelry, and money. I have toured these areas and come across the Sardiyyin Arabs of the Hawran. I inquired near them and they pointed out to me the Zahalni horses left to them which were the offspring of the ones they had captured in Zahleh. Up to now, they still call these horses the Zahalni.

The outcome also spelled doom for the Christians of the Mountain and Greater Syria. The defeat of unconquerable Zahleh meant the loss of their last refuge and hope. "The fall of Zahleh brings to its utmost the consternation of Christians who rightly saw, in the preservation of this town, the last support of all of Christian Lebanon," commented the French consul general, on June 21; while the British vice-consul in Sidon commented on the fall of Zahleh that "many Christians have, in consequence, determined to leave Syria."[92] Abkarius wrote:

> The taking of Zahleh was an event of importance for the Christians in every place [throughout the land] because it had been their main support, and [now] was [an element of] power to their foes because it inspired them with a desire for [the possession of] all their cities and towns.[93]

The taking of Zahleh was also an equally great cause for celebration among the Druzes and Muslims of Greater Syria. It established the unquestioned superiority of the Druzes over the Christians and left the entire Mountain in their hands. To the Muslims of the interior, punishing Zahalni arrogance was a source of great satisfaction. The *Kitab al-ahzan* describes how the Damascenes decorated their shops and rejoiced over the great victory. Al-Sayyid Muhammad Abu'l Su'ud al-Hasibi, a notable of Damascus, wrote in his memoirs: "Even before Zahleh was conquered, people [in Damascus] began to inquire daily: 'Have they conquered Zahleh?' 'Why have they not conquered it?' It seemed to them to be a matter of reconquering the Morea [Peloponnese]; so much had they suffered from the people of Zahleh and heard of their sly deeds."[94] When the news of the fall of Zahleh finally reached Damascus, he also tells us the Damascenes lit lanterns and decorated their houses in celebration "as if it were Ramadan." Although he deplored the excesses of 1860 and his father forbade the lighting of lanterns when Zahleh fell, he understood why others reacted as they did to what he saw as Zahalni insolence and ambition.[95]

The fall of Zahleh escalated the anarchy. The conquerors returned to lay waste the plains again. Bands of Shi'is and Sunnis from Baalbek took advantage of the disorder to settle scores and to loot. They attacked Christian villages, "pillaging their property and burning their houses and churches, and carrying away the cattle and the crops." Thirty-four villages of the Beqaa and Baalbek area were repeatedly sacked. Baalbek, the seat of Faris Agha Qadro, the local civil governor of the district, and the local headquarters of Husni Bey, the Ottoman colonel in command of a battalion of the regular imperial troops, was then attacked.

Old quarrels between the Ottoman authorities and the local Harfush chiefs were behind the attack. According to the Greek Catholic bishop of the district, the assault was led by members of the Harfush clan who earlier had been outlawed by the Ottoman government. They launched a surprise attack against the civil governor. He survived, but a number of his retainers did not. The Ottoman army did not interfere to save him or the population.

Class differences also played a role. The troops sent from Damascus to Baalbek to lift this siege consisted of 400 irregulars "enrolled among the lawless class of Damascus, chiefly Kurds notorious for their licentiousness." Notwithstanding the bias against the Kurds, it is obvious that draftees may have contributed to the tensions. Under the command of Hassan Agha Yazigi, these "wicked troops were the greatest scourge of the Christians who had remained in their homes." In subsequent weeks, the troops stationed in Baalbek renewed the looting and violence against the bishop's house and other residences.[96]

The fall of Zahleh and the destruction of Baalbek made the Druze the victors, but they fought on. They attacked Deir al-Qamar yet again and sacked it on June 20 or 21. Its surrender on June 2 from the first attack had protected it from destruction, for at the beginning of the civil war attacks on property and life were selective. Now, however, all restraints had disappeared. When the Druzes returned from the sack of Zahleh, they fell upon Deir al-Qamar, symbol of Christian wealth, power, and status in the Mountain and laid it waste.

The massacre at Deir al-Qamar was the worst in the civil war. The Druze chronicler Abu Shaqra called it "an enormous national calamity, [and] an unfortunate event of unprecedented magnitude in modern Lebanese history. My pen would disdain from recording happenings as confused as these, were it not for the compelling necessity to investigate historical truths."[97] In contrast to the provocative Zahalni, as soon as the war broke out, the people of Deir al-Qamar had sent delegation after delegation to Druze shaykhs and Ottoman officials and appealed to the European consuls for protection. Then after the people had resigned themselves to defeat, had surrendered, and appealed to the Druzes for mercy, they were attacked.

Some of the town's influential citizens had been able to escape before the attack. Jibra'il and Rufa'il, for example, two members of the Mishaqa family, were taken to Mukhtara by Sa'id Janbalat, with a number of friends and the Catholic metropolitan of Deir al-Qamar and Beit al-Din. Rufa'il later returned to Deir al-Qamar on business and then decided to take his family to Beirut, where his brother Ibrahim had settled after the clashes of 1841 and his son Khalil worked as dragoman for the British consulate. Rufa'il's plans, however, were at first thwarted by Tahir Pasha, a general who, after the troubles at Deir al-Qamar at the beginning of June, had been sent from Beirut with a hundred soldiers to keep the peace, and who prevented the Christians from leaving, and by the Druze shaykhs who were reluctant to meet with him. Rufa'il's brother Ibrahim appealed to the British consul general who, in turn, appealed to the Nakad shaykhs who helped Rufa'il and his family to leave and reach Beirut safely.[98] Thousands were not so fortunate. They remained, hanging on to every rumor of disaster in the Mountain, of reassurances by Ottoman authorities, Druze shaykhs, or consular representatives.

At first the Druzes simply prevented anyone from entering or leaving the town and withheld supplies. As more and more Druzes appeared in the town's principal quarters and spread among the houses, they told the inhabitants that they had been sent by their shaykhs to guard the houses of the principal families. They moved from house to house and shop to shop, and next they began to pillage abandoned shops and warehouses.

The townsfolk's response was fainthearted. Abkarius complains that they did nothing to oppose the Druzes and, instead, "[looked] to the Lord of Heaven for relief." Actually, they tried to enlist Ottoman protection as the Druzes closed in. Three times their notables met with Tahir Pasha, twice at his palace at Beit al-Din and once in Deir al-Qamar. They suspected him of striking a bargain with the Druzes, and he in turn suspected them of supporting the Beirut Committee, which was stirring up Christians against Druzes. They assured him they had taken no part in the committee's activities and had nothing to do with its supporters in the Mountain. He then assured them of his protection as long as they did not leave town. He also met with Druze delegates.[99]

Two developments appeared to improve the situation, just as Tahir Pasha prepared to leave for Beirut. An apparent reconciliation between Christians and Druzes took place, and reinforcements in the form of some 500 infantrymen arrived from Sidon. Tahir Pasha assembled the notables and the officers of the troops stationed at Beit al-Din and of those just arrived from Sidon. To all of them he recommended calm, and the public crier went through the streets with his reassurances. Soldiers patrolled the streets and guarded the grain supply.

After Tahir Pasha's departure, however, the Christians appealed to Mustafa Shukri Efendi, the local governor and commander of the Ottoman garrison who was only half an hour's march away and had 400 soldiers with him. He claimed he had no authority to attack the Druzes and could not otherwise restrain them.

At some point during this tense period that preceded the attack on Deir al-Qamar, the Christians were disarmed although it is not clear how. Either the Druzes confiscated the Christians' weapons when they entered town, as some claimed, or, as others had it, the authorities ordered a general disarmament. Some say Mustafa Shukri Efendi suggested that the Christians surrender their arms and take refuge in the serai. Others say Tahir Pasha before he left town had asked the population to disarm, and then "the very day Tahir Pasha finished disarming the Christians, the Druzes came in to slaughter them like sheep."[100]

In any case the inhabitants appeared resigned to the overwhelming superiority of the imperial forces and of Druzes all around them. Unlike the Christians in other districts, theirs was truly a minority position in the heartland of the Druze Shuf. In addition, they had been cut off from news of the outside world for days, which must have added to their confusion and defeatism. The few who resisted had their arms taken by force. They hurried to the serai for refuge with their families and valuables, as rumors reached them of Druzes murdering Christians, including monks. Some sought help from Druze friends.[101]

The lack of a central authority added to their problem. The efforts of local Ottoman officials at controlling the situation as it deteriorated were feeble. The French consul general in Beirut, who was critical of the Ottomans' role in the civil war, reported that after the Druzes arrived the governor of Deir al-Qamar immediately came out of his palace with his officers and admonished the Christians not to go anywhere or touch their arms.[102] The governor's invitation to surrender their arms and seek refuge in the serai took on sinister designs after the massacres, but he may simply have been afraid they would provoke the Druzes. Several complaints by Ottoman authorities about the Beirut Committee and Christian provocation indicate they believed that restraining the Christians was the only way to prevent trouble. Perhaps it was all the governor could do. In retrospect it is possible to agree with the Christians that the Druzes should have been more forcefully prevented from gathering in town, but it is equally easy to see the precariousness of the Ottoman situation.

And if the governor had no power, all the more helpless were those under his command. As the Druzes came into Deir al-Qamar, one captain of the local regular troops with 15 soldiers and the Druze shaykh Khattar Nakad "civilly" requested the Druzes they met to leave, and then passed on to another house or quarter. When an American missionary named Mr Bird asked the guards of his house why they did not prevent the Druzes from coming into town, they answered, "They had no orders to interfere with a single Druze whatever he may do and if they take any steps it is only a sham." Other soldiers were accused of simply joining in the pillaging.[103]

Before sunset, a priest and a man named Habib Bahout were killed at the gate of the serai. More Christians rushed to the serai or to the most strongly built houses. About 200 sought refuge in the military barracks of Beit al-Din, but most barracks were soon evacuated by the troops. Many hid in the governor's house. Throughout the night, the Druzes arrived from all directions.[104]

By dawn on Wednesday, June 20, it was clear that Deir al-Qamar would fall to the Druzes. Two hours before sunrise, Druzes from Baaqline, Manasif, Shahahir, Arqub, Ammatur, Ain al-Tineh, Mukhtara, Batma, and Jdaideh moved on the town. According to Abu Shaqra, the 4,000 soldiers in the town, demoralized by the news of Zahleh's fall, offered no resistance. Since the Christians had already been disarmed and gathered in the serai, they fell prey to their attackers in their houses and inside the serai.[105]

The massacre continued for the next two days. Thousands were killed. The *kavass* (armed footman) of the Prussian consulate arrived at Deir al-Qamar during the massacre and saw bazaars and streets strewn with corpses; he guessed the number at 2,000. Only people who had friends among the Druzes escaped and were saved.[106]

Christian sources accused the Druzes of attacking women, but their objectivity is questionable. The French consul general, for example, was so hostile that one must treat his comments about Druzes with care. He claimed that even nuns were attacked; the two agents of Mr Bird recalled females were abused. Even Abkarius claimed the Druzes carried off girls and matrons alike, tore off their veils, and "examined the women in parts of their bodies which cannot be mentioned, a thing without precedent [even] among the barbarian riff-raff of past ages or present." Aqiqi said that some women and children escaped, but the attackers "killed every male they found." Abu Shaqra, who did not hesitate to admit to the horrors of the massacre at Deir al-Qamar perpetrated by his co-religionists, on the other hand said that women were untouched; the Druze men did not so much as make inappropriate remarks to them. He cites only one case where a woman was touched, and even then that was innocent: a village Druze from far away, not knowing that Christian women did not cover their heads, took his turban and covered the bare head of a Christian woman.[107]

After the massacre the town was sacked and destroyed. Abu Shaqra, who maintained that the Druzes had no part in the sack of Zahleh, admitted that at Deir al-Qamar vast quantities of jewelry, goods, and horses were carried off. There was an abundance of precious goods because the town was so wealthy and, as Cyril Graham remarked, "used to comfort and luxury." Houses were ransacked and then set afire, shops were emptied, valuables were unearthed and carried away. The looters loaded pack animals with booty and left town.[108]

One of the last houses to be destroyed was that of Khalil Shawish, the secretary of the Druze *qaymaqam* of southern Lebanon, who was known to be under the protection of Shaykh Bashir Nakad. His house sheltered some 300 people and was guarded by soldiers. Despite large sums offered to Bashir Nakad to ensure the continued protection of the house, however, in the end he declined to protect it further. A relative of the Druze *qaymaqam* led Shawish and the members of his family away; the remaining men and boys were killed by the Druzes and the soldiers. The house was then looted and burned.[109]

One house targeted for attack was left untouched. Three thousand men led by Shaykh Qasim Imad surrounded the house of the Reverend Mr Bird and demanded the surrender of its 20 occupants. Just then a Druze Hamada chief arrived with a proclamation from the Ottoman pasha. It ordered the Druze to leave town when three guns were fired from the serai. Simultaneously, Mr Bird himself arrived at his besieged home with some of Nakad's followers and a safe conduct given to them in the presence of the pasha. The three guns were fired; Sa'id Janbalat and the Ottoman colonel arrived with Hamadas and some troops. Shaykh Janbalat promised Mr Bird that his house would not be attacked. The clergyman then left Deir al-Qamar for Abey with the others and from there they were escorted to Beirut.[110]

The richest and most prosperous town of the Shuf had been leveled. Stripped and mutilated bodies were scattered in gutters, streets, what was left of vaults, bazaars, and houses, in front of the Ottoman barracks and in the serai. Many of the dead were wounded on their right hands and on their necks, perhaps because the victims had instinctively raised their arms to parry the blows that felled them. "Blood flowed in rivers," wrote Mishaqa. When the men and male children in the serai were killed "the blood in the court was a foot deep," reported the Reverend Mr Bird. Abkarius wrote that "blood ran like water" in this unprecented disaster. Churchill went even further: "The blood at length rose above the ankles, flowed along the gutters, gushed out of the water spouts, and gurgled through the streets."[111]

The violence spread beyond Deir al-Qamar. Just outside the town, at the barracks of Beit al-Din where Christians were known to have sought shelter, the Druzes attacked. The troops offered no resistance. There was little they could have done. Four hundred men were stationed at Beit al-Din, and the Druzes numbered several thousand. The Druzes raided and torched the countryside.

Finally, the Ottoman authorities, with the help of some Druze shaykhs, moved to end the destruction. The governor general Khurshid Pasha returned to Beit al-Din and the next day ordered a cease-fire: any Druzes who disobeyed would be seized and sent to the gallows at Acre and their chief held responsible. The order was ignored until the Druze chiefs arrived with the proclamation and ended the fighting with a signal from the serai. Sa'id Janbalat, Nakad, the Hamada chiefs and the Ottoman colonel were then able to restore order and, in doing so, to end the most violent phase of the civil war in the Mountain.[112]

The events in the Lebanon immediately heightened unrest everywhere in Greater Syria, as groups joined to attack others or fought one another. On the whole, safety was directly correlated to distance from the warring districts of Mount Lebanon and to a show of force by the local Ottoman authorities. Along the Syrian coast, the presence of warships proved settling. It helped maintain peace in Jaffa, Haifa, Acre, Sidon, Tyre, Beirut, and Tripoli, although some of them who were closest to the war zone suffered from the aftershocks it generated, especially when refugees began to arrive. Tyre and Sidon were on the brink of civil war and were the scene of violence, but Beirut, further up the coast, remained relatively calm, although it almost succumbed.

By 1860, Beirut had become the center of power and commerce on the Syrian coast and had replaced Sidon as the center of the *vilayet*. First, during the Egyptian occupation of Syria in the 1830s and then after the restitution of Ottoman rule in 1840, it was the administrative headquarters for all of Mount Lebanon, after the semi-autonomous Shihab rule had come to an end and was replaced by a dual Ottoman governorship for north and south Mount Lebanon. Beginning in the 1830s one by one the European consulates moved to Beirut, followed by European commerce. The city's population, estimated to be between 6,000 and 8,000 before 1836, quadrupled between 1830 and 1850.[113] In the nineteenth century, Beirut had broken the confines of its city walls, and limited by the Mediterranean sea to its west and north, had expanded southwest, south, and east, into the surrounding countryside where, by the late 1850s, the majority of the town's population resided.[114]

During the civil war much of the Mountain's Christian maneuvering was orchestrated from Beirut; to Beirut came defeated Christian factions and refugees fleeing the war. Neither the city's facilities nor the authorities were equipped to provide shelter or deal with the shortages caused by the arrival of these tens of thousands of destitute refugees. They camped out in the quarantine area, schools, hospitals, and open spaces, gardens, and cemeteries. Relief was organized haphazardly at first, then more systematically, by the government, foreign institutions, and local charitable organizations and individuals, both Muslim and Christian. By the end of the fighting, the population had more than doubled again with the influx of refugees from the civil war of 1860. Most of these immigrants were Christians – Maronite, Greek Orthodox, and Greek Catholic – in contrast to the mostly Sunni Muslims and Greek Orthodox Christians already there.

News of Christian defeats in the Mountain and of Muslim attacks on Christians in Sidon and Tyre reached Beirut in the first week of June, and the Beiruti Christians panicked. Their co-religionists in the Mountain had been their safeguard and now that their protectors needed protection, they were certain an attack in Beirut was imminent.[115]

Their worst fears seemed about to be confirmed on June 23, when a fight broke out between a Christian refugee and a Muslim in which the Muslim was killed. Immediately armed Muslim mobs marched to the governor's palace demanding the life of the murderer and threatening to kill every Christian in Beirut if he was not turned over to them. Khurshid Pasha, the governor, was in fact not there. He had gone to Deir al-Qamar; but the acting governor, Isma'il Pasha, had the Christian – or at least a Christian – arrested. He swore he was innocent, but he was tried on the spot.

By that time the mob seemed to be in control of the city,[116] and it grew more and more violent. Several Christians were knocked to the ground; others were beaten; at least one was hit over the head. Some Europeans were roughed up as well. Bentivoglio, the French consul, went to the serai to see the dead Muslim and had a sword brandished in his face by a relative of the dead man. Two Englishman were threatened with pistols and one was heaped with abuse.[117]

The Christians locked themselves in their homes awaiting slaughter, and the Westerners shared their panic. "Beirut is now in danger. Druses are surrounding it. The Moslems are in arms, and declare that they will now kill the Christians of this place. Today the city is filled with Turkish troops – and an insurrection is greatly feared by all Christians of native and foreign birth."[118]

Isma'il Pasha took decisive steps to contain the crisis. On the day of the outbreak, an Ottoman man-of-war filled with troops had arrived at Beirut and, despite the profound distrust the Christians and some of the Europeans felt toward them, Isma'il Pasha posted Ottoman soldiers around the city. At the same time, the pasha mollified the mob by finding the accused man guilty and condemning him to death. He then consulted with the consular corps assembled in the British consul general Noel Moore's office. They knew that the death sentence could not be carried out without the governor's approval, and that approval could not be obtained until Khurshid Pasha returned from Deir al-Qamar in three days' time. Isma'il

Pasha argued that he could not wait that long – the safety of the town depended on an immediate execution – and essentially asked the consuls to sanction it.

The agreement between the acting governor and the consuls resolved the crisis. The consuls refused to sanction a death sentence against the accused Christian directly, but they agreed that, in the absence of the governor, Isma'il Pasha had full powers to act as the governor would have acted, had he been present. Isma'il Pasha then told the consuls that without action the crisis would reach proportions compared to which the execution of one man would be minor indeed. He was prepared to call out the army and bombard the town, and that would destroy all parties alike. He then left the consuls and ordered the death sentence to be carried out against the condemned Christian an hour after sunset. The accused protested his innocence to the end, but innocent or guilty he had served his purpose. The pasha's quick response – only twelve hours had elapsed between the death of the Muslim and the execution of his alleged murderer – and the agreement between the Ottoman and European representatives in Beirut had effectively ended the threat of civil war in the city.[119]

The Christians persisted in their belief that the authorities were plotting their downfall, however, even after the violence had been averted. For days Christians trusted neither Ottoman, nor Muslim, nor Druze. "It would be difficult to describe ... the intense panic that has seized the Christians of Beyrout," wrote Moore on June 26, "they have acquired the conviction that the fate of the population of Deir el-Kamar awaits them at the hands of the Turkish Authorities and troops the Moslems of the town and the Druzes." Hundreds left for Malta, Alexandria, or anywhere away from Syria, just as thousands of refugees continued to arrive at Beirut. A stream of rumors kept up the tension and fed both the fears of the innocent and the ugly mood of the violent. Refugees publicly bemoaned their lost ones; armed bands roamed the streets; commerce was at a complete standstill.[120]

In the southern regions of Syria, the situation remained under control in June and July 1860, despite a palpable increase in sectarian hostility. In northern Palestine, on the whole Bedouin chiefs ensured the peace. In Jerusalem, Nablus, and Acre the authorities imposed stern military measures which helped keep the peace.[121] In Bethlehem, peace was more difficult to maintain, despite traditions of economic cooperation among religious groups. At the end of June 1860, trouble arose when a Christian handed a Muslim a gold napoleon as part payment for a camel-load of wheat. The Muslim rejected it, saying he could not accept money from infidels. The Christian retorted that he would report to the French consul that French money had been refused. The Muslim then beat up the Christian and called upon a soldier to lock the beaten man up, which was done.[122]

Just south of Mount Lebanon close to the warring districts, looting and clashes went on, although sporadically compared to the mixed districts of the Mountain, with Shi'is allied with Druzes against Christian villagers, or Shi'is acting on their own, or most rarely, Shi'is against Druzes. At the end of June and in the first days of July 1860, the Shi'is in the hills first joined the Druzes to plunder neighboring Christian villages and then continued on their own. The large village of Bassa, on the edge of the Acre plain, and the village of Kfar Biraan near Safed were plundered, and three Christians were killed in the latter. At the same time, Shi'is and Druzes fought one another. North of these villages, at Jbaa near Sidon, Druzes attacked and wounded the religious chief of all the Shi'is of the region, provoking war between the two sects.[123]

In Latakia, Antioch, and Aleppo, local authorities kept firm control on the situation, as they also did in Homs and Hama.[124] It was more difficult to maintain control in Aleppo, which had been the theater of sectarian clashes in 1850.[125] The mass of the population had rejected its leaders. The governor had been recalled, and he lost interest in the town and shut himself away in his harem claiming ill health. The provincial council was in disarray because the year before they exploited the general scarcity by speculating in grain to enrich themselves. Jews and Muslims were fighting over some land on which a mosque had been built. The Christians, a minority of some 17,000 among a Muslim population of some 100,000, were also tense. Only the military governor Umar Pasha appeared to have the intention of preserving order, but he had barely 1,000 soldiers, was new at his post, and had not yet developed a network of support in the town.[126]

By the last days of June, the "Muslim rabble" (as the British consul called them) of the town were holding nightly meetings to make, so the authorities suspected, seditious plans. When the authorities sent two companies of infantry to disperse one of the meetings, the rioters fired at the soldiers, wounding four of them and driving them all away. The Christians, too afraid to fight, paid others to protect them; by the last few days of June they had collected 20,000 piastres for that purpose. In the end, violence was averted, however; leading Muslims organized a sort of police force to monitor public order, and the bishop encouraged his parishioners to cooperate with them.[127] Damascus was less fortunate. There the situation grew steadily worse.

CHAPTER 4

THE DAMASCUS "INCIDENT"

News of the war in Lebanon trickled into Damascus first in sketchy reports and then in more gruesome and graphic detail. People seized upon any scrap of news that came their way and anxiously waited for the post from Beirut that brought the latest reports. These reports were then circulated, amplified, and distorted in the marketplaces, houses, mosques, and churches in every quarter and corner of the city. The stream of rumors was relentless and continuous. "The excitement provoked by the contest in Lebanon rather augments," wrote James Brant, the British consul in Damascus, on June 4, "but more from rumors than positive news." As the days went by he became more and more confounded by the numerous and often conflicting reports and did not know what to believe.[1]

In early June, Lanusse, the chief secretary at the French consulate and acting French consul and Belgian vice-consul in Damascus, repeated rumors of Christian victory that circulated in the city, a victory so decisive that the Druzes were reported to have demanded reinforcements. The Hawran and the villages around Damascus provided a considerable contingent. Soon, however, these stories of Christian victories and Druze defeats were replaced by better-founded reports of crushing Christian defeats and massacres.[2]

The rumors about what was happening in the Mountain quickly became intertwined with, and inseparable from, the rumors about what was going on in Damascus. Among the local Christians and Europeans, they featured Muslim and Druze plots; among the Muslims, the rumors were apt to be the same except that the intended victims were Muslims and the perpetrators European powers and their sympathizers. Among the Christians, it was rumored that the Druzes had sent to Ahmad Pasha, the governor of Damascus, a list of 72 Christians they wanted handed over. Other sinister stories were whispered from door to door at night by Lanusse, or so Brant complained, causing panic among the Christians. Among the Muslims, the version was that the Christians had drawn up a petition signed by 72 of their notables demanding a Christian king be set up to rule over Zahleh and Lebanon. Still other rumors concerned attacks on mosques by Christians.[3]

Mishaqa was particularly astonished by the Muslim panic because the balance of force was so overwhelmingly on the Muslim side. They had weapons including cannons, and they held the citadel. Rare was the Christian who possessed so much as a hunting rifle; they were such pacifists, he tells us, that most of them didn't even have the courage to kill their own chicken but took it to the butcher to do the job for them. But Muslim fears were real, especially *vis-à-vis* the Europeans, particularly the French and Russians. The local Christians were in part mistrusted as instruments of these foreigners.[4]

As the war spread from the mixed districts of southern Lebanon to the Anti-Lebanon and the Beqaa and Baalbek regions closer to Damascus, the Damascenes became more directly involved. Men were sent, or volunteered to go, to the warring districts. In June, troops were dispatched from Damascus to the Anti-Lebanon, deepening the involvement of the city in the war, generating other cycles of speculation, fear, and tension, and exposing the soldiers and civilians alike to the abuse and loss of innocence that the sights of war can produce, which they brought back with them to Damascus. Some quarters of the city also responded by sending men: the inhabitants of the outer Salihiya quarter armed themselves and marched out to attack Zahleh; others were expected to follow their example.[5]

The majority of Damascenes, however, did not become directly involved in the war until after the frightened and miserable Christian refugees began to arrive in the city. Threatened by the Druzes, the Christian inhabitants of the small village of Zabadani had left their homes on the morning of June 13 under Ottoman escort and reached Damascus the same day; it is probable that other Christian villagers between the Anti-Lebanon and Damascus followed the same route. A few of the male survivors of the massacres at Hasbaiya and Rashaiya also made their way to Damascus, but most of the survivors from there were women and children. "After the massacres at Rashaiya and Hasbaiya, the town of Damascus had received a great number of refugees from these towns and all the surrounding villages," wrote Maxime Outrey, French consul in Damascus who arrived in Syria after the civil war, landing in Beirut on July 19 and sending his first report from Damascus on July 28. Brant was more precise when he estimated that between 3,000 and 4,000 refugees were in Damascus by late June, most of them Greek Orthodox widows and children. About 2,000 strangers had taken refuge in the mosque. Robson – an Irish Presbyterian missionary who had been living in Damascus for 18 years –

estimated the refugees at 5,000 or 6,000. Both estimates seem within range; the 7,000 figure suggested by the anonymous Christian author of the *Kitab al-ahzan* is probably too high.[6]

Peasant families were also stranded in Damascus because of unsafe roads and a political situation too volatile for them to risk returning home. They had traveled from what Mishaqa simply referred to as "the white mountains"[7] to help with the harvest in the villages around Damascus and Hawran. Unable to return, they sought refuge in the city. How many there were is uncertain, but according to Mishaqa, Damascus was filled with them.[8]

The combination of refugees and stranded peasants caused overcrowded conditions, especially in the Christian quarter of Damascus, which was jammed with outsiders. The congestion demoralized the local population, which was confronted with the hardships of dislocation. Refugees with nothing but the clothes on their backs, sometimes ragged and barefoot, often destitute and unable even to buy bread, were a depressing sight.

The local population were pressed for aid. Damascene Christians did all they could to help the refugees despite their own hardships and numerous poor. The various local churches, chiefly the Greek Orthodox and the Greek Catholics, carried most of the burden, but many individuals also contributed generously including Muslim notables. Among them was Emir Abd al-Qadir (1808–83), the Algerian hero who had resisted the French conquest of Algeria between 1830 and 1847, and had retired to Damascus in 1855 where he lived the remainder of his life. He gave money to the widows of the Shihab emirs. Another benefactor was Ahmad al-Hasibi. In the memoirs of his son Abu'l Su'ud, who witnessed the events of 1860 as a young man and wrote about them several years later, we learn that he sheltered the widows of the Shihab emirs and their children, first in his own home and then in a house in the Qanawat quarter of Damascus. Other Muslim notables of Ahmad al-Hasibi's acquaintance – Abd Agha al-Tinawi, Muhammad Agha Nimr, Shaykh Muhammad Qatana, and al-Sayyid Hasan – helped feed them.[9] The European consulates also contributed to refugee relief. Perhaps to entice his government into authorizing some funds for the refugees, the British consul mentioned that the French consul had contributed handsomely, with what was rumored to be about £100 sterling.[10]

But the demand for relief was so great that private charity provided little more than shelter to a few, a bakery for their use, and free distribution of bread for a scanty meal, at a cost Brant estimated to be £30 to £40 a day. Most of the refugees remained without shelter, sleeping in stables and lanes around the churches, "with no bed save the ground and no cover save the sky." During the day, women and children could be seen roaming the streets begging, constant reminders to all Damascenes that war was nearby.[11] This tended to polarize the Damascene population because, despite the relief provided by many Muslim notables, for some the refugees were seen to be a threat. On the streets random acts of hostility towards Christians – particularly the refugees themselves – were commonplace. Such reactions are common when refugees and minorities in any society become more visible and, hence, more threatening.

Relations continued to deteriorate between the Damascene Muslims and Christians in June and early July, especially after the massacres of Hasbaiya and Rashaiya and the takeover of Zahleh. Violence increased, and people began to worry for the first time since the beginning of the war in the Lebanon that there would be trouble in Damascus. After the crushing defeat of Zahleh, the majority no longer felt that the situation was still under control. The anonymous author of *Kitab al-ahzan* wrote that insults against the Christians multiplied after the refugees from the war-torn regions arrived and the Damascene Muslims showed no sympathy for their plight. The *Kitab al-ahzan* was written soon after the civil war, probably between late 1860–61 and 1864, probably by a Christian member of the Damascus business community. It is openly anti-Muslim, but even Mishaqa, who was far more even-handed, noted the increasing animosity among the city's Muslims and Druzes toward its Christian population. Pragmatist and conciliator that he was, he was careful to distinguish between "reasonable" and "ignorant" Damascenes in both camps. The indignation of the Muslim ignorant against the Christians continued to grow.[12]

Lanusse firmly believed that the Christians were in terrible danger and predicted the worst. Brant, in contrast, underestimated the sectarian hostility that was building up in the city and called Lanusse an alarmist. In his opinion, there was "no fear of the Muslim inhabitants molesting the Christians," especially if the authorities acted firmly. But even he mentioned hostility and abuse, threatening language, and ill-treatment.[13]

When the news of Zahleh's defeat reached Damascus and the Muslims began to celebrate, lighting lanterns and fires in the quarters and marketplaces, their rejoicing had much to do with the end to the threat Zahleh had posed to the interests of Damascene grain and livestock merchants. Mishaqa remarked ironically that when the news of Zahleh's fate reached Damascus, "you would have thought the [Ottoman] Empire had conquered Russia." But it did not help Muslim–Christian relations. Some of the Muslim notables tried without success to stop the celebration. One of them was Mahmud Efendi Hamza, a learned man knowledgeable in

European science, who had been called to mediate between Druzes and Christians in Zahleh; another was Ahmad Hasibi.[14]

The turmoil in Damascus now grew after Zahleh's defeat, but measures could still have been taken to neutralize the hostilities, and many tried. Abd al-Qadir made the rounds of the ulema, Muslim notables, and the leaders of the various quarters in an effort to prevent violence. He also kept in close touch with Lanusse at the French consulate. As a hero of the Algerian resistance, he had both the status and the power to play an exceptional role, and he tried every diplomatic means at his disposal to control the situation. Lanusse tells us that he watched over the security of Christians and Europeans in the city "night and day" and Mishaqa writes that there was not a single leader of the city – ulema, agha, or village shaykh – with whom Abd al-Qadir did not consult. Twice in June he was said to have avoided disaster. But he also prepared the city for the worst. On June 19, he began to set up his defenses in case the Christian quarter was attacked. He surrounded himself with trained men and prepared his band of Algerian followers to act as Christian protectors. He approached Lanusse for funds to arm 1,000 men, and after some hesitation Lanusse gave him *carte blanche* to spend what was needed. He was discreet in his defensive preparations, but they were probably known.[15]

While Abd al-Qadir was making the rounds, the European consuls were pressuring Ahmad Pasha to bring the survivors of the massacres of Hasbaiya and Rashaiya to Damascus, to strengthen Ottoman garrisons in the Baalbek area, and to maintain order in the city. In the third week of June, the consuls asked to be allowed to attend the joint assembly of the *majlis* (great council) and the military authorities to hear what was being proposed to ensure order. They delegated the Austrian consul and a viceconsul of Greece, a Mr Yorgaki, who spoke Turkish and knew the Turks, to arrange an audience with Ahmad Pasha to convey their wishes and concerns. After the battle of Zahleh, the most senior of the consuls met again at the British consulate to draw up another request for measures to maintain order. On the whole, however, most of the consuls did not share Lanusse's alarm or at least did little about it. Their inaction may have wasted precious time, but Damascus was far more immune to European pressures than Beirut, and it is unlikely they could have achieved very much in any case. Outrey was probably right when he concluded that in the end their influence was slight and that a more energetic stand would not have made much difference.[16]

The one individual who had the power to alter the course of events at that stage was Ahmad Pasha, but he took only a few precautions. In early June 1860, he increased the guards in the Christian quarter and prohibited the sale or supply of arms to either Christians or Druzes fighting in Mount Lebanon. In early July, in great haste and at night, 14 cannons were placed in the upper parts of the citadel. Cannons were also mounted on the gate of the Umayyad Mosque, the most important mosque of Damascus, during Friday prayer, and Hasibi tells us that the pasha did the same thing at the gates of other mosques.[17]

It is just possible that not only Ahmad Pasha, but everyone else in charge, simply failed to notice the ugly mood in Damascus on the eve of the riots. To every query by the consuls, he answered that the situation was under control, offered reassurances for the safety of the city, and insisted that there would be no disaster. The pasha repeatedly reassured people that Damascus was in no danger; the *majlis* failed to collaborate either with him or the European consuls, whose request for a meeting had been rejected; Brant and others completely overlooked the gravity of the situation and contented themselves with platitudes and vague reassurances when the fate of thousands was at stake.[18]

In the absence of enlightened guidance and foresight, the situation became palpably tense as the al-Adha feast grew near. On June 29 and 30, Christians panicked when they heard rejoicing over the fall of Zahleh. They felt trapped in the city; no place was safe. In a matter of days, "they seemed to have yielded up the rights and liberties which they had gained during the last twenty-seven years." They stopped riding into the city; they put up with humiliation, insult, even assault; they stayed away from cafés, promenades, gardens, and other public places; they relinquished all their rights to collect debts or other claims against Muslims, and neglected their businesses. So convinced were they that the attack would come at al-Adha that during the four days of the feast, they hid at home, which slowed government business almost to a standstill, as most of its clerks were Christian.[19]

To the relief of the Christians, al-Adha came and went peacefully. Soldiers guarded the Christian quarter which was reassuring, at least until its inhabitants realized that many of those very soldiers included officers and privates who had probably taken part in the massacres in the Anti-Lebanon. They placated the soldiers who guarded them with food, drink, and presents. When nothing happened they "began to reappear from their hidings, diamonds, gold came out of hidings where they had been buried, and everyone thought the alarm was over."[20]

For about eight days, the city remained calm, while the Druzes encircled the city, crowding its northern suburbs. A considerable number of armed Druzes were also reported inside it. Rumors continued to circulate. Talks between representatives of various groups continued and Abd al-Qadir continued to make the rounds of city notables, but "ulemas, notables, the authorities themselves, all swore to Abd al-Qadir that nothing was to be feared." Spokesmen from the Christian quarter met with Muslim notables, among them Mustafa Bey al-Hawasali, who visited three prominent Christians – Hanna Frayj, Antun Shami, and Mitri Shalhub – and reassured them that they could sleep with open doors and have nothing to fear; he himself would guarantee their safety.[21] Reassured, the Christians returned to some semblance of daily routine. The government ordered Christian clerks back to work at the serai, and they returned on Monday, July 9. Shopkeepers opened their stalls in the marketplace, tradesmen went to work, and children were sent to school.[22]

One small incident then ended the uneasy peace. On July 9 (or possibly on the preceding day), some Muslim boys began playing pranks; they marked the doors of Christian houses with signs; hung crosses around the necks of dogs or tied them to their tails; and all over the streets in every corner of the city marked crosses in chalk and charcoal, so that Christian passers-by had no choice but to step on them, and when they did were taunted and insulted. One anonymous Turkish source remarked that "these insults were not of such a nature as would naturally occur to these boys but they must have been instructed by some of the leaders of the sedition." Hanna Frayj, Antun Shami, and Mitri Shalhub had an interview with Ahmad Pasha, and they reported the incidents.[23]

It was Ahmed Pasha's misfortune to be both firm and indecisive at the wrong times. In a gesture which to some was ill-timed and to others malevolent, he and his chief of internal security – probably a military officer named Akif Agha – even after a meeting with a group of Muslim notables (according to Abkarius) decided to punish the boys publicly. Near Bab al-Barid, at the western entrance to the Umayyad Mosque, the officer in charge of internal security seized two or three or perhaps a few more of the boys, including the sons of notable and respected Muslim families, and had them taken to the serai where they were shackled, "treating them like convicts." Each was given a broom "as if they were scavengers," and they were then taken to the Christian quarter where they were ordered to sweep the streets.[24]

This act was uncharacteristically firm, and the consequence was violence. Those who previously had begged the government to act promptly and decisively now blamed it for being too hasty. As the procession crossed town, Muslims asked the soldiers what was going on. A crowd soon formed. The brother of one of the boys, a shopkeeper near Bab al-Barid by the name of Abd al-Karim al-Samman, fueled the fury of the crowd, which subsequently earned him the nickname of *al-sha"al* "firestarter," by shouting at the guards to release the boys. When they did not, he seized the poles holding the lock of his shop door and went after the soldiers and the chained boys. Relatives, friends, neighbors, and passers-by followed him. The soldiers were beaten and the boys released, but al-Sha"al continued to inflame the crowd, shouting that Muslims had endured enough since the Egyptian occupation and that it was time for them to rise up and avenge themselves on their Christian enemies.[25]

As soon as the boys were set free, the shops near the Umayyad Mosque and in the marketplace shut down within minutes and their occupants rushed towards the Christian quarter. Others went to the Umayyad Mosque, consulted with the people inside – including a prominent notable and a learned Islamic scholar by the name of Abdallah ibn Sa'id al-Halabi who was later put under arrest – took or ignored their advice, and came out shouting slogans against the Christians.[26]

News of what was happening quickly spread through the suburbs. People came to the Christian quarter from the Shagur, a suburb outside the south city wall; the Maidan quarter, the large suburb on the southwest a mile and a half away; and from Salihiya, a large suburban village two miles northwest of the city. The inhabitants of the surrounding villages poured into the city. Most sources emphasize the role these outsiders played in the violence, though whether to improve relations between Damascenes by blaming outsiders or because it was true is unclear. Druzes and Muslims from surrounding villages also poured into town for days. Over a thousand Druzes rushed to the city, some from Geramana, a village two miles distant; Kurds, Muslim villagers, and city rowdies from the Maidan all ran to the scene. But no Druze chiefs or any regular Druze force appeared. Estimates of the mob that attacked the Christian quarter range from 20,000 to 50,000. As with most such estimates, these tell us more about the anxiety of those who feared the crowd than about its actual size.[27]

Hasibi, an eyewitness to the event in his youth, implies that the government, and in particular an officer of the irregular troops named Salim Agha al-Mahayni who worked for internal security, actually started the massacre. The anonymous Turkish source agrees, claiming to have seen Salim Agha coming from the Maidan quarter with a mob of its worst ruffians toward the Christian quarter. About the time the captured boys were released, Salim Agha was in the Umayyad Mosque with thirty men. When they heard the noise of the crowd around the boys, Salim Agha and his recruits ran out of the mosque. The crowd did not realize that they were soldiers; assuming they were an attacking mob, they closed their shops and ran.

Hasibi then went from the Suq al-Arwam (to the right of what is today

MAP THREE

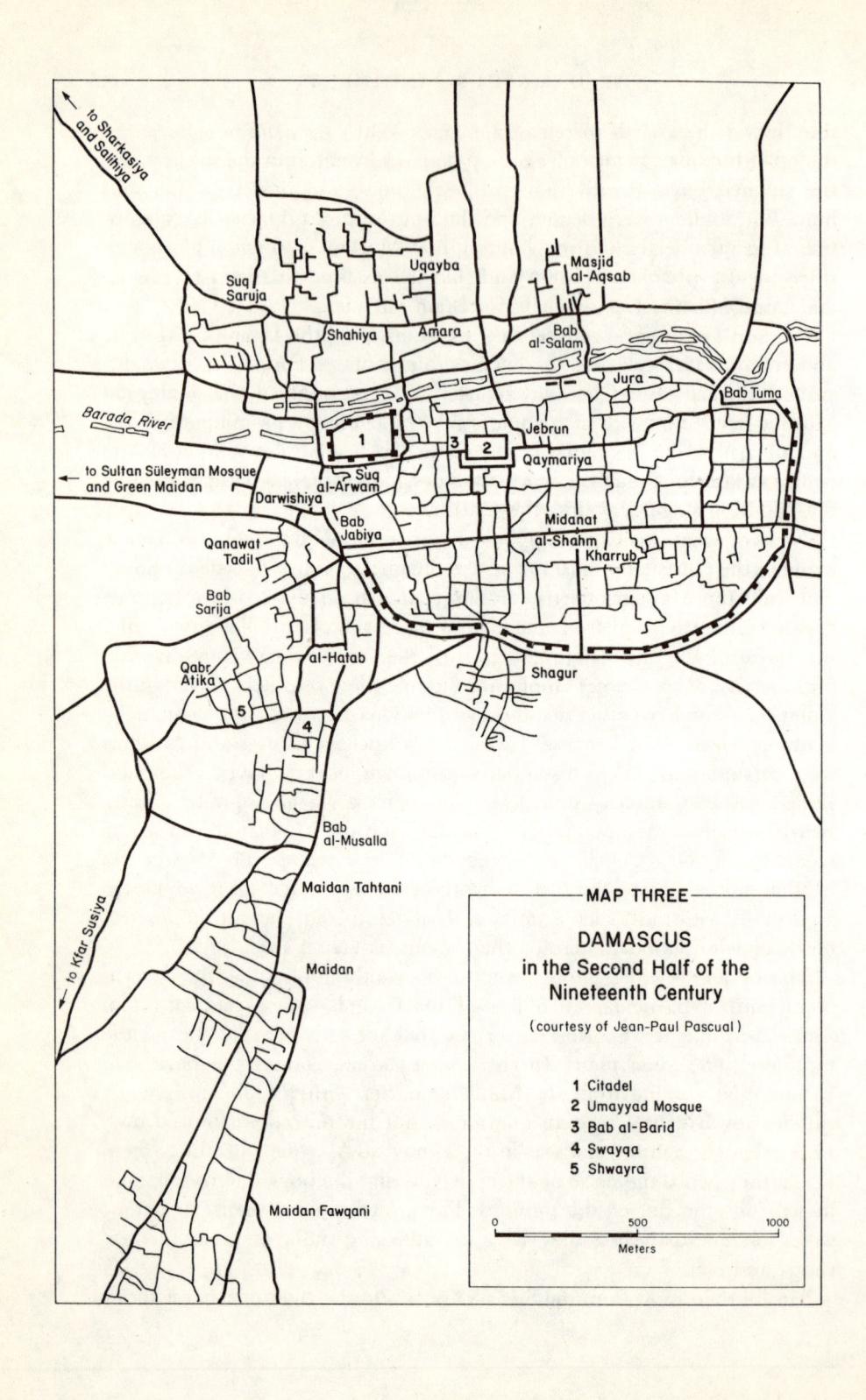

DAMASCUS
in the Second Half of the
Nineteenth Century

(courtesy of Jean-Paul Pascual)

1 Citadel
2 Umayyad Mosque
3 Bab al-Barid
4 Swayqa
5 Shwayra

the Hamidiya Suq) to the Qanawat quarter and sat in front of a coffee house with the leader of that quarter, a man by the name of Rashid. They stopped every armed man, disarmed him, and brought him into the coffee house until a merchant wailed, "Woe onto you, people of the Qanawat, you are sitting still when more than forty Muslims have been killed." In response, the men left. Hasibi then went home where a Christian clerk by the name of Antun Basha Abu Basil started crying and kissing Hasibi's hands and feet, concerned about his son and family. Implying he would go to the Christian quarter to rescue the family, Hasibi then armed himself and left the house with Sayyid Hasan al-Bahnasi and other members of his quarter. They reached the house of Abd al-Qadir near the Christian quarter and watched the dense mob crowding the street leading into the quarter, held back by some troops. The mood of the crowd was ugly. When Hasibi sensed that, he turned around and did not return to the Christian quarter until the riots had ended. But he saw enough to realize that there were "as many people as there is sand," among them troublemakers of every kind and that they were on the verge of attacking the Christian quarter.[28]

The rioters seized whatever weapons they could lay their hands on, but, except for the irregular troops, they were poorly armed. No more than one in twenty had a real weapon; mostly they held sticks and clubs; a number carried battle-axes, a few had swords, and even fewer had muskets or pistols, many of which were of little use. Even so, they were better equipped than the Christians, who aside from a few fowling-pieces and pistols, had no arms at all. There was not a sword or axe among them.

What the rioters lacked in ammunition they made up for in determination. The Masjid al-Aqsab gates leading into the Christian quarter were shut to prevent people from that quarter from joining the insurgents, but a band of Kurds from the Salihiya quarter broke them down. In no time, excited, quarrelsome, and angry unarmed men, children, and even women rushed to the Christian quarter, shouting abuse.[29]

When they arrived, an Ottoman colonel by the name of Salih Zaki Bey Miralay, whose men were guarding a part of the Christian quarter, ordered his men to fire on the crowd. One discharge was fired into the mob and one cannon was fired into the air. That one round of gunfire wounded or killed two people and momentarily checked the mob. It was, however, not enough to stop them, and it may even have worsened their mood. The Greek Orthodox church and the roofs of the covered bazaar were set ablaze; inspired by the sight, they set about burning down houses.[30]

Had the troops persevered against the rioters, or had the government interfered in any way at that stage, they might have been held in check. But because the troops held their fire after that initial round, the mob regained its confidence. Mishaqa claims that Zaki Bey was even ordered back to his quarters in the citadel and punished for firing on the crowd.[31] In any case, the most elementary precautions were not taken. The anonymous Turkish source writes:

> Had these city police and people of the Meidan who were enrolled as guards kept the heads of the streets leading to the Christian quarter, and bolted the gates of the quarter and fired upon the invaders, and endeavoured to turn them back and prevent them from entering the Christian quarter like the regular troops, the affair would not have arrived at such a pass but would probably have been soon stopped.[32]

The troops in the Christian quarter reportedly received orders to withdraw and by five o'clock in the afternoon none were left to defend the quarter. Brant was not aware that the cannons sent to the Christian quarter had been fired even once. He wrote that they were never used and that during the massacres the troops fired only a few shots without effect.[33]

The soldiers then began to join the rioters – some say they were even in the forefront, as their officers lost all control of their men and the security forces failed to maintain order. Lanusse accused the chief of police (*tufenkji bashi*) of even encouraging his troops to attack the Christian quarter, and the chiefs of the irregular troops did the same. Hasibi wrote that the troops under the command of a colonel named Muhammad Sa'id Bey together with some Kurds started to plunder, kill, and rape, and the officers were unable to stop them. The exception was Mustafa Bey al-Hawasili, an influential Sunni notable and paramilitary chieftain from Bab Tuma, whose troops took part in the riots. He did his best to restrain the crowd, only to be deserted by his own men. The troops of Salim Agha al-Mahayni and Mustafa Bey al-Hawasili, Kurdish irregulars under Muhammad Sa'id Bey, and the *zaptiye* (police) were among the first and most active participants in the riots.[34]

The local authorities were absent. No officer of rank headed any of the detachments of troops that were "occasionally sent out" during the riots. "Neither Ahmad Pasha, nor the members of the great council, not one ulema, nor anyone closely or distantly related to the government, appeared on the streets or made the least effort to stop the disorder." Members of the *majlis* stayed away. "No one of the aforementioned members and leading men said to any one 'desist'." Ahmad Pasha never left the serai. He seems to have spent most of his time in meetings, but he did not act.[35]

The angry mob attacked at several points at once, first looting and burning, then killing. The houses of the rich Christians were attacked first; then those adjoining. Then the Greek Orthodox church and patriarchate were plundered of their ornament and plate, robes and money. Other religious and charitable institutions suffered a similar fate, including the Greek Catholic patriarch's residence and the Armenian church. A church bell was removed and placed upside down in the middle of an old cross engraved on the pavement of a street leading to the Umayyad Mosque. A leper hospice in Damascus was attacked and burned together with its inmates.[36]

As they went, the mob would first break down the door of a house with axes, then attack the men inside with clubs, sticks, axes, daggers, swords, and occasionally guns. Then they would plunder the house of furniture, clothes, food, goods, and any hidden valuables and cash. They would threaten the women and the children to make them tell where the men or valuables were hidden and snatch, sometimes brutally, their jewelry off their bodies. They sometimes carried off the girls and young women of the household. They stripped the house down to its doors, windows, shutters, and paneling. Even the firewood and charcoal, the marble on the floors, and the timber on the roofs were carted off. Camels, horses, mules, and donkeys were used to remove what the looters could not carry. Finally, when it had been cleared out, the house would be set on fire. When the spoils were divided up, the best armed and most important of the attackers were given first choice; they were followed by successive parties of "the lower rabble, the unarmed, the poor, the weak, the women, and even children."[37]

Foreign consulates were an early target, a measure of Muslim belief in foreign plots and resentment against the humiliations inflicted on them by the Western powers. Probably because of the Crimean war,[38] which between 1853 and 1856 had pitted Russia against the Ottoman empire, the Russian consulate, in the center of the Christian quarter, was the first to be attacked, looted, and set on fire. Khalil Shehadi, the dragoman at the Russian consulate, was killed. Two of the servants escaped by hiding in a cellar where they remained for four days without food or drink, while the house burned over their heads. The French consulate, "particularly resented,"[39] was the next to go. Its occupants disguised themselves and escaped to Abd al-Qadir's residence.

The insurrection had begun while Abd al-Qadir was on his way back from the village of Ashrafiya some three to four hours' journey from Damascus, to which it was said the Druzes had invited him to come to an understanding. In retrospect, it seemed to Outrey and probably Abd al-Qadir himself that he had been deliberately enticed out of Damascus. He managed to return in time to provide protection to the consuls, for the Russian and Greek consuls also sought refuge with him. The Dutch, Austrian, and Belgian consulates were broken into and burned down, as was the house of an American missionary named Frazer, who escaped with his family before the attack. None of the inhabitants of his house was hurt. The Dutch consul and his family had fled before his house was attacked and the others were away. The American consulate was also burned, and its consul, Abdu Costi, a Damascene, beaten and left for dead.[40]

The Prussian consulate, near Suq al-Arwam outside the Christian quarter, and the English consulate, north of the Umayyad Mosque in a Muslim quarter, both escaped attack. Smylie Robson, an English missionary in the Christian quarter, described the terrible scenes around him in a letter to Brant written shortly after the riots broke out (at "¼ past 5 o'clock"). He wondered whether "perhaps in your quarter you see nothing of all this most shameful and horrible business." His letter brings to life the panic of the Europeans in Damascus:

> For the last two hours and a half, the street past my house has presented a most terrible scene, first the rush and running of men armed, unarmed, boys, women, shouts, imprecations on the infidel Christians, cries of "kill them, butcher them, plunder, burn, leave not one, not a house, not anything: Fear not the soldiers, fear nothing, the soldiers will not meddle with you." ... they were right. Nobody has interfered. Men, women and boys, aged and soldiers for more than two hours have been carrying every sort of thing past my house, like fiends from hell ... I know not the moment when some of these plunderers and murderers who are passing my door without ceasing will recollect that this is the house of a Frank and a Christian, and stop to rob it and murder us. I have no hope that this will end today or tonight.

For the moment he had enough bread in the house and would remain indoors, however insecure that was:

> I cannot go to your house. Could I go with my wife and servants into the midst of armed ruffians crying and thirsting for blood? To open my door would be as much as my life is worth ... My neighbours offer to hide me and my property. What dependence can be placed on them?

To him, the only choice was to "remain where I am and leave the event to God."[41]

> Where is your Pasha now? Fifty men could have put the insurrection down. Has any attempt been made to preserve the lives of the Sultan's subjects, or the subjects of other Powers? ... Will the government not make any effort to

stop this disgraceful as well as wicked outrage? Will it remain perfectly passive? Or is the government at the bottom of it all? If the government remains indifferent, the night will be worse than the day.

From Brant's invitation to Robson to move to the consulate, he concluded "that the state of affairs must be very different in your Quarter from what it is here as you would not think of proposing to me to appear outside my house." After the riots, Brant himself assumed that he had been saved because his residence was in the Muslim quarter, where it became a refuge for the Austrian vice-consul and his wife, a couple from the Marcopoli Aleppine family of Venetian origins and about 200 refugees.[42]

William Graham, an Irish Presbyterian missionary, was detained in Damascus by Robson, who blamed himself for it later, and when the riots broke out, he and a member of the Misk family found refuge in the Christian quarter in the house of Mustafa Bey al-Hawasili. Graham later left Hawasili's house for a more secure one. For a while no one knew where he was, but eventually they learned that he had been killed on his way to the English consulate. His killer openly admitted his crime and excused himself by saying that he thought Graham was a consul.[43]

Various European missions in Damascus were attacked. The eight Spanish Franciscans of Terra Santa locked themselves up in their convent with a few friends and refused to answer the door, a fatal mistake, as on three occasions they ignored the Algerian followers of Abd al-Qadir who pounded on the door, offering to escort them to a safer place. The next day, they were attacked; one of them left the convent and was run down and killed; the rest were killed in the convent which was sacked and burned. The French Lazarists were luckier; their monastery would have been more difficult to invade but in any case Abd al-Qadir's men rescued them before any attack. The French Sisters of Charity were also rescued and escaped late at night, under the greatest difficulties, with the 150 children in their care.[44]

The merchants, shopkeepers, government clerks, shop clerks, stonecutters and masons who had gone back to work were caught in the Muslim part of the city. When the mob began to gather, they tried to escape. Some reached home, some were killed in the streets, some fled to the English, French, and Prussian consulates, some ran to Abd al-Qadir's house, or to the houses of Muslim partners and acquaintances, or to nearby khans. Most were seized by the troops and taken to the citadel.

Inside the Christian quarter some fled to churches, to the Austrian consulate, or to the houses of rich neighbors; none of these places proved to be safe. Many hid in closets, latrines and outhouses, cellars, or on housetops; but they were soon discovered and dragged out of hiding. A number hid in wells, and most of those did survive and were rescued by Abd al-Qadir's men a few days later. A few escaped by jumping from roof to roof and hiding in ruined houses. A few left the city entirely, but some among those were attacked by peasants and either killed or forcibly converted to Islam. Many Christians who lived at Bab Sharqi fled with the metropolitan of the Syriac Catholics to the safety of the Greek Orthodox monastery in the village of Saidnaya. When they reached the monastery they found Christians from the village already hiding there. The monastery was attacked, but with no success.

Some Christians used disguise to escape. The men who dressed up as women were generally found out, but a few pretended to be rioters and escaped carrying pieces of furniture or other plunder. Some fled from one Muslim house to another. A number perished using that route, but some were saved. Few families were together when the attack came, and often days passed before one member of a family found out what had happened to the rest.[45]

For eight days and nights, the plunder and killing continued, but the first day, Monday, and the following Wednesday were the worst. From two in the afternoon until long after sunset, the violence continued unabated. On the first day, most rioters grabbed their plunder, killed people, and left, but some continued throughout the night. By then fire had spread, engulfing several hundred houses. At dawn the main body of attackers returned and continued their task without interruption until evening. Then there was a lull, because little was left to seize.

On this second day, almost all the Christian shops in the main bazaars were looted. By sunset, nothing was left but the stones and fragments of timber of burning houses and a few rooms the flames had not yet reached. The Christians left in the quarter were all in hiding.

On Wednesday, a rumor that Christians had attacked some Muslims provoked new brutality. In the Salihiya quarter word spread that some Muslim builders, at work extinguishing a fire before it reached Shaykh Abdallah al-Halabi's house, had been shot by Christians hiding in a Muslim's house nearby. Brant confirms that this was so because the Muslims were brought to his house to tend their wounds. The attackers turned out to be a group of Christian workers who had panicked when the crowd of firefighters appeared, thinking they had come to attack the house. The Muslim owner had armed them to defend it. They shot and wounded some men before they were themselves killed.

The incident lent new intensity to the attack on Christians: even Brant, who mentioned plunder more than murder in the first two days of the riots, had to acknowledge by the third that every Christian who was found on that fateful Wednesday had been killed. The Muslims, including some Kurds, rushed toward the Christian quarter and surrounded Abd al-Qadir's house where many Christians were hiding. The emir came out escorted by his followers and threatened to fire on the crowd. It withdrew but moved on to other Muslim houses where Christians had been given protection and demanded that they be handed over. It became more and more difficult to continue protecting the Christians. Several hundred of them were rounded up and killed.[46]

In the days that followed, the killing tapered off and looting was reduced to the few remaining doors, timbers, and pieces of marble that could still be found in the ruins. After a week, there was nothing left to plunder. Only the khans in the bazaars were left untouched and the property of Christians there was undisturbed. The fires went out the following week when there was nothing left to burn. The stone and mudbrick houses in Damascus did not burn easily. The fires must have been rekindled over and over.[47]

Mikha'il Mishaqa, by then a vice-consul for the United States, was awakened from his nap on July 9 and told that the city's Muslims were attacking the Christians. He looked onto the street, and saw people running madly. He locked the door and waited for the consul's Muslim *kavass* to arrive. Two assistants of the precinct officer brought to him a man who had taken refuge at the officer's house. When the *kavass* arrived, Mikha'il sent him to Abd al-Qadir to ask for an escort. The six men assigned to him could not reach his house, however; they had been given no arms and the streets were full of rioters. Mikha'il said he would supply the weapons.[48]

While they waited, insurgents attacked the house, broke down the locked door with axes, and entered the outer part of the house and the garden. They fired through the grille into the house and began to batter the inside door. Mikha'il did not dare to wait any longer for Abd al-Qadir's escort and slipped out the back way. He had the presence of mind to bring money and the common sense not to arm himself. Accompanied by his *kavass* with a sword, his nine-year-old son Ibrahim, and his six-year-old daughter, he fled, leaving behind his wife and her nursing infant, his wife's mother, and her aunt.

Mikha'il was almost immediately faced with a group of insurgents who ran at him brandishing weapons. He threw some money at them and headed for another street, as they knocked each other down fighting over coins. Again he was faced with armed rebels, again he escaped by throwing money, but he had "death behind [him] and before [him]." He went into a back street, only to come face to face with more armed men. This time he had nowhere to run. They surrounded him, as his children screamed. One of the attackers hit his daughter with an axe, another shot Mikha'il from a distance of six paces and missed. He was not shot at again because the crowd was too dense, but he was wounded by an axe blow on his temple and a cudgel blow on his face and arm.

His wits saved him once more. He told his tormentors to take him to a certain officer with whom he had important business. Some people in the crowd knew who he was and said they ought to do as he told them, which they did, after stripping him of all his cash, watch, and even head-dress. His *kavass* went with him, but he was separated from his children. He eventually was settled into the house of one of the officer's men, after another near escape from death with a sickle.

Sitting in the desolate upper apartment where he waited, listening to the sounds of gunfire, houses burning, and crowds in the streets, was for Mikha'il in many ways more agonizing than his experiences earlier in the afternoon. Alone with his *kavass* and an old landlady, in an obscure place, he agonized over the fate of his family. Suspicions began to assail him. He worried that the officer who had brought him there planned to come back after dark and kill him. He saw through the window that other Christians of no higher status than his own were being taken to the officer's house for refuge, while he was being kept in that house alone. He thought the end had come when someone knocked on the door. In fact, it was the officer's nephew, a Muslim friend by the name of Sayyid Muhammad al-Sawtari, and followers of Abd al-Qadir who had come to rescue him. They dressed him in a North African robe, took him first to the emir's house, and then to Sawtari's house. For Mikha'il the worst was over.

Dimitri Debbas, then a young man of 21, was caught in town near Bab al-Barid. He rushed to his shop in a khan near Bab Tuma, locked its door, and from his hiding place saw "hundreds of thousands" rushing about with weapons and sticks. There were four people with him. "We stayed till sunset, we cried bitter tears, we had no escape, and we were afraid they would attack us in the khan and kill us. When it got dark, each of us was afraid to go out for fear we would be attacked and crushed like ants." Finally Dimitri crossed himself, undid his belt, tore its cloth in two, wrapped half of it around his head like a turban and the other half around his waist, put his faith into God's hands, and opened the door of the khan. He merged with the crowd and kept moving until he reached the house of Abdallah Shurbaji, agha of the quarter, where thousands of Christian men and women had sought refuge "pressed together like cheese."[49]

It turned out to be a long night. He watched goings and comings from his hiding place, awaiting the worst. He heard the men entrusted with guarding Bab Tuma come to Abdallah Shurbaji to complain that they were not getting their share of the loot. Abdallah Shurbaji told them to go and do as they wished, but not in Bab Tuma because there he was responsible. In the course of the night, the house became more and more crowded and Abdallah Shurbaji began to complain that it was being ruined. He summoned Muslim notables and entrusted the important Christians in his house to their care. Like Mishaqa, Debbas was sensitive to matters of precedence; like him, he distrusted the man who had given him asylum; and he became more and more certain that once the Christian notables had departed, the rest of them would be killed. He mingled among the notables, and left the house with them.

They were first taken to the house of another Muslim notable, Abdallah Efendi al-Imadi, but it was too crowded and in the morning they went on to the house of Abdallah al-Halabi. Dimitri went along, his arms bare and his forehead covered with a white belt. The sun had come out, and the city had filled with villagers. At the intersection, the crowd was so thick that it had backed up into the streets and no one at all was able to move. The streets were so jammed that Brant's *kavass*es could not get through.[50] He heard that the missionary Graham and a Damascene named Ibrahim Medawwar had been killed. "It was a horrifying moment, we deeply felt despair." Then Dimitri noticed that another Muslim notable, Abduh Efendi Khayr, had opened a small door in the large gate to his house to let in three Christian notables in service at the serai. Dimitri raced after them and slipped in. They were all "trembling souls assuming this was the last minute in [their] lives." The rioters began banging on the door and firing shots. They called out, "Oh Abduh, deliver the Christians to us," and threatened to burn down the house.

Its owner ignored them and led his guests up the stairs and through two ornate rooms into a third, where 30 to 40 Christians had already assembled. Among them, Dimitri saw his nephew Esber Yazigi. He went over and sat down in front of him. At first, his nephew did not recognize him: he saw a man with a white turban and took him for a Druze. When he realized the man next to him was his uncle, he began to weep. He seized Dimitri by the hand and said, "Uncle, I will not leave your side: we will either die or live together." Dimitri remained with his nephew for the rest of his adventures.

On Wednesday afternoon, Abdallah Efendi al-Imadi, a Muslim notable, sent the Christians under Muslim protection to the house of Abdallah al-Halabi. Dimitri, holding his nephew's hand, was among them. In the evening, loaves and half-loaves were handed out to each of the refugees. After that, Halabi withdrew to his chamber and prayed.

On Thursday, Ahmad Pasha summoned the Muslim notables to the serai and demanded they hand over the Christians in their charge – for execution, Dimitri was convinced. The Muslim notables adamantly refused, but agreed to the compromise of sending them for protection to the citadel. Halabi was gone for the whole day and the Christians anxiously awaited his return. When he came home, 180 refugees were assembled and Halabi's brother, Shaykh Salih, took them to a hall, closed the door, and said that no one was to raise his voice. They could hear the people of the Salihiya quarter outside in the street trying to extinguish a fire before it reached Halabi's house (this must be a reference to the after-effects of the fateful Wednesday when word spread that Muslim builders had been fired upon by Christians hiding in a Muslim's house, which led to the killing of hundreds of Christians dragged out of hiding).

The assembled group of Christians replied to Shaykh Salih, "Protect us or release us; in the basest of houses, we would have found protection." People from the Salihiya quarter knocked on the door, came in and went up to the roof while the shaykh tried to quiet the people down. It was "a horrible hour," remembered Dimitri, who worried also at the sight of the shaykh deliberating with some Christian notables near the hall where the Christians had been assembled. Then the shaykh escorted these notables to the women's quarters, and Dimitri and other Christians ran behind them, fearful that they and the Christian women were going to be saved and the rest of the men killed. Some 300 women were assembled in the women's quarter, and among them were notables dressed up like women. Dimitri and the other men quickly followed suit and put on women's garments. At that point, Shaykh Salih arrived with some of his followers, and they started to undress the Christians and to shout at them: You unbelievers, now you are posing as women in the shaykh's house? The Christians began to pray "the prayer of death," for they saw themselves about to be slaughtered.

Then 180 Christians were taken to a room about 15 x 20 feet, far too small for the purpose, but they were all squeezed into it. They protested, but were told to be silent or the people from the Salihiya would hear and come kill them. The Christians shouted back they were going to die from hunger and thirst, anyway; they were given water and urged to calm down. Dimitri gave water to every man in the group. An eight-year-old boy then began to cry from hunger, and Dimitri had to stifle his cries so the "evildoers" would not hear him. Gunshots could be heard all afternoon.

"We were about to die from heat, hunger, thirst, fear, and lack of air," wrote Dimitri, when the news came from Shaykh Abdallah al-Halabi that the Christians were to be taken to the citadel. A number were escorted there, but Dimitri remained in hiding in the shaykh's house, fearful that at the citadel they would meet the same fate as the Christians of Hasbaiya, Rashaiya, and Deir al-Qamar. At last, an elderly man by the name of Hajj al-Bakri, who used to export cloth to Aleppo for Dimitri's father, swore by touching his beard that Dimitri would be safe at the citadel. Convinced at last, Dimitri went. He was the last to leave Halabi's house. Escorted by Ottoman troops, he was again besieged by doubt, but the soldiers hit the men with rifle butts when they stepped out of line so he made no effort to escape. Another did run away and was killed by the mob. At last, the Christians reached the citadel to join the thousands already there.

Of all the Muslims who came to the aid of the Christians, none played a greater role than Abd al-Qadir. His rescue operations were critical to the Christian population. Brant, who had failed to see trouble coming, wrote on July 11 that people were convinced that the government would not help them. Reports had first circulated that authorities were coming from Beirut, but they did not appear, and "from hope everyone [was] plunged in[to] despair." Abd al-Qadir was their only real hope.[51]

When the violence began, Abd al-Qadir's house by one of the town's gates near the Christian quarter had been encircled with armed Algerians, and Christians were taken into it by the hundreds. Armed Algerians were also used to rescue Europeans and local Christians; the men searched the streets for them, took the wounded to the military hospital and led the able-bodied to Abd al-Qadir's house.

For weeks after the riots, Abd al-Qadir's followers continued to guard people in and out of Damascus, as thousands of Christians left for the Syrian coast escorted by his Algerians and Druzes. The first convoy of 500 to 600 Christians was arranged by Lanusse and Abd al-Qadir. Thousands more followed.

During that time, Abd al-Qadir's men also offered protection to Europeans in Damascus. Cyril Graham, who came there in late July, was escorted into town by 60 Algerians and 15 Druzes. An additional 15 of Abd al-Qadir's men met Graham and his party at Dimas. This protection may have been unnecessary once the reign of violence was over, but it made all the difference while it raged. Brant estimated that Abd al-Qadir's Algerians saved thousands. Lanusse credited him with 11,000 lives saved, some in his house, some in his quarter, and the largest number in the serai. Outrey added another thousand or two to that.[52] The anonymous author of *Hasr al-litham* mentions that in the midst of all the savagery, the emir remained "a man of great stature, a hero." Mishaqa added, "The

Christians would have despaired of a strong hand to protect them from the impending disaster were it not for the manliness and highmindedness of the Sharif Emir Abd al-Qadir al-Jazayiri, who was anxious to preserve the good name of his religion. This outstanding man, whose excellence was well known to the kings and inhabitants of the earth, never rested a moment in his attempts to allay the revolt." Abkarius called him "the magnanimous and most noble personage of illustrious rank, the glorious, highly honored lord, the master of all sciences in the highest degree, the climber in dignity to the most exalted functions, the possessor of surpassing excellence and of pure, undefiled lineage." Historians have since attributed all sorts of designs to Abd al-Qadir's actions; but to those seeking to escape death, he was quite simply a savior.[53]

He was not the only one, however. Mishaqa and Debbas both found refuge with Muslim notables, as clearly did scores of others. How many Christians owed their lives to Damascene Muslims is not known, but they constituted "a rather considerable number" of families according to Outrey, who is not likely to have given Muslims more credit than they deserved. Neither was the author of *Kitab al-ahzan*, who also mentioned that many Muslims sheltered Christian friends and business partners. Among them he named al-Sayyid Mahmud Efendi Hamza and his brother Sharif As'ad Efendi Hamza, the son of Ahmad Agha al-Yusif, Abdallah Efendi al-Imadi, a merchant named Uthman Jabri, and someone named Faris Agha. The same point is made by Ibrahim Arbili, a Greek Orthodox emigrant to the United States, whose memoirs describe the massacres of 1860 in Damascus. He tells us that his father, Yusuf Arbili, a physician, survived partly with the help of Mahmud al-Kudari, a humble Muslim grocer whose family he treated; and that many Muslims rescued Christians. Mishaqa "saw none more zealous and compassionate" than Salim Agha Shurbaji al-Mahayni, Sa'id Agha al-Nuri, and Umar Agha al-Abid who, despite the lawlessness and ferocity of the Maidan rabble, kept their quarter under control and protected its Christians from harm, rescuing hundreds of people and bringing them into their houses. Mishaqa also praised al-Sayyid Mahmud Efendi Hamza and his brother, As'ad, Shaykh Salim al-Attar, whom he described as an important member of the ulema, and "many religious and virtuous Muslims" who took Christians into their homes, following the example of Abd al-Qadir. In all, he estimated that "these pious Muslims of various classes" saved 16,000 Christians. Hasibi, while admitting that some upper-class notables had played a part in the massacres, generally distinguished between the helpful attitude of many of the Damascene notables and the destructive populace:[54]

Honorable citizens rescued Christians and gave them refuge in their homes ... The main body of the Christian survivors was brought to the house of our master, Shaykh Abdallah al-Halabi. Nearly one thousand persons were daily brought to his house, from where some were taken to the citadel and others to Muslim homes.[55]

One Turkish source denies that others acted as well as Abd al-Qadir. "In that distress there was no one but he and his followers who made any effort to save the Christians." "It is true," he adds, "that some persons among the Muslims took from the Christian quarter a few men, women, and children, and they also took some persons to their houses from the castle – asking the privilege of taking them as tho [sic] they had merciful intentions towards them;" but then he says, "Alas! for these poor people what harm and torture they inflicted upon them in their houses." He claims the Christians were taken to Muslim houses so that they would reveal where they had hidden their valuables. Some were then returned to the castle, others were compelled to become Muslims. A number of women and children were carried off. He himself was present and witnessed "persons of the lowest class" picking out children and taking them off. No doubt some did take advantage of the chaos, but that Christians were housed merely to be coerced is very unlikely. It is clear that thousands of Christians escaped with Muslims' help.[56]

Not just this group, but most of the Christians who had escaped from the embattled Christian quarter had ended up in the citadel. At first, many assumed, as Debbas had, that the government was sending people to the citadel to have them massacred, as had been done at Hasbaiya, Rashaiya, and Deir al-Qamar, and even Muslims who had encouraged the Christians to go there as their houses filled to the bursting were secretly uneasy. Ahmad Pasha himself, on the fourth day of the riots, said that the safety of the Christians there could not be guaranteed. Hasibi's father and Abdallah Bey al-Azm, who belonged to a leading family and had encouraged Christians to leave his palace for the citadel, sensed that by doing so the Muslims were being asked to approve the betrayal of the Christians in the citadel in the event of an attack. They protested that they would leave Damascus first. They were reassured, and, as it turned out, the citadel remained the safest place to be in those eventful July days.[57]

The calamity that befell the Christians of Damascus, despite probable exaggerations on the part of both local and foreign observers, is not unlike what had occurred in Aleppo ten years earlier. Both incidents share with the events of Mount Lebanon a variety of causes affecting the society and economy. In Aleppo and Damascus, tension among the religious communities had been building up again as a result of the privileges granted to the Christians by Egyptian rule in Syria in the 1830s, the Ottoman declaration of equality among all subjects during the period of the Tanzimat, the enforcement of conscription on Muslims and the exemption of non-Muslims from it, and most important, the growing disparity in wealth between the haves, among whom figured the Christians, and the have-nots, the majority of whom were Muslim craftsmen and shopkeepers. This probably explains why craftsmen and shopkeepers figure so prominently in the list of persons executed by the Ottomans for their guilt in attacking the wealthy Christian quarter of Bab Tuma. In Aleppo, likewise, the rebels who perpetrated the massacres were mostly drawn from the peripheral poor quarters of Bab al-Nayrab, Banqusa, and Qarliq, inhabited mostly by Kurds, Turkomans, and Bedouins who had suffered from the dislocation of the caravan trade. As in Damascus, they directed their attacks against the wealthy Christians who inhabited the quarters of Judayda and Salibeh. Most of the Christians were Greek Catholics who had commercial relations with Europeans. In Damascus, the poor Christians of the Maidan quarter were not molested and Jews of both Damascus and Aleppo were spared. The primary motive behind the riots was not religious fanaticism – after all, the various religious communities had lived with one another in peace for centuries – but the growing gap between the rich and the poor.[58]

CHAPTER 5

INTERNATIONAL RESPONSE

The Ottoman reaction to the first news of the Syrian massacres was consternation. The eruption of violence in other parts of the empire during the 1850s had been a source of great embarrassment and concern to the government and, in addition, the news of the fighting in Mount Lebanon arrived on top of other reports of tension in eastern Europe and elsewhere. Reports of civil war in Mount Lebanon first reached Istanbul on June 7; on July 1, the last mail to the capital brought news of the fighting in Deir al-Qamar and Zahleh.[1] "And when the news of the massacres in the Lebanon reached the ears of [his] Majesty the Sultan Abd al-Majid Khan, it gave great pain to his Majesty and compassion for his subjects took hold of him," wrote Abkarius, though he was not there to witness the sultan's "abundant" and "sincere tears."[2] Witnesses closer to the seat of power confirm that the news was regarded as alarming. Dr Barozzi, the court physician and informant for Charles Jean de la Valette, French ambassador to the Porte, kept a diary in which he reported that the Ottoman ministers were dismayed at the news from Syria. The pashas Ali and Rushdi were "stunned and demoralized," and the pashas Ali and Fuad were furious at the perpetrators of trouble. Riza Pasha, the pro-French minister of war, was criticized for having depleted Syria's armed contingents. Some officials blamed Russia, but it was fear of France that moved the government to react. People worried that the costs of the crisis would be hard to meet, and it threatened to worsen and destabilize the empire. Rumors were rampant and contradictory reports circulated widely and spread confusion.[3]

The European diplomatic corps in Istanbul were informed of the Syrian crisis before their governments were and consequently had no instructions as to how to react. Some thought they might have been able to prevent the bloodshed; La Valette, for example, thought he might have avoided "the horrible scenes" by pressuring the Porte to act, had he been alerted earlier to the danger. He had been displeased with the quality of Bentivoglio's reports from Beirut, for they had not prepared him for the civil war and, once it occurred, did not give him the information he needed to help him sort out contradictory reports and claims from Syria and Istanbul. "How is all this going to end?" wrote La Valette on June 20, "all hell is breaking loose."[4]

In the face of unconfirmed and contradictory reports, the ambassadors fell back on their various standard positions *vis-à-vis* the Ottomans and one another. "Everyone is giving advice to the Porte," La Valette reported; "the diplomatic corps is outdoing itself." The Russians had warned about the dangers of the Tanzimat reforms and now seemed vindicated. Bulwer, the British ambassador "looks desperate," wrote La Valette. This new jolt to the status quo threatened the precarious balance of power among the various nations contending for influence in the empire.[5]

The Ottoman government itself, however, moved with alacrity, if only to undermine any European (especially French) excuse for further intervention in its affairs. Although at times it had been paralyzed by lack of money and by bureaucratic inefficiency, this time the Ottomans dealt with the crisis which, in their opinion was most likely the work of outsiders. Before the Europeans could make a move, the Ottoman authorities had got the Maronites and Druzes to sign a peace treaty, reprimanded their own officials for not keeping the peace, and sent instructions to the governors of the various provinces and to the commander of forces of the army of Anatolia urging them to keep the peace in their districts. Murder, the sultan reminded them, was contrary to Islamic law and to his benevolent and paternal sentiments toward his subjects. He warned them that they would be held responsible for any murder and pillage against Christians. It was their duty to understand the extent of their duties, maintain calm at all times, watch day and night, realize that their country was facing critical and dangerous times, and devote themselves entirely to preventing new embarrassments against all Ottoman subjects. If these officials got wind of bad blood between Muslims and Christians, they should immediately take measures to prevent conflict at all costs.[6]

The sultan also sent a letter to the ambassadors to express his sorrow at the news from Syria, and he promised to exert all his power to reestablish order and security, severely punish the guilty parties, and render justice. Ottoman agents were instructed to warn against "overblown news and ill-intentioned and erroneous opinions." In response, these agents monitored reactions to Ottoman initiatives, lobbied at the courts of Europe, and defended their government against any bad press. They accused the Russian press of printing slander, the French press of exaggeration and hostility, the Belgian press of being alarmist. They were more neutral toward Austrian and British coverage. They followed parliamentary debates in Europe and welcomed signs of approval.[7]

The Ottomans could not win the propaganda war in Europe, but they did their best. Their agents were certain that "malevolence started such slander." They blamed Western machinations for fomenting trouble in Syria and argued that the Sublime Porte could not be held responsible for "mysterious troubles prepared and fed by foreign agents." "What matters to us is to prove to the world that we remain masters of our own household."[8]

The second Ottoman initiative was military. In June, before the fall of Zahleh, four battalions had been sent from Istanbul and two from Crete, so that before the news of a massacre in Damascus had even reached Istanbul, some 6,000 men were already on their way to Syria in three Ottoman men-of-war and a ship-of-the-line under the command of Admiral Mustafa Naili Pasha, commander-in-chief of the sultan's naval forces in the Mediterranean. In July, the Ottomans also replaced Ahmad Pasha by Mu'ammar Pasha, previously governor of Smyrna, as governor of Damascus who was to maintain order until an Ottoman special envoy to Syria arrived.[9]

For that envoy, the government needed someone of exceptional international stature, loyal to it, and acceptable to the Europeans. They went to great lengths to appoint the right person, with the credibility of Ottoman rule and the boundaries of European interference in Syria on the line. Their first choice was a career officer named Mehmet Namık Pasha.

On paper, Namık Pasha certainly deserved to be considered. In the course of a long career that was to stretch over the reigns of Sultans Mahmud II, Abdulmejid, Abdulaziz, and Abdulhamid II, he served as field marshal (*mushir*), minister of war, commander-in-chief (*serasker*), and provincial governor (*vali*). Born in Konya in 1804, he entered the army during the reign of Sultan Mahmud II, and was sent as a youth to Paris where he learned French and had military training that led to rapid promotion. In 1832 he was made a general and sent as an ambassador to London where he spent about a year. On his return, he rose to the rank of general of a division (*ferik*) then field marshal. He also served in the war academy (*harbiye*) established in 1834. He was commander of the forces in Syria in 1844, in Iraq and the Hijaz in 1849, and governor of Baghdad in 1852. He was also commander of Tophane (the arsenal of ordinance), minister of commerce, governor of Bursa and Kastamonu, commander of the forces in Arabia for a second time, president of the military council (*shura*), and commander of the *hassa* (Arabic, *khāssa*), the special imperial troops that guarded the sultan. In 1860, he became commander-in-chief for the first time. After that he was appointed as commander-in-chief on two other occasions and was twice minister of marine. In 1877 he was elected a member of the senate created that year, and when he died in 1892 he was recognized as the most senior Ottoman minister and field marshal. He knew Arabic, French, and English.[10]

All the promise of his early career, however, could not get Namık Pasha the approval of Europe to his appointment as special commissioner to Syria in 1860. The viziers Ali and Fuad Pasha favored his nomination on the grounds that he could exercise authority over Syria's populations, as demonstrated by how orderly the province had been under his command. However, the French and especially the British objected to him on the grounds that he may have been responsible for the killings of Europeans and other Christians in Jedda on June 15, 1858. Tensions had grown in Jedda between Hijazi Muslims, other Muslims, and Christians locked into commercial rivalries, exacerbated by struggles of power among leading emirs and a high turnover of governors (between 1850 and 1858, Jedda had had five different governors). In October 1857, Namık Pasha arrived as governor, and the following June, while he was in Mecca planning a pilgrimage, a dispute over the nationality of a ship in the Jedda harbor ended in the death of 22 people; all but one were Christian foreigners or foreign protégés and they included the British vice-consul and the French consul and his wife. The governor, the British, and the French continued to quarrel over who was responsible, and on July 25 the British bombarded Jedda in retaliation and several local officials lost their jobs. The Ottoman, British, and French governments argued over compensation for losses incurred, and although they settled their differences in 1860, litigation over individual claims lasted for years and the memory was far from dead.[11]

Bulwer in particular was adamant in his opposition, and he recommended instead a certain Umar Pasha. He knew that Namık Pasha was anxious to vindicate himself over the Jedda incident, and conceded that he was considered able, brave, and honest. He also acknowledged that the pasha had not even been in Jedda at the time of the trouble and may have acted with "vigor and discretion" when he returned. Nonetheless he also had heard that, according to other people, the pasha had not done enough. Bulwer also objected to the appointment of the pasha on the grounds that the indemnities to European victims of the Jedda outbreak had not been settled and the matter was still pending. In Damascus, Brant fed Bulwer the news that Namık Pasha had not been popular with non-Muslims in Syria, and therefore his appointment neither inspired confidence nor was seen as evidence of benevolent intentions on the part of the Porte towards its *ra'aya*s.[12]

La Valette shared Bulwer's reservations and suggested in his stead an officer named Tassif Pasha. But when he declined for reasons of health, La Valette found himself unable to recommend another candidate. He too opposed Namık Pasha's nomination on the grounds that France and England still awaited reparations for the Jedda massacres. He wrote to Thouvenel that, in the light of that incident, the "strange" nomination would constitute "a breach of all propriety." La Valette asked Thouvenel to let the Ottoman viziers know of the irritation and pain such a nomination would cause, and later thanked him for his help. On another occasion, La Valette mentioned that Namık Pasha was known for his "fanaticism" and, to reinforce the point, remarked that the pasha's son-in-law was "worthy of him" and was none other than Tahir Pasha who had "distinguished himself" at Deir al-Qamar in 1860.[13]

All this European interference worked, but ironically it ended up serving Ottoman interests better than European ones, for the Ottomans gave up and the official they chose instead turned out to be a far more formidable antagonist to European ambitions than Namık Pasha would probably have been. On July 8, the sultan appointed Fuad Pasha as envoy extraordinary to Syria with full powers over both civil and military matters in the region, and sent him off with 15,000 to 16,000 men. Halim Pasha, president of the council of war and reputed to be brave and energetic, was to accompany him as commander-in-chief of the Syrian army, and Namık Pasha was to fill the post vacated by Halim Pasha. Despite their financial limitations, the Ottomans found funds for Fuad Pasha's mission by "[emptying] the cash box of the ministry of Finance of the sparse amount of money it contained." The Porte also sent wheat with Fuad Pasha to Beirut.[14]

The sultan used the occasion of Fuad Pasha's appointment to reiterate his unhappiness about the events in Syria and to make known the unlimited powers he bestowed on Fuad Pasha for his mission. The firman stated that he was "much displeased out of compassion for the people" at the news of civil war between Maronites and Druzes, that he looked only with compassion upon his subjects regardless of differences of religion, so that they all may enjoy security, comfort, happiness, and tranquility, and that his greatest aim and earnest desire was that "no party should molest another or trespass upon its rights in any way." As for Fuad's mission, it was completely open-ended:[15]

> You, my vizier full of intelligence, one of the glorious ministers and of the great advisers of our empire, possess all our imperial trust. Our imperial irade, full with justice, calls for your nomination with full powers to this important mission. The needed number of troops has been set aside. Immediately proceed to Syria, with your perfect knowledge of our affairs, your

skillfulness, your zeal, and your loyalty. In Syria, surround yourself with all civil and military authorities, and take all necessary measures to put an immediate stop to all discord between Maronites and Druzes, and bring back rest and tranquility to the populations. As to those who dared spread human blood, after looking into the matter punish them on the spot, in accordance with our laws. In short, we trust your intelligence and sagacity with full powers, civil as well as military, to take the necessary measures to push aside all difficulties.

Fuad Pasha was 45 years old when he was sent to Beirut, and had all the *savoir faire* and charm of the true diplomat. Tall, handsome, and expansive, he had a great deal of presence and was widely known for his wit. The son of a famous poet, Kececizade Izzet Molla, and from a well-known family, Fuad Pasha had started his career as a *littérateur* and a poet. Then his father fell out of favor with Sultan Mahmud II, who confiscated the family property, and Fuad turned to the study of medicine for four years, after which he was named doctor of the admiralty and accompanied Admiral Tahir Pasha on a campaign to Tripoli. He then joined the translation bureau at the Porte and spent a few years preparing himself for a diplomatic career by studying history, modern languages, international law, and political economy.

Fluent French helped him rise rapidly through the ranks of the translation bureau to become, together with his lifelong colleague Ali Pasha, a protégé of Mustafa Reshid Pasha. He was minister of the interior at 34 and foreign minister for the first time at 37; in 1851, he wrote part of the first modern Turkish grammar; in 1854 he was appointed to the new Tanzimat council which he presided over in 1857. He served three years as first secretary of the embassy in London and went on special missions to Madrid, Bucharest, St Petersburg, Cairo, and Paris.[16]

The European ambassadors wanted to attach European delegates to the commission, but Fuad and Ali Pasha refused. The mission was said to include Abro Efendi, director of French correspondence at the ministry of foreign affairs and, in the opinion of one correspondent, "one of the most intelligent functionaries of the Porte;" Franco Nasri Efendi, director of the disputed claims office, a Catholic of Syrian origin who also had the reputation of being intelligent, and was put in charge of the distribution of relief; Danish Efendi, of whom we know little except that he was young and trusted by Fuad Pasha, Şirvanizade Mehmet Rüstü Pasha who in 1863 became governor of Damascus, and Constant Efendi and Arzuman Efendi, experienced secretaries and translators. The Ottoman attachés included Shawqat Efendi, first secretary. Fuad's aides-de-camp were lieutenant-colonels Hasan Bey (O'Reilly) – an Irish mercenary who had served under the king of Sardinia and with the Hungarians before entering Ottoman service – his chief of staff, Ra'uf Bey, and officers Mustafa Efendi and Jamil Bey.[17]

Fuad Pasha left for Syria on Thursday, July 12, on the *Taif*, an Ottoman warship, accompanied by two corvettes and two gunboats and, given the government's limited resources, generously supplied with troops and funds. He also had the backing of most of the European ambassadors.[18]

During a refueling stop at Cyprus, Fuad Pasha heard of the massacres in Damascus. They could only complicate his already delicate mission, which the pasha understood to be both humanitarian and punitive. The news increased the sense of urgency. He was acutely aware of his enormous responsibilities, considered his task "so heavy," and planned to "fulfill my duties with uprightness [underlined in original text] to extricate my country from the crisis that the sad and painful events of that Province have created."[19]

He reached Beirut on July 17 and immediately issued a declaration that he would put the fear of God in the hearts of the unruly and lawless. He voiced the indignation of the Ottoman government at the news of the civil war and its opposition to anyone who, for whatever reason or in any way, harmed the rights of others. Anyone who disregarded his orders would be considered a rebel. All excesses and hostilities would stop immediately. "I have come with an imperial commission, independent and extraordinary, to punish those who committed these crimes," he declared. "The nature of my powers is evident from the superior firman which was addressed to me. It conveys the justice of his imperial highness the Sultan who gives asylum to the oppressed and inflicts punishments on oppressors. I will perform my duty with perfect impartiality." He then went on to say that with compassion and equity he would provide relief for destitute families, and that all hostilities must cease everywhere. The imperial troops under his command would punish anyone who went against his orders or began to fight. He also announced that he was setting up extraordinary means to hear about criminal actions and he invited "every one, small or big, to let us know freely his grievances and we will lend him our attention."[20]

The challenges facing Fuad Pasha in Syria were enormous. He had to be both a civilian and military leader, command the army, punish the guilty and render justice, organize relief for the victims of civil war and help rebuild towns and villages, bring back order and local trust in Ottoman rule.[21] The most formidable challenges he faced came not from the divided populations of a troubled province but from outside it, in the form of European diplomatic and military powers. Fuad Pasha was to preside over an international commission that would include European representatives who commanded more funds, troops, and power than his government and were outraged by the death of innocent bystanders. Fuad Pasha also had to fend off the vigorous French thrust for political and military influence in the area and, more generally, deal with the politics, rivalries, and colonial ambitions of Europe in Syria.

News of the Syrian crisis had been slow to reach Europe; telegrams from Beirut had to be sent via Smyrna, where the telegraph station nearest to Beirut was located. Until the news arrived, the only European response had come from ambassadors in Istanbul. They ordered ships to sail to Syria. On June 13 a small French squadron anchored in Beirut, and on June 25 a small number of French marines landed in Sidon to protect its French khan.[22]

Knowledge of the massacres of Christians in Mount Lebanon was widespread by July. In the beginning, Western observers in Syria attributed the war to a whole range of factors that included violence on the part of the local population, whether Christian or Druze, but by July the Christians had become the pitiable victims of civil conflict. The European, especially the French, press was outraged at what it portrayed as the indiscriminate and brutal slaying of Christians at the hands of Druzes, Muslims, and the Ottoman army.[23]

The European governments reacted swiftly. At their head was France's Napoleon III. Since becoming elected president of the Second Republic, in 1848, and especially since his accession to power as emperor of the French in 1852, Napoleon had concentrated on a number of policies that at home strengthened unity and prosperity at the cost of democracy and abroad maintained and improved French prestige by revising treaties disadvantageous to France, supporting nationalistic aspirations among subjects of larger empires, and maintaining and improving relations with the other Great Powers, particularly Britain. Although he supported the Ottoman empire because its collapse would upset the European balance of power, he also supported nationalist and minority rights and posed as the protector of Christians, particularly the Maronites of Lebanon.[24]

France's involvement in the Middle East in the 1850s laid the foundations for its reaction to the Syrian crisis of 1860. The Crimean war (1853-6) was an important landmark in the "Eastern Question" which centered around the decline and possible collapse of the Ottoman empire and the rival concerns and ambitions of the Great Powers as to how such a collapse would affect the European balance of power. The war broke out when Russia claimed to be the protector of the Greek Orthodox in the Ottoman empire, and was opposed by British, French, Austrian, Prussian, and Ottoman alliance against those ambitions. It sealed France's cooperation with Britain, setting aside their rivalries, renewed France's prestige in Europe and abroad, and reasserted France's commitment to the Roman Catholic and other Christian subjects of the Ottoman empire. The war also opened a new phase in Napoleon III's involvement as the avowed champion of national and minority rights in the Ottoman empire. The Syrian crisis of 1860 offered him a new opportunity to demonstrate that role.[25]

However committed Napoleon III was to protect Eastern Christians, the first priority of his Middle Eastern policy was to act in concert with Europe, particularly Britain. In May 1860 before the news of the Syrian civil war had reached the French government, Prince Alexander Gorshakov, the Russian foreign minister since 1856, had proposed a joint Franco-Russian action in the defense of Christians in the Ottoman empire. Napoleon Auguste Lannes, Duc de Montebello, the French ambassador to Russia, thought that other European powers should also be involved.[26]

The first reports of the May and June wars in Lebanon reached Paris in June and were forwarded to Napoleon III who was in Baden. They were contradictory and confused. By the beginning of July, all the reports sent from Bentivoglio in Beirut were received by the French foreign minister Edouard-Antoine Thouvenel. Thouvenel had only been minister since January but he was an experienced diplomat and knowledgeable about Ottoman affairs since he had been ambassador to the Porte between 1855 and 1860. He sent the first official French response, which consisted of "grave concern" over the possibility that the French-protected Maronites' most sacred rights had been violated and that massacres in other parts of the Ottoman empire might be encouraged.[27]

On July 5, Thouvenel met with Lord Cowley, Britain's ambassador to France, to discuss how they should go about quelling the unrest and, when that was accomplished, revising Lebanon's system of government in place since 1842. "I am not yet talking of an expedition," he added (although, in fact, he talked just "as a man who was already considering it," commented the historian Pierre de la Gorce, author of a three-volume study of the Second Empire). Thouvenel proposed that warships monitor the Syrian coast and that a commission representing the five Great Powers be sent to Syria to investigate. The following day, Thouvenel sent a telegram to the French ambassadors in London, Vienna, St Petersburg, and Berlin, directing them to inform the British, Austrian, Russian, and Prussian governments of his initiative and to support it. He also requested the Ottoman government to take the measures necessary to restore order. Since the powers had collaborated with the Porte in 1842 in creating the administrative system of Lebanon, he argued that the present French initiative was in no way either new or threatening to the independence of the Ottoman empire.

Thouvenel then proposed that an international commission made up of delegates from the Great Powers and the Porte be appointed. It would investigate the causes of the disturbances, the degree of responsibility of local chiefs and administration, the means of compensating the victims, and, in recommendations submitted to the Great Powers, the measures to be taken to avoid a recurrence. The French government also sent French warships under the command of Rear Admiral Jehenne to Beirut, as did the British under the command of Vice-Admiral Martin. Ships from other European powers and the Ottoman fleet met them at Beirut.[28]

This first French initiative would probably have resulted in little further action had it not been for the Damascus riots, news of which reached Europe a week later. Thouvenel met with Napoleon III and they decided that France would intervene. On July 20, an expeditionary corps for Syria was formed by cabinet decision.[29]

Historians have debated Napoleon III's motives in intervening in Syria. There is always, of course, the possibility that Napoleon III and Thouvenel were genuinely concerned over the fate of the people there. More likely is that the emperor seized an opportunity to assert French prestige and influence and to conduct a foreign policy more decisive than the July Monarchy before him to distract attention from his unproductive Italian adventure in 1859–60. In the summer of 1860, an Anglo–French force had defended newly acquired commercial privileges in China, and this too may have strengthened his resolve to be aggressive *vis-à-vis* the Ottoman empire.[30]

The historian Marcel Emerit, in an article published in 1952, argued that there were two cornerstones of Napoleon's policy: the first was the completion of the Suez canal in Egypt, which Ferdinand de Lesseps, a French entrepreneur and a former member of the French consular service, had begun in 1859 in the face of British and Ottoman opposition, five years after he obtained from the Egyptian Khedive Sa'id his first concession to build it and four years before he received the Ottoman sultan's ratification of the project. The second was the silk trade. In the 1850s, France needed to import raw silk from Syria, partly because of a crisis in the French textile industry. Emerit argued that to protect the canal and the silk trade, Napoleon III had encouraged any rebellious movements that weakened Ottoman rule. Since the mid-1850s the French had nurtured Abd al-Qadir, the Algerian emir and French protégé who had saved so many lives in Damascus in 1860. Emerit claimed that they had a plan to make him the ruler of an Arab kingdom that would stretch from Syria and Mesopotamia to the Arabian peninsula, and would constitute a buffer state between Egypt – where the French had control of the Suez canal at stake – and Anatolia, where the Ottoman resistance to the canal was centered. The creation of that buffer state would force the Ottomans to stop interfering with the Suez project and would enhance French economic and other interests in the region as a whole.[31]

Whatever his motives, Napoleon III had "a penchant for conference diplomacy," as the historian William Echard remarked. Having decided on military intervention, the emperor and Thouvenel lost no time in lobbying other Great Powers to support it. Napoleon III instructed Victor Fialin Persigny, French ambassador to the Court of St James since 1859, to argue to the British government that the intervention had to be European-wide and that France did not want to intervene in Syria unilaterally, but would only act as Europe's agent and with the full backing of the rest of the Great Powers. It would also prefer a joint European expedition.[32]

The British, however, were wary of the French initiative. They first thought the war was just yet another outburst of the endemic sectarian hostilities in Mount Lebanon. Once Damascus suffered bloodshed, however, they were afraid that the crisis would provide Napoleon III with an excuse to interfere. Lord Palmerston, then prime minister, did not trust Napoleon, a distrust fueled by the recent French annexation of Nice and Savoy. He was also suspicious of French ambitions in the Ottoman empire, not least of Lesseps's Suez canal project.

The British response to French eagerness was consequently distinctly cold. On July 5 when Cowley met with Thouvenel, he had discouraged interference because he was afraid that Napoleon III was using the crisis for his own benefit. He deplored what had happened in Lebanon, but he pointed out that in many instances the Maronites had provoked the violence and that Christians had been the sole source of the reporting that was reaching Europe, so it was probably biased.

As the month went by and Europe seemed more and more unlikely to remain aloof, the British tried to contain, if they could not stop, the scope of the French initiative. On July 18, the British cabinet decided to impose conditions demanding that a formal convention between the five Great Powers and the Ottoman government was required. The cabinet also decided that, instead of joining the French in an expeditionary force, Britain would only increase its naval presence on the Syrian coast. Aware that Austria claimed to be a protector of Roman Catholics in the Ottoman empire and consequently could be used as a counterweight, the British cabinet took the position that, although Russian and Prussian troops need not join the French in their military intervention, Austrian troops might do so if that became necessary.[33]

The next day, Thouvenel telegraphed French representatives in Vienna, St Petersburg, Berlin, and Istanbul to propose a conference in Paris to discuss a draft of a convention that would regulate the intervention in Syria of a European – mostly French – military force that would collaborate with the Ottoman authorities to restore order. To counter British objections, Napoleon claimed that he was motivated only by humanitarian principles, that he did not wish to intervene, as it would be costly and would reopen the "Eastern Question," but that he owed it to his own public opinion to react to the attacks on Christians and on French consulates and religious missions in Syria. No doubt, these arguments did little to reassure Palmerston, who only hoped that Fuad Pasha would restore order before the French could get there. On July 21, Palmerston informed Persigny that the Maronites and Druzes had just concluded a peace that made an expedition unnecessary, to which Thouvenel replied that peace between Maronites and Druzes did not diminish the need for intervention. The French had decided it was necessary, not because of Mount Lebanon but because of Damascus, where the French consulate had been sacked and Christians, including French missionaries, had been murdered by Muslim extremists.[34]

On July 25 the British cabinet finally agreed to intervention, but still with conditions. One continued to be that a convention between the five Great Powers and the Porte be signed first. .The others were that the Ottoman government formally request a European military intervention, and that, once they did, it be limited to six months. That the British continued to feel uneasy about the French was clear from a note written by Lord John Russell, then foreign secretary, to Palmerston on July 27 telling him that he had decided to support intervention not because he trusted the French but because European public opinion was in favor of the expedition and he feared the dangers for Britain of a Russian–French alliance, supported by Austria and Prussia. "We have been with Russia against France (1840) and with France against Russia (1854), but we have never had to oppose both, and in so rotten a cause it would be terrible work."[35]

The other Great Powers responded more readily to French diplomatic efforts. French relations with Austria had somewhat improved since Napoleon first intervened in Italy, and the Austrians may have wanted to keep up the rapprochement and perhaps to accumulate some credit if they ever needed an excuse to intervene on behalf of Christians in other parts of the Ottoman empire. In any case, the Austrian government believed that it was Thouvenel and not Napoleon III who was pressing for intervention. The Russians had suggested some form of intervention as early as May, even before the crisis had attracted world attention. Prussia's national aspirations made it advantageous to support a supporter of nationalism, as Napoleon III was.[36]

On July 26, Thouvenel succeeded in gathering in Paris French, British, Russian, Austrian, and Ottoman representatives to discuss the Syrian crisis, but they disagreed over the scope of intervention. Two days later they met again. Russia, which in May had suggested to Napoleon III a joint intervention on behalf of the Christian population in Syria, now proposed that the five Great Powers act essentially as overseers, pressuring the Ottoman empire to improve the condition of its Christian subjects and intervening wherever there was trouble. The British would, of course, have none of that, which suited the Ottomans. The Austrians supported the Russian proposal, but the French, although favorably disposed towards it, were concerned that it would detract from the immediate issue at hand – that of a military intervention in Syria.[37]

To placate British concerns, Thouvenel proposed two protocols as a compromise. One addressed the issue raised by Russia, but in a way Britain had approved in the past. It consisted in reiterating the request already embodied in the treaty of March 30, 1856, which had concluded the Crimean war, that the Ottoman government reform the conditions under which its Christians lived. The conditions for intervention in Syria were embodied in the other protocol, dated August 3, which was ratified by the convention of September 5. Thouvenel's proposal to appoint a commission to investigate the Syrian crisis was accepted. Composed of representatives from the Great Powers, it opened its sessions in Beirut on October 5.[38]

The French won approval for military intervention in Syria, but at a price. The protocol agreed to their presence there, but also imposed controls on its duration and their freedom of action. Its seven articles stipulated: (1) A European military force of up to 12,000 soldiers would be sent to Syria to help reestablish order. (2) Napoleon III would provide half that number. If more were needed, the Great Powers without delay would agree with the Porte on which countries among them would provide troops. (3) Upon arriving in Syria, the expedition's commander would contact the Porte's extraordinary commissioner, so as to take all measures necessary to occupy the positions that would allow the execution of the mission. (4) The British, Austrian, French, Prussian, and Russian rulers would allow sufficient naval forces to monitor the Syrian coast so as to insure its tranquility. (5) The European expeditionary force would stay in Syria for no more than six months, which the Powers believed to be sufficient to pacify the area. (6) The Ottoman government would cover the army's subsistence and supplies in so far as it was able. (7) Finally, the convention should be ratified in Paris within five weeks or as close to that time as possible.[39] In effect, although France had received European approval of its expedition to Syria, it was to act in the name of all the signatories, not to threaten or undermine the Ottoman empire but, on the contrary, to act in conjunction with its ruler to defend its best interests and those of its Christian subjects.

Marquis General Charles de Beaufort d'Hautpoul was appointed commander-in-chief of the French expedition, perhaps because he had served in the 1830s as chief of staff for Ibrahim Pasha during the Egyptian campaigns in Syria.[40] He was sent, however, not simply as a French general, but essentially as Europe's representative. Thouvenel made every effort to see that he had freedom of action. The instructions he conveyed to Beaufort through the French minister of war were to cooperate with the Ottomans but at the same time to act as freely as circumstances in Syria would permit. He wrote to Admiral Hamelin, secretary of state for the marine and responsible for the war ministry, that the object of Beaufort's mission, like that of the naval officers sent to the Syrian coast, was to take "prompt and energetic measures" to put an end to the bloodshed and to punish those who had attacked Christians. Thouvenel then noted that, by the terms of article 3 of the protocol of August, Beaufort should get in touch with Fuad Pasha as soon as he arrived in Syria so that the two of them could combine forces though, even after that, General de Beaufort was "nonetheless totally free to exercise judgment in anything that concerns the honor of our flag and the safety of our expeditionary corps. As long as he explains his actions to the representative of the Turkish government, he remains free to adopt the measures and to occupy the positions that he deems necessary."[41]

Hamelin's instructions left Beaufort room for independent action, but also clearly limited its scope. It was not his mission to conquer or occupy; the mission was "remedial and temporary," a response to public sentiment and to the profound pity inspired by the misery of the Christians of the East. Beaufort was to consult with Fuad Pasha on the measures to be taken. If the pasha lacked firmness or energy in implementing the measures needed, Beaufort should "press him strongly or, if needed, feel free to act on your own within the limits of your program." Beaufort was not to march on Damascus unless he were certain he could do so usefully and without any risks. In brief, he wrote, the emperor wanted "your little army corps" to act as a mobile column that could bring justice anywhere in the country. It will catch, judge, and punish the guilty, return to the Christians their confiscated goods, disarm the Druzes, and force on them reparations as indemnity to the victims of the insurrection. The expedition would thus appear as an obvious act of justice. "It will be short and the emperor will be very satisfied if it could return in two months having accomplished its work."[42]

There were slight variations in how the decision-makers in Paris phrased their instructions to Beaufort, and definite vagueness as to the ways in which the mission to Syria should be carried out. That left him with some freedom as to how he would choose to interpret his mission.

Under Beaufort's command, some 6,000 soldiers, drawn principally from camps in Châlons-sur-Marne, were sent to Marseilles and Toulon to embark for Syria. On August 7, Napoleon III, reviewing some of the departing troops, delivered a speech in which he stressed France's special role in the Syrian crisis:[43]

> Soldiers, you are departing for Syria, and France happily salutes an expedition which has one purpose only, that of making the rights of justice and humanity triumph. For you are not going in order to wage war against any nation but to help the Sultan bring back to obedience subjects blinded by a fanaticism from another century. You will do your duty in this far away land, rich in memories, and you will show yourselves the dignified children of these heroes who gloriously brought the banner of Christ to that land. You are not going away in large numbers, but your courage and your prestige will make up for that for today, wherever flies the flag of France, nations know that there is a noble cause preceding it and a noble people following it.

We have some idea of what the voyage to Beirut was like for the soldiers from an account by Baptistin Poujoulat, a Frenchman who was returning to Syria which he had visited 25 years earlier, in order, as he put it, to study it anew. Before reaching Syria – indeed, probably before leaving France – Poujoulat had made up his mind that the Ottomans had been guilty of, at best, negligence and that, as he put it unequivocally, "Syria is French territory."[44]

He left for Syria on August 6, 1860, on the steamer *Le Borysthène* of the Messageries Maritimes, together with some 400 men of the 16th battalion of light infantry (*chasseurs à pied*) of Vincennes, 12 of their officers, the medical corps of the army, the commissariat (*intendance*), and almost all the general administrative staff of the French expedition. The trip was acutely uncomfortable. Poujoulat was seasick and the heat was unbearable both on the deck where the soldiers lived and in the cabins, which were "sweating-rooms where one cannot breathe." But it takes more than discomfort or strict discipline to dampen the enthusiasm of youth and the soldiers laughed, joked, and at night sang: "Do not fear the cannon, it is not worth it. From the shoulder-strap to the troubadour is less difference than people might feel. To others in your turn perhaps you will say: conscripts carry your arms! March to rhythm! Run to victory!" The soldiers spoke of Turks and Druzes as villains who should be taught a lesson; the only topic of conversation was Syria.[45]

Staff-colonel Osmont had been sent ahead to prepare the way for their arrival. He arrived in Beirut on July 30, 1860, and immediately began to tackle the problem of how to billet 6,000 to 12,000 men in the town; he had to assume that the expedition could eventually reach that number. He decided to camp them in a pine forest two kilometers south of town. It was on the way to Damascus, had adequate space, shade, and air circulation. Some Ottoman troops had already camped there, but Isma'il Pasha, in charge of the Ottoman troops in Beirut, agreed to accommodate the French.[46] Osmont found that the water supply was insufficient in Beirut. Drinking water either came from tanks or had to be transported on donkeys from the numerous wells located around the town. The wells around the pine forest could provide sufficient drinking water, however, and "Beirut's river," some ten kilometers from town, could supply river water via aqueduct to be used for the horses and laundry. Osmont found that the meat market could provide ample supplies of good quality lamb and beef. Wine could be gotten from Cyprus, although it would have a "small taste of resin," local flour was of poor quality and in short supply, but rice was available in Beirut or Alexandria, straw was short, wood was plentiful, warehouses for supplies were easy to find, and medical care could be provided by the hospitals attached to the missions of St Vincent de Paul.[47]

Osmont also found that there were no roads in the country capable of moving transport or artillery. One road was being built (the carriage road between Beirut and Damascus, the construction of which had began in 1859 and was completed in 1863), transport could be arranged between Beirut and whatever point the road had reached (Araya). The problem was that the French company in charge of the project had a 50-year lease and monopoly on all transport by wagon and car.

On August 2, the French administrative personnel and equipment arrived in Beirut. Osmont visited the local authorities in the company of Bentivoglio, the French consul general, to clear the way for the troops to disembark. The pasha objected that he had not received any official instructions from either Fuad Pasha or from the Sublime Porte about any French expedition, but in the end he agreed that the equipment could be unloaded and stored in warehouses, so long as it not be used until orders came from the capital. The French had all to remain on board until then, but would be allowed to go ashore in the line of duty. Osmont wrote to his superiors in France that he felt confident that in a matter of a few days all would be cleared with the local authorities, since on 25 July the French ambassador in Istanbul had announced that the sultan had agreed to France's propositions. Nonetheless, Osmont was anxious to see the troops arrive, and he worried about rumors that they would not come.[48]

Osmont also established contact with the French colony in Beirut. In addition to Bentivoglio, he had as his local contact Edmond de Perthuis, a French entrepreneur living in Beirut who was a former marine officer and an Orléanist. He had left France after the revolution of 1848 to settle in Syria, where he represented the Messageries Maritimes, the most important French steamship line servicing the Mediterranean, and also organized important construction projects, including the Beirut–Damascus road. (He later supervised the improvement of Beirut's harbor between 1890 and 1895.) The day after Osmont's arrival, it had been Perthuis who took him scouting for a place to put the troops around the suburbs including the pine forest.[49]

Le Borysthène arrived in Beirut early in the morning of August 16, a month almost to the day after the arrival of Fuad Pasha. By then the harbor was already crowded with some 30 European warships and three Ottoman vessels. They were soon joined by *L'Amérique*, also of the Messageries Maritimes, the vessel carrying Beaufort, his general staff, and more troops: the 400 remaining men of the 16th battalion of light infantrymen of Vincennes, 300 men of the line, and 500 sappers, in all, some 1,500 to 1,800 men out of the 6,000 total. By August 22, the infantry and artillery had arrived; only the cavalry was missing and they continued coming for another month.[50]

A considerable crowd watched the troops disembark; they were uncharacteristically silent and reserved at the extraordinary sight of French troops landing in an Ottoman province. Rumors among Europeans had it that their arrival would provoke riots, but the debarkation proceeded smoothly. Muslim boatmen from Beirut refused to bring French ammunition to shore, but their gesture against the foreign presence was more symbolic than effective. European boats were quickly made available to Jehenne, the French admiral supervising the landing.[51]

Once ashore, the troops made a more chaotic than grand entry under the blazing August sun; they set up camp for the day near the beach outside town. At six in the evening they began their march towards the pine forest, a walk of an hour and a half. They were exhausted from the march to Marseilles and 12 days at sea, and burdened with packs and arms – although some let local people carry these for them. The heat was oppressive. Poujoulat referred to their march as "martial," but described the soldiers as sweaty and exhausted. The Countess de Perthuis, Edmond's mother, found it embarrassing that the Zouaves were in disarray and let local people carry their packs.[52]

People lined the way or watched from the terraces of their houses as the soldiers marched by. Many were jubilant, but with the restraint suitable for the arrival of armed foreigners on Ottoman soil and for the mixed feelings it provoked among others. Hundreds of women, partly veiled and partly hidden behind bushes, crossed themselves, placed their hands on their hearts, lifted their faces in thanks to heaven.

The newcomers knew as little about the people amassed to watch their arrival as the latter knew about them. The soldiers could not tell a Muslim from a Christian from a Druze. Men expressed joy or watched with grim expressions. If they appeared joyful then they must be Christian; if they looked grim then they must be Muslim; Ottoman soldiers were easy to spot. The soldiers mistook Syrian Christians for Muslims because of their headdress and because the women hid behind veils: the soldiers had associated veiling with Muslims and did not realize that these were Christian women. The Zouaves had no more sense of how to behave in their new surroundings than the Ottoman soldiers they despised. Some of them seemed drunk, and in Syria drunkenness was uncommon though, in time, the presence of the troops led to the spread of taverns in Beirut. They accosted women on the way and made rude remarks that drove "our gentlemen to urge us to leave the terrace [and go indoors]," wrote Madame de Perthuis. "Everyone is scandalized at this entry," she added.

The people watching them arrive were equally ignorant. They were baffled by the Zouaves' fezzes and turbans and were intensely curious. For days they discussed the encampment, and for much longer they made the pine forest the destination of all their leisure rides.[53]

Beaufort had been the first to disembark, and he had been met by Bentivoglio who had arranged to take him to Perthuis's house. Beaufort, however, brought with him four of his officers. Louise, Perthuis's wife and the daughter-in-law of the countess who left us her memoirs, prepared an impromptu luncheon for this unexpected party. Food was difficult to find in the market, since all provisions had been bought up to feed the arriving troops. Although the officers accompanying Beaufort showed appreciation for the hospitality, Beaufort himself was as boorish as was typical of him. Madame de Perthuis remarked that he was in a "rotten mood" and complained "as if he were in an inn" instead of a private home that the meal was late, although it had been served at 11.30 in the morning. Beaufort ate and ran: "That is how the leader of the French army sent to help the Christians makes contact with his compatriots who, if I dare say so, until now have shown themselves the most devoted in helping the Christians. Instead of the pleasant relations which we had anticipated ... from that day dates impolite incidents and a lack of tact on the part of General Beaufort the causes of which we never understood." To her his behavior was so inexplicable that she wondered whether he had received orders from Paris to avoid the Perthuis family, or whether he did not wish to ally himself with Orléanists like themselves in order not to compromise in some way the emperor's government.[54]

Whether or not Beaufort disapproved of their politics, it became evident that he was often rude, as he amply demonstrated in his dealings. Ottoman–French relations would have been difficult even if Beaufort had been graceful; it did not help, however, that he had no tact at all. The anonymous witness who left us his descriptions of the French expedition in *Souvenirs de Syrie* commented that Beaufort's functions required him to be "a military man combined with a diplomat;" unfortunately, Beaufort was certainly the first and as certainly not the second. In instructing him, Hamelin had written that the emperor counted "no less on your prudence than on your military qualities." Of prudence Beaufort had none.[55]

Beaufort was, however, fully aware of the importance of his mission. His instructions were vague enough for him to read into them what he wanted, and he wanted to play an important role in Syria and keep the French troops there as long as he could. He did not see his mission in the context of Ottoman rule, but as just another in a long line of French responsibilities in the East that began with the Crusades. As he told his troops on August 7:

> Defenders of all the noble and great causes, the Emperor has decided that, in the name of civilized Europe, you will go to Syria to help the Sultan's troops avenge humanity disgracefully vilified. It is a beautiful mission of which you are proud and of which you will show yourselves worthy. In these famous lands Christianity was born, and Godefroy de Bouillon and the Crusaders, general Bonaparte, and the heroic soldiers of the Republic honored themselves. There, you will find again glorious and patriotic memories. The whole of Europe wishes you well and follows closely your mission. Whatever happens, I have the sure hope that the French Emperor will be pleased with you.[56]

The problem was that Beaufort's understanding of his mission clashed with Fuad Pasha's. The pasha had been sent to Syria to gain three objectives: to repress the revolt, rebuild the damage, and reorganize the region. Beaufort arrived with the same goals. Each man thought they were his responsibility, and each man's ideas about how they were to be carried out were vastly different. Fuad Pasha wanted to combine harsh punishment in Damascus with leniency in Mount Lebanon. Beaufort set out to punish every guilty Druze. Fuad Pasha believed the Christians had been responsible for starting the war in the Mountain, both through their religious leaders and through their own aggression. Beaufort regarded the Christians as innocent victims. These differences resulted in disagreements over reparations. Fuad Pasha believed that the Christians received fair and adequate compensation for their losses, especially in the light of the government's shortages of money and personnel. Beaufort regarded Ottoman compensation policies as unsatisfactory and believed that the aid the French expedition's material help gave to the Christians had been the only help they had. They disagreed, as well, about Syria's future organization. Fuad Pasha would reorganize Lebanon within the context of Ottoman policies of centralization; Beaufort favored the return of the semi-autonomous days of the Shihab emirate.[57]

Tensions between the two men had to do, then, with broad issues of policy. The Ottomans, including Fuad Pasha, were unhappy to see the French expedition arrive. They did all they could to prevent it and then, when it took place, they tried to contain it by allowing it to be helpful in practical matters but powerless in decision-making. Thanks to Fuad Pasha, they were able to use the French with great political cunning. Although the French were certain of their superiority and of the nobility of their mission, the Ottomans turned out to be superior politicians – at least, when it came to the power struggle between Fuad Pasha and Beaufort. The Ottomans first tried to stop the expedition by lobbying in Istanbul, Europe, and Syria. Then, after he arrived in Syria, Fuad Pasha sent Hasan Bey, his chief of staff and a friend of Bentivoglio, to ask the French consul general to try and stop the expedition. To indulge Fuad Pasha, Bentivoglio wrote a letter to La Valette to that effect but he fully expected and hoped that his request would have no result, as he very much wished the expedition to take place.[58]

The French got back at the Ottomans by constantly criticizing them in general, and Fuad Pasha in particular. La Valette admitted that at first he had supported the pasha's appointment and eagerly encouraged him to go to Syria. After the pasha arrived in Syria, an unspecified Ottoman source suggests that La Valette was pleased with him and referred to him as Turkey's savior. However, by the end of October, the ambassador was irritated because the pasha tried to portray the French troops as "perfectly useless" for enforcing the repressive measures taken in Syria, when in the opinion of the French ambassador they were indispensable to their effectiveness. "It is not from here that one can control Fuad Pasha," observed La Valette, but rather "from Beirut or Damascus" that this could be accomplished, with the help of the French commissioner or other agents. He added that there was a gap between the pasha's vigorous words and his indecisive actions, and complained that in Syria Fuad Pasha was using some of his cunning against the French, and his words lacked honesty and clarity. By January 1861, the ambassador was openly hostile. He wrote that Fuad Pasha lacked the perseverance, firmness, and uprightness indispensable to his mission, that neither his previous record nor his current conduct in Syria justified Europe's trust in him. In his opinion, Fuad Pasha was too concerned with the impression his acts made abroad, and had been severe with the guilty parties in Syria only at the beginning. The real reason for La Valette's change of heart most probably lay in his next criticism, namely that Fuad Pasha, in so far as his personality allowed, had shared "in the hostile passions against the French expedition."[59]

Relations between the French and the Ottomans were not improved by the conflict in personalities. Fuad Pasha's sense of humor was celebrated; Beaufort had not an ounce of humor. Fuad Pasha had the subtlety and tact of the polished diplomat; Beaufort had the directness and bluntness of the military man. Fuad Pasha could bide his time; Beaufort exploded with impatience. On the battlefield, Beaufort would have carried the day; in the game of politics, there was not a doubt who had the upper hand. Beaufort had to order the French evacuation very much *à contrecœur*.

And yet, there was something almost endearing about the gruff, self-righteous soldier. He cared about justice, albeit in black-and-white terms of good Christians versus bad Druzes and Muslims. He detested frivolity: soon after his arrival he was scandalized that the Austrian consulate held a ball, thinking it was indecent to waltz in the face of so much misfortune, unable to appreciate, as the Countess de Perthuis did, that some might welcome the break after weeks of hardship and fear. However much he was convinced of the superiority of his mission over any Ottoman one in Syria, he was too correct a soldier to ignore his orders. He simply saw the Ottomans as subservient to representatives of France and patronized them. He instructed his men to "behave decently towards Turkish soldiers and get used to treating them like comrades in arms."[60]

From his first days in Syria, Fuad Pasha outmaneuvered Beaufort and stifled his initiative. Publicly he said only that the French had come with the Sultan's permission and that the general population should join the government in welcoming them. He instructed Mustafa Pasha to put notices all over the Syrian coastline announcing the arrival of the French expedition, in order to forestall panic or rumor. The announcement was circulated on August 3 that, as a result of the massacres in Damascus, France was sending some auxiliary troops to the sultan to help pacify

Syria and that people should not be alarmed when they arrived. This announcement was read at the serai, sent to the Muslim notables in Syria, to the consuls of England and France, and to the admirals commanding the fleet offshore. On August 4, two steamships were sent, one south to Jaffa and the other north to Alexandretta (Iskandarun) to make the same announcement.[61]

When the troops arrived, Fuad Pasha sent a platoon of Ottoman soldiers accompanied by an army band to the garrison in Beirut to escort them. Poujoulat was irritated that Ottoman soldiers marched ahead of the French on their way to their camp and he made fun of their heavy gait, although his compatriots were not making a very military impression either, as they were exhausted from their crossing to Syria.[62]

Beaufort was anxious to proceed without delay to Damascus, but he could not leave until the cavalry had arrived. The delay worried him for days, as did the need to organize and settle the expeditionary force, but he was left with no other choice but to wait in Beirut. He wrote to Fuad Pasha in Damascus. On August 27, he had received a letter in which the pasha assured him that all was calm and his presence there was not needed. The pasha also put at Beaufort's disposal Ra'uf Bey, his aide-de-camp, and a cavalry squadron. Undeterred, Beaufort wrote that if he could reach Damascus his goal would be to come to a complete and immediate agreement with the pasha. He also planned to write again to Fuad Pasha "in very precise language" regarding the assistance he should render in order to obtain immediate results.[63]

Beaufort continued to keep Fuad Pasha informed, both in person and through his aides, as to what he needed and what he planned to do, but the pasha ignored what did not suit him and made it difficult for Beaufort to move. The general complained to no avail. In the end he never did get his troops to Damascus, nor play any role there, although well into the winter of 1861 he still had expectations. He thought the corps would be sent on campaigns to the Anti-Lebanon, the Hawran, or the interior, but Fuad Pasha never let that happen.[64]

Beaufort shifted his attention to Mount Lebanon, where a limited French initiative would be less unacceptable to Fuad Pasha and where he was impatient to act before the bad weather. Unable to leave Beirut, Beaufort sent Lieutenant-colonel Chanzy to Damascus as August drew to a close. Chanzy was to convey to Fuad Pasha the difficulties of keeping the French forces inactive and to stress the urgency of their need to intervene in Mount Lebanon. The pasha was a great listener, as the French found out, but he frustrated Beaufort by assigning no role to the French: "As I predicted," commented Beaufort, who had not yet met the pasha to size him up, "Chanzy found Fuad Pasha taking refuge behind the affairs of Damascus not to discuss yet those of Lebanon," by which he really meant those of the French forces. At that point Beaufort had been in Beirut less than three weeks, but was already finding it impossible to accept inaction in the face of all that needed to be done, or to let things drag on and allow the French to be immobilized in Beirut.[65]

Fuad Pasha allowed Chanzy four hours of his time only to send him back with the promise that he would come to Beirut on September 6 or 7 for discussions. On September 9, he still had not come and Beaufort accused him of avoiding him, but the pasha came the following morning. By September 12 they had had their discussion and in a few days Beaufort was to take his army to Mount Lebanon, with a mobile column. But it took two more meetings with the pasha before Beaufort was clear on what his sphere of activities would be, and it was not until September 19 that he finally learned what the pasha proposed: he was to occupy and protect a position on the Beirut–Damascus road which had never been in the least danger of attack and Christian villages that had never been in the least threatened.[66]

Beaufort objected, and Fuad Pasha found him another assignment, but its details were so vague he should have figured out he was not to play a significant military role. For a while, he even seemed confident that he and Fuad Pasha were "completely in agreement." The pasha was to go to Sidon to move four battalions of infantrymen to Deir al-Qamar, while Beaufort would march directly to Deir al-Qamar and set up camp north of it. The Christians could then return to their villages behind the army which would protect them against the Druzes, and Beaufort would decide with Fuad Pasha how to deploy the two armies in order to capture the Druzes.[67]

On September 27, Beaufort received a letter from Fuad Pasha informing him that these plans had changed: instead of marching towards Deir al-Qamar, the pasha had gone to Jezzine where he left his infantry and then set up camp at or near Mashgara on the eastern slope of Mount Lebanon and the entrance to a main pass into the Beqaa plain. He had sent Isma'il Pasha and some troops to Mukhtara, the Janbalat home in the Shuf, to put him in touch with Beaufort and safeguard the Christians returning to their villages. By October 4, Beaufort believed that the pasha had gone back on his word and was doing all he could to keep Beaufort away from the Beqaa region, although they had initially agreed that the French could stay on one side of the Litani river. On October 20, Beaufort reported that Fuad Pasha, acting on his own, had taken troops to the Hawran.[68]

In the meantime, Beaufort himself had moved some of his troops to Mount Lebanon. On September 25, he left for Deir al-Qamar with 2,400 infantrymen, a mountain battery, and 40 cavalrymen as escort made up of spahis and hussars. Colonel d'Arricau left for Ain Sofar with 12 companies to deploy his battalions in the Mountain. The light cavalry was left behind in Beirut and then ordered to move to Qabb Elias in the Mountain, from where it could monitor the Beqaa valley and Jabal Sheikh. Beaufort settled Colonel d'Arricau at the palace of Beit al-Din because, as he explained, its location would give the French forces admirable military and hygienic advantages and, combined with the Ottoman forces sent to Mukhtara and left at Jezzine, it would also make it possible to monitor the country and stay connected to Beirut. He felt confident that he had positioned his troops in such a way that they would be able to encircle the Druze Mountain and continue to provide support to the Ottoman troops on their way to the Mountain.[69]

The general then toured the countryside between Beirut, Deir al-Qamar, and Qabb Elias which formed a hypothetical triangle and were the main locations of his expeditionary force. He stationed troops at these locations and at smaller ones, and kept others mobile. To seal off all escape routes for Druzes on the run, he surrounded their areas in south Lebanon with three companies of light infantrymen from a camp at Betlun, three companies of Zouaves under Colonel Osmont, his chief of staff, and one of the two battalions at Deir al-Qamar under Colonel d'Arricau. He himself took with him a mobile column of a company of light infantrymen and three companies of Zouaves to villages of the mixed districts such as Baisur, Abey, Kfar Matta. Leaving his infantry there, he continued on to other villages. He met with *'uqqal*s, sized up any potential resistance, and found none. The Druzes were so frightened it was unlikely they would make a move. He also met a number of Ottoman functionaries, including Ahmad Pasha who had come to Mukhtara at Fuad Pasha's request. Fuad Pasha was once again in Damascus, but came back to Qabb Elias on October 23 to meet with Beaufort before going to Beirut.[70]

Only one minor exchange of fire occurred in Beaufort's entire tour of the Mountain, which was an embarrassment for a self-important general anxious to defeat the Druzes in battle. On the march to Abey, the battalion leaving Beit al-Din was shot at a few times by some villagers from Kfar Faqud armed with rifles. The soldiers fired back two shots and killed one Druze. The villagers immediately rushed to the soldiers begging for mercy.

Beaufort went back to Beirut on October 24, having "established calm and security." The troops had met frightened Druzes on the run and destitute Christians. Should the need to act militarily arise "again," however,

Qabb Elias and Beit al-Din were occupied by the French forces and they could move quickly to the Beqaa or to any other part of the Mountain.[71]

Beaufort continued to keep a close watch on the mixed districts and the plains around Beirut. He was in close touch with his officers in the Mountain and toured it regularly. On November 4, he wrote that he had ordered six companies of the line to move from Beit al-Din to Deir al-Qamar, and four élite companies to leave Beirut on November 5: two to settle for the winter at Baabda, ten kilometers from Beirut, and two with special missions, one to Hammana and the other to Btater. He also had left at Qabb Elias 12 companies, and he sent three of them to Zahleh where they were housed in a church (Catholic, most probably) and at the bishop's residence. Two others were billeted in an old fortress dominating the village of Qabb Elias, and seven lived in tents (the last one may have been sent to Zahleh, it is not completely clear from the text). Some of the mountain artillery and squadrons of light infantry remained at Qabb Elias. Beaufort also moved detachments of the engineering corps between Beirut, Beit al-Din, and Qabb Elias. A battalion of light infantry and battalions of Zouaves remained at Beirut's pine forest camp.[72]

Beaufort also distributed troops along the coast south of Beirut. On December 12, 1860, he visited Sidon with an escort of cavalrymen and spahis, stationed some in the town's outskirts, and ordered 100 infantrymen to remain in the French khan in town, where the vice-consul at Sidon, his staff, some Sisters of Charity and fathers of the Convent of the Holy Land were staying; it also housed a hospital and an orphanage. At the end of the month, Beaufort announced that he was about to visit Btater, Qabb Elias, Zahleh, and Hammana again. On April 9, he left for a tour of Kisrawan in the north of the Mountain, and on April 21 for another one of the mixed districts in the south and then also visited Sidon and Sur on the coast. In early May he went back for a tour of the north.[73]

The French forces finally found some outlet for their energies in relief and reconstruction work, but the lack of combat was still hard to bear, especially since Beaufort so despised the administrative and military abilities of the Ottomans, and missed no opportunity to say so. Shortly after the troops moved to the Mountain, he boasted that the French had done more cleaning up in a few days than the Ottomans had done in four months. He criticized the Ottomans for not going after fugitive Druzes whom he wanted to chase down. "Everywhere, the Turkish agent was powerless," he noted after a tour of the mixed districts in October 1860. Rarely, did he praise an Ottoman functionary.[74]

Stifled in his ambition to play a major military role, Beaufort turned his attention to the local political situation and tried to interfere with the work of other European officials in Syria. Although it was the French consul general's place to report on local politics and on representatives of the Great Powers or the Ottoman government, Beaufort sent his own reports. He kept the minister of war informed of who was replacing whom in local government, as administrative shuffles began after the war, and of what political setup he thought would be best for the Mountain. Although he was not a member of the international commission, he thought of it as a European one. In October he complained that Fuad Pasha was reorganizing Mount Lebanon when, in Beaufort's opinion, it was the job of the commission to do that. He pushed his favorites for local office, and condemned candidates he disapproved of. He and his officers discussed the reorganization of Mount Lebanon with various commissioners. His views differed from those of the British and, in his opinion, "The project of France is the only one that can insure a future of order and tranquility in Lebanon."[75]

In September 1860, just over a month after his arrival in Syria, Beaufort had already come to the conclusion that Fuad Pasha's objective was to eliminate French influence, not by openly opposing French measures, but by blocking them, creating delays, and putting up obstructions. He repeated the same accusation in January, adding that this had been the intention of his government all along. Beaufort criticized Fuad Pasha for not accepting his military help, complaining that "despite all the advances I have made, despite the excessive moderation which I show in all matters for over six weeks," the pasha "persists in his bad will towards us and one can expect from him neither frankness nor good will." He was certain that "Fuad Pasha's evident goal is to annihilate all action, all influence on our part." He believed that the pasha lied: in the face of persistent reassurances that the situation was under control in Damascus and that his presence there was not needed, Beaufort claimed that Outrey reported that the situation had never been worse.

In March, he reported that at Barouk in the Mountain, Fuad Pasha had assembled Christians and Druzes and reproached the Christian population for taking their grievances to the French, who were not qualified to deal with the affairs of the country. In April and May, he complained again of the impotence, ill will, injustice, and machinations of the Turks.[76] Beaufort blamed Fuad Pasha for much of that inaction and complained of Ottoman ill will and interference. He wrote that the pasha was unable to object openly to his course of action, but he could impede it. He also accused him of trying to undo whatever influence Beaufort had: after Beaufort had toured the Mountain in May 1861, Ottoman agents had, he claimed, visited every locality he had gone to and discounted his message that Europe was responsible for the Mountain's reorganization. Beaufort was certain that Fuad Pasha was also doing his best to hinder the work of the European commission in Beirut. Repeatedly he complained that although he kept the pasha informed of every movement of his troops, the pasha never reciprocated. He could not establish complete authority even within the confines of Mount Lebanon where the French were tolerated, because the pasha established an Ottoman camp every time he established a French one, "no doubt to prove that our presence at this point is becoming useless."[77]

When the French expeditionary force was about to leave Syria in May, Beaufort was still complaining about the lack of military action. On June 1, in a general order to the troops, he congratulated them on their selfless and successful mission and their excellent performance despite poor quarters, lack of amusements, a hard winter, an exceptionally hot summer, and the "inaction that weighed on you." "I do not need to tell you how much I regret not having had the happy opportunity to lead you in combat."[78]

From the moment Beaufort set foot in Beirut to the moment he left, he was frustrated by Fuad Pasha and his subordinates, who preempted as many of his moves as they could to limit French advances. Madame de Perthuis sized the situation up when she wrote: "The fact is that the general de Beaufort is bad tempered (*a de l'humeur*), and will continue to be so, his ambition is not satiated, he arrives too late, the Turkish army arrived before he did and Fuad Pasha, who is not wasting any time, has achieved all the work that he hoped would bring him glory."[79]

As the months went by, Fuad Pasha remained suave toward Beaufort despite his reservations about the French presence in Syria. Although undoubtedly aware that the French were criticizing him and his mission, in September 1860 he wrote to Thouvenel that he had received the latter's two "affectionate" letters and that he welcomed all the benevolence from good friends and honorable men "like yourself" carrying out his burdensome duty. Surely tongue-in-cheek, Fuad Pasha then added, "I had the privilege of meeting General de Beaufort and of appreciating his good and kindly dispositions towards us. He is a man I will very easily get along with, I hope, and what I will do on my end will make him pleased with me."[80]

Fuad Pasha was extremely weary of Beaufort and the expedition he led. He confided in Lord Dufferin, the British commissioner, that the general's impatience made him uneasy. Any premature movement by the French troops could compromise his handling of the Druzes. He could hope only to induce Beaufort to wait until the European commissioners had arrived. Although the French were aware that Fuad Pasha disapproved of their presence and that he had said as much in private,[81] he never said so publicly; that would have been out of character for the polished politician and diplomat. But he checked or undermined Beaufort's plans, kept his distance, and was evasive with his answers whenever the general or his officers confronted him. He gave away as little as possible, discussed as little as possible, ignored all their requests for action, and their hints that French presence was indispensable to tranquility in the Mountain.[82]

Other Ottoman officials shared his feelings. A diplomat stationed in Berlin expressed delight at the news that Fuad Pasha was taking charge of the situation and told a member of the Prussian cabinet that in his opinion the French expeditionary force would find nothing to do but "to applaud Fuad Pasha's conduct and success."[83]

The antipathy between Fuad Pasha and Beaufort trickled down into the ranks on both sides and occasionally resulted in "incidents." An Ottoman officer resigned because Beaufort had somehow hurt his feelings; another was reprimanded for insulting the French vice-consul; two Ottoman soldiers were accused of insulting a French soldier. The French criticized Ottoman ineptitude; the Ottomans accused the French of spreading false rumors.[84] Some of the soldiers were undisciplined and rowdy, and Beaufort issued a general order reminding them that they must follow strict discipline and not forget the dignity of their uniform; he reprimanded them for looting the property of people already in misery.[85]

Beaufort wanted the expeditionary corps to stay beyond its original mandate of six months, Fuad Pasha wanted it to leave. In January and February, Beaufort became extremely worried when he heard that his troops were about to depart. He complained that both Fuad Pasha himself and his Ottoman agents were spreading rumors that the troops were leaving, and he tried to stop the rumors everywhere he could. In March, when the six months were almost up, he ordered two squadrons of light cavalry to go to the valley of the Litani river and Hasbaiya and make a good impression on the region and "to refute the rumors spreading more and more in the interior that, at the request of Turkey backed by England, French troops are leaving Syria." In Beirut, probably much to Beaufort's irritation, the stories continued to circulate, and he reported that they caused such alarm among the Christian population that about 100 families had fled to Greece and the Aegean islands. The officers under Beaufort reported that the Christians were discouraged and the Mountain stirred up over the talk of French departure.[86]

Beaufort had to prove that the French presence was necessary for local stability in order to remain. He mentioned in his reports that there was political ferment, assassinations in the Mountain, the marking of crosses on shops in Beirut's bazaars at night, unrest in and emigration from Damascus, and continued unrest in the Anti-Lebanon. Even when he reported that calm prevailed he judged it deceptive. The Ottoman authorities were intimidating the Christians in some districts. Fuad Pasha was pushing for direct Ottoman rule in the Mountain; the French expeditionary corps would of course discourage that effort.[87]

On his side, Fuad Pasha was resisting all French arguments to prolong their stay. He denied that there was any unrest in the areas where Beaufort and d'Arricau reported it. He no doubt assumed that the French were stirring it up themselves or at least spreading unease to keep themselves there, but he wrote to Beaufort that he thought the rumors were being spread by the small opposition party who were distributing flyers to keep everyone stirred up. They posted placards on the walls and churches of Damascus, spread stories about a prophecy in Beirut, started talk of underhanded dealings. In fact, he said, tranquility prevailed, but he would send Isma'il Pasha on a tour of the Mountain to conduct a rigorous inquiry into the matter and reassure the French. Beaufort criticized Isma'il Pasha's inspection tour as too brief and superficial and accused the pasha of belittling the facts.[88]

Beaufort and Fuad Pasha continued to argue over how restless or calm the countryside was as they jockeyed for position over whether or not the French would stay in the country. Beaufort visited Kisrawan in April and reported Ottoman interference; they were encouraging local divisions that could help them impose their will on the population. The people, Beaufort claimed, were worried at the prospect that the French forces might leave. When he informed Fuad Pasha the pasha replied that the government could not be held responsible for a situation in the north of Mount Lebanon that it could not have prevented and that, in any case, calm would prevail there as elsewhere. Beaufort described the reply as showing "the *impudence* [original emphasis] of the Ottoman authority" in asserting its will and depicting in a favorable light a situation that in reality was deplorable. On April 21, he toured the mixed districts and reported that the situation was very bleak. The Christians of Damascus were worried and the Druzes and Muslims of the Hawran had still gone unpunished for their crimes.[89]

The future of the expedition depended, however, not on two rivals but on the decision-makers in Europe. By the winter of 1861, Napoleon III had no wish to keep his troops in Syria indefinitely, though he did want them to remain there until the international commission had decided on Lebanon's future organization. The French would be given the credit and their presence would appear to have borne results: "Napoleon had gone to the aid of the Maronites and the mission must not appear fruitless."[90] In January, Thouvenel first requested the Great Powers to extend the French mandate. On February 19, at a high level meeting, the British and Ottoman representatives vetoed the French request (it was supported by Russia), because it set no definite date for the departure. The Ottomans proposed May 1 as the terminal date and it was agreed to by all parties. Thouvenel set to work and got it pushed up to June 5. That decision was incorporated in a convention dated March 15, 1861. The French had failed to avoid a definite deadline. As it happened, however, the commission ended its task on May 4, so in effect they had achieved their purpose.[91]

But not Beaufort's. In April, he heard that he had an extension until June 5, and he thought that the French expedition would be "unable to accomplish in the two months left what it has been unable to accomplish in almost eight."[92] As the date of departure approached, the French tried some last-minute efforts to put it off. The foreign colony in Beirut signed a petition to the Great Powers asking for its indefinite prolongation. Beaufort then accused the Ottomans of spreading new rumors. When some 2,700 Ottoman troops disembarked in Beirut in April, Beaufort complained that they told the local Muslims that they had been sent to force the French out if they refused to leave.[93]

Outrey, the French consul in Damascus, voiced Beaufort's frustration when he wrote, "Here we are at the fatal date and the mountain sends us the echoes of its despair." He then mentioned the despair of local Christians at the impending French departure and commented, "I know how much the sight of daily harrowing scenes is painful to us and unfortunately the news from Constantinople is not of a nature to give us solace." He was also irritated by what he saw as the French government's indifference to the situation in Syria: "I do not know by what fatality the question of Syria seems to have become odious to Paris. It is evident that they want to be rid of it at any price." He ended by saying how much he would have liked to shake Beaufort's hand, but that things were too critical for him to abandon his post and take leave of the general.[94]

Others shared the impression that the French government had abandoned the corps. The anonymous author of *Souvenirs de Syrie* wrote that the French expedition was "sacrificed" by Napoleon III to please the British, who wished the occupation to end:

> We say "sacrificed" because the French army had to condemn itself to an almost total inaction, because faced with humiliating suspicions and accusations of all kinds, it was obliged to leave the country without having rendered the services it had been sent from such great distance to accomplish.

The superior officers of this small army, some of whom were of the highest merit, such as general Ducrot and colonel Chanzy, did not hide the painful impressions they took back with them to France.[95]

The last French battalion in the Mountain left on June 7, and Beaufort sent word from this "sad country" (*malheureux pays*) that he and his men were about to depart. "We have no more detachments in the interior," he wrote, "and in three or four days all the Expeditionary Corps will have left Syria." One consolation awaited the general and his men: along the roads on which the troops traveled on their way to Beirut, the Christians and Druzes lined up to greet them and express regrets at their departure. Beaufort commented, "The farewells of the Christians, their despair, their tears, the eager demonstrations of the Druzes themselves are enough proof of the liking that our brave soldiers inspired to all and of the regrets that France leaves behind in this sad country, where the memory of its generous intervention and of the good it has done will never be erased."[96]

Fuad Pasha remained master of the situation until the last French soldier left Syria. Backed by his full powers and the troops at his disposal, with an iron will he had demonstrated that he did not need the French force sent to assist him. Yet till the end he cloaked that will with the impeccable correctness and outward graciousness of a host. On Beaufort's last day in Beirut, the pasha invited the French general to dinner. These farewells could not fail to amuse those present because everyone knew that Fuad Pasha had done all he could to speed the parting French and that Beaufort resented it. Nonetheless, he sat through protestations of regret by Fuad Pasha, who hid his joy in dreary dejection. He even said that it was not those who left who were to be pitied, but those who stayed behind. He then ordered his Ottoman officials to take their leave of the general, and they subjected him to such a battery of farewells that Beaufort was said to cry: "Indeed! I have to hug this one too! We will never finish. Decidedly Fuad Pasha does not want to let me leave!"[97] Beaufort, the first to disembark in August 1860, was the last to embark on June 10, 1861. Until his last hour on Syrian soil he remained a prey to the Ottoman master of politics and a victim of his own vanity and clumsiness.

CHAPTER 6

RETRIBUTION AND THE RESTORATION OF ORDER IN DAMASCUS

The July riots left the Christian quarter of Damascus in ruins. Cyril Graham in a dispatch dated July 26 wrote:

> This afternoon, I went *all through the Christian quarter*, I went into all the finest houses – houses which I had been in a few weeks ago when they were the show houses of Damascus, now nothing but the walls remain in many cases not above 5 or 6 feet high from the ground. In many the bodies lay unburied and the stench generally was horrid for all the wells were full of bodies. I saw a head alone here and there, and limbs lying alone and in one house the dogs were still at work; 2 houses were on fire, only the night before last, I think, the Muslims set fire to some houses. In short *the whole Christian quarter is burned not one house remains untouched*, the only Christian houses which have been saved are those in the Muslim quarters, and all these have been gutted and plundered.

Hasr al-litham records that "nothing was left in the Christian quarter except a head being hit by a hail of bullets coming from the rifles of soldiers, a chest being stumped by the feet of horses, bodies burnt by fire and turned to ashes, and the screams of children and women."[1]

The statistical data are no less extreme. Estimates range so widely that they agree only in conveying a grim picture of the extent of the damage incurred. All inhabitants of the quarter were either dead or had vanished. Estimates of the dead range from 500 to 10,000, but the vast majority of them hover at the mid-point between those two extremes.[2]

Estimates of the damage incurred vary as well, but all agree that it was enormous. According to one report, 1,500 houses were robbed, and only one left untouched; some 200 other houses were plundered but were too close to Muslim houses to be burned; the rest of the quarter – some 1,200 or 1,300 houses in all and every church, school, and convent – was in ruins. Other reports estimate about 3,000 houses in the Christian quarter and another 300 houses in the Muslim quarter were plundered and burned. In September 1860, Robson estimated that the lowest, and perhaps most accurate, estimate of the loss of property was between 300,000 and 400,000 purses (150–200 million piastres, since 500 piastres equaled one purse). The quarter, once so rich and prosperous, had been reduced to "a pile of ashes under which lay thousands of bodies."[3]

The riots also left in their wake a general demoralization of the entire population of Damascus. One of the oldest centers of Arab and Muslim culture had suffered from an outburst of hatred unparalleled in its history as an Ottoman province; Hasibi's efforts to exonerate his family from any role in the massacres reflected the shame and amazement of many Muslims at what had happened. For the Christians who survived, major difficulties lay ahead. The riots had ended, but the problem of how to survive was just beginning.

Most of the Christian refugees in the citadel were women and children, at the sight of whom all, including Fuad Pasha who arrived in Damascus on July 29, were deeply moved. For the first two days, they had insufficient food and little in the way of shelter. When he arrived at the citadel, Dimitri Debbas found thousands and thousands of them in utter despair. It was a sight "like the Day of Judgment" with women screaming, some in labor, most in fear, and wounded men howling from pain. Two days later, the men were separated from the women, and he heard "crying, wailing, farewells, and tumult, like Sodom and Gomorrah." For weeks, the refugees were not supplied with basic necessities – half-starved and half-naked, they survived on coarse bread and cucumbers. Some lived in tents; scores slept on the bare ground, covered with the rags they wore. During the day they endured the relentless summer sun; at night they were exposed to the chill evening air; this combination brought sickness and death. The stench alone was sufficient to make one sick. The survivors clung to anyone who appeared to have any authority. Cyril Graham, who arrived in Damascus with Outrey on July 25, was "nearly torn to pieces" when he went to survey the situation.[4]

There were other threats as well: a Muslim butcher was executed for trying to poison the Christians in the citadel. The Druzes were reportedly threatening to attack it. The refugees did not know where relatives and loved ones were or what the future held in store.[5]

Dimitri Debbas says the refugees would not have survived at all, were it not for three "miracles." The first was that Hashim Agha, the officer in charge of the citadel, was a compassionate man who provided protection and looked after their well-being as best he could. Dimitri goes so far as to accuse Ahmad Pasha, governor of Damascus, of asking Hashim Agha to let the Druzes from al-Maidan "protect," that is to say kill, the Christians in the citadel, but that the agha refused to turn them over, using the excuse that the pasha was a military governor who commanded soldiers, but that he, the agha, was responsible for the citadel which was the property of the sultan, and that he would not deliver over a single person. It is unlikely that such an exchange ever occurred, and even if it did, Dimitri would certainly not have been in a position to hear it. But that such a story circulated among the refugees in the citadel speaks of their trust in Hashim Agha. Dimitri also tells us that the agha closed the gates of the citadel, released its iron chains, placed guards at the entrances, and then went to the top of the citadel and turned the cannons towards the city.

The second miracle was that the Muslim notables of the Maidan quarter sided with the Christians. They assembled the people and warned them not to harm the Christians, lest they themselves be harmed. The third miracle was that Emir Abd al-Qadir and his men also provided the Christians with protection.

A fourth miracle, one that Dimitri did not mention, was the fortitude that enabled him and thousands of other refugees to survive at all. Even under the worst of conditions they struggled on. In a civil war with no heroes and no cause, they were the closest thing to being heroes and to having a worthy cause. History recounts the role of the Ottomans, the French, and other Europeans in settling the peace in Lebanon and Syria in the civil war in 1860, but does not often remind us of the stories handed down from generation to generation, telling of the misfortunes ordinary people endured.

The Christians in the citadel also owed their survival to the impromptu relief measures. So desperate was their condition that there was no time to organize the effort. Lanusse hired a bakery at the expense of the French government to bake bread for people housed at Abd al-Qadir's house and in the citadel. The bakery was still at work when Outrey came to Damascus at the end of July. Outrey himself sent food daily to the citadel to keep the people from starving. By then, it was distributed in an orderly fashion since several churchmen had taken things in hand. A Lazarist father by the name of Najeau and priests from other communities oversaw its distribution. The consulate also provided food for the Christians still living with Muslims around the town and the hundred or so still at Outrey's house. The French consulate had spared no expense either for food or clothing, a precedent set in Aleppo after the riots of 1850 when the French consul was said to have distributed some 200,000 francs (5 million piastres).

The British consulate also helped, but it did not have the resources to do so on a large scale. Brant entreated his government to send more aid when the demands on him became too heavy, but they did nothing in Damascus. In Beirut, however, they supervised the formation of a very active Anglo-American Relief Committee.[6]

At first the local authorities did not have the means to provide relief. On July 16 the new governor Muʿammar Pasha arrived in Damascus to replace the disgraced Ahmad Pasha. He was followed the day after by Khalid Pasha, a general in command of an army division and of the police. The government had in the first days supplied bread and tents, but had since done little because the treasury was empty and neither Muʿammar Pasha nor Khalid Pasha brought money with them. Brant regarded the financial situation as insoluble: "The Christians have nothing left, the Jews have been applied to, but many of the richest I know will scarcely be persuaded to advance what they may have in reserve. The Government has already borrowed nearly all that the capitalists possessed; were confidence fully restored I dare say some might still be found, but the degree of confidence necessary cannot be expected just yet."[7]

Fuad Pasha had all the power, and when he arrived Outrey told him that the French consulate could not continue to feed the refugees. He immediately gave orders that the refugees be given a ration of bread (half an oke or 1⅜ lbs) and that each adult be given a half-piastre (50 paras or 2s.6d.) a day. These were to be distributed under the supervision of committees of Christian notables. That ration seemed adequate to Outrey. Fuad Pasha expressed official regret that the French consulate had been obliged to provide for the victims of the riots, and he offered to reimburse them, an offer which probably was not accepted.[8]

The refugees themselves felt that survival depended on emigration: the best way to help them was to get them out and soon. Even if their security had been guaranteed, they had neither shelter nor the means to resume their lives there. In this they had the sympathy of the European consuls, who also doubted whether Damascus was a safe place for them. On July 16, although calm had been restored, Brant wrote that "after what we have witnessed no one can say that we are safe from one hour to another." Two days later, he wrote that it seemed to be the general determination among both European and local Christians, including the consuls, that they should leave for Beirut as soon as practicable. About the same time, the Russian consul general in Beirut told Outrey that he believed all consulates and their nationals should withdraw to Beirut, and Outrey wrote to Lanusse that he should come with French nationals to the coast, if it became impossible to remain in Damascus.[9]

Outrey considered the possibility of abandoning the French consulate entirely. Before Fuad Pasha arrived in Damascus, Outrey wrote that the

European consuls all impatiently awaited him, but that if he temporized, "we will have to withdraw all the Christians to the coast and ourselves withdraw to Beirut" to await orders from their various governments. He added that he would try to avoid this and that he hoped such a move would not be made in panic. Later, when Beirut began to overflow with refugees, the consuls in Damascus began to discourage people from emigrating, but in late July 1860 they were being encouraged to leave, and the consuls themselves considered departing.[10]

The first caravan of refugees left for Beirut on July 16 or 17 under a Druze and Algerian escort. The first group had been chosen on the basis of connections and money, since Fuad Pasha and Outrey decided that the first convoy should be made up of people who had the means to reach Beirut. Dimitri Debbas, after he learned that the better-off Christians had the advantage, decided to join their caravan. He had no shoes or money, but he acquired the first by stealing them, and went without the second. The caravan he found included most of the notables of the city. They traveled on horseback; Dimitri went with the humbler citizens on foot.[11]

This caravan was soon followed by others, all of them organized with the cooperation of Abd al-Qadir, the consuls, and the Ottoman authorities. At this point, Fuad Pasha did not object to the Christians' emigrating, whether elsewhere in or outside Syria, and made no move to stop them, although he had the authority to do so. Noel Moore, the British consul general in Beirut, wrote that the pasha had even offered a government escort to any refugees in the citadel who wished to leave:

> Fuad Pasha has understood that never will it be possible to convince people who have experienced such horrors to remain in Damascus, where they have no means of livelihood and where time is needed for them to have the courage to start again their activities. For the moment, a total migration is necessary, and little by little, when confidence is restored, undoubtedly they will return on their own, to claim their lands or the ruins of their houses.[12]

Three or four convoys took the refugees to cities along the coast, some possibly even to Cyprus. The Christians left Damascus in thousands. By November, few were left. Despite plans to send them to other cities along the coast however, most of them ended up in Beirut.[13]

Sending the Christians to safety was only one of many problems that faced the government in Damascus. It had also to impose order and punish the guilty and to do so firmly and quickly if public confidence was to be restored. After Mu'ammar Pasha arrived that very evening he notified the population by public crier that the government's authority was restored and that carrying arms was henceforth controlled. The gates of the city were guarded. The city began to return to life. Shops opened, and tradesmen went about their business.[14]

Mu'ammar Pasha's efforts to enforce law and maintain order were not entirely successful. He put Khalid Pasha in charge of the city's police, changed all the guards, and increased the city's patrols, but his new regulations were not enforced. Brant, at first more optimistic than Lanusse, complained about idle talk, groundless fears, and the anxiety of poor, panic-stricken people, but soon he too began to worry that the government was not acting firmly enough. He told the pasha that his orders were not being carried out, that the city's gates were left unguarded, and that strangers walked about in the city armed.[15]

The truth was that Mu'ammar Pasha was in no position to act decisively. He was first of all a newcomer, and knew neither the language nor whom to trust. Consequently, he had to take his time to decide what was the most prudent course. He trusted neither the military nor the civil authorities he found in Damascus. The troops were partly composed of local recruits. He doubted the *majlis* would obey him, although its members had assured him that it would. He trusted only Khalid Pasha and the 2,000 troops who had arrived with him.

Mu'ammar Pasha's concerns were real; he was a prudent and shrewd man, and under less precarious circumstances his careful calculations might have been correct. However, in this volatile and tense atmosphere, quick and decisive steps were needed. When Mu'ammar Pasha did not take them, confidence in him evaporated.[16] Violence was so close to the surface that rumors continued to destabilize the city. It was widely believed that Ahmad Pasha was plotting to kill off the Christians, not only those that remained in Damascus, but in Homs and Hama as well, and that massacres had already occurred in those two cities. It was also rumored that the Ottoman irregular cavalry, mostly Kurds in a garrison at Baalbek, together with Metwalis and Sunnis of the district, had fallen upon the Christians, plundered houses, abused women, driven the people away or made them embrace Islam, and burned 20 churches and two convents.[17]

By Saturday, the suq had closed down, a sure sign that people expected further trouble. Whatever confidence the Christians had gained from the arrival of the pasha had faded. Once more people began carrying arms. When they realized that some of the measures Mu'ammar Pasha had ordered had not been carried out, "the turbulent began to raise their heads and to encourage each other by spreading reports that the Pasha had done and could do nothing." Some began to fear a second massacre. On July 27, the rumor was spread that 70 Christians were plotting to burn the Umayyad Mosque. A number of Christians panicked and ran to the citadel from the Maidan quarter. The city was once again on the brink of war.[18]

The Muslims were also very concerned about the possibility of foreign occupation that had been heightened by the impending French expedition to Syria. A shaykh of the Anaza tribe told Cyril Graham that more bloodshed was unlikely unless there was a foreign occupation, but if that happened, the people from the Hawran and the Arabs would fall upon the town. Graham concurred in this opinion and believed that only Mu'ammar Pasha's arrival prevented the citadel from being the scene of yet another massacre.[19]

The European consuls thought they would be singled out for attack. Even the usually imperturbable Brant, though skeptical that there would be a second massacre, began to explain the riots as a sign of Muslim "fanaticism." Lanusse, Outrey, Bambino, who was the French consular agent in Hama, Robson, and Graham all expected the worst. They never went anywhere unescorted. So far, all they had suffered were occasional insults, but they still were convinced that the Muslims regretted having let them escape. Outrey prepared his consulate for a siege, stocked up on arms, and arranged for Abd al-Qadir to come to his aid in the event of an attack and to keep him informed in the meantime, precautions meant to "insure that the French consulate will not be an easy bargain."[20]

Hope was riveted on the arrival of Fuad Pasha. The Ottoman government instructed its ambassadors to let the Europeans know that the mission had its full support and that French agents in Syria should give him their cooperation. The French ambassador knew that Fuad Pasha would be supported by thousands of troops led by Halim Pasha, and he mentions that they were under Fuad Pasha's orders to stay away from the city until Fuad Pasha himself arrived.

Graham came across this army encamped in the Beqaa valley, and was irritated by the delay,[21] but Fuad Pasha no doubt ordered it to enhance the effect of his own entry into the city, which was indeed a spectacular show of force. He had left Beirut two days earlier, on July 27, with most of his retinue, two battalions, and six pieces of artillery. By the time he reached Damascus, these had joined up with Halim Pasha and his 3,000 troops. "When [he] arrived, all thoughts of resistance disappeared as if by magic, and I do not think I am mistaken when I say the entire city trembles in fear of its just punishment."[22]

Fuad Pasha proceeded to demonstrate to everyone that he had full powers and planned to use them. He told the consuls that he had matters in hand and that interference was unnecessary. He would impose justice and order and would execute everyone found guilty and exile the rest. He would even bomb and set fire to Damascus, if that was what it took.[23] He particularly needed a show of force to impress the French. He did not want the expeditionary force to come anywhere near Damascus and he would do what had to be done in Damascus to stop them. The tactic seemed to work, for Osmont remarked that Fuad Pasha seemed master of the situation.[24]

The pasha also called in all his generals and told them that he would punish anyone who threatened order. He had already used his powers to "imprison one *mushir*, impoverish one *vali*, and put in chains superior officers," and "the first [among you] who will fail to do his duty will be ruthlessly shot."[25] His subordinates knew that he meant every word and that he had declared that he would gun down the population if it dared to revolt against him.[26] Fuad Pasha was equally stern with the *majlis*. They must report the names of all who provoked, or partook in, the massacres and to collaborate in their punishment.[27]

The day after the pasha's arrival all of Damascus was occupied by troops. Military commissions had already been set up to arrest rioters. The consulates were busily drawing up confidential lists of all those whom they knew to have taken part in the insurrection, as were the leading Christian and Muslim citizens in each quarter. These lists became the basis on which the military commissions proceeded to make arrests.[28]

A proclamation issued two days after his arrival announced the pasha's order to the public. In it, he denounced their conduct; ordered all those who had stolen property to hand it over or risk severe punishment; all those who had abducted men, women, or children to give them up, regardless of whether in the meantime they had converted to Islam or married Muslims. No excuse would be accepted for not obeying the proclamation.[29]

The round-up began on August 3, when 330 people were arrested. The number had risen to 500 on August 4, and to 800 by four or five days later.[30] The city's Muslims were in a panic. "Everybody was in alarm," wrote Brant, "and all were clinging to Europeans in order to obtain a good word from them." Those arrested were mainly the lowborn, including petty criminals; Fuad Pasha moved first against them before turning to what he referred to as the "superior social class."[31]

The accused were delivered to an extraordinary tribunal made up of Ottoman functionaries brought from Istanbul. They interrogated the suspects and judged them guilty or innocent. On August 20, 167 people were publicly executed, undoubtedly to instill fear and obedience in the Damascenes. Of those executed, 57 were hanged and displayed for days in the bazaars, and on the streets and gates. The remaining 110, most of these members of the irregular cavalry, were shot.[32]

The Damascenes looked on as the 110 men, tied together and with their arms pinioned behind their backs, were led to a public square called the Green Maidan, west of the nearby Süleyman Mosque, escorted by two battalions of riflemen from the Imperial Guards. They were followed by their women and children, who were not allowed to approach them until they reached their destination. There, still shackled together, they were lined up and given five minutes for their last words to their families and to prepare for death. Their hands were then untied; the two battalions of riflemen were drawn up at a distance of some 15 paces from the men, commanded to face them and, at the appropriate signal from their commander Khalid Pasha, fired. Most of the victims fell, but 30 remained standing. A second discharge brought them down. When a doctor was sent in to check whether everyone was dead, another 30 were found to be still alive. They were shot again, but not before two of them had tried to escape over a high wall. Two cavalry officers caught up with them and cut them down with their swords; it took a second blow to kill one of them, and it broke the soldier's sword in two. When all the prisoners were dead Khalid Pasha retired with his soldiers, leaving behind a small detachment of cavalry to watch the bodies until they had been taken away by the families, some on people's backs, others on biers, and others on pack animals.[33]

Another 145 prisoners were exiled, 186 were put to work on the construction of the road, 83 were condemned to death *in absentia*. A levy of 2,000 men was imposed on the city – by September 8, 1,000 had already been sent to Beirut on their way to Istanbul, since the conscripts were required to serve elsewhere in the empire.

For weeks on end the arrests went on and sentences were carried out. On August 25, 270 men arrived in Beirut on their way to Istanbul to serve a sentence of forced labor. On September 19, the Damascenes woke up to find nine men found guilty of murder hanging in various parts of the city, among them the murderer of the Reverend William Graham. By mid-October, the extraordinary tribunal at Damascus was still carrying out sentences. By early 1861 another 181 had been condemned to death and executed and 146 sent to exile for life.[34]

The men who attacked the Christian quarter were for the most part of the lower and middle classes, judging by a list of the condemned. Certainly they were the ones punished most severely. Of the 181 men on the list, 82 were irregulars (2 of them retired) and 1 an army deserter; 21 were unemployed, 5 were merchants (*négociants*), 2 were identified simply as tradesmen (*marchands*), 1 as a small tradesman, 1 as a cloth tradesman, 1 as a silk tradesman, 1 as a shoe salesman, 1 as a bead tradesman, 1 as a varnisher,

2 as druggists, 1 as a swimmer, 3 as butchers, 1 as a seller of soft drinks, 2 as lemonade sellers, 2 as tobacco salesmen, 4 as farmers, one of whom lived three hours' journey from Damascus, 1 as a carpenter, 4 as gardeners, 3 as barbers, 3 as camel drivers, 1 as a quarter leader, 3 as grocers, 1 as a vegetable salesman, 1 as an engraver, 1 as a wood cutter, 1 as an ophthalmologist, 1 as a police employee, 1 as a dyer, 1 as a bread seller, 2 as *kavas*ses at the Prussian consulate. The remaining 25 were not identified.[35]

They came from the popular quarters of Damascus or from its outskirts; a few were from further away – 35 came from Salihiya, 27 from Bab Tuma, 17 from Qanawat, 19 from Midanat al-Shahm, 11 from Shagur, 9 from Qaymariya, 7 from Suq Saruja, 6 from Bab al-Barid, 5 from Swayqa, 2 each from Bab al-Musalla, Arab Mahallessi, Bab al-Sarija, Amara, Sheikh Darwish, Kfar Mishqi, Uqayba, Bab al-Salam, Maidan Fawqani (Upper Maidan), Wavla or Navla, and 1 each from Kfar Susiya (a village near Damascus), Maidan Tahtani (Lower Maidan), Zuqaq al-Hatab, Qabr Atika, Masjid al-Aqsab, Sakieh, Darwishiya, Zeyer, Djibroun (probably Jirun), and areas simply referred to as Maidan and Chemie (probably Madrasa Shamiya in Suq Saruja). The domicile of 11 is only given as Damascus; and of 3 is not given. Two came from Rashaiya, 1 from Hasbaiya, 1 from Deir (now Beit) Jina.[36]

The 146 exiled men were also mainly lower class. Out of the 146, 91 were jobless or only irregularly employed. Twelve were declared to have no profession. The rest included 4 irregular soldiers, and 1 listed as excluded from military service, 4 druggists, 3 lemonade sellers, 3 sellers of vegetables, 3 confectioners, 3 heads of khans, 2 shoemakers, 2 butchers, 2 grocers, and 1 employee in the coffee house, an eye doctor, a cook, a cloth printer, a maker of boxes, a tobacco tradesman, a linen tradesman, a biscuit tradesman, a tradesman in grapes, a tradesman in nuts, a tradesman in chemical products, a cobbler, a tinsmith, a pastry seller, a farmer, a bricklayer, a customs employee, a horse dealer, a tool maker, and a barber.

They too came from poor quarters in Damascus and from its suburbs and nearby villages. Eighteen were listed simply as from Damascus. Twenty-one came from the Qanawat quarter, 11 from Swayqa, 10 from Midanat al-Shahm, 10 from Bab Tuma, 10 from the lower Maidan (al-Tahtani), 9 from Bab al-Sarija, 8 from Qaymariya, 7 from Qabr Atika, 5 from Amara, 5 from Bab al-Jabiya, 4 from al-Kharrub, 3 from Salihiya, 3 from Uqayba, 2 from Naqqashat, 2 from Shwayra, 2 from Upper Maidan (al-Fawqani), 2 from Djebroun, 2 from Darwishiya, and one from Bab al-Musalla, Masjid al-Aqsab, Makashan, Zuqaq al-Hatab, Taadil, Bab al-Barid, Sharkasiya in Salihiya, Shagur, Jura, and the village of Duma.

A few, the merchants and the doctors for example, may have been men of some means. The historian Abdul-Karim Rafeq has investigated the law-court registers of Damascus and found that among the guilty were people of some status, though not necessarily wealthy. Of five civilians and three military men executed in August 1860, only one was an artisan, the rest were people of means. They included Muhammad Rashid al-Badawi, former head man (*mukhtar*) of the Qanawat quarter, and Mustafa Bey al-Hawasili, a retired army officer who at the time of the riots had been appointed by the governor as commander of 100 local police. Rafeq also discovered that six of the eight were in financial straits and heavily in debt to Christian creditors, suggesting that this provided them with a motive for attacking Christians.[37]

The preponderant role played by lower-class Damascenes in the riots is only part of the explanation for why they made up the majority of those condemned to death or exile. The other is that the government chose to be relatively lenient with the upper class, though they certainly arrested some. In the beginning of August for example, Fuad Pasha told Moore that he would begin to mete out punishment to the influential when he had finished rounding up the mob. True to his word, arrests of the notables began when he had finished the executions of the common people in August. The seizure of the conscripts also continued. Within a month, all the members of the *majlis* and most of the notables had been arrested. By October 26, 230 men had been arrested according to Dufferin, among them were Shaykh Abdallah al-Halabi and other rich and influential men.[38] Once arrested, however, they were treated by the authorities with a deference that was irritating to the Europeans, yet understandable since they carried weight the authorities could not ignore. It was bad enough that they had been arrested at all, and the Ottomans realized that, even if the Europeans did not.

The treatment of Shaykh Abdallah al-Halabi, the most prominent among them, was particularly galling to the Europeans, who believed he had been the principal instigator of the massacre. His house had not been searched, and he received visitors as he pleased (in the opinion of Brant, undoubtedly so that he could "carry out his machinations as if free"). Later he was sent into exile. De Rehfues, the Prussian member of the international commission, complained that Shaykh Abdallah traveled from Damascus to Beirut, not with the other prisoners, but in a "pompous carriage, with a large retinue, and in conditions of comfort which contrast with the usual mode of transport of condemned people." What de Rehfues and other Europeans did not appreciate, and what the Ottoman authorities did, was that the humiliation of arrest was itself sufficient punishment for such a pillar of society.[39]

The authorities were equally careful in their handling of the trials involving notables. To prove culpability was an arduous job. Fuad Pasha insisted on proof, and the European consuls on punishment; the pasha argued that he could find no positive evidence against the notables, and the consuls argued that the evidence they had would have been sufficient to hang any one else. Brant, for example, singles out the Mufti Ghazzi Efendi and Shaykh Abdallah al-Halabi as undeniably encouraging Muslims to commit excesses.

The European consuls could not do much except complain, however. The trials of the notables took place in private, and European observers were in no position to assess the evidence or, for that matter, to know anything of what went on. Brant thought they were so obviously guilty that no evidence against them was needed, and he acknowledged that hard evidence was difficult to come by. He commented that some people thought that the pasha could have been less scrupulous and settled for the evidence he had, as it was difficult to obtain all the evidence required under law. He speculated that Fuad Pasha had not anticipated how difficult it would be to obtain proof, nor the number of respectable people who thwarted his efforts at every step. He added: "Although it is certain that above 5,000 persons have been massacred in broad daylight or by the light of blazing houses, yet nobody will testify to having witnessed a murder committed, or will recognize a single man guilty of such a crime."[40]

In mid-October, Abro Efendi informed the European commission in Beirut that despite the most meticulous inquiries, no proof whatsoever could be found to condemn the notables, and that in the absence of such proof perpetual exile was the most serious punishment they could justify. In another session of the commission, he reiterated the same point and added that the only guilt firmly established was that the notables had done nothing to prevent the riot. On October 19, the members of the *majlis*, who earlier had been let out of confinement on parole, were taken in custody once again. They included Abdallah al-Azm, Abd al-Qadir Hamza, and Abd al-Hadi al-Umari. They, together with the mufti Umar al-Ghazzi, Ahmad al-Hasibi, Ali al-Azm, Abdallah Bey (al-Azm), son of Nasuh Pasha, all of the *majlis*, and Shaykh Abdallah al-Halabi – 13 men in all – were sent to Beirut under military guard, on their way to prison in Cyprus.[41]

Punishing officers of the Ottoman army suspected of having been involved in the riots was another delicate matter. The arrest and condemnation of irregulars and low-ranking army recruits had been swift and had generated no controversy. That of their superior officers, however, involved assigning ultimate responsibility for the massacres; it also was mixed up with struggles for influence within Ottoman circles as well as between Ottomans and Europeans.

The case of Ahmad Pasha illustrates the problems well. The pasha's motives are known to us principally through his critics, since the Ottoman archives on the civil war have not been fully explored. But we do know that although after the event, the Ottoman government, European representatives, and local sources all denounced the pasha, before the riots they were more divided in their assessment of his role. From early June, Lanusse mistrusted his intentions, basing his suspicions on information gathered from influential men. Lanusse and others around him – probably Abd al-Qadir among them – were convinced that Ahmad Pasha wanted the Damascene Christians destroyed and he wanted the Muslims to be blamed for it, discredited, and accused of fanaticism. According to this theory, Ahmad Pasha had been trying to arouse the Muslim populace against the Christians long before the riots, and was also plotting to allow the Druzes into Damascus so they too could attack the Christians. Then he would lock himself in the citadel and bomb the city. According to another version, Ahmad Pasha was accused by the French of plotting a massacre and making it known to the European consuls that he believed France, specifically Lanusse, and Russia had provoked the civil war in Lebanon.[42]

Brant, who seemed to have advised and cooperated with Ahmad Pasha, dismissed Lanusse's accusations. He alleged no ill will on Ahmad Pasha's part, though he did find him weak and indecisive, and therefore disregarded the warnings about a massacre and the rumors about the role in it that Ahmad Pasha would assume. It must have cost him a great deal after the riots to have to admit that the pasha's actions during the riots gave "at least plausibility to the opinion strongly maintained by some that the whole affair was a plot of his [Ahmad Pasha's] contrivance." Although Brant still would not admit to a plot, "so many reasons and facts are adduced that my reason is staggered and I must suspend coming to a decision until a rigid examination of the facts has been made, and competent witnesses [have] made their depositions."[43]

In the summer of 1860 Ahmad Pasha's influence did not match his power, and his relations with the population were ambivalent. He enjoyed some popularity among the Damascene populace, particularly in the beginning of his tenure. Mishaqa tells us that when he was appointed governor in 1860, "he got along very well with everyone," and Lanusse implies that the pasha had some influence over the people. Tensions seem to have developed quickly, however, between Ahmad Pasha and the city's notables. The well-connected and influential Abd al-Qadir mistrusted him and warned the French against him. Members of the *majlis* also seem to have had their differences with him. Lanusse tells us that in vain the *majlis* tried to warn the pasha about the impending catastrophe, but that he refused to listen. Brant also heard from Lanusse that the *majlis* mistrusted the pasha and that the feeling was mutual.[44]

Personal considerations reportedly lay behind this mutual distrust. Lanusse claimed that Ahmad Pasha's father-in-law, Selim Pasha, had been killed by the Damascenes while he was governor of the city 30 years earlier, and Ahmad Pasha wanted revenge. Brant complained that this legend had been widely circulated by Lanusse and other French emissaries, but he dismissed it as a "mere fabrication," adding that Ahmad Pasha never even had a father-in-law named Selim Pasha, that the pasha's wife had been dead many years, that he never remarried, and that his family at that time consisted of his mother and two sons. Lanusse, however, may not have started the rumor, as Brant accused him of doing, but picked it up from the Damascenes. Dimitri Debbas gives a variation of the story when he says that Ahmad Pasha sought the destruction of Damascus "because, according to hearsay, his maternal uncle was Selim Pasha who was killed by the Damascene Muslims." Dimitri was not particularly well connected to European circles in Damascus, so the rumors he heard also probably originated among the Damascenes.[45]

A more immediate and likely cause for animosity between Ahmad Pasha and the Damascene notables may have been, as Lanusse told Brant, that the notables had complained about Ahmad Pasha's rule and tried to get him recalled, and that the pasha had sought revenge on the Damascenes for this betrayal. Ahmad Pasha's relations with the Ottoman government were also not good. Bulwer, the British ambassador to the Porte in 1860 was later to write, "It would seem that he [Ahmad Pasha] was at the time on bad terms with the government at home, having offered his resignation when some troops had been withdrawn from him, and his resignation having been accepted." Discrediting the government may thus have been another motive for stirring up trouble.[46] Before the riots, then, Ahmad Pasha's appointment in Damascus was in fact coming to an end, and his relations both with the Damascenes and with the Ottoman government were probably strained.[47]

What is certain is that Ahmad Pasha did little to prevent the violence once it began, and the few measures he took made things worse. The irregular troops selected to guard the Christian quarter were lawless and rowdy men recruited in Syria. Their fellow recruits were rumored to have looted and killed in the Lebanon and Anti-Lebanon, and they were more a source of danger than protection. Twenty days before the riots Ahmad Pasha and the *majlis* appointed "some worthless fellows and base people" as officers and policemen. They in turn collected a number of "the lowest and basest fellows," supplied them with arms, and appointed them to guard the Christian quarter, an action that encouraged the Damascenes to prepare for an uprising, rather than deterring them from it.[48]

When Ahmad Pasha had cannons mounted at the gate of the Umayyad and other mosques, that too stirred up Muslim hostility against the Christians, because it suggested the Muslims were in danger from Christian treachery; the pasha's actions made Muslims wonder about Christian intentions and created "a great doubt."[49]

Other measures were simply not taken at all. The seven gates of Damascus were left unguarded despite the numbers of Druzes gathered outside the city. A cannon and 50 men at each gate would have sufficed to keep them there. Brant says that after the riots the pasha had boasted about his secret police, but when Brant asked the pasha why they had not informed him of the "plots" in town, the pasha had no answer. The historian Gökbilgin notes that the pasha could have gone with the members of the *majlis* to the Christian quarter to restrain the attackers, but that he did not even go as far as the gate of his own citadel which was 100 feet away from him. He also tells us that after the riots Fuad Pasha found out that Ahmad Pasha had not called in troops stationed in the Hawran because they might have looted provisions, but even that would have been far preferable to the loss of life that took place.[50]

Why Ahmad Pasha did not try harder to safeguard the city is a matter of speculation. To those who believe he was preparing a massacre, the answer is obvious: a weakly defended city was an advantage. On the other hand, if the pasha was innocent of such designs, why did he not take precautions when he himself claimed that the European powers were plotting to provoke civil war in Syria? When Brant asked him this question, he answered that "it would have been useless as the plot was prepared, and had not this pretext been found some other would have served the purpose."[51]

Other more practical considerations may have played a role. The troops at the disposal of the authorities in Damascus were perhaps insufficient for the purpose, though the idea that there were only 400 was rejected by Moore, the British consul general in Beirut, after the riots. It was "understated rather than the contrary," Moore claimed, that in the two *pashaliks* of Beirut and Damascus there could have been no less than 4,000 Ottoman regulars, and that in Damascus alone, there were some 1,500 regular troops, cavalry, and infantry, and as many irregulars. Moore's statement was undoubtedly in part a reaction to the post-civil war tendency to underestimate the number of troops in Syria in an Ottoman effort to clear its forces of responsibility for the civil war.[52]

In contrast to Moore's calculations after the war, Lanusse and Brant remarked on how few troops there were in the city, as early as June, and the troops had been further depleted just before the riots broke out; some had been sent to Mount Lebanon and others had left for the *hajj*. The story that surfaced after the riots that differences had developed between Ahmad Pasha and the Ottoman government over the withdrawal of troops from his command – the same differences that reportedly had occasioned the pasha's removal from his post – also suggest that the forces in Damascus were inadequate.[53]

Internal security was probably poor as well. The commanding officer in Damascus was sometimes in charge of internal security, as was Khalid Pasha, for example. How it operated before the riots is, however, unclear. Sources mention an officer who functioned as a chief of police and captains, officers, and subordinates appointed arbitrarily, but people seemed to regard them more as a danger than as protection. There also may have been a secret police. It was mentioned once by Brant, but none of the French ever referred to it.[54]

The ability of the troops in Damascus to maintain order was further undermined by where they were stationed. Most of the regular troops were billeted in the serai where Ahmad Pasha's headquarters were located, which deprived the rest of the city of protection. Brant wrote that the pasha kept the most reliable soldiers there, to ensure his own safety, and sent the less dependable irregular troops to guard the Christians. He was afraid of the irregulars and wanted to keep them some distance away. This fear in itself constituted yet another source of weakness in the city's defenses, since any mistrust between commander and troops can only increase the inefficiency of both.[55]

That Brant could even suggest that Ahmad Pasha was afraid of his own troops provides another reason why Damascus was so inadequately protected. The pasha was a poor leader. He did not get along with the *majlis*, the consuls, or the soldiers in his charge. At best, he was indecisive, a fatal shortcoming under duress because it creates the impression that no one is really in command. He sent mixed signals to those around him, and his pronouncements did not support his actions: he promised to send troops to help the Anti-Lebanon and did nothing; he claimed the Europeans were plotting in Syria but did nothing about that either; he vacillated between assuring the people that there was no danger and implying that civil war was imminent.

The cumulative effect of this equivocal and inconsistent language and conduct was to allow the lawless to assume they could get away with murder, encourage speculation about the pasha's real intentions, and generate what Brant acknowledged to be "a general distrust of His Excellency." Even if the pasha was innocent of any plan to attack the Christians, he certainly did nothing either to prevent it or to establish trust among local leaders. On the other hand, if he planned the outbreak, he failed to anticipate all its ramifications and did not protect himself with a better display of efficiency or neutrality. In the end, however, although his willful participation in the riots cannot be proved, there is no doubt that he was a weak man, unable to cope with crisis or, for that matter, to do anything, whether for good or evil, effectively.[56]

Whether by design or neglect, Ahmad Pasha had been involved in the humiliation of the Ottoman state and had been in part responsible for European interference. Fuad Pasha, however, had to weigh that point against the dangers of admitting to the world that responsibility for what had happened ultimately lay with an Ottoman official just at the time when he was convinced that the European powers were eager to use the massacres as an excuse for interfering further in the affairs of the empire. In addition, although Fuad Pasha was perfectly aware of Ahmad Pasha's failures during the riots, he also knew of Ahmad's record before his appointment in Syria and of his reputation as an able commander: he had been one of the first officers of the general staff and served as director at the war academy, which won him the nickname of "Nazir" ("minister," but here it means director); then, in 1854, as chief of the general staff of the Rumelia army with the rank of general, he had distinguished himself in war against Russia. Fuad Pasha had known Ahmad Pasha for years, and that must have made it difficult to participate in his downfall.[57]

Fuad Pasha started his mission in Syria by showing very little sympathy for Ahmad Pasha. When he first arrived in Syria in July, he ordered Ahmad to come to Beirut to surrender. When Ahmad arrived, he had already made two tactical errors. He came in the company of Osman Bey and Muhammad Ali Bey, the officers who had commanded the garrisons of Hasbaiya and of Rashaiya during the massacres there, and he introduced them to Fuad Pasha as men of distinction. Fuad Pasha ordered them to be taken away and interrogated. Then in a desperate gesture Ahmad Pasha threw himself at Fuad Pasha's feet in a bid to win his sympathy. He said that he was concerned over the pasha's safety in Damascus. Abro Efendi, who witnessed the interview, thought that Ahmad Pasha was a coward who was behaving stupidly, an opinion which Fuad Pasha must have shared. Dissatisfied with Ahmad Pasha's answers, Fuad Pasha ordered his arrest, took his sword away from him, and sent him off to Istanbul for trial.[58]

Sending Ahmad Pasha to Istanbul may have been a gesture of clemency. At least it upset the Europeans who were afraid that Ahmad Pasha would be judged more leniently in the Ottoman capital than he would have been in Damascus. It is also just possible that Fuad Pasha was less interested in protecting Ahmad Pasha than he was in giving the Ottoman government a chance to investigate whether the massacres had their origin in an opposition group. Outrey, for one, believed in the conspiracy theory and argued against Ahmad Pasha's execution because the death of the pasha would eliminate the only known link with it.[59]

Whatever the rationale, the Ottoman government did not take advantage of it; they stripped him of his rank, threw him out of the army, and sent him back to Syria for trial. Bulwer reports that he was unpopular at the Porte and that in Ottoman circles he had always been regarded as a coward, not "the usual defect of a Turk." However, that does not explain how Ahmad Pasha had been appointed governor of Damascus and commander of the army in the first place. Clearly, he must have had some support in Ottoman circles but, just as clearly, he must have lost it. After the riots, he had also alienated people by blaming others.[60]

On the evening of August 15 he was back in Damascus. When he was brought before the council which questioned him that evening and the following days, he was addressed simply as Ahmad Agha. The trial itself took place behind closed doors. The secrecy surrounding it provoked speculation, but resulted in no public revelations either about the causes of the massacres or about Ahmad's role in them. According to Bulwer, Fuad Pasha expected to find out "whether the outbreak was a plot concocted long beforehand or whether it was only suppressed fanatical feeling which burst out through the occurrence of purely accidental circumstances." Whether he discovered anything or not is not known.[61]

By the beginning of September, with the sentence against Ahmad not yet pronounced, it had become apparent that Fuad Pasha was reluctant to sentence him to death. He admitted to Dufferin that Ahmad deserved the death penalty but he nonetheless argued against it on the grounds that his conduct as governor had been exemplary before the riots. During the trial, Moore had been skeptical that Ahmad would ever be executed, because such a punishment would shock the Muslim people as well as the army. However, what was at issue was not Ahmad's local popularity, which was nonexistent, or the Ottoman ability to execute a senior officer for reasons of state – that principle had its place in sultanic law – but rather the predicament of giving the death penalty to an officer who, until the riots, had had a distinguished record. Perhaps, Fuad Pasha's hesitation reflected the sensitivity of the situation, as well as distress at the fall of an old colleague.[62]

Fuad Pasha also had to take into account European pressure in favor of the death penalty. Without it European meddling would only increase. Dufferin made a special trip to Damascus to persuade the pasha, arguing that the greater the vigor he showed, the weaker the excuse for the European commissioners to usurp his authority. That argument, or Dufferin's pressure, or a combination of both must in the end have seemed more pressing than his own preference. He decided in favor of the death penalty.

On Friday, September 7, at a meeting over which he presided, the military tribunal in Damascus ordered that Ahmad Pasha, Osman Bey, who had commanded the garrison at Hasbaiya, Muhammad Ali Bey, who had commanded (*binbashi*) the garrison at Rashaiya, and Ali Bey, who had been in charge of the Christian quarter during the riots, be executed by firing squad. At the same meeting, another Muhammad Ali Agha, who had been second in command at the garrison at Hasbaiya, was discharged and sentenced to life imprisonment.[63]

The execution of Ahmad Pasha and his colleagues was not public, like that of low-ranking army officers, but there were spectators. They were shot in the barracks square. Ahmad Pasha was said to have commented that his blood could be claimed if that solved the troubles of the government, and to have died with a courage that in his governorship he had been accused of lacking. He calmly said his prayers on the place of execution and asked to have his hands and eyes free. His request was denied; his arms were pinioned, his eyes bandaged, and he fell dead upon the first volley discharged.[64]

The execution of Ahmad Pasha and his fellow officers established beyond doubt how far the government was ready to go to punish those involved in the riots. The people who witnessed the execution wept and others shared their feelings. Abd al-Razzaq al-Bitar, in his biographical dictionary of Damascus, referred to the pasha as *al-shahid* (the martyr), and Isma'il Hami Danişmend, a modern Turkish biographer, described him as an honorable soldier who was the victim of state necessity. Beaufort commented that the execution of Ahmad Pasha, three colonels, and a major of the army of Syria made a deep impression on the whole country. It was also a turning point. From then on, army officers accused of crimes were treated more leniently. The trials of the accused in the Mountain, which took place months after those in Damascus, showed that the government was much more reluctant to deal harshly with the Druzes. Many had their sentences commuted.[65]

Fuad Pasha also argued in favor of prison terms or leniency for a number of commanding officers brought to trial and found guilty. In July of 1860, the pasha arrested three officers, Abdul Salam Bey, the lieutenant colonel who commanded the garrison at Deir al-Qamar, Havis Agha, a major under him, and the lieutenant colonel at Beit al-Din. The tribunal in Damascus ordered the death sentence, but the execution was postponed on the grounds the guilty could help build the case against other Druzes.[66]

In the same month, Khurshid Pasha, governor general of Sidon at the time of the civil war, was arrested and replaced by Admiral Mustafa Pasha. To the surprise – not to say disapproval – of the European commissioners, Fuad Pasha sent Khurshid Pasha to Latakia from where he was to go on to Istanbul for trial. But Khurshid, like Ahmad Pasha, was sent back. He was tried in Beirut by a special tribunal in September.

Dufferin found this tribunal more trustworthy than the one sitting in Damascus, possibly because it was more open to British influence. It was presided over by the new governor general of the Sidon province, another Ahmad Pasha, who had earlier served as governor of Smyrna and who had the reputation of being both able and honest. It was composed of Admiral Mustafa Pasha, the mufti of Beirut, Abro Efendi, Hamid Bey, an accountant for the province, and Hasan Bey.

In November, Fuad Pasha asked Dufferin whether the international commission would intercede for the commutation of Khurshid Pasha's sentence, should he be found guilty and condemned to death. Dufferin was surprised that Fuad Pasha wanted to save Khurshid Pasha's life, and he advised him against protecting a man whose guilt was so universally recognized. Fuad Pasha, however, must have found other ways to lighten Khurshid Pasha's sentence. In December, the tribunal, having heard Khurshid Pasha's defense against all accusations, found him guilty of failing to suppress disorder rather than of causing it. He was sentenced to life in prison.[67]

Three other officers were also condemned to life imprisonment. They were Tahir Pasha, military commander of the armed forces under Khurshid Pasha; Süleyman Nuri Bey, a colonel sent to rescue Zahleh which he never reached; and Ahmad Efendi, controller of property at Beirut and agent representing the Druzes and the Christians to the local government. In addition, one Ali Wasfi Efendi was sentenced to prison, deprived of his rank, and dismissed from public service. These sentences were lighter than those of the leading Druzes whom the same tribunal condemned to death, although eventually they, too, ended up with lighter sentences. Other officers were either given light sentences, or exonerated. One Shakir Pasha, for example, was acquitted in Damascus by the same military tribunal that condemned Ahmad Pasha to death. Lower-ranking officers were probably able to get away with lighter sentences because they carried out orders and because they did not arouse the same scrutiny and interest among the European commissioners that their superiors received.[68]

The merciless punishment of the common people and the more lenient treatment of the guilty notables and high-ranking officers were the most obvious, but not the only, signs of the government's determination to reassert its control over the country and of how far it was prepared to go to do so. In Damascus Khalid Pasha had the streets patrolled at night and ordered that lanterns be hung in front of the houses at regular intervals. The gates of the quarters were repaired and the entrances to the city closely guarded. The troops were on semi-alert: half of them slept while the other half patrolled the city under orders to fire at the slightest sign of trouble. The artillery was kept in readiness. Colonel Gessler, a Prussian artillery instructor in the Ottoman service, said that no officer could have carried out his duties better than Khalid Pasha.[69]

The authorities also tried, but with less conviction, to disarm the Damascenes. In November 1860, notice was posted that all arms were to be brought to a collection point and that a fine and six months' imprisonment would be inflicted on those who did not comply. The measure was only partly successful. Only a small portion of the population complied. Fuad Pasha expressed his determination to enforce disarmament, but he did not act as if he meant it. No measures were taken to ensure its implementation, which would in any case have been extremely difficult. The pasha may have been confident that the city was under control, or he may have decided to spare its population further humiliation. Disarmament did not even have the support of some. The Algerians who had protected the Christians during the riots partly because they had the arms to do so, argued against it. Their French supporters considered taking arms away more likely to cause trouble than to quell it. In any case, by December, disarmament was, for all practical purposes, forgotten.[70]

As order was restored, Fuad Pasha turned to other problems. From the start, his agenda in Damascus had included compensation for the victims and reconstruction of the Christian quarter. He turned his attention to these matters with the same energy he had displayed in reestablishing order. Immediate palliatives were also required before these could be tackled. He took several emergency measures. He made medical help available. A military school was turned into a hospital for Christian women, and the army hospital kept for other sick and wounded. A commission was created to distribute food and money to the Christians. A regulation posted on August 15 ordered all the population to hand over to the authorities Christians – some 500 by one estimate – who had been forced to embrace Islam; failure to comply was punished by death. These Christians were now required to resume their original faith.[71]

An entire Muslim quarter of the city was evacuated in July, after Fuad

Pasha arrived, to vacate 80 houses for Christians whose own homes had been destroyed. In September three more Muslim quarters were put at the Christians' disposal after they had been evacuated and placed under guard. A house was made available to serve as a church for all Christian denominations.[72] Houses only partially damaged were repaired and made available to Christians. Four to five hundred houses in need of repair, about half of which belonged to Christians and the rest to Muslims, were fixed up and turned over to them.[73]

The Christians did not all take advantage of these measures, however. Some preferred not to stay in Damascus. When Fuad Pasha offered to move the Christians in the citadel to private houses, they at first declined. But as time went on and news of the hardships involved in traveling to the coast began to trickle back to those still in the citadel, some had second thoughts. The government also began to discourage emigration. In late August, it announced that it would stop furnishing pack animals and horses to Christians leaving for the coast. By late November, Christians had to have permission to leave, though some departed clandestinely. In the end, perhaps a few thousand Christians remained and took advantage of the houses put at their disposal. In the first week of September, they were settling into them. By September 20, no refugees were left in the citadel.[74]

Although orders had also been given to clear the Christian quarter, it lay in ruins, with corpses and rubble in collapsed houses and streets blocked with wreckage that in some places had accumulated as high as six feet. It was not until December – and only then because Fuad Pasha was imminently expecting a visit from the European commissioners – that 1,000 laborers and 200 animals were put to work. Many of the streets were cleared, and the corpses buried in the Christian burial ground outside town.[75] In January, Fuad Pasha called on the Christians to form a general commission or council to superintend building operations. This council under the supervision of Şirvanizade Mehmet Rüstü Pasha, a member of Fuad Pasha's mission, was composed of eight Christian delegates from the various denominations, a spokesman for the Greek Orthodox and Catholic patriarchates of Damascus, two Muslims not compromised during the riots and chosen by the Christians, a staff officer of the army, and an architect. The council was constituted after some difficulties and in April the work was about to begin on the first project, a block of houses belonging to the poor. Christian superintendents and laborers were to do the the work, and the government was to furnish all the material required for reconstruction. Some 130,000 trees had already been cut to supply timber, and the costs of the project were to be charged to the general indemnity fund, instead of to the owners of houses.[76] By October, houses were still in short supply and the Christian quarter still not rebuilt. Fuad Pasha suggested that Christians of the various rites meet with the commission to decide how to speed things up. In one day, the commission questioned 18 of them. The solution was to set up four commissions, so that decisions could be made about the number of houses to be built and work could go on simultaneously in different parts of the Christian quarter. Each commission had six members: one notable and two architects each from the Christian and from the government side; the Christian members were selected by the whole community. Under this system, the Christians interviewed by the commission had estimated that the work could be completed in about 30 days.[77]

None of the problems created by the riots were resolved quickly or easily, largely because they involved expenses which the government could not afford. The distribution of bread and cash to refugees in itself amounted to five or six million piastres a month. A list of the funds distributed to Christians in August 1860 amounted to 1,289,933 piastres; 323,015 piastres of which were distributed to 5,536 Damascene refugees; 157,667 piastres to 4,944 refugees from Deir al-Qamar, Hasbaiya, and Rashaiya; 207,251 piastres for miscellaneous expenses including those of the imperial hospital lodging 1,200 to 2,000 people; and 600,000 piastres to Damascene Christians (probably the bread and cash rations). By the first week of October, however, the allowance of money to the Christians was much in arrears and many had not received anything for 20 days, a situation that recurred in February 1861, and no doubt at other times as well. The excuse given for the delay was that the public treasury was empty, an explanation Brant found believable. So did Dufferin, "In as much as Fuad Pasha is absolutely penniless and whatever sum he can scrap together would be insufficient even to roof the Villages of the Lebanon."[78]

In the absence of money, the solution the government came up with was to seize stolen property and give it back to its owners, not as reparations but as a relief measure. In the three Muslim quarters evacuated to lodge Christians, looted objects including blankets and other necessities were seized and distributed to Christians. The requisition of stolen property continued even after Fuad Pasha left for Beirut in early September 1860. In early November, numerous stolen objects had been repossessed.[79]

When the stolen goods ran out, Fuad Pasha turned to Muslim property. The bedding shortage was remedied by requisitioning 2,000 to 3,000 mattresses from the Muslims. This partially solved the shortages, but by December the Christians were still very badly supplied with beds and with charcoal, which the government could only distribute in small quantities.[80]

Although the recovery of plundered goods helped solve some immediate problems, it also helped generate some new ones. Fuad Pasha claimed at one of the meetings of the international commission that confiscation was contrary to the laws of the empire and, consequently, that he needed the approval of the central government to carry it out. It is difficult to believe that Fuad Pasha was under any such restriction: after all, he had claimed full powers when it suited him. More likely, he used this tactic to limit the amount of confiscation that went on, as the pressure from the European commissioners to extract more and more from the Muslim population continued unabated.[81]

Recovering plundered goods also raised problems of distribution and assessment. It was in the government's interest to set the value of returned property high, because that lessened the amount of compensation owed; it was in the interest of the victims to do the opposite. There also was no way of ascertaining whether those claiming the goods had ever actually owned them, and that contributed to tension within the Christian community. People with influence were given the best things at fair prices; the poor received worthless goods at exorbitant prices or else declined to accept them. That generated dissatisfaction toward the government as well.[82]

Since efforts to pay the Christians in goods were only partially successful, it became even more imperative to try to find ways to raise cash. That was, however, easier said than done, given the poverty of the central treasury and the collapse of confidence in the economy of Damascus. It required difficult and approximate assessments of the financial resources of the Damascenes; long and arduous deliberations of the international commission; slow and patient behind-the-scenes negotiations among Fuad Pasha, commissioners, Damascene Muslims, and other groups.

One of the problems was to determine who was eligible for indemnities. Three categories of recipients were established: Christian subjects of the Ottoman empire, whether or not they enjoyed the status of Great Power protégés, foreigners with losses of real property, and religious institutions. The next problem was to determine how to pay it. The commission considered two methods: payment in one lump sum to be determined somewhat arbitrarily, and payment on a case-by-case basis to determine how much indemnity to allocate to each individual. The second option seemed to present insurmountable difficulties, and the first promised the advantages of quick payments, so the commission adopted it.[83]

The commission then had to decide how large that lump-sum payment should be. After much deliberation, it recommended to the Sublime Porte that 150,000,000 piastres constitute the settlement of the Damascene indemnities, to be divided among the victims. In a protocol of March 5,

1861, the Sublime Porte approved the commission's plan according to a classification made in proportion to their losses. At the same time, it excused itself from paying more than 75,000,000 piastres – half the sum – because of budgetary constraints.[84]

Although Fuad Pasha had at first acquiesced to the total indemnity recommended by the commission to the Porte, he had second thoughts about it in the summer of 1861, probably in large part because of the government's share of the burden. The European commissioners believed that 150,000,000 piastres was a moderate and reasonable amount, but Fuad Pasha was determined it would be lower. While the European commissioners were in Istanbul, he met with a group of Damascene Muslims and Jews who complained that the indemnity was too high and that the Christians' losses did not amount to more than about 45,000,000 piastres, a figure in sharp contrast to the one the Christians gave.[85]

In the summer of 1861, E.J. Rogers, who had replaced Brant as British consul in Damascus, asked representatives from the various Christian sects to estimate their losses. In an admittedly exaggerated estimate, they assessed their total losses in moveable and immoveable property at no less than 200 million piastres, including churches and convents, and about half that sum if church losses were excluded. The estimate was based on the state of their property at the time of the outbreak and it also included a considerable amount of stolen property. From that amount, about 50,000 purses could be deducted for the value of water, ground, and houses only partially destroyed.[86] Fuad Pasha chose to believe the Damascene Muslims and Jews, and settled on the sum of 45,000,000 piastres. If the Christians refused to settle for that amount, he would require them to submit proof of greater value to commissions composed of both Christian and government representatives.[87]

The Ottoman government and the commission then had to figure out how to raise the indemnity. One way was to sell exemption fees for 20,000 piastres to Muslims wishing to avoid military service. To be eligible one had to belong to a "noble" family and not be among the levy of 2,000 recruits imposed on Damascus after the riots.[88] A more promising method was to find ways to tax the Damascene population. The commission imposed a special fine on those in any way compromised in the riot and an extraordinary tax on non-Christian property. The latter applied to all non-Christians, whether or not they had taken part in the riots.

In the spring of 1861, Fuad Pasha issued proclamations to the inhabitants of the *pashalik*. The city was to provide 25,000 purses, of which 16,500 would be imposed as an extraordinary general tax and 8,500 would be collected from people believed to have participated in the massacres.

From this amount, the government would deduct 7,000 purses which the city had already provided, either in kind or in cash, broken down into 2,000 purses for the clearing of the Christian quarter, 4,500 purses for the value of trees used for lumber, and 500 purses already collected as part of the general extraordinary tax. The balance – 18,000 purses – was to be collected at once. To achieve that, the local government divided Damascus into eight quarters, and appointed special councils for each in charge of assessing the criminal tax and making sure every house contributed to it equitably. All Christians and any Muslims known to have aided Christians were absolved from payment.[89]

The rest of the *pashalik* was levied 35,000 purses; 4,328 from Baalbek; 4,861 from al-Jaydur; 8,229 from Jabal Druze; 2,441 from Hasbaiya; 1,761 from Rashaiya; 2,167 from Hama; 433 from Homs; 275 from Hosn al-Akrad; 216 from Marj (Maarrat?) al-Numan; 475 from Qnaitra; and 118 from Iki Kabouli. From these sums, the government would deduct expenses already incurred by these areas for relief, wood, support of the troops, or payments already made towards the extraordinary tax.[90]

The apportionment of this fine had been heatedly debated for months, both inside and outside the commission, before these figures were agreed upon. As with the overall indemnity, the sum proposed by Fuad Pasha was much lower than what was proposed by some of the European commissioners. In August 1860, the pasha told a group of Damascene Muslims that he would impose a fine of 25,000,000 piastres; in the fall of 1860, he argued in front of the commission in favor of a fine of 35 million piastres (£291,000 or 7 million French francs).[91]

This last sum was based on one of the budgets prepared for discussion before the commission. It had been drawn up by a Christian Damascene who estimated that the city had some 13,356 Muslim households; 7,600 Muslim-owned shops or coffee houses; 58 public baths; 73 mills; 22 khans; and 669 gardens. By imposing a tax of 1,000 piastres per house, 750 piastres per shop, 10,000 piastres per bath, 2,000 piastres per mill, 15,000 piastres per khan, and 2,000 piastres per garden, it would be possible to collect 21,450,000 piastres. In addition, a contribution of 13,550,000 piastres could be collected from wealthy people, on the basis of reliable approximations of their incomes. In all, the 35 million piastres proposed could be collected.[92]

The European consuls and commissioners argued for much higher fines. Brant believed that £5 million sterling (625 million piastres) would scarcely cover the destruction and loss of property; Dufferin, an influential member of the commission who on the whole tended to be closer to Fuad Pasha's positions than the other commissioners, suggested £250,000 (31,250,000 piastres). De Rehfues, the Prussian commissioner, was convinced that Damascus, a rich city, together with Mount Lebanon and Sidon, could raise 100 million piastres. Beclard, a French colleague, at first supported him and argued that the fine should fall mostly on the rich, but changed his mind after consultation with Outrey on the city's resources and called for an indemnity of 35 million piastres collected in a week. He later modified that stand as well, suggesting two-thirds of it be collected in a month, using the threat of ordering the French army to come within a few miles of the city gates.[93]

Fuad Pasha did not want to destroy the city's future economic growth, and the sums quoted by de Rehfues would have been out of all proportion to the city's resources. In Mount Lebanon, he noted, all the land was concentrated in the hands of a few families, while the remainder was tilled by poor tenants, Sidon had almost no capital to speak of, and although there were rich people in Damascus, their wealth was tied up in landed property which could only slowly be converted into cash. Thousands of Damascenes would fail to pay and the government would then be forced to seize the land and other possessions, and to put in jail those who had none. How was the government to feed all these people once they were seized? Further, Fuad Pasha argued, the arrest and exile of the wealthiest Damascenes would create an economic and social vacuum in the city: their property would be seized, they would have to be replaced by men from outside the city. They were not responsible for the riots and could not be penalized for them; nor could they force others to pay, since they lacked the power of the notables they had replaced. Finally, although some of the rich might agree to pay, they had no power to make others follow their example.[94]

Dufferin believed that no more than 10 million piastres could be levied per month, and that 50 million was the most that could be demanded altogether without permanently destroying the city's economy. Others argued for other sums and varying periods of time for their collection. Eventually, the commission agreed on a sum of 40 million to be collected in eight months from an estimated population of 35,000 adult males (out of a total Muslim population of 125,000), or 1,142 piastres per adult male, a sum close to the 35 million piastres Fuad Pasha had proposed. The pasha had once more managed to get his way.[95]

Collection did not prove easy. By November 1861, almost a year after the commission set the total, 30,000 men had provided no more than 12.5 million piastres. Fuad Pasha reduced the sum in the summer of 1861; the portion of it to be collected as a fine must also have been reduced. Perhaps too the Damascenes simply could not, or would not, pay, and the overworked authorities could not force them to. In any case, for one reason or another, the full 40 million piastres was never collected: Fuad Pasha had been closer to the mark than his European colleagues in estimating what the Damascene Muslims could, or would, hand over.[96]

The authorities also sought to collect part of the extraordinary tax from the rest of the non-Christian population. The Druzes in the *pashalik* of Damascus were assessed 7 million piastres. Considering their numbers and their role in Damascus riots, they ended up with a fine that was higher than that for the Damascene Muslims, particularly since they were also fined for their involvement in the civil war in Mount Lebanon.[97]

The Jews were also given a sum to contribute. The Jewish community was not large, but it included families who had grown rich in the nineteenth century, partly by lending money to the provincial treasury. Since they had not suffered losses from the riots, the local authorities had approached them for money and were rejected. The authorities may well have imposed a fine to achieve the same end.[98] The Jews had been left unharmed during the riots; few had been involved in them, though one was sentenced to death for the murder of a Christian. Under British pressure, however, the sentence was not carried out; Fuad Pasha commuted the sentence to imprisonment, and eventually the man was exonerated and released. Other Jews had been detained, but not many. They had to pay the fine nonetheless.[99]

The British, who had many Jewish protégés, argued that aside from the guilty, the Jews should be exempt from the fine levied on those compromised in the riots, but Fuad Pasha had no instructions to exempt Jews from the fine all non-Christians had been asked to pay. He also wanted to collect a general real-estate tax from the Jews, including those who were British subjects and protégés,[100] but that involved the rights of foreigners in the empire, which posed problems for him. Finally he reached an agreement with them in the fall of 1861 that they would pay a "voluntary contribution" of 150,000 piastres. Fraser described "the settlement of this delicate question by Fuad Pasha in a manner not less satisfactory than ingenious." The treasury had devised yet another method of finding money.[101]

The non-Christian residents of Damascus, including the Algerians, who had helped the Christians during the riots, were exempt from the special fine. Exemption lists were drawn up by Abd al-Qadir and submitted to Fuad Pasha. About 2,000 Muslim Damascenes were on the lists and were spared taxation. Among them were many ordinary people of whom we know only that they showed exceptional kindness to the Christians during their ordeal. Fraser and Robson listed two inhabitants from the Matnet al-Sham (Midanat al-Shahm) quarter, Hajj Hasan al-Ashya and his son Hajj Isma'il. Rogers's list has six names, including Sayyid Muhammad Id Bayazid who helped many Christians. Four of them were probably recommended to him by Jane Digby, the daughter of a British admiral, who had left a husband and had a string of lovers before she was 40; then she married a Bedouin shaykh and spent the rest of her life happily dividing her time between Damascus and the desert.[102]

The extraordinary fine levied on the non-Christians was never collected in full. Because it was levied in proportion to land revenue it fell most heavily on property owners whose real estate had been most seriously damaged during the riots, or landlords who, although they had property in Damascus, may not have actually lived there, and on widows and minors with property in their names. The mobs who were acknowledged to have been the principal perpetrators of the massacres escaped the tax almost entirely. There was also no mechanism to enforce the regulations among the rich, especially since much of their wealth was tied up in land.[103]

In many ways, the problems raised by the extraordinary fine imposed on non-Christians were the most difficult to deal with. The punitive aspect of the fine may have contributed to convincing the Damascenes that Fuad Pasha and the Ottoman government meant to discourage any recurrence of sectarian trouble, but it also rekindled old resentments and generated new ones. Non-Christians resented the burden of the in-kind and cash taxes they were subject to, especially those who had remained aloof from the riots. They had not been consulted, and the decision had been made by the government and by foreigners meddling in their lives. They made counterproposals, but little attention was paid to them. Their leaders had been exiled and the new appointees to public office did not understand them. They had no effective protectors left.[104]

To put up with the practical burdens of the fine was bad enough, but to live with its implications was still more painful. Were all the non-Christian Damascenes liable to a fine because, in effect, they were all guilty? Even today, it is still a sensitive subject. Many accounts reveal an awareness of the moral implications of what happened, and they try to rationalize, explain, or simply cope with them. It can be argued, Fraser wrote, that the resident proprietors were as guilty as the infuriated and fanatical mob for not having done a better job of suppressing the outbreak, even though there were extenuating circumstances which hindered them from intervening. The authorities did not oppose the insurgents, and whether one attributed that neglect of duty to connivance, apathy, or fear, the effect on the silent and well-disposed majority of Damascenes was the same. Some became convinced that the authorities were pleased with the turn of events and consequently that their services were unwanted. Others felt that if they went to the Christian quarter, armed or not, sinister motives would be attributed to their presence there. Still others feared for their lives. As a result, though the majority were not involved in the outbreak, they were accountable because they acquiesced in it. Whether they felt outraged, embarrassed, or unmoved by the accusations levied against them, they could not ignore them.[105]

Once the fine was collected, what portion of those funds actually reached the Christians is a matter of speculation, but it is clear the difficulties did not stop at collection. Most of the problems with disbursement can be laid at the door of greed, too few funds, and inconsistently estimated compensation. The government could not satisfy claimants, and the difficulties in assessing the validity of individual claims were insurmountable. It took almost a year to produce a list of the rates at which individual claims had been appraised. When this list became public in June 1861, "a good deal of public outcry" was raised by Christians against what they claimed to be injustice and insufficient awards. They complained that the distribution of indemnity had been prepared without consultation and that it was unworkable. The indemnities had been fixed using general rules, but rules can be bent, and they were, to the detriment of the needy. Some people – usually influential ones – received much more than they lost and accepted it with alacrity, while others received much less than their due and rejected it. In many cases, the sums allotted did not amount to more than 10 or 20 percent of the losses sustained – or so it was claimed over and over again.[106]

Objections also were raised over two aspects of the indemnity plan, both of which were undoubtedly attributable primarily to the emptiness of the public treasury. One was that installments were to be paid at intervals exceeding one year; and the other was that one-quarter of the indemnity was to be paid in timber – a stipulation which did not benefit those unwilling to rebuild their houses, or those planning not to resettle in Damascus.[107]

Fuad Pasha faced these objections with some of his own. He accused foreign agents of stirring up dissatisfaction through the clergy. With his usual efficiency, however, he broke the deadlock. He recognized that there were errors on the list, explained them by the great similarity in names of claimants, and had them rectified. Then he summoned the Christian patriarchs, remonstrated with them, and, using the well-tried device of committees, "appointed as many commissions as should be necessary" to investigate the claims of anyone dissatisfied with the indemnity proposed to them. An inquiry was ordered into the claims of those who declined the indemnity they had been offered. Fuad Pasha engaged to pay at once all those whose losses of personal property did not exceed 5,000 piastres: in practice, that meant the poor whose whole indemnity could be settled by one cash payment.[108]

Among the Damascenes who recouped some of their riches through indemnity was Dimitri Debbas, who had returned from exile in Cyprus to collect his money. There was enough of it for him and his family to settle in Beirut and launch a new business in the manufacture of silk. Like him, many returned to collect their indemnities and to use them to start their lives over.[109]

A list of the allotments made to the various classes of workmen gives some indication of the range of indemnity received by the working class. The city's Christian workmen were divided into eight categories: carvers in wood or stone, masons and builders, painters, carpenters, barbers, watermen, spinners, and journeymen. Each of these categories was then subdivided into eight classes of indemnity, in all likelihood in accordance to the skills and status of the workmen. In the first class, indemnities ranged from 25,000 piastres to 13,000: carvers, painters, barbers, and spinners received the highest sum; masons and builders, carpenters, and watermen received 20,000 piastres; and journeymen 13,000 piastres. In the second class, the allotments were distributed differently. Some of the categories of workmen who had received equal indemnity in the first class, did not in the second. Only the spinners received 17,000 piastres; carvers, painters, and barbers received 14,000 piastres; masons, builders, and carpenters received 12,000 piastres, watermen 10,000; which was what journeymen – the lowest paid workers in the first class – also received. In the third class, spinners came on top again, this time together with carvers, for an allocation of 10,000 piastres; masons and builders, carpenters, and barbers received 9,000 piastres; journeymen 8,500; and watermen 7,500. In the fourth class, carvers, painters, and spinners received 8,000 piastres; journeymen received 6,500; masons and builders, carpenters, and barbers received 6,000 piastres; and watermen 5,500. In the fifth class, carvers, painters, and spinners received 5,000 piastres; journeymen 4,500; masons and builders, carpenters, barbers, and watermen received 4,000 piastres. In the sixth class, carvers, painters, carpenters, and spinners received 3,500 piastres; journeymen 3,000; masons and builders, barbers, and watermen 2,500. In the seventh class, the allocations went down to 1,500 for all workmen, except journeymen who received 2,000 piastres. Other journeymen received allocations of 1,000 piastres each and constituted the eighth class all by themselves.[110]

Despite their modesty, these sums could represent substantial help. In

December 1860, the workmen cleaning the Christian quarter were paid from seven to eight piastres a day. One can assume these workmen were unskilled laborers; nonetheless, the modesty of their wages gives us a sense that for some, at least, the indemnities equaled months of pay.[111]

Although the settlements left many dissatisfied, most of the claims had been settled by the end of the year. By June, many of the principal Christians of the city had accepted the amount offered, which is consistent with the allegation that those with influence were offered more than they deserved. Their number cannot have been high, however, because by October, only 167 people had reportedly accepted the government's offers. Most Christians had turned down the first offer, no doubt in the hope of receiving a larger one. Eventually, some of them may have found satisfaction; others may have decided to settle for little rather than lose all. In any case, by December, only about 250 to 300 unsettled claims remained, and Rogers expected that they would be resolved within the next five or six months. On December 26, he wrote from Damascus that the allocation of indemnities had afforded general satisfaction.[112]

The settlement of indemnities ended the effort to solve the most critical after-effects of the Damascene outbreak. Coupled with other immediate measures taken and in large part implemented to provide relief to Christians, deal with other emergencies, and punish culprits, it constituted an impressive achievement. Even the European critics of Fuad Pasha gave him credit for his rebuilding measures, particularly when they were compared to those taken in Mount Lebanon. He had acted firmly and swiftly and had reestablished order. He did have some advantages. He had an open mandate from the Ottoman government. It is in Damascus that he started implementing his mission to Syria, and perhaps at this early stage of his mission, he wanted to make sure no European – especially no Frenchman – seized the initiative from him. Ottoman control of the Syrian interior had always been tighter than its control over Mount Lebanon. When the pasha turned his attention there, he had to deal with the French military, British defense of Druze culprits, and established traditions of autonomy that were absent in Damascus. By that time he probably was balancing the advantages of harsh punishments against the disadvantages of upsetting the social equilibrium in favor of the Christians, an outcome impossible in Damascus. Finally, the conflict in Damascus was urban and localized, easier to control and to reshape than were the districts of Mount Lebanon. Problems remained in practically every area of post-riot Damascus, but as much as could be done was done.

CHAPTER 7

RECONSTRUCTION AND THE RESTORATION OF ORDER IN MOUNT LEBANON

The war left vast areas of Mount Lebanon totally devastated. Two hundred villages had been plundered and burned, cattle and crops carried off or burned. The stench of the abandoned dead and burned-out buildings spread over the deserted land. In some places the attackers had prolonged the immediate hardship of war by cutting down the mulberry trees that supplied the population's livelihood. In the Metn district, the important village of Hammana was flattened and almost every tree had disappeared. A year later, Rashaiya in the Anti-Lebanon was still in ruins; only the serai was standing, and even it was stained with blood and filled with bodies, half-buried under rubbish. Because the serai was uninhabitable the Turkish army had been garrisoned in the few houses left standing.[1]

Conditions in Hasbaiya were worse. Evidence of fire and massacre remained everywhere; every building was damaged. Only the Protestant church stood unscathed. The serai, the site of the first great massacre of the war, lay in ruins, half of it totally destroyed. The corpses left from the slaughter still lay piled in pits near its main gate. If such desolation still prevailed almost a year after the war, one can hardly imagine the misery of the previous spring and summer.[2]

In the Anti-Lebanon, in the spring of 1861, only 10 Christian families, too poor to flee, could be found in Hasbaiya and 40 in Rashaiya. All the rest had gone to the coast. Of the Druze inhabitants in Rashaiya, only a few hundred remained. Entire villages were deserted.[3]

Worse than the ruined landscape was the plight of the Mountain population deprived of food and shelter. In Deir al-Qamar, people were dying of hunger. In Beit al-Din, Kfar Nabrakh, and al-Fretu al-Baruk, the situation was no better.[4]

To the miseries of the homeless and hungry can be added the terrors caused by the thieves and outlaws who overran the countryside. Scarcity combined with anarchy invites crime, and desperation and greed generated hordes of criminals who made life even more difficult than it already was. Thieves did not observe sectarian boundaries; hunger and misery destroy loyalty; hoodlums favored attacking members of other sects, but when none were available they attacked their own. Their loot was often so modest it gives a good indication of just how desperately poor the area had become.

Crime was equally common in all the districts affected by the war. Robbery and murder were reported in the important village of Ain Sofar, south of the Beirut–Damascus road. Around Baalbek, villagers trying to salvage what remained of their crops were attacked by marauders. In the mixed districts, Druze villages were plundered along the road the French military expedition traveled on its way to the Mountain. The looters were among the Christians returning to the Mountain in the wake of the French column. The Druze villages of Ain Hanu, Ainab, Bshiftine, Kfar Katra, Brih, Kfar Nabaa, Kfar Tin, and the country around Deir al-Qamar all suffered from them. Abandoned houses were picked clean; goats, oxen, and cattle driven off. At Qabb Elias, two horses belonging to Christian farmers were taken from an open field at night. Six Christians on their way to the cattle market in al-Huleh were robbed by a band of ten Druzes who found 3,000 piastres on them. The wife of Marun Yusuf of Wadi al-Sed, a Christian villager in the mixed districts, was on her way back from Beit al-Din where she went to sell eggs and milk, when she was set upon one afternoon and robbed of eight francs (200 piastres) in the valley under Kfar Nabrakh. Near Jezzine, bands of highwaymen robbed passers-by.[5] Some of the highwaymen became well known for their boldness. One, a Christian from the village of Shwayfat, with a band of companions robbed and sometimes murdered those who had the misfortune to run into him. In April 1861, he set upon a group on its way from Deir al-Qamar to Beirut with oil for the government. Ahmad Pasha, the new governor-general of the *vilayet* of Sidon, offered 100 francs (2,500 piastres) for his capture.[6]

In the poor and remote areas south of Lebanon and the Anti-Lebanon, where central control of any sort was nil, looting was probably worse. In the Hawran, Druze and Muslim refugees reportedly lived by looting the villages around Jabal Sheikh. On one of these raids, Muslim tribesmen and Druzes from Leja carried off three or four thousand goats from the villages of Reineh, Arneh, and Hinj in Jabal Sheikh. In Quat Yusuf, south of Jabal Sheikh, the Druzes of the Hawran also denuded the town of its goats – this time 1,300 animals belonging mainly to Christians, but some also to Druzes. In the villages of Sahmaya and Ashrafiya, the looters left nothing behind when they retreated into the Hawran. In Dnaibeh, Kfar

Danis, and Ahibar, they repeatedly subjected the people to demands for tribute. Ransom was extorted even from the most impoverished villagers.[7]

South of the Lebanon conditions were no better. In the village of Khiam in the Marjayun district, Muslims and Druzes from Leja walked off with 500 goats and 150 oxen belonging to Christians and Shi'is (Metwalis). "At every instant," Beaufort wrote, "I am told of new thefts and new assassinations." Even allowing for exaggeration in order to justify keeping French troops in the area, the number of reported incidents is sufficient to indicate that lawlessness had been one of the prices for the war in the Mountain.[8]

Women shared in the suffering. Though their own lives had for the most part been spared, wives, mothers, and sisters wept for their lost menfolk and for the punishments and reprisals facing those who survived. Their misery found expression in public demonstration. As the gunfire receded, the wailing of the women intensified. Ritual wailing is an unnerving sound to the unwary Westerner accustomed to associating grief with reserve and self-control. The wailing of the women grieving for their lost husbands and sons and their shrieks demanding sympathy and justice unnerved many a soldier in the French expedition. It was a persistent reminder of what had come to pass.

The women were left unprotected to provide for themselves. Many fled to the coast. For those who remained behind conditions were appalling. In Hasbaiya, except for about half a dozen men, only women and children remained amidst the destruction. In Deir al-Qamar, only women and children were left in a town deprived of all its resources. In Beit al-Din, 40 widows and children were left helpless. Four kilometers away, in a place called Ain Azima, women were attacked by some 20 Druzes who broke down the doors of the house they were in, searching for men. In this case the men were alive but sleeping in safety some distance away. They had left the women to take care of the silkworms which had not been destroyed by the war.[9]

Violence also remained commonplace. In the early spring of 1861, a Druze from the village of Mazer in the Shuf was found dead near al-Bothmi. Apparently, it was a crime of passion and the murderer another Druze. A Christian, possibly from Mukhtara or Maasriti, was killed and left by the roadside. Four Christians, then three more, then one more, all from the village of Bmahrin were rounded up, accused of murder, and sent to jail in Beirut. A colonel of the French expeditionary force appealed five times to Ahmad Pasha on their behalf, on the assumption that they were innocent, but there were sufficient grounds to judge them guilty. A Druze from Ammatur was found murdered in the plain of Marj Bisri, on the boundary between the Shuf and Iqlim Jezzine. In Ain Sofar, a body was found so disfigured it was impossible to identify. The body of a Druze was found near Shwayfat. Two men were found murdered between Baalbek and Zahleh, and one in the village of Ramliyeh in the northern Arqub. In these cases the murderers were never found. Revenge – the need to settle scores – was the greatest threat to the prospects for continued peace, but it was also inevitable in closely knit societies where blood ties ran deep and family honor was a powerful motive force.[10]

Some of the murders were inadvertently encouraged by the presence of foreign powers in Syria. Although the Ottoman authorities and the European officials went out of their way to appear neutral, rightly or wrongly they were seen by the local population as either protectors or enemies, depending on who was doing the talking. The Christians regarded the French expeditionary forces in the Mountain as their protectors. They returned to their villages behind the French troops, and looted abandoned Druze houses with impunity. They also used their French connections to deceive the Druzes. In September 1860, for example, a messenger was sent from Beirut with a letter to a French colonel of the expeditionary force who had just arrived in Btater. The messenger was waylaid by Ghandur Bey, a Christian leader in Btater, who told him to tell some Druzes that the message he had brought directed the French troops to attack the Druzes the next day and they should be advised to flee their villages, which of course they did. The Christians then came in and looted their houses without interference. The incident was reported by one of the Portalis brothers, a family of French silk traders in Lebanon with a factory in Btater, who tells us that the same trick also had been pulled on Druzes elsewhere in the Mountain.[11]

Even the pro-Christian French officers had to admit that some of the local Christians went too far. Although they were sometimes surprised that the crimes were not worse than they were, they acknowledged that their very presence in the area encouraged local Christians to attack the Druzes, cause "disorder," kill, and loot abandoned Druze houses. Portalis also wrote to Beaufort that Christians had taken advantage of the march of the French expeditionary forces to the Mountain in September 1860, and had killed 25 to 30 Druzes.[12] Fuad Pasha also wrote to Beaufort that the Druzes were suffering from "a natural" Christian resentment. Everywhere, the Druzes were hounded and attacked. Druze peasants could not plough their fields without being pounced upon. Not a week went by without assault or murders being reported to the authorities. Ahmad Pasha complained that known Christian outlaws had found refuge with the French expeditionary forces, both at the main French camp in the pine forest and at Baabdat in the Metn district. Ahmad Pasha diplomatically chose to assume that the French commanders were unaware of it.[13]

These sectarian episodes continued for at least a year after the civil war itself had ended. Although tradition required respect for elders, a Christian from Deir al-Qamar shot and wounded an old Druze neighbor. A Druze was killed at Kawkaba by a Christian from Rashaiya, when he realized he must be the murderer of his son and two brothers because he was wearing the clothes of his victims. A Muslim named Ali Tami was found murdered near his village of al-Burjayn in the district of Iqlim al-Kharrub. During the civil war, he had burned Dahir Nassif, a Christian from Deir al-Qamar. Now it was his turn at the hands of the dead man's relatives.[14]

Although the Druzes were in no position to be aggressors when the wrath of Ottomans and Europeans alike kept them on the run, they were not blameless either. The Christians sought vengeance; the Druzes were afraid of it. Some attacks on Christians were apparently simply retaliation for attacks on Druzes. In early spring 1861, at Qalaa on the Beirut–Damascus road, a Christian from Kfar Quq was killed by a band of Druzes. In the Beqaa valley, at Mishdil at the outlet of the Wadi Arir, a caravan of Christians was attacked by armed Druzes, and one of them was wounded. In the mixed districts, small bands of armed Druzes attacked hamlets at night and spread terror among the farmers in the isolated houses. In a village in the Arqub, a Christian was attacked and mortally wounded in front of his family by four masked men. On his deathbed, he identified them as Druzes from Kfar Nabrakh. A Christian from Fwara near Kfar Nabrakh and another in the village of Sharun were killed the same way. Sometimes Christians and Druzes simply brawled. In Abey a Christian was hit with a hatchet.[15]

To bring an end to misery and lawlessness in the Mountain the authorities, with European help and local cooperation, had to act on several fronts, often simultaneously: they had to provide immediate relief and compensation, rebuild settlements in the destroyed areas, punish the guilty and reinstate the rule of law, and reestablish a secure and lasting administrative structure.

Along the coast and in the Mountain's northern districts the thousands of refugees required immediate relief measures. The war-scarred districts of the Mountain itself were temporarily ignored, because most of them were deserted and reconstruction could wait. Energies and resources first had to be channeled to help the living. So much had to be done that neither the personnel nor the resources at the disposal of the authorities, the Europeans, and local benevolent groups were adequate for the task.

The government-sponsored relief effort began when Fuad Pasha arrived in Beirut on July 17. Although he concentrated on Damascus, he took some immediate relief measures for the Mountain. He sent groups out to visit villages, assess the cost of reconstruction, and dispense food and money. He also distributed 5,000 piastres in Deir al-Qamar sometime in the late summer of 1860 and appointed a deputy lieutenant-governor (*mutesallim*) and committees to oversee the rebuilding of houses in Deir al-Qamar and other towns and in the villages of the districts of Manasif, Jurd, and Arqub.[16]

The lack of funds was a continual problem. The Ottoman empire had been in serious financial trouble even before the civil war began. So depleted was the Syrian treasury that no discretionary funds remained. The customs revenues that came into Beirut were used for the most pressing needs. Funds reserved for the troops were diverted to more urgent requirements. Out of 2.5 million piastres sent from Istanbul for the troops in Syria, Fuad Pasha withheld 2.25 million piastres to rebuild villages, but even that was insufficient. A summary of the expenses incurred, compiled by Fuad Pasha, shows that over 4.5 million piastres had been spent by October 1860. In addition daily relief and building costs totaled 1,289,933 piastres, more than the revenues generated from Beirut customs and from funds originally earmarked for the troops. Other unspecified expenditures added another 1,531,344 piastres to that total. In October, the government had to raise some 2,350,000 piastres "in a short time," and it is safe to assume that its expenses continued to exceed revenues in the months that followed. So strained was the local treasury that an Ottoman relief committee had to borrow 50,000 piastres from the French expeditionary forces – and was slow to pay it back.[17]

The scarcity of resources led authorities to take from the Druzes and give to the Christians just as they made the Muslims in Damascus pay reparations and provide homeless Christians with shelter until new houses could be built. Druze-owned dwellings, including vacant ones, were put at the disposal of Christians; and measures were taken to return looted objects. Fuad Pasha confiscated Druze grain in the Beqaa valley and distributed it to the Christians on the plain; wherever the authorities found grain depots, they seized them for distribution. The Druzes were also required to share other food supplies. In the Beqaa, mules belonging to Druzes were requisitioned for Christian use. All Druze and Muslim villages were ordered to provide Christians with wood. Druze property, including that of Sa'id Janbalat, the richest of the Druze landowners, was confiscated and leased out to Christians.[18]

Indemnities were also apparently promised and sometimes paid. The details are difficult to trace, because the sources mention indemnities principally when they were not paid in full or at all. It is clear, however, that when they were paid it was more apt to be in Damascus, where a greater Ottoman commitment, fewer victims, and perhaps a higher standard of living made the law easier to enforce than in the Mountain. Complaints were lodged with the French agents that lost goods were undervalued and that the indemnity was correspondingly insufficient. The blankets, utensils, and other supplies made available to refugees when they returned home were subtracted from what was owed them, making the payment even smaller than it already was. The refugees of course tended to overvalue their lost possessions which, added to all the indignities of their situation, made them difficult to satisfy.[19]

The relationship between shortage of funds and inadequate relief and reconstruction measures was obvious to all. The pragmatic Fuad Pasha, who was continually trying to convey hard facts to the not always realistic European commissioners, stressed that financial problems "paralyzed good intentions." In the months immediately following the civil war, it became evident to the Westerners that lack of funds explained why the authorities did not provide more relief than they did in the war-devastated districts. Starvation in Deir al-Qamar in October 1860 was attributed by Beaufort directly to lack of money. Less than two months after his arrival in Syria, Beaufort had realized that the question of indemnity had reached a stalemate because the treasury was empty, and that for the same reasons, the authorities were unable to distribute relief. By then, even the resources made available for relief by subscriptions from Europe were drying up, and in any case, they went primarily to refugees on the coast, rather than to those few remaining in the war-torn districts.[20]

Efforts to raise money in Lebanon as in Damascus by levying fines and taxes on the local Muslim population also failed. To enthusiastic proposals by European commissioners that taxes for reconstruction totaling 100 million piastres be taken from the Muslims and Druzes, Fuad Pasha answered that they had no resources, and such a sum could only be collected over a long period of time. In towns such as Sidon, no money was available. In the Druze sections of Mount Lebanon, most of the people were tenants, not landlords. That he was correct became increasingly evident within a few months. In December 1860, he reported that the tax imposed on the Druzes was proving so difficult to collect that he had ceased to try. Other policies designed to raise money for the Christians ran into similar difficulties. The confiscation of grain owned by Druzes in the Beqaa for distribution among the Christians was apparently not carried out systematically. The land taken away from Sa'id Janbalat to be rented to Christians had by April 1861 been taken back and leased out to Janbalat's representatives, whose rents were paid by the British major and agent Fraser.[21]

Given these difficulties, although food and relief were a high priority the most basic relief measures such as food could not be always be sustained. In October 1860, for example, Beaufort obtained from the authorities "a rather considerable" consignment of flour for the inhabitants who had returned to the Mountain and the bakers who had resettled there. Items such as mattresses and bedspreads were distributed.[22] But in the mixed districts of the Mountain and in the Anti-Lebanon (one of the most neglected areas), people continued to starve. In Rashaiya, the Christian population had received no relief and was still starving in the ruined town in March. Giving the Christians Druze houses was no solution either; those available were barely more than huts and insufficient for entire families, and many Christians refused to live in them.[23]

To fend off French interference Fuad Pasha and his subordinates repeatedly drew attention to the limits of the human and material facilities at their disposal. The French were aware of them but chose to ignore them when they assessed the shortcomings of relief and reconstruction measures. They were fond of pointing to the lack of solutions provided by the authorities; to the drying up of resources for the victims of war; and to the impotence and ill-will of the Turks, ignoring the fact that Fuad Pasha was doing the best he could with what he had.[24]

The lack of funds also turned a remedy into yet another problem: the Ottoman troops ordered to police the areas where they were stationed went unpaid, and like any unpaid soldiers became hazards themselves. By March 1861, they had not been paid for 34 months; only their food rations were doled out. Not surprisingly they held up people, extorted money, and destroyed terraces for firewood.[25] Occasionally they became so out of control that the local authorities had to step in. On June 3, 1861, a Christian girl from Abey was taking water to her father who was mending the road between Deir al-Qamar and Beirut, when three Ottoman soldiers spied her. Two of them decided to molest her, but the third refused to join them and left. They gagged her, tore off her clothes and were trying to rape her when a local Christian happened by and rescued her. The soldiers ran to the village of Ainab. The rescuer was beaten up by yet another soldier. The authorities acted swiftly. The soldier who beat the rescuer was flogged, and the molesters found guilty of rape and publicly executed. Umar Pasha told the troops that any further breaches of that sort would be dealt with in the same way and promised the villagers that he would protect them as long as they did not break the peace. The incident made a great impression; the villagers later said that in 30 years they had seen nothing like it.[26]

More generally, Fuad Pasha did his best to police troubled spots and to redress grievances and reassure the Christians of the mixed districts. When some parish priests from the villages of Abey and Freidis were reportedly mistreated by Turkish soldiers, the soldiers were put in prison. When Christians complained that their testimony was not admitted by the authorities and that Druze followers of runaway chiefs had appeared in a village, Fuad Pasha sent Isma'il Pasha to inquire into the matter, even though he did not believe the allegations. When he toured the Mountain, he listened to complaints "with his usual eagerness," and took steps to respond to them. When he was away he had the local authorities read his proclamations, full of goodwill toward the Christians and promises for the future.[27]

At the same time, he warned them not to break the law. He was weary of their provoking the Druzes and their intrigues with foreigners, especially the French. He was convinced that the clergy was stirring up trouble and tried to counteract it by ordering them to urge calm and obedience. He also issued warnings which were posted in the major cities of Syria, printed in the Arabic newspaper of Beirut, and read in all public meetings, reminding the population that the government of the Sublime Porte and his own extraordinary mission in Syria had done all in its power to eliminate trouble in Mount Lebanon, and that it was the duty of the subjects of the Sublime Porte to wait quietly and confidently for the benefits the government condescended to give them. In harsher tones, he informed them that the government would "spill the last drop of blood of its employees before allowing them to give his subjects so much as a bloody nose" and would put a stop to the threats of the daring and to intrigues which might disturb peace. He admonished the population that it was the duty of every man to concern himself exclusively with his home and his business; he should help make the country prosperous, avoid reprehensible acts, and obey the orders of the local authorities under the Sublime Porte.[28]

Restitution to Christians of stolen property continued to be a bone of contention between the French and the Ottomans. Although Fuad Pasha initiated the policy of restitution, the zeal of the French in implementing it went beyond his original intentions. In November 1860, Beaufort reported that the Druzes had returned most of what had been taken from the Christians, despite difficulties raised by the Ottomans. In the following month, a concerted policy had been worked out between the Ottomans and the French. Beaufort acknowledged that Fuad Pasha and his agents were actually helping.[29] Wrote Aqiqi: "Fuad Pasha dealt with matters as gently as possible by making financial compensation and soothing people's feelings, until he had given everyone satisfaction. He ... dispensed a large sum of money in indemnities for what had been burned and stolen. He took a great amount of money from the Druzes and the Muslims."[30]

Although there were those among the French military expedition to Syria who were willing to admit that the Ottomans played an important role in reconstruction, French enthusiasm for Fuad Pasha's policies waned after the first months. The need to rebuild the Mountain led to an uneasy alliance between the authorities and the French expeditionary forces. Often Fuad Pasha initiated a policy, and the French carried it out. They would have preferred complete control, but the strong hand of Fuad Pasha and their limited resources made it impossible. They had to settle for an aggressive implementation policy and incessant criticism from the Ottoman authorities. They reciprocated with criticism of the pasha's relief and reconstruction measures because he insisted on ignoring the French and they wished to appear indispensable.

The Ottomans and the French managed, nonetheless, to achieve a great deal and, in the process, even cooperated. One urgent job was the disinfecting and clearing of towns and the rebuilding of roads. French soldiers assumed these tasks, the condition of roads being a natural priority for an army on the move. Among their achievements was the improvement of the road between Deir al-Qamar and Beit al-Din; it became a muleteer road and reestablished contact between those two important centers.[31]

The Ottoman authorities and the French expeditionary forces also rebuilt houses. Fuad Pasha appointed a committee to supervise the project; the French commandant Cerez, battalion commander of the First Algerian Tirailleurs attached to Beaufort's general staff, reorganized the committee to make it more efficient. Workers, wood, and tools were sent to Deir al-Qamar, and by October 1860, houses were being built in Hammana. In Zahleh, almost all the crop terraces had been reconstructed, and everywhere houses were going up, sometimes with the help of their former inhabitants.[32]

The reconstruction of Deir al-Qamar gives some indication of the problems involved in bringing the villages and towns of Mount Lebanon back to life. Beaufort visited it in September 1860, when houses lay in ruins and corpses were piled in the streets. He moved his camp as far away as possible to avoid infection in case of an epidemic and got reconstruction underway. But difficulties kept cropping up: shortages in building material – especially lumber – and the rainy season caused delays. The population continued to shrink as people left for the coast where relief was better organized, and the consequent scarcity of labor hindered rebuilding and slowed down street clearing. Bureaucratic red tape also slowed reconstruction. But the scarcity of money did most to delay rebuilding. By January 1861, for example, Deir al-Qamar had received 300,000 piastres from the government for reconstruction. Beaufort estimated the amount needed at 750,000.

When relief was regarded as inadequate, the inhabitants refused to cooperate, and that slowed the process too. In October 1860, Marun Latif, a local Christian spokesman and a respected member of the community, rejected the wheat sent to Deir al-Qamar on the grounds that the measure used by the man distributing the grain was incorrect. As so much else, the matter had to be sent to Fuad Pasha for arbitration. Other Deir al-Qamaris complained that the wheat they had could not be milled until the aqueduct which supplied the mill with water could be repaired.

There were quarrels over who should pay for burying the dead; in one case the argument was over a sum of 456 piastres, which in those times was considerable. Muhammad Agha, the Ottoman representative, refused to pay either the cost of the limestone used in the serai or for the labor involved in burying the dead elsewhere.

Despite all this, everyone contributed to the town's rebuilding. Fuad Pasha himself is often given credit for having begun reconstruction of Deir al-Qamar with state funds. In October the European relief committees contributed 20,000 francs (500,000 piastres) to the reconstruction of Deir al-Qamar and the villages of adjoining districts.[33] Townsmen and villagers also helped. Fuad Pasha set up local governments in every village and town, each composed of a president, two elected assessors, and a *majlis* of five elected members. In Deir al-Qamar, the municipality was headed by Marun Latif. Its functions included burying the dead, disinfecting the town, and clearing the streets. The *majlis*'s job was to settle any disputes that arose and establish local militias.[34]

By April, Deir al-Qamar had recovered from its devastation and regained some of its population. Beaufort found it transformed: "Where I had left only bodies and ruins, streets, rebuilt houses, and open shops can already be seen; industry is picking up and the French committee has already reestablished a sizable number of silk looms."[35]

The reconstruction of Zahleh took longer. Sometime in the winter or early spring of 1861, Yusuf Karam sent a representative to take command of Zahleh and in effect to preempt the functions of the municipality, but he quickly learned that no outsider could bring together the divided population or impose his will on it. He soon gave up and departed, leaving the town leaderless. When Beaufort arrived in April 1861, he found that aside from paying a few insignificant indemnities for fires and other kinds of destruction, the Ottomans had made no headway in the town's revival. Beaufort himself brought troops to Zahleh to help clear the town and reorganize it as they had done in Deir al-Qamar. He set up a municipal government composed of Maronite, Greek Catholic, and Greek Orthodox Zahalni, for which he took credit, and which the pasha approved in a letter dated October 11, 1861.

Beaufort then turned to Abro Efendi, Fuad Pasha's close associate, who represented him at the sessions of the international commission at Beirut, to take the necessary steps to obtain relief for the Zahalni and to remedy the situation created by the confiscation of the Druze grain in the Beqaa valley. The Zahalni had been forbidden to dispose of their grain in the Baalbek district, which meant they could not trade. They had also been forbidden to cut wood in the nearby forests. Beaufort asked Abro Efendi to lift these restrictions on the Zahalni, and he apparently agreed for there were no further complaints on the subject in his subsequent correspondence. The complaints were replaced by others saying that Christians with French help had cut trees all over Mount Lebanon in an unwarranted and "wholesale manner." But slowly Zahleh too rose from its ruins, and by April 1862 it had an estimated 6,174 inhabitants and 2,207 rebuilt houses and it seemed for the moment to have ceased to be a source of concern for the Ottoman authorities in Mount Lebanon.[36]

The number of people who returned to their areas of origin provided an indication of the faith people had in the future. Without that faith all reconstruction efforts would fail for lack of manpower. How to encourage it was the problem, and the authorities disagreed on the solution. The Ottomans believed the French presence drove the local population to mistrust them by suggesting the government was unable to maintain order. The French, on the other hand, believed their presence to be indispensable, because it reassured the Christians, especially those who still needed aid and sought the punishment of the perpetrators of the civil war. The French agreed, however, that men had to be enticed back to do the work of reconstruction. At least one French officer even admitted the Ottomans had done "all they could" to convince people to return to, or stay in, the Mountain.[37]

Short of forcing the refugees to go home and those that remained behind to stay there – and no one had the means to do that – no official efforts were spared to encourage resettlement. Announcements from Fuad Pasha expressing the government's goodwill toward the people and promises of a better future were read out in towns and villages; similar statements were issued by various foreign and local groups working on solving the refugee problem; pressure was put on local secular and religious leaders to use their influence to keep people home, and various reconstruction measures served the same end. Exactly how successful they were is difficult to ascertain: as we have seen, Christians returned to their villages in the wake of the French troops; three or four thousand of them came back in September 1860, and probably more in the following months as reconstruction measures got under way. By April 1861, about 1,800 people had returned to Jezzine alone to look after their silk crops and to seek indemnities.[38]

In general, the efforts to bring back the refugees and to restrain further emigration were not very successful, essentially because people had no trust in the ability of anyone to protect them. Christians did not trust the authorities and minded the presence – however peaceful – of any Druzes. In June 1861, four Druzes and their wives, with loaded donkeys, came to Deir al-Qamar under Turkish escort to bring wood to the English school in town. As they were quietly eating their soup with the soldiers, Christian women gathered around them and shouted abuse. Umar Pasha rushed over from the serai with several Turkish officers to calm the women down. He retreated in the face of their onslaught. The French officers then sent the women on their way, but with difficulty. The women complained that if the pasha could not keep the Druzes out of Deir al-Qamar even while the French soldiers were there, there was no hope when they departed. The French, of course, found the argument useful, but the Christians in fact trusted no one, and remained for the most part reluctant to return home.

Attempts by bishops to persuade Christians to stay in the mixed districts often also failed, mainly because, as the Christians of Beit al-Din told a French officer, the advice of their bishops and patriarchs had been more harmful than useful during the war. People also realized that appeals of this sort by their churchmen were often made under pressure from the government and that some religious leaders even defied authority and urged people to emigrate, about which Fuad Pasha and the French officers both complained. Long after the war, for example, d'Arricau tells us that people were leaving Deir al-Qamar and Beit al-Din at the instigation of their bishop, even though the French troops were still there to protect them. In late May and June 1861, the indefatigable Bishop Tubiyya Awn of Beirut, who had already been accused of stirring up the Maronites on earlier occasions, called on Christians to come at once to Beirut.[39]

When the French finally departed in June 1861, the situation grew worse. As they began to decamp the Christians too talked of emigration. Public meetings were held at Deir al-Qamar. French reports to the French ministry of war predicted that the resettled Christians in the Mountain would again flee. British reports confirm that Christians intended to abandon their villages and head for the coast despite efforts to reassure them. In fact despite all the talk, the departure of the French had very little permanent effect, but since resettlement had been limited to begin with, the Christian population of Mount Lebanon was still only a fraction of what it had been before the civil war.[40]

Even fewer Druzes than Christians returned to the mixed districts. They certainly had no reason to return, convinced as they were that the Ottomans, the French expeditionary force, and the Christians were all out to destroy them. In the summer of 1860 they had left for Hawran with their families and possessions. A year later, their villages in the mixed districts remained deserted.[41]

Although the Europeans were inclined to accuse the Ottomans of favoring the Druzes, the Druzes themselves did not think so. Those who had fought ignored appeals from Fuad Pasha himself, not to mention his subordinates, to trust the authorities and give themselves up; any Druzes remaining in the mixed districts were quick to disappear at the slightest sign of trouble. When the Druzes of Baaqline were summoned to the serai by Fuad Pasha in June 1861, they ran away, and only returned under cover of darkness.[42]

The Druzes were even more afraid of the French. When French troops first arrived in Syria, the fighters fled, and everyone else gave themselves up. Druze deputations continually visited French official representatives to show their good faith. In October, when the French troops marched up the Mountain, the armed Druzes again ran away, while the *'uqqal* and village chiefs protested their good faith. The same thing happened in Abey and in Kfar Matta. By April 1861, the French thought the Druzes had become somewhat less apprehensive, but they continued to try to neutralize them.[43]

Population figures are few for nineteenth-century Lebanon, and they are even harder to come by for the period right after the war. We do have some statistics for Deir al-Qamar, however, and from them can gain some idea of both the losses and the recovery of population in the area generally. On the eve of the war Deir al-Qamar probably had around 7,000 to 10,000 people; in October that number had been reduced to 182 men, 109 women, and 95 children, for a total of 386. Then the town was cleaned up and rebuilt, and the numbers began to rise. By April 1, it had 1,318; by April 6, 1,325; on April 26, 1,343. By May 6 the total was down to 1,310 and by May 12 to 1,233. The rest of the month it fluctuated between 1,233 and 1,231. By May 26, it had gone up again to 1,267, still below that of April.

Among them in April were 149–151 women with husbands and grown-up daughters, 236–239 widows, 297–306 children with parents, and 85 orphans. There also were 2 gunsmiths, 8 barbers, 9 butchers, 2 bakers, 1 embroiderer, 5 coffee-makers, 6 coppersmiths, 55–56 shoemakers, 3 tinsmiths, 11 soapmakers, 16 blacksmiths, 36 ploughmen, 17 masons, 17 merchants of combustibles, 59–60 merchants of manufactured goods, 2 chickpea dealers, 23 unspecified merchants (wholesalers or traders in several goods), 8 farriers, 8 carpenters, 23 muleteers, 21 goldsmiths, 34–35 lacemakers, 1 saddler, 21–23 tailors, 6 tanners, 6–8 dyers, 126–129 weavers, and 25–26 people whose jobs were unspecified.[44]

Skills among the remaining population were also out of balance: there were too many shoemakers left, for example – 56 in all. By May 26 only 42 remained. The number of weavers, who in normal times were in great demand, dropped from 129 on April 26 to 114 a month later. Among those who left in May were barbers, butchers, shoemakers, soapmakers, masons, blacksmiths, merchants of fuel and of manufactured goods, other merchants, muleteers, lacemakers, tailors, dyers, weavers, and unskilled workers. But those who returned also included shoemakers, lacemakers, weavers, and unskilled workers; and new arrivals included a couple of goldsmiths. In addition in both lists there were of course women and children. In those months of April and May, no fluctuations occurred among the number of gunsmiths (2), bakers (2), embroiderers (1), coffee-makers (5), coppersmiths (6), tinsmiths (3), ploughmen (36), chickpea merchants (2), farriers (8), carpenters (8), saddlers (1), and tanners (6). There were also 85 orphans in both months.[45]

In June, as the departure of French troops approached, Fuad Pasha took steps to keep the folks who had returned to Deir al-Qamar from leaving it again. He received the town's most prominent men and assured them he would accede to any reasonable request to ensure peace. He ordered Umar Pasha to move his headquarters from Mukhtara to Deir al-Qamar (eventually it was established in Beit al-Din). He established a local police force of 50 armed Christians and issued a proclamation forbidding Druzes to enter the town.[46] Despite these efforts, the population of Deir al-Qamar fell again that month as the departure of French troops caused a momentary flight. Among the people who left were what Fraser called "hangers on," that is people who lived off the French and saw no point in staying on without them. In any case, by June 7, only 100 men and 200 women were left, many of whom stayed behind to feed the silkworms.[47]

The return of lasting security depended partly on the punishment of civil war criminals in the Mountain, which proved difficult to achieve for a

RESTORATION OF ORDER IN MOUNT LEBANON

year after the end of hostilities. The ability of the authorities to punish the lawless was unclear. The restoration of order depended on an adequate army, as Ottoman troops were regularly called upon to act as police. Fuad Pasha had more troops at his disposal than the governors of the provinces of Syria normally did, because of the exceptional circumstances that had brought him to the area in the first place, and because of the high rank he held in the imperial administration. More had been sent to the area after the war ended. An Ottoman battalion had arrived from Istanbul in August 1860 and was stationed at Ain Sofar on the Beirut–Damascus road, and twelve more battalions came from Anatolia in October to reinforce the garrison in Damascus. Five ships brought two regiments of cavalry and five or six hundred horses in April. Two infantry regiments arrived in Beirut on April 21 and four more arrived on April 29, two from the regular troops (*nizam*), and two from the reserves.[48]

Although all these soldiers certainly exceeded normal peacetime forces, the number was still insufficient for the task at hand. Fraser wrote that they were "amply sufficient in the hands of such a man as Fuad Pasha," probably because he was bent on proving that French troops were unnecessary in Syria, but the fact was that, though Fuad Pasha used his troops sparingly, he could not muster sufficient force both to police and punish and to restore order. Because of the empire's financial straits, the troops in Syria had to be sufficient for the task at hand. Most were garrisoned in large cities and sent out when trouble appeared. Eight thousand were stationed in Damascus, five to six thousand in the much smaller town of Rashaiya. Eight hundred troops were spread out between the plain of Baalbek and, further north, the town of Homs. Four to five thousand were sent to Kiswa and Khuraikeb. There were other garrisons at Qabb Elias and Ain Sofar, and a few hundred troops were stationed along the Syrian coast.[49]

Fuad Pasha's shortage of troops was in part caused by the nature of the territory he had to police. Central control had for centuries been frustrated by the topography of the Lebanon and Anti-Lebanon ranges, particularly the Anti-Lebanon where many of the perpetrators of the civil war had gone into hiding. Unlike Damascus, where the Ottomans had been entrenched for centuries, the Anti-Lebanon was remote from central control, and the inaccessible terrain discouraged it.[50]

Even if the number of troops at Fuad Pasha's disposal had been sufficient to go after all the guilty parties in Mount Lebanon, it was difficult to ascertain who they were – certainly more difficult than was the case in Damascus. There, Fuad Pasha had been both harsh and swift in meting out punishment, but in the Mountain he appeared to stall, intent on settling the affairs of Damascus before involving himself with the Druzes of Lebanon. The nature of the conflict and the heterogeneity of the Mountain's population meant that any punishment that would alleviate Christian anxieties would correspondingly intensify Druze ones. Doing nothing, however, was having the opposite effect. A lenient policy toward the Druzes would provoke the Christians; dealing with them severely would satisfy the Christians but drive the Druzes away.

Although the Druzes had won the civil war, the Christians had helped start it – in contrast to the situation in Damascus where the Christians had clearly been a defenseless minority, and their role had not been lost on the Ottomans. For that reason some tried to discourage the authorities from being too severe with the Druzes. They included Abd al-Qadir, who reportedly advised Fuad Pasha against extreme severity,[51] and the British officials in Syria, especially Lord Dufferin, who championed the Druze cause, in part to counteract French support of Maronites and Catholics. Dufferin and his subordinates argued that the Christians had to bear their share of responsibility, as did the Turkish officials who had been implicated and who deserved to be punished before the Druzes did. The vacillating policies that resulted sent mixed messages to the people. Even though the Europeans wanted a stable Lebanon, they continued to contribute to its instability.

This lack of a firm policy left the Druzes not knowing what to expect. Sometimes the Ottomans threatened them; sometimes they promised them advantages. Some were pursued; others were given positions of authority. In September 1860, Yusuf Abd al-Malik, one of the Druzes who was believed to have led an attack against Deir al-Qamar on August 14, 1859, was given horsemen by the authorities and told to guard the road to Damascus.[52] Acts such as this probably won over a number of rebels and helped control them, but also sent mixed messages, especially when the authorities also tried to impose their will on the Druzes by conducting punitive expeditions against them. These expeditions were carried out when the French pressured the Ottomans to move against the Druzes. In September 1860, Ottoman and French troops joined forces to march against the Druzes of the mixed districts, but no battle ensued. Fuad Pasha probably only intended a show of force, or was trying to placate Beaufort who insisted that he be included in punitive expeditions against the Druzes.

The Ottomans acted alone in the Hawran, the Druze bastion where many had sought refuge, including some 25 armed men from Hasbaiya and Rashaiya, another 1,000 from Damascus, and 3,000 locals. In August 1860, an Ottoman battalion was sent against the Druzes hiding in the Anti-Lebanon. From Beirut, it went by sea to Sidon and then overland to

Nabatiyeh and Hasbaiya. Halim Pasha marched from Damascus for the same destination with some 3,000 men. This expedition did not, however, establish Ottoman control over the interior. In September, Fuad Pasha closed the Druze access roads to the Hawran and then a month later sent troops to the Hawran to push the Druzes out of Lebanon. By February, they still did not control the Anti-Lebanon, but they kept an eye on it in the person of Khalid Pasha who commanded the Syrian army. In the end, none of these expeditions amounted to much. In Beaufort's opinion Fuad Pasha had given up on military operations by the spring because his troops were insufficient and dispersed and he did not want to risk defeat.[53]

Fuad Pasha began his efforts to mete out punishment by having Christian delegates draw up lists of the most guilty Druzes. Hundreds of names were submitted. In the Metn district alone, for example, 472 Druzes were accused, and other lists probably had as many or more names.[54] This was done in September 1860 when, after a delay of almost two months from his arrival in Syria which the French later complained allowed many of the guilty to make their escape, Fuad Pasha set up extraordinary tribunals at Beirut and Mukhtara to judge the accused Druzes. On September 15, 1860, a proclamation was issued warning the Druzes in exile in the Anti-Lebanon that they had to give themselves up within five days or be counted as rebels and treated accordingly. None had surrendered by the deadline, but two days later eleven or so decided to come forward. They arrived at the house of the Druze *qaymaqam*, and Fuad Pasha put them under arrest. Among them was Sa'id Janbalat, unanimously regarded as the most influential of the Druze leaders. Other prominent captives were Hasan Talhuq, Karam Abu Nakad, Id al-Fahun, Asad Hamad, Qasim Husayn al-Din, the emirs Mulhim and Hamed, and Yusuf Abd al-Malik. This last prisoner had been described as being in the good graces of the Ottomans, obviously not for long.[55]

French observers judged the trials that followed as a travesty of justice. A French captain stationed at Deir al-Qamar wrote in January, 1861:

> It is a real comedy the broad outlines of which are the following, from what I gather: Fuad Pasha asks every Druze: Were you present at the events at Deir el Qamar?
> Answer. No. – Did you go to Zahleh?
> Answer. No. – Did you go to Hammana?
> Answer. No. – Did you go elsewhere?
> Answer. I did not leave my village during the war. – To the Christians he says: Do you have witnesses that the Druzes who are present here have killed and looted in your villages and burned your houses?
> Answer. No, since we escaped not to be killed ourselves. – However,

Turkish law demands witnesses and I cannot condemn [anyone] without their evidence.[56]

Nonetheless, some of them were punished, occasionally harshly. Sentenced to death were 11 Druze chiefs and notables in prison at Beirut, and 58 prisoners at Mukhtara. Others were deported: 150 Druzes were brought to Beirut from Mukhtara on March 12 and sent to Crete and Tripoli (Libya) on March 16. Another 245 were deported to Tripoli on March 18. The names of 248 Druzes condemned to deportation or imprisonment were submitted to an international commission meeting in Beirut in the spring of 1861. Of them 159 were sentenced to temporary exile; 55 to a one-year exile; 6 to two years; 17 to six years; 9 to detention for nine years; and 2 to detention in a fortress for twelve years.[57]

Exile was the punishment for "having been" or "accused of having been" at the scene of a massacre – though the word itself was rarely used; most often massacres were referred to as "events." The language used was cautious because it was so difficult to prove anything, unless the accused admitted their guilt, which they rarely did, though some admitted they were "at the scene." The language is so vague, in fact, that it is difficult to know why the sentences varied. What appear to be the same crimes carried very different sentences. Probably the trials themselves clarified degrees of guilt that are masked by the language of the record. The heaviest sentences fell on the names most often listed, or where evidence was clear.

Among those sentenced to temporary exile were 15 who had been present at Hasbaiya; another 5 accused of murder at Hasbaiya; 13 present at Rashaiya; another 2 accused of looting at Rashaiya; and 7 accused of murder at Rashaiya. Ten were sentenced for "being present" at both Hasbaiya and Rashaiya; 4 for being present at Rashaiya and Kenakir; 2 for being present at the first massacre at Deir al-Qamar; another 6 for murder during the first massacre at Deir al-Qamar; and 1 for murder at the same massacre and at Jezzine. Two owed their exile to their presence at the second massacre at Deir al-Qamar; 2 others for murder at the massacres at Deir al-Qamar – it is not specified when; 1 for his presence at Dahr al-Baidar and Jezzine; and 1 for being at Zahleh and Jezzine. Nineteen were sentenced for murder at Jezzine; 1 for admitting his presence there and for being accused of murder; another for being a leader of criminals at Jezzine; and yet another for looting at Jezzine. One was exiled for his presence at both Zahleh and Sabbaghin; another for his presence at Zahleh and Dahr al-Baidar; 7 for their presence at Zahleh; 37 for murder at Zahleh; 2 for being at both Zahleh and Hasbaiya; 1 for being at both Zahleh and Jezzine; 7 for murder at Zahleh and Jezzine; 2 for their presence at Zahleh and Deir al-Qamar; and 2 others for murder at Zahleh and Deir al-Qamar. One had been at massacres at Ain Meassir; 5 were simply accused of murder; and 1 of being a leader in "the events."[58]

Those sentenced to one-year and two-year exiles were presumably accused of more serious crimes in the events of 1860, although the summary of the case against them often differs little from that of men only temporarily exiled. Among those sentenced to one-year exile, one received his sentence for having participated in the events at Hasbaiya; another for those at Rashaiya; 4 for taking part in the events of Jezzine and 6 more for murder there; 11 for being at Zahleh and 3 more for murders there; 1 for being accused of having been present at Zahleh and of looting at Sahbin; 4 for participation in the first massacre at Deir al-Qamar; 1 for massacres in Jahiliyeh; and 23 were accused of murder. Those condemned to two-year exiles included 2 for being at Rashaiya, 1 for being at both Jezzine and Zahleh, and 3 for murder.[59]

Sentences of six-, nine-, and twelve-year exiles seemed attributable to having been in more than one place where the war had been fought or presumably for more serious crimes. Seventeen were condemned to six years: 3 of them for being been at Hasbaiya (1 for looting, 1 for participation, and 1 for having been there); 1 for being a leader and for his presence at Rashaiya; 1 for being in Jezzine; 2 for participation at both Zahleh and Jezzine; 2 for being at both Zahleh and the second massacre at Deir al-Qamar; 2 for murders in the same two locations; 5 for the second massacre at Deir al-Qamar, and 1 for murders at Zahleh. Condemned to nine years in exile was one prisoner for admitting he participated in the events at Hasbaiya and in its looting; 1 for murder at Rashaiya; 1 for being at both massacres and for killing three Christians in his house; 1 for murders at Jezzine, Zahleh, and Deir al-Qamar; one for being at the second massacre at Deir al-Qamar; 1 for being at the two massacres at Deir al-Qamar; 1 for both Deir al-Qamar and Sidon; 1 for several murders; and another for instigating disturbances and several murders. Finally, 1 of the two sentenced to twelve years of exile was described as a leader of criminals and murderers; the other as being present at the two massacres at Deir al-Qamar.[60]

Those condemned to death were held responsible for the acts of the entire community in the civil war. The particular accusations against them varied, but in essence they amounted to a consensus among the authorities that they were in charge. Most prominent among them was Sa'id Janbalat. Husayn Talhuq was second; he was the oldest among them (he was 70 at the time of sentencing) and was found guilty of having been armed during the attacks on Hadeth and Baabda. The other condemned men included Hassim (Hassib?) Nakad, accused of being present at the first conflict in the vicinity of Deir al-Qamar; Asad Imad, present at the siege of Zahleh; Emir Muhammad Qasim Raslan, present at the attack at Hadeth; Salim Janbalat, accused of heading a band of marauders who pillaged and mistreated women in Jezzine; Jamal al-Din Hamdan; Muhy al-Din Shibli, murderer of the father superior of the convent of Ammiq; Ali Sa'id; and Bashir Miri Nakad.[61]

However harsh or lenient these sentences, few were actually imposed. French observers complained that sentences were either rescinded or reduced to a minimum, and that well-known offenders were freed solely on the grounds that they did not appear on any of the lists of guilty Druzes and, consequently, escaped punishment. In Abey, for example, of the 33 people arrested, only one was still in prison in January, 1861. All the members of the Abu Nakad family who had been accused of participating in the civil war were freed after a first inquiry by the judge sent from Beirut (presumably to Mukhtara, where one of the two extraordinary tribunals met). In the Metn, out of the original list of 472, only 49 were arrested and only 4 of those brought to trial. In the prison at Mukhtara, only people who were described as "nonentities" remained by January 1861.[62]

Some of these complaints were probably justified, but certainly not all. Fuad Pasha claimed that no effort had been spared to bring the guilty Druzes to justice. He talked of the proclamations he had issued to the Druzes and the military expeditions he had led against them. He argued that he had preferred to organize the country and pacify the Christians before confronting the Druzes because taking them head on from the beginning would have interfered with his resettlement policies. It also would have driven the Druzes away and, given the difficult terrain, it would not have been easy to cordon them. By November, however, the opportune moment had come, because by then the Druzes had felt confident enough to return to their villages where he was able to find them.[63]

This apparent leniency can be justified on several grounds. There was reason to be suspicious of any Christian accusation. The tribunals often did not have sufficient evidence to find a suspect guilty. Yusuf Abd al-Malik, one of the arrested Druze leaders, was acquitted for lack of evidence by the extraordinary tribunal at Beirut; only after his acquittal was a letter with his seal discovered that implicated him. It was signed by members of the Talhuq and Abd al-Malik families, and addressed to Khattar al-Imad, still in hiding in the Hawran. In this case Yusuf was then retried and sentenced to exile, but that episode illustrates some of the difficulties facing Fuad Pasha and the courts.[64]

There are also hints that a less judicious policy would have driven the Druzes to desperation. In January 1861, Isma'il al-Atrash, the renowned Druze leader from the Hawran, raided the villages of Bassir (Bisri?) and Shabab (Beit Shebab?) in the mixed districts to take 400 hostages to exchange for Druzes in prison in Mukhtara. Fuad Pasha sent Mustafa Pasha to attack Atrash and protect the Christians, but it showed that the possibility of a Druze resurgence was omnipresent.[65]

The Ottoman officials publicly deplored the slowness of justice just as some of the Europeans did, but they blamed it on European meddling. Yusuf Abd al-Malik, the only Druze leader to be acquitted by the extraordinary court at Beirut, was freed because of favorable testimony by some French silkspinners, whose property he had protected during the civil war, and by an American missionary who lived in Mount Lebanon. When he was subsequently sentenced to exile on the basis of new evidence, he was again rescued by European intervention. He was already on board a ship on his way into exile when Dufferin interceded on his behalf, despite believing that, unlike other Druze leaders, he was more friendly to the French than to the British. Dufferin did so because he believed that the new evidence was unconvincing and introduced too late. "A long discussion" followed between Fuad Pasha and Dufferin, but in the end, Fuad Pasha countermanded the decree of exile and ordered Abd al-Malik to be returned to shore.[66]

This kind of European interference was common and included obstruction when it came to death sentences. The international commission insisted on reviewing the cases of all those the tribunals had tried and sentenced for various crimes in Mukhtara and Beirut. When it came to death sentences, Fuad Pasha was ready to proceed with the executions, but the Europeans argued against their timing. At one point the French pressed for immediate executions, but Dufferin insisted they not take place before the Turks found guilty by the commission had been punished. Although the French blamed Fuad Pasha for delays, there is no question that they were caused by European interference.[67]

In the end, although some sentences, especially those involving deportations, were carried out, the Druzes got off lightly. Compared with the numbers originally accused of war crimes, the number deported or sentenced to death was relatively small. By March 1861, court proceedings against the Druzes had closed, and those who had not been found guilty had been sent home. The Druzes stripped of their privileges were to get them back. Those who had been deported were protected by Fuad Pasha's instructions that they not be treated harshly, and the pasha promised to protect their families while they were gone. The British commissioner also instructed the British consul at Tripoli to watch over the Druze exiles there.

None of the death sentences were carried out. The central government commuted them all. Two of those sentenced to death – Muhy al-Din Shibli and Bashir Miri Nakad – were exiled to Belgrade instead, as were some of the other Druzes. According to Fraser, Fuad Pasha thought these two deserved the death sentence, but now deprived of that option he punished them with exile.[68]

A general amnesty was contemplated. In November 1860 the international commission discussed it. In May 1861, Fuad Pasha declared to Dufferin that he would proclaim a general amnesty as soon as the mufti returned bringing the Porte's decision regarding sentences referred to it for approval. The only Druzes unaffected by the amnesty would be those still in hiding in the Hawran.[69] The amnesty was delayed, however. One problem was what to do with the people who had leased land taken from the Druzes. The government would have to pay them indemnities which, of course, it could not do; lack of funds had been the reason the lands had been rented out in the first place. When the British pressed for the restoration of confiscated lands to their Druze owners, the Ottomans, to gain time, fell back on the argument that the Druzes had to pay their fines before their lands could be restored. In June 1861, Fuad Pasha told Fraser that he intended to impose a heavy fine upon the Druze nation, the amount of which was still to be determined. Until it was paid, he would retain the Druze lands as a guarantee.[70]

The government was not earning much revenue from the confiscated land. The rich who could afford to pay for the land were the very people who had been deprived of it and the tenants who had leased it were in no position to pay more than their leases. The government received some £10,000 (1,250,000 piastres) in rents, a pittance, according to Major Fraser, being the equivalent of a year's income from the estate of Sa'id Janbalat alone.[71]

The financial problems for the Ottomans in pardoning the Druzes are in fact well illustrated in the Janbalat example. Sa'id Janbalat's family could not regain control of its lands, even though the government had more than once agreed to return them and had lost revenues on the leases. In June 1861, the government was still auctioning the coming year's harvest and the Mukhtara estate had not been restored to the family.[72] Fuad Pasha first considered solving the problem by allowing private arrangements between the landowners and the tenants, but then he found another solution. In July 1861 the tenants were summoned to Beirut to discuss how to cancel their two-year leases and Fuad Pasha had the leased estates restored to their owners.[73]

Like many other sensitive decisions, the matter of fines levied against the Druzes was passed on to the authorities in Istanbul. Beclard, the French commissioner, supported the idea of a fine to help repay Christians for their losses; the British opposed it, on the grounds the Druzes had suffered enough. By August 1861, even before Druze property was confiscated, its produce had been withheld and that taken together with Druze losses since Fuad Pasha had arrived in Syria amounted to more than 20 million piastres (£160,000), an enormous sum for a Druze population of no more than 7,000. Any further levy would ruin them completely. He calculated that per capita the sum was nearly seven times as great as the 12.5 million piastres paid out by the Muslims of Damascus, despite what he considered to be their greater guilt. They had neither been provoked by the Christians, as the Druzes of Mount Lebanon had, nor had they been exposed to pillage. While French and British agents argued about how much to tax the Druzes, Fuad Pasha claimed to be waiting for instructions from the Sublime Porte.[74]

The Druzes lost immeasurably as well in terms of pride and honor. Although many arrested and imprisoned were freed, as a nation they had been put on trial and humiliated. Their honored leaders, most prominently Sa'id Janbalat, had been treated as criminals. Janbalat had given himself up in September 1860 and was confined to the barracks prison in Beirut, first in a cell by himself and then, at his request, with a cousin Salim Janbalat. By prison standards he was privileged. His cell was large and had two glazed windows to the west. A raised wooden platform along one side served as a bed and divan. But by the standards of his rank and status, he was in a wretched condition.[75]

He was also deprived of his property; Fuad Pasha had confiscated everything that could be converted into money. Even before his trial had begun, some of his horses had been sold and a considerable portion of his harvest auctioned. Fuad Pasha's justification was that the starvation threatening the Christian population had required quick action. Should time prove sequestration of Druze property inappropriate, the government could make the necessary reparations. Even Dufferin admitted the plan was not "altogether devoid of sense," and indeed Fuad Pasha's swift initiative did save the situation there. The Janbalat family seat at Mukhtara was occupied by Ottoman officials and other confiscated property was rented to Christians until July 1861 when Umar Pasha, who had occupied Mukhtara since its sequestration, was ordered to evacuate the Ottoman personnel and troops. Eventually, thanks in part to British pressure in Istanbul, it was restored to the Janbalat family.[76]

By April 1861, imprisonment, humiliation, the daily expectation of a death warrant, and generally delicate health had taken their toll on Sa'id Janbalat. Dr Pestalozza, the Ottoman quarantine medical officer at Beirut, reported that Janbalat had second-degree phthisis (tuberculosis), that his quarters were not adequate for the treatment he needed; and that he should be removed to better accommodations. So important was the prisoner that he was visited by a whole array of doctors in addition to Pestalozza: Pincoffs, a member of the Royal College of Physicians; Dobrowolski, a civil physician; Suquet, a French medical officer; Colmant, the principal medical officer of the French expedition; and Cauvin, a surgeon from *l'Eclaireur*, a ship anchored in the harbor. They found him emaciated and they agreed that he was suffering from advanced tuberculosis (a disease that reportedly ran in his family), was feverish, and suffering from insomnia and pain. Confinement and anxiety had encouraged the rapid progress of his disease. The doctors could not do much for him, but recommended he be taken home and nursed by his family; he was not expected to live more than two months. Ahmad Pasha ordered him taken to a room in the barracks which was spacious, well ventilated, and comfortable. Surrounded by his children and the women of his family, he was attended daily by Dr Pestalozza.[77]

"It is a lamentable thing that after so long a period of suspense the career of this unfortunate man should be destined to so tragic a termination," wrote Dufferin in April 1861. In May, Dufferin paid him a visit and found him dying. Accompanying Dufferin was a British official, E.T. Rogers, who had never met Janbalat before. He found him on a sofa in a corner of a room in his new quarters, looking very ill and breathing with difficulty. When Rogers ended his visit, Janbalat was too weak to walk with him to the door and simply stood up to bid him farewell. Kissing the hand of his visitor, Janbalat asked whether he would ever be sent back to the barracks and expressed the wish to be allowed, after his recovery, to go to England to live and die there, as he had "already seen too much of the Osmanli government."[78] On the morning of May 11, 1861, he died without a struggle, to a background of loud and continual laments of the Janbalat women. Dufferin looked after his wife and children until they were reinstated in their estate at Mukhtara.[79]

Janbalat's death introduced an anxious time for the Druzes. They had lost all their leaders. He left two sons, clearly too young to lead the community. Two other Druze chiefs – Husayn Talhuq, a spokesman for the Druzes (nicknamed their "consul" according to Beaufort), an old man in his seventies, and Muhammad Arslan, who had served as Druze *qaymaqam* – were in prison and sick. Their death sentences were first commuted to life imprisonment and then allowed to lapse, but they were not allowed to assume the Druze leadership. The erosive policies of Bashir II against the Druzes, the years of turmoil, and the humiliation and political defeat which followed the Druze military victories in 1860 left them without a candidate for leadership.[80]

From the start, Sa'id Janbalat had been at a particular disadvantage – his prominence made him the target for anyone wishing to make an example of the Druzes. In February 1861 Dufferin wrote that Janbalat's fate was a foregone conclusion and that a majority of his colleagues were prejudiced against him: "There is scarcely one class in the community to which he is not obnoxious. The Turks, and Christians, and even a party among the Druzes themselves equally desire his ruin."[81] This animosity colored his trial, according to the British. Christian witnesses summoned by Janbalat to testify in his favor unexpectedly testified against him. Dufferin accused Bentivoglio, the French consul general, of having bullied witnesses into reversing their testimony. On at least one thing – the shortcomings of the judicial system – Dufferin agreed with his French colleagues, but in his eyes, it allowed undue French influence on the proceedings. "So little regard is paid to the truth in this country, that the prospect of a very slender and remote advantage is enough to secure any amount of perjury," he commented, adding:

> The effect upon the native mind of a mere whisper from a Consul is known to be so forcible, so acute are the least intelligent in detecting the hidden intention of a leading question, that persons in Count Bentivoglio's position should be careful not to act in such a way as unwittingly to lay themselves open to the charge of tampering with evidence on which is to depend the life of a human being.[82]

Even without the influenced witnesses, however, Janbalat probably had little chance of coming out of his trial unscathed. Dufferin was correct in saying that the verdict was a foregone conclusion. Janbalat was accused of: (1) sending letters to the people of Jezzine falsely promising them security; (2) giving his word to Tahir Pasha that no harm would befall the inhabitants of Deir al-Qamar; (3) receiving Isma'il al-Atrash and his followers on their return from the sack of Zahleh; (4) sending the Druze chief Ali Hamada to Hasbaiya under the pretext of conducting his sister Nayifa to Mukhtara, but in reality to massacre Christians there; (5) commissioning one of his men, Zayd al-Din, to behead Emir Sa'ad al-Din Shihab at Hasbaiya and subsequently rewarding the executioner.[83] None of his accusers claimed that Janbalat had been present when the events occurred. They were damning to the prisoner because they implied he had condoned the massacres. The last three accusations were the most serious; if either of the last two could be proven, Janbalat would be given the death penalty.

Janbalat's supporters with Dufferin in their lead argued that Janbalat had acted in good faith and was being tried unjustly. Dufferin dismissed the first two accusations as unimportant: the letters to the people of Jezzine were injunctions to maintain the peace, not promises of protection; and it had been proved "over and over again" that other Druze chiefs had inspired the massacre at Deir al-Qamar. The charge was simply an effort to shift the blame away from the Ottoman authorities to the Druze leaders; it was not what actually happened. Dufferin also argued it was unjust to make Janbalat responsible for events in a town outside his jurisdiction and garrisoned by Ottoman troops; even witnesses for the prosecution admitted that Janbalat had proposed to place his family under the protection of the officer in command at Beit al-Din and had entreated the inhabitants of Deir al-Qamar not to surrender their arms and not to allow Tahir Pasha to leave town. So committed was Dufferin to the cause of Janbalat and the Druzes and so eager was he to clear them of responsibility, that he consistently shifted the blame onto Turkish officers even though he was generally an Ottoman supporter.

Dufferin also argued against the more serious allegations, as Janbalat did. To welcome Isma'il al-Atrash at Mukhtara was not evidence of complicity. Neither was it possible to prove Janbalat's complicity in the massacres of the Hawran. It was alleged that he had sent his wife's veil to Isma'il al-Atrash to indicate his support, but no one could prove it. On the contrary, Dufferin claimed, Janbalat had sent word to the government that Isma'il al-Atrash had come to Mukhtara and that he had been more embarrassed than pleased to see him. Janbalat had received Atrash with honors, but only because he had no choice in the matter, given his position and the rules of hospitality. The Druzes believed they were threatened by the Christians. Isma'il al-Atrash and his followers had burned, pillaged, and destroyed on their way to Mukhtara; but though an assassin to his enemies, he was a deliverer from Christian aggressors to his followers. No Druze chief, however indisposed he may have been towards Atrash's excesses, could refuse to receive him.

As for the fourth accusation, no one could prove Ali Hamada or any other Druzes had come to Hasbaiya on the day of the massacre. Hamada was an associate of Janbalat, but not his dependant; he was a leading shaykh of a rival family openly hostile to the Janbalats, who had buried the sword at a time of common danger. He and his followers acted independently; no one could make Sa'id Janbalat responsible for their acts. If anything, Janbalat had made himself unpopular with them by his moderation. Nor could proof be found of who beheaded Emir Sa'ad al-Din Shihab. Two other Druzes had been condemned for the same crime by a tribunal at Mukhtara, based on the testimony of one woman.

That Sa'id Janbalat had sympathized with the Druzes is probable; that he had not been an impartial spectator was not in doubt; that he was indifferent to atrocities against the Christians is possible; but there was no proof he orchestrated the events or took part in them. To claim otherwise was to attribute to him more power than he had. Although his wealth made him important in times of peace, it did not place him above other Druze chiefs nor protect his property in time of war.[84]

Not only was Sa'id Janbalat innocent, argued Dufferin, but he had desired peace from the first, stayed at home, and saved hundreds of Christians. Referring to him and to other Druze leaders in prison, Dufferin asked: "Are these men to be treated as murderers?" He obviously presented his case very convincingly, because the commissioners ended up by referring the matter to the Ottoman sultan. That pleased Dufferin, who thought the more tranquil atmosphere of the capital would counteract the passions and prejudices of the court at Beirut. No doubt he was counting on Bulwer, the British ambassador in Istanbul, to exert pressure along the lines he advocated.[85]

Sa'id Janbalat himself believed he was a victim of circumstance. His trial had been conducted improperly; many of his answers were not even recorded. He had tried to prevent trouble in 1860, not provoke it. He had watched the intrigues of Christians and the preparations for war of the rival Druze faction, the Yazbakis, and, foreseeing violence, had warned the government that unless he was provided with support, matters could become very serious. After repeated entreaties, he had been informed that a pasha had been sent to Deir al-Qamar and an officer to Zahleh with full powers to prevent bloodshed. When Tahir Pasha came to Deir al-Qamar and demanded from Sa'id a guarantee for the security of the town, he refused to give it. When Tahir Pasha said he intended to return to Beirut, Janbalat had pressed him to remain and prevent the massacre that was otherwise inevitable and had advised the notables of the town to do likewise, to no avail.[86]

What was at stake at Janbalat's trial, and the reason it received so much attention, was the fate not simply of a prominent leader, but of the Druze nation. Were they responsible for the events of 1860 or not? The debate has never ended. The Christians blame the Druzes; the Druzes believe they were the victims of Christian provocation. Both agree that the government and its local representatives were wrong, but that does not make their mutual accusations less deeply felt. That guilt and responsibility are still burning issues is shown by how reluctant people are to write about, or discuss, the subject up to the present day.

In Mount Lebanon, lack of leadership is more apt to provoke new conflicts than to achieve peace. Economic hardship for thousands of dislocated and dispossessed mountaineers, isolated acts of looting and murder, insecurity, revenge and settling of scores, all generated new tensions and conflicts. The solution could not come from the devastated, weakened victims of war. It could only come from the decision-makers in Beirut and Istanbul.

CHAPTER 8

THE PEACE SETTLEMENT

Beirut was still a city on edge in the summer and fall of 1860 and hence an unlikely theater for peace negotiations. In July, the news about the massacre in Damascus had begun to circulate and panic among the Christians in Beirut reached a new height. Captain Paynter, an officer on the British ship *Exmouth* anchored in the harbor, wrote that after the tragedy in Damascus the exodus of Christians from Beirut was so general that the governor had had to prohibit anyone from leaving the port. He assured the people that they had nothing to fear, as he had 5,000 troops ready to defend them against any Muslim uprising. Several of the English residents sent their families away anyway, as unrest and fright were "continuously uppermost in their thoughts." Paynter himself was convinced that Beirut was safe, and he proved right. The presence of high-ranking Ottoman and European representatives, soldiers, European warships, and Muslim goodwill, all contributed to containing the situation.[1]

It was in the still uneasy atmosphere in Beirut that peace negotiations began on July 12, 1860. Damascus was still in flames when a peace treaty was signed between the Druzes and Christians of Mount Lebanon, represented by local authorities, two *qaymaqam*s, and various emirs, *muqataʿji*s, *majli*s members, notables, and other deputies. The treaty optimistically based its peace on "oblivion of the past," a phrase also used without success after the sectarian clashes of 1845 in the Mountain. The treaty invoked divine assistance and the good intentions of all concerned to work toward the establishment of harmony and the end to disorder. It then declared that all acts from the beginning of the war to the present were "not liable to any claim or pretension on either side, neither at present nor in the future." This statement too proved fruitless; claims and counterclaims on either side were put forward repeatedly, filling countless hours of debate both within and outside the international commission (see appendix).[2]

The treaty was also only the beginning. Ending the war proved to be an awesome task, assisted by the presence of Ottoman and European ships in Beirut's harbor and of French troops in Lebanon, and made possible by the cooperation of Fuad Pasha and European commissioners who, with their governments' mission, all converged on Beirut to settle the Syrian crisis.

The cast of characters involved in the peace talks was as varied and diverse as the issues they had to resolve, but perhaps none proved more charismatic than Fuad Pasha. He stole the show and emerged as the principal power broker in Mount Lebanon. Through ingenious diplomatic maneuvers and a skillful combination of persuasion and coercion he imposed his will on the Europeans, who were unprepared for him, armed as they had been with moral outrage at the fate of Syria's Christians, strengthened by the backing of European might, and convinced of their own economic, moral, and cultural superiority.

Fuad Pasha was a match for just about any diplomat of his time. His charm entrapped most who met him. When Brant met Fuad Pasha for the first time in Damascus, he found the pasha frank and energetic, and could not help but trust his apparent sincerity.[3] Within a month, he was claiming that Fuad Pasha was the only energetic and enlightened Ottoman pasha he had ever met. When, for the first time, the pasha joined his European colleagues in session Dufferin wrote of him:

> Nothing could have been more skilful, conciliatory, or dignified than the manner in which Fuad Pasha proceeded to establish his official relations with us, and, it was rather amusing to observe the change in tone in our discussions, which the courtesy of his own manners insensibly imposed. He is now, as it were, a man fighting with his face in the sun and from a lower level, but did the justice of his cause but equalize the chances of position, it is evident he would be more than a match for his present opponents. His powers of conciliation are very great, and I have remarked that the persons most indisposed to him, when admitted to his intimacy, have always in some degree succumbed to the plausibility of his representations and the charm of his manners.[4]

Fuad Pasha was so skillful at masking his determination under an easygoing and pleasing exterior that some made the mistake of underestimating him. The Damascene *majlis*, for example, had begun by treating him as some kind of underling; had procrastinated in carrying out his orders; or even objected to them. He was soon receiving the cooperation he demanded. Beaufort, too, began by underestimating Fuad Pasha. Even those who knew better sometimes fell into the trap of assuming Fuad Pasha lacked resolve. La Valette had. Bulwer recognized the pasha as "a man of courage, and even genius," but worried that he would not be forceful enough.[5]

One reason Fuad Pasha was effective in Syria was that he lined up British support, particularly Dufferin's, on his own side. Dufferin was the only other commanding personality among the Beirut-based peacemakers. The rest of the Europeans lacked natural authority and remained in the background, while the struggle for influence over the resolution of the civil war continued.

Frederick Temple Hamilton-Temple-Blackwood, fifth baron Dufferin and Clandeboye, first Marquis of Dufferin and Ava, was 34 years old when he was appointed British commissioner to Syria on July 30, 1860, to assist Sir Henry Lytton Bulwer, the British ambassador to the Porte, in the inquiry into the causes of the civil war, and also to draw up a scheme to improve the governance of Syria. He was born in Florence to a family of Irish peers. One of his forebears on his mother's side was the playwright Sheridan. Educated at Eton College and, with distinction, at Christ Church, Oxford, Dufferin left the university in 1846 and spent the next ten years taking care of his Irish estates, widening his circle of friends, and traveling to the Near East. He was one of the lords-in-waiting to Queen Victoria during the Liberal cabinets of 1849–52 and 1854–8 and was given his first diplomatic post in 1855, as attaché to Lord John Russell's mission to Vienna to end the Crimean war. By 1860, he had a reputation as a distinguished speaker and had written a book about a yacht trip to Iceland. Dufferin's first major appointment to Syria in 1860 justified the promise of his early career. He went on to hold many important posts, including governor general of Canada, ambassador to Russia, and viceroy of India.[6]

From the moment he arrived on September 2, 1860, Dufferin imposed himself on the local scene. "Your rank and position place you beyond all jealousy. You will be esteemed at heart by all employees," Cyril Graham had written to him before he arrived in Syria, but Dufferin's personality contributed at least as much as his rank and position to the attention he attracted. He was both forceful and engaging; most of the time, he combined frankness and determination with tact and a conciliatory style; at times, however, he could be blunt, but would then apologize with simplicity and candor. Most people were drawn to him, and he disarmed even those who disagreed with him. Both Beaufort and Beclard, the French commissioner whom he frequently opposed, were very favorably impressed. He was a fast learner, and patient with the frustrations that accompanied undertaking his new job. Having stayed up one night until 3.00 AM and the next until 1.00 AM, he commented that "it is not that there is much to do, as that so many people waste one's time unprofitably."[7] In November, Dufferin wrote to Fraser in Damascus that he apologized for his hurried note: "but the plot here is thickening so, I never can get out for more than an hour's ride."

Lord Dufferin supported Fuad Pasha's mission fully; he was opposed to the French military presence in Syria and to their favoring the Maronites; he defended Druze interests. These stands were all consistent with Britain's overall policy in Syria, but Dufferin's style and preferences came through in the ways in which, and the degrees to which, he followed particular policies. He had been sent to Syria with only the most general instructions. "Your instructions are scanty [wrote James Graham]; and much is left to your own tact and sound judgement on the spot ... Moderate counsels, conciliatory manners, strict adherence to justice tempered with mercy, are the rules and safe guides of your conduct."[8] The Foreign Office gave him guidelines to which he was expected to adhere: secure future peace for Syria; work for a speedy and impartial administration of justice; seek no territorial acquisition, no exclusive influence, no separate commercial advantages, and see to it none were acquired by any of the Great Powers. Lord John Russell instructed him that communications with Beaufort should came from the commission as a body and not from any individual.

With this free rein, Dufferin was able to impose his views, especially those related to the fate of the guilty Druzes and to the future of the Druze nation. The Druzes had a long association with the British, and they found an exceptional champion in Dufferin who blocked any effort to inflict on them harsh punishment from either British colleagues or Fuad Pasha for their role in the civil war. He argued that weakening the Druze would only strengthen the French and their Maronite clients. He threatened Fuad Pasha with an alliance between England and the same French, however, if the pasha allowed the Druzes to be punished too severely. "Please speak strongly to Fuad Pasha," he wrote to Fraser. "Hint to him that if I see he is determined to go to extremities with the Druze aristocracy and landed proprietors, I shall be disposed to come to terms with the French, and that as I am the only friend he has, it is likely to go badly for him." At other times, he was less polite. Fraser had irritated Dufferin who believed that he had encouraged Fuad Pasha to "sacrifice the Druzes" and turn Lebanon into "a French fortress" by suggesting that the system of mixed districts be destroyed. Fraser later denied Dufferin's accusations; Dufferin eventually apologized but not before he had admonished him:[9]

> Pray do not encourage Fuad Pasha in such ideas ... I thought I had explained my views to you quite clearly on this subject. It is a point of such importance that the public service requires the plainest speaking. You yourself are very frank, and I myself am inclined to be equally so. I therefore

must request you to hold to F[uad] P[asha] language the exact contrary to that which you seem to have held towards him on this subject. Let him understand if there is a question of behaving towards the Druzes with such injustice; if the policy of extradition from the Mountain and the Anti-Lebanon, with which the Christians inaugurated the war is to be completed by the Turks, that I shall immediately come to an understanding with France, and unite those two nations [i.e. Druzes and Maronites], whom the Turks have been perpetually endeavouring to destroy by pitting one against the other, into an independent body protected by the guarantee of Europe against the encroachments of their enemies.

Dufferin was protecting the Druzes not simply to block the French. Concern over too much French influence was shared by the very people he was admonishing for being too severe. He had become personally involved with the Druzes' fate, partly because he was inclined on occasion to adopt lost causes. Although he was a ruthless landlord in Ireland, he could show concern for the disinherited in other places. The novelty of his task may also have had something of the commitment of the novice diplomat in it.[10] Dufferin argued for clemency, and, when Janbalat fell ill, for his freedom. When Janbalat died, he saw to his widow's protection. Dufferin left Syria in May 1861, shortly after Janbalat's death, a fitting moment for his departure. He had devoted so much energy to Janbalat's case that it was as good a time as any to terminate Dufferin's commitment to the Druze cause.

Dufferin's support of Fuad Pasha did not mean that he always agreed with him or never tried to pressure him. Dufferin championed the victims of guilty Turkish officers, but Fuad Pasha favored leniency for these officers. As soon as Dufferin arrived, he had gone to Damascus to see Fuad Pasha, and to witness the execution of those officers. When Dufferin agreed with the pasha, he spoke of his independence of mind; when he differed with him, he complained of his "trying to keep [in] well at Const[antino]ple and to throw dirt in our eyes," and of his unwillingness to "throw himself honestly and with no reserve" in the Commission's hands. On these occasions, Dufferin's peremptory tone was born of frustration rather than lack of esteem, the frustration of a stubborn man who had met his match. Not even as strong a man as Dufferin, backed by as strong a power as Britain, could dictate to Fuad Pasha. The two, however, cooperated far more often than they disagreed, and this powerful alliance lay behind the successful resolution of the civil war.[11]

The conditions under which Dufferin, Fuad Pasha, and the other commissioners worked were very difficult. Each of them was bound by his own government's foreign policy. All had been given the same two guidelines:

punish the guilty parties and restore order in Syria. But there were important differences in their relations with the Porte, and those differences made carrying out these general instructions difficult in practice. The French stressed the guilt of the Ottoman authorities in Syria, and the British the necessity of blocking any imperial designs on the part of the other Great Powers (i.e., France). Beclard, the French consul general in Alexandria who had been appointed French commissioner to Syria in August 1860, was instructed to cooperate with the other commissioners, look into the causes of the civil war, assess the responsibility of the leaders of the rebellion and "of the agents of the [Ottoman] administration," look for solutions to the disasters suffered by the Christians, and ensure future order and security in Syria. Fuad Pasha had the arduous task of making sure that the Ottoman empire retained control of its Syrian province.[12]

The commissioners were also aware that the civil war had attracted a great deal of attention in the European press, where it had been portrayed as a massacre of Christians by fanatical Muslims. For some of the commissioners, therefore, public outrage at home coincided with their governments' foreign policies, but for others it did not, and that placed additional burdens on their mission. Beclard's task was made easier by the fact that both the French government and the public were critical of Muslim rule and its consequences for Syria's Christians, particularly France's protégés, the Maronites. In the case of Dufferin, however, staunch British support of Ottoman rule did not coincide with public outrage at Muslim "fanaticism", and that created some embarrassments for the British Foreign Office. For example, it was very eager to discourage the publication of a letter from Cyril Graham to Dufferin which presented the Druzes as the first aggressors, the Damascene Muslims as fanatics, and the local Ottoman authorities as guilty and irresponsible. Graham took the position that Britain could not justify allowing Turkey ever again to rule the Syrian province; instead, as he put it in another letter to Dufferin on August 6, 1860, "Turkey *must* fall, *will* fall." Graham had hoped to be appointed British commissioner, but opinions so contrary to those of the foreign office defeated him. Dufferin got the appointment and more than fulfilled the expectations of his government.[13]

The commissioners had also to contend with the situation in Syria, where the problems caused by the war were urgent. At no time could they get away from the plight of the refugees wherever they went, but especially in Beirut where most of the refugees had ended up. The problems stared them in the face. At the same time, men and money were short and limited what the commissioners could accomplish. Their task was not made easier by the competition between the Ottoman and French armies in

Syria which, as far as the commissioners were concerned, was just another problem to be added to the rest.

The European commissioners had been welcomed by a guard of honor when they disembarked. Dufferin was the first to arrive – on an Ottoman vessel, which caused a small sensation as it was taken as a sign of his support for the Ottoman government. He was followed by M. Beclard on September 12 and by E.P. Novikow, the Russian commissioner, the day after. De Rehfues, the Prussian, was last to arrive. De Weckbecker, the Austrian commissioner, was already living in Beirut as Austrian consul general, although in mid-September it was announced that his appointment had been canceled, and that he had been replaced by someone named Count Ludolf. In the end, de Weckbecker stayed on as Austrian commissioner.[14]

The commissioners met for the first time on September 26, at Novikow's house. At first, they took turns presiding over the meetings, but on the grounds that they were on Ottoman territory, most of the time Fuad Pasha, or when he was absent Abro Efendi, ended up presiding. Although the commission visited Damascus, their deliberations went on in Beirut until they were recalled to Istanbul. They left Beirut on May 11, 1861, and did not return to Syria until late June. They reconvened on July 9, 1861, Fuad Pasha again presiding. The following November, they left for Istanbul again, returning to resume their meetings in December. By then they had convened 42 times. The membership remained the same except that Fraser replaced Dufferin in May of 1861.[15]

Whether the commissioners agreed or disagreed depended on the issues. Beclard and Dufferin, especially in the beginning, disagreed about the purpose of their mission. The French commissioner and his ambassador in Istanbul found Dufferin in a surprisingly "bad mood" over the Christians. They claimed that in the first six weeks or so, he had been exclusively concerned with strengthening Muslim rule, which he regarded as the key to security in Syria. The French ambassador gave credit to Beclard for reminding Dufferin that the official aim of the commission might be to help reestablish the sultan's authority, but its real purpose was to come to the aid of the Christians who had been "abandoned by the very government which was supposed to protect them."[16]

Alliances developed among the commissioners. In addition to Fuad Pasha and Dufferin, there was Beclard and de Rehfues against Dufferin. De Weckbecker tended to stay on his own, as did Novikow, and both tended toward leniency. De Weckbecker's moderation might have been attributable to his being the only one among the commissioners who was a local official. He was disliked by Moore, the British consul general, but

Moore was not a member of the commission. Moore objected to de Weckbecker's appointment as commissioner on the grounds that local residents would have biases and preconceived opinions, and that the Austrian was particularly prone to both.[17]

The obligation to work as a team also proved difficult because even when they could agree, the home governments opposed the agreement. At one point the Prussian and Austrian commissioners refused to go along with division of Mount Lebanon into different "circumscriptions" (territories with marked-out borders), a move that Dufferin had come to favor, because they had been instructed to advocate a Lebanon under a single Christian governor dependent on the Sublime Porte instead. Foreign and distant governments were immune to Dufferin's persuasive powers and could not be manipulated to support the policies he endorsed. He complained that the European governments, having appointed the international commission, were now nullifying any agreement it reached by demanding results that had no connection with reality.[18]

It is always more difficult to reach a consensus than to dictate as an individual, and there were times when Fuad Pasha would have much preferred to have done away with the commission altogether. On June 28, 1861, he complained to Fraser that he saw no point in the European commissioners' returning to Syria; in his opinion there was nothing left to discuss. He was right in the sense that most of the commission's task had been accomplished, as Dufferin's departure had indicated. However, the commission continued to convene for months in an effort to tie up loose ends.[19]

It was understandable, however, that Fuad Pasha became weary of the European commissioners. They had given him many reasons for exasperation. He, and in his absence Abro Efendi, had to contend with their relentless impatience. He was continually attacked by all of them, even those who agreed with his policies. They were impossible to satisfy. Whatever the Ottoman special envoy accomplished, they demanded more. They kept coming up with new ideas which were all generated to serve the same end: to control decisions and initiatives. When the punishment of the guilty Damascenes was a main item on Fuad Pasha's agenda, they wanted to deliberate in Damascus. When Mount Lebanon was on the agenda, they proposed to move to Mukhtara. Anywhere Fuad Pasha went, they wanted to follow so as not to be left out. They interfered in controversial trials, including Khurshid Pasha's. They complained of being prevented from exercising their right of interference, though they certainly tried to enforce it. As far as Fuad Pasha and Abro Efendi were concerned, the commission behaved purely and simply "like a plaintiff" and presented "a lot of senseless questions as if the government was on trial."[20]

The commissioners also had a difficult task. They were confronted with three kinds of problem. The first centered on housing, indemnity, and war-relief problems which needed immediate attention. The second dealt with determining responsibility for the civil war – who had caused it and how – and then punishing the guilty. The third was to decide how the area, particularly Mount Lebanon, should be administered in the future to prevent a recurrence of civil war.

The commission began its deliberations with the question of relief. The first step taken was to appoint committees. Three relief committees had already appeared haphazardly but nonetheless had provided a great deal of material help to the refugees. In October 1860, Moore, the Greek consul Canaris, and Perthuis who headed these committees, were brought before the commission.

The commission decided that they, together with de Weckbecker, who was to preside over an Austrian relief committee yet to be formed, and Novikow, who was to do the same for a Russian committee, would together constitute a central relief committee, which would receive its "impulse" directly from the commission, and would coordinate the use and distribution of donations. The committee and the five it oversaw would also estimate the costs of rebuilding houses and use these estimates to determine relief distribution, but would stay clear of assessing damages. The commission reserved for itself the task of dealing with questions of damage and reparations.[21]

Surprisingly, this seemingly hopeless tangle of committees accomplished a great deal. One reason may have been that relief was one area of activity where Fuad Pasha did not mind European intervention. He did not raise objections and, if anything, he encouraged European initiative. The rest of the commissioners also agreed on the need for relief, if not on its extent, especially the indemnities to be paid; but these issues were negotiable and limited in any case by what was in the treasury. The broad consensus among the commissioners, combined with the reconstruction projects already underway in the mixed districts under the supervision of the French expedition, yielded immediate results in several areas.

The commission received and evaluated reports of Fuad Pasha's relief efforts in Mount Lebanon, including the distribution of grain and other necessities, the restitution of stolen goods, and all other aspects of government-sponsored relief. It kept up pressure on the authorities with continual inquiries about how many people were actually benefiting from relief, how many houses and villages had been rebuilt, whether relief was interrupted, and if so, where and why; and whether Christians in the mixed districts or the Anti-Lebanon were returning or not.[22]

Of all the issues discussed by the commissioners, that of assigning ultimate responsibility for the war was both the most sensitive and the most central. They began by distinguishing between three categories of criminal: those responsible for the massacres, the leaders of bands, and assassins.[23] In practice these must have been difficult distinctions to maintain, but by creating them the commissioners clearly wanted at least to try to differentiate between those who caused the civil war and those who simply got swept up in its violence. Those in the first category were thought to be the most guilty.

Assigning ultimate responsibility for the war affected both the understanding of the past and planning for the future. It asked how and why relations between centuries-old communities had so broken down. It risked deepening wounds that had not yet healed, as the moral and practical suffering of the war was far from over. It had practical consequences, as well, in terms of the amounts and sources of indemnity and other compensations to the war's victims. Finally, and perhaps the gravest source of concern, it would influence decisions regarding the future of Syria and the share various communities would have in the political settlement under consideration.

For months on end, the commissioners debated the issue of who was responsible for the war but throughout it all each of them held positions which rarely, if ever, wavered. Their minds had been made up either before they came to Syria or soon after. No serious doubts or changes of mind resulted from the arguments of the prosecutors and defendants in trial after trial and interview after interview. To the contrary, they remained remarkably consistent in their interpretations of what had happened during the war, and who was to be blamed for it.

The role of the Ottoman authorities both in Damascus and in Mount Lebanon and of the Druzes and Christians in Mount Lebanon were at issue. The guilt of the Damascenes was not seriously questioned; it was practically the only subject on which the commissioners showed unanimity, although each might place different weight on whether the mob's behavior was due to "fanaticism" alone or some other cause. Brant, who failed to find any Muslim fanaticism before the massacres, decided it was the cause of all the troubles in that city afterward. Dufferin too dismissed the motives of the Damascenes as "simply fanatical." Fuad Pasha said it had no cause or provocation, and constituted a crime which was punishable by the law of the empire.[24]

The European commissioners placed responsibility for the massacres on the local Ottoman authorities. These representatives from France, Great Britain, Prussia, and Russia took the position that government responsibility was total. The French had from the very beginning been critical of the Ottoman authorities whom they accused not only of neglect and partiality, but of willfully fueling the conflict. La Valette complained that they let matters deteriorate and their policy was devoid of foresight, and then pitted the Druzes against the Christians. Abd al-Qadir reflected the French opinion when he told Moore, after the war, that "it was easier to move the Mountain to the sea than to reform the [Ottoman] functionaries."[25]

French agents, both then and later, collected local statements in support of their critical position against the Ottoman authorities. Muhammad Agha Suwaydan, an old and respected local leader in the district of Hasi, and a member of the influential Muslim Suwaydan family prominent in the districts of Homs and Hama, two years after the civil war confided to a French agent that the Ottoman authorities had planned the massacres, and had expected them to spread all over Syria. When they occurred, he had armed all the men in his area and sent the men of his family at their head to protect the Christian villages. Subsequently he had refused to serve the Ottoman government. "Hatred of the Osmanlis is today general," he added, "Druzes, Bedouins, Ansaris, all understand that their divisions only benefit the Turks," and "the time is not far away when Syria will be rid of the Turks," with foreign help if necessary. His French listener must have sympathized with his views, but the Ottomans still controlled the area despite the French, so it is not surprising that he also doubted that Ottoman rule in Syria could be ended.[26]

Dufferin, in contrast to the French, unquestionably supported Ottoman suzerainty over Syria, but even he was vehement in blaming the local Ottoman authorities for the massacres. In an interpellation to Fuad Pasha at the commission's meeting on November 10, 1860, he set up his own three classes of criminals and put at the top of his hierarchy in crime, which also included Damascene Muslims and Druzes, Turkish officers and magistrates who, by their apathy or connivance with the Druzes or the Sunnis, had "intensified the horror of what it was their duty to prevent." The European commissioner's conviction that the blame for the civil war lay with the local authorities was shared by their consular colleagues in Beirut, though some of them distinguished between the early phases of the war in Mount Lebanon, when local factions alone were involved, and the massacres at Hasbaiya, Rashaiya, and Deir al-Qamar, which were condoned or encouraged by Ottoman officers.[27]

Some of the European commissioners blamed the Ottoman authorities in Istanbul, but on that sensitive issue they were neither explicit nor in agreement. The French questioned the ability of any Ottoman official to behave responsibly and made no distinction between local authorities and their superiors in Istanbul. Their premise was that the Ottomans, wherever they were, were no longer fit to rule.

The British position was more complex. Local British agents believed one thing and their government wanted them to say another. Moore had blamed the local authorities and implied that the Porte was behind it all, for which he had been rebuked by Bulwer who clarified the British official position in his remonstrance, but admitted reluctantly that some of the Ottoman agents may possibly have been involved. Moore could "rest assured that neither Aali [sic] nor Fuad Pasha are either so wicked or so stupid as to have dabbled in such designs," and rumors to the contrary should be discouraged. He told Moore not to give "too easy credence to exaggerated stories of plots and massacres."

Still, the doubts of British representatives in Syria did not die down completely. Dufferin wrote Bulwer that the outbreaks in Mount Lebanon had gone awry in large part by Ottoman design. The execution of their plan had been left to the local authorities but, in his opinion, the Ottoman government was behind them.[28] He repeated this opinion more than once, and his stand was far closer to that of his French colleagues than he probably acknowledged. His motives were different, however; he wanted to shift the blame from the Druzes to their superiors, while the French wanted to undermine Ottoman rule:

> There can be little doubt but that the late massacres and all the wars, quarrels, and disturbances, which have agitated the Lebanon for the last 15 years, may be attributed to the dissatisfaction of the Turkish Government with the partial autonomy it enjoyed. Their policy has been to prove the Scheme adopted by the Great Powers in 1845 impossible. With this object in view they stimulated as occasion served the chronic animosity existing between Maronites and Druzes.
>
> In proportion as Foreign influences exalted the arrogance of the Christians, this independence became more insufferable to the Turks, and a determination was arrived at to inflict on them through the instrumentality of the Druzes a [more] severe measure of chastisement than they had yet received. What happened at Hasbeya, Rasheya and Deir el Kamr was an exaggeration of the plan. Khourshid Pasha and his accomplices were incapable of carrying so subtle a policy into execution, the play was overacted, and an 'esclandre' took place.[29]

The possibility that a plot by some faction in Istanbul lay behind the war was never openly discussed in the commission's meetings and in the end was never either confirmed or disproved. However, all the European commissioners, as well as Fuad Pasha,[30] were aware that many people believed in it.

Fuad Pasha and his retinue certainly admitted among themselves that Ottoman officials bore responsibility for the massacres. After an inquiry into the massacres around Sidon, Abro Efendi concluded that the local authorities had been neither active nor impartial, in fact they had encouraged Christians to fear their massacre. There was evidence, Fuad wrote, that soldiers had sided with Muslim mobs in attacking Christians:

> During this uproar the authorities made no effort whatsoever to stop the disturbances. The inquiry [into what happened] had concluded that the authorities nad the means to check the murderers and the perturbances of public order. In spite of their obligations, these authorities instead rather encouraged the chaos by their embarrassed and partial attitude.[31]

Fuad Pasha and his colleagues were, however, far more ambivalent than their European colleagues about the degree of guilt to be assigned to the Ottoman local authorities. Fuad Pasha kept the commissioners from participating in the trials of the Turkish officers accused of failing to fulfill their duties during the civil war, and his (less successful) efforts to commute the death sentences of Ahmad Pasha and others reflected his belief that the punishment was too harsh. He acknowledged that they had failed to perform their duty, but no evidence had been adduced that justified capital punishment. Articles 56 and 57 of the penal code reserved that penalty to three categories of criminals: those who organized and led a plot aimed at provoking one segment of the population to attack another; the leadership of such a plot, and members of an armed band, who carried out assassinations. Contrary to what Abro Efendi had privately admitted, in the sessions of the commission Fuad Pasha consistently denied accusations that the local authorities had discriminated against the Christians or connived with the Druze aggressors. Abro Efendi opposed punishing the rank-and-file soldiers in the garrisons at Hasbaiya, Rashaiya, and Deir al-Qamar too harshly, arguing that they had simply followed orders, and their superiors had already been punished for their crimes.[32]

The officers in charge of Ottoman troops in the affected areas defended themselves as best they could. Khurshid Pasha, the governor of Sidon, argued passionately that he had done all that was in his power to contain the outbreak and that he had taken every step in consultation with the local *majlis*. When he heard that armed bands were assembling in the Mountain, he had immediately dispatched his own agents to disperse them and appealed to their leaders to go home. When these efforts failed, he used both force and diplomacy: he sent out his best soldiers to Hazmiyeh; and at the same time sent Christian and Muslim emissaries to the two factions in the Mountain. In order not to deplete Sidon or Tripoli of their defenses, he sought reinforcements from Nablus as the center of a district in Palestine transferred from Damascus to Sidon in the course of the Tanzimat reorganization of the Syrian province. He then led 250 cavalry and 100 regular infantrymen to the camp at Hazmiyeh. When Khurshid Pasha learned that war had actually broken out, he sent part of his forces against the aggressors – including the Druzes whom he was accused of encouraging – and even ordered the artillery to fire.

In Khurshid Pasha's opinion, if the war had not been contained, it was not because of his lack of initiative or because he took insufficient measures, but because the military resources at his disposal were too limited. Commanders at the Beqaa and other strategic locations simply had no troops to spare for trouble spots outside their command. Despite enlistments, the army was undermanned and unable to deal with a crisis. Fuad Pasha acknowledged that Khurshid Pasha's position had been unenviable. His sense of responsibility in the face of the difficulties with which he had to deal had led him to offer his resignation on three occasions, but each time the Porte had turned it down.[33]

Extenuating circumstances could also be cited. The local authorities had lacked troops, funds, and just about every resource needed to contain the outbreak. Ahmad Pasha may have been grossly negligent in Damascus where the situation was relatively clear-cut; in Mount Lebanon, Khurshid Pasha had a particularly complex and delicate situation on his hands, given the troubled history of the preceding two decades, the number and hostile relations of the sects involved, and the resources at his disposal.

Even the shortcomings of the local governors and their subordinates could be partly excused by institutions that discouraged independence and initiative among middle-rank governors and army commanders. It would have taken daring and leadership to initiate punitive measures against troublemakers in Mount Lebanon very early on without orders from superiors in Istanbul. It would have been practically impossible, once war broke out, to come out openly and unequivocally on one side or another, or to exercise the sort of comprehensive and swift justice that only someone of the rank, character, and stature of Fuad Pasha was able to impose – and even he met with obstacles from all directions. The quality of men the system invited into its middle-level bureaucracy and army discouraged initiative, particularly in the middle decades of the nineteenth century when a concerted effort at reasserting central power had weakened local governors, shortened their tenure in office, and stripped them of power. Initiative, which any bureaucracy or army discourages, was further weakened in the Ottoman empire by both tradition and by innovations introduced in that period. The lack of initiative that made the middle-ranking bureaucrats and officers so compliant was exactly what made them so ineffectual in times of crisis, and they cannot be blamed for the very characteristics the system instilled in them. They realized too late what was happening around them, and then they found themselves ill-equipped to deal with it. They were mediocre men where greatness was required.

Nor were the local authorities alone in their failure to gauge the situation correctly. The European consuls, though more than willing to blame the local authorities, had themselves misread the situation and failed to see the dangers ahead. La Valette was taken aback by the events in Syria; Bentivoglio in Beirut so misjudged the gravity of the situation in Mount Lebanon that he was accused by the Christians of being exceptionally indifferent for a French consul. Brant failed to assess the gravity of the situation in Damascus, a mistake in judgment that had serious consequences. He had not anticipated the calamities as clearly as some of his colleagues had done, but Bulwer remarked that if all the consuls had been as tranquil as Brant had been, perhaps the "trifling disturbance" would not have "swell[ed] into a riot."[34]

Fuad Pasha and the other Ottoman officials placed responsibility for the civil war not so much with the local representatives as with the Syrian people who, they pointed out, had long cultivated sectarian animosities. Khurshid Pasha and his staff, Fuad Pasha, Abro Efendi, and others among Fuad Pasha's assistants all harped on the theme, especially the Christian–Druze hostilities in Mount Lebanon, but sometimes Christian–Muslim animosity as well. Abro Efendi, for example, explained the Sidon outbreaks in terms of old hatreds between local Muslims and Christians.[35]

The Ottomans regarded the Druzes in Mount Lebanon as less blameworthy than the Christians, a position that provoked controversy among the commissioners, who were agreed that the Druzes were culpable at Hasbaiya, Rashaiya, and Deir al-Qamar and only disagreed on whether the Druzes had been dragged into the war or had themselves provoked it. Some of them believed that at least in the early phases massacres attributed to them were really victories over an aggressor who had been equally armed and equally bellicose.

The Ottoman position (shared by Dufferin although perhaps not by all the British agents in Syria) was that the Druzes were not responsible either for starting the war or for its consequences. To Fuad Pasha, they were certainly less guilty than the Damascenes, where one segment of the population had risen against another with no cause or provocation. At least in Mount Lebanon, the Druzes had more than sufficient provocation. Of this the pasha was firmly though dispassionately convinced. Dufferin was by contrast passionate indeed on the subject, pointing to the 150,000

Christians who attacked the 35,000 Druzes in Mount Lebanon, an inequality that did not stop the Christians from demanding the heads of 4,500 Druzes (Mount Lebanon's entire taxpaying population) after the civil war. If the Druzes had won, it was because they were united and better trained than their enemies, not because they had wanted to fight. They had had no choice but to defend themselves. Self-defense was demanded by natural law, according to Dufferin, and it should not be confused with the subsequent massacres allowed by the Ottoman garrisons. Men who had taken part in a war started by their enemies were not assassins.[36]

The rest of the European commissioners were mixed in their opinions, but even the most adamant ended by taking moderate stands on punishment. De Weckbecker, a moderate, concluded that there was no evidence to show that the Druzes had started the war. The war in Mount Lebanon was between two peoples; the solidarity, good organization, and leadership of the Druzes gave them easy victories that were only later blemished by deplorable excesses. Novikow, on the other hand, did not believe that there had been a civil war at all; he thought the Druzes were guilty of murdering unresisting Christians. He was pragmatic when it came to punishment, however, and recommended deportation and leniency for most. De Rehfues and, even more, Beclard firmly believed in the guilt of the Druzes and that their leaders should be punished, but in the end they did not object to leniency for the rank and file. In short, although the commissioners might disagree on the role of the Druzes, they were able to reach a consensus on what constituted suitable punishment and to them it was a moderate one. To the Druzes, who of course regarded themselves as innocent, the sentences against their people were both harsh and unjustified, but considering where the commissioners started, the sentences against the Druzes were surprisingly light.

This leniency had several explanations: the speed and severity with which Fuad Pasha dealt with the perpetrators in Damascus took much of the pressure off the commissioners; they wanted to blame the authorities and the leaders, not the ordinary people; the actual evidence they listened to for months on end must have had its effect; the negotiations that undoubtedly took place behind the scenes over every vote and decision influenced the outcome. Finally they must have realized that any judgment they recommended had to be acceptable to the Druzes, if future peace was to be assured. Dufferin and Fuad Pasha also no doubt deserve some credit for the outcome.[37]

Among the local population, the Ottomans most blamed the Maronite Christians of Mount Lebanon and their supporters, not only for starting the civil war but for having done so to undermine the government. During and after the war the Ottomans made these views amply clear. Khurshid Pasha believed in a plot by the Maronite clergy and the Shihabs to restore the Shihab rule that had ended in 1842. According to La Valette, in June 1860, Fuad Pasha told the ambassador that the Maronites had been the original aggressors because the Maronite patriarch and shaykhs had decided the time was ripe for "un mouvement contre la Porte."[38] In June 1860, Khurshid Pasha had complained to La Valette that his agents in Mount Lebanon had reported to him that the rebellious Maronites in the Mountain refused to calm down and had begun to fight and, by so doing, had forced the Druzes to retaliate. He blamed local Maronite priests for inciting the Christians to rebellion, with the consent of their clerical superiors. The Ottoman government made this the official view during and after the war, and had no qualms about blaming the Maronites for giving "the signal for war."[39]

The Ottoman officials were particularly bitter about the "Beirut Committee." Its original purpose may have been to protect Maronite interests, but many believed that its principal aim was to provoke the Druzes to war. Khurshid Pasha referred to it as the "National Committee," suggesting that it had some national aspirations for the Maronite community. Its members were Mansur Tiyan, a member of Beirut's Grand Council, Naʿum Kayfani, a merchant under foreign protection, Asad Sabit, the dragoman in the Prussian consulate; several merchants and foreign protégés. There was no doubt in the Ottomans' mind that the rebellion was orchestrated by the Beirut Committee with the approval of Bishop Tubiyya.[40]

When war first broke out in Mount Lebanon, Ottoman officials blamed it on the committee. In May 1860, Wasfi Efendi, Khurshid Pasha's secretary, met with Moore, the British consul general, and attributed the "state of disorder" in the Mountain to "the machinations of a Committee of Christians organized and sitting in Beirut," some of them Ottoman subjects under foreign protection. In June, Khurshid Pasha blamed the committee for stirring up Christians all over Mount Lebanon, and claimed that when he discussed the matter with the bishop (presumably Tubiyya Awn), the latter told him that the "movement" had as its only aim the "liberation of his brothers in creed from slavery" and that appeals had been made all over the country inviting Maronites to "join the association." In Khurshid Pasha's opinion, the committee had more to do with the outbreak of civil war than did ancient rancor between the communities of the Mountain.[41]

Bishop Tubiyya headed the Ottoman list of Maronite agitators who constituted the Beirut committee. He was said to be the author of a memorandum sent by the Christians of the mixed districts to the Sublime Porte, blaming the local authorities for the deteriorating situation in the Mountain.[42]

The British officials in Syria shared this belief. Brant described the conduct of the Christians of Mount Lebanon in the years preceding the war as intolerant and provocative. He distinguished between the war in which Maronites and Druzes were concerned and the massacres of Hasbaiya, Rashaiya, and Deir al-Qamar. Fraser believed that Christians had participated in reprisals as actively as the Druzes had in the early phases of the civil war. Dufferin repeatedly blamed the Maronites – even when he referred to the aggressiveness of "Christians" he usually meant the Maronites. On one occasion, he said it was wrong to speak of the Christians as if they were "saintly martyrs," when in fact they were "as savage and bloodthirsty in their traditional warfare as any of their pagan neighbors [the Druzes]."

Dufferin had not always held those views – when he had first arrived in Syria, he had been outraged at the atrocities committed against the Christians. But in time he had discovered that there were two sides to the story and modified his opinion. However criminal the excesses committed by the Druzes, the provocations had come from the Christians. The Maronites had gathered armed men in various parts of the Mountain; their spiritual leaders had circulated inflammatory leaflets; a central committee of very questionable character had been established in Beirut. There was even reason to believe that they had twisted arms to involve reluctant Christians in their holy war. Dufferin supported his accusations with facts and figures; custom-house returns proved that over 120,000 rounds of ammunition and 20,000 guns had been imported by the Maronites into Mount Lebanon between January 1857 and the spring of 1860. In vintage Dufferin style, he wrote that "this time at all events, it was the lamb who dirtied the stream, and if the wolf standing lower down took it amiss, it must thank its own folly for the consequences."[43]

British officials also regarded Bishop Tubiyya as the principal instigator of Maronite aggression and blamed him for obstructing the road to peace in the Mountain. Dufferin portrayed him as unscrupulous, ambitious, fond of intrigue, "the worst specimen of a medieval ecclesiastic." His influence was sinister, and Dufferin argued that his removal from the country was a necessary preliminary step to achieving peace. Even the French consul agreed on that point. Some of the British officials tried to back these accusations with evidence. In June 1861, Fraser reported that Bishop Tubiyya, together with another Maronite bishop by the name of Butros, publicly circulated letters to the Christians inviting them to remain in their villages, but privately called upon the same Christians to leave the Mountain at once for Beirut.[44]

The bishop's influence continued to worry Ottoman and British agents after the events. His house had become a rallying point for collecting petitions for the return of Shihab rule. At the same time, Fuad Pasha, pragmatist that he was, used Tubiyya's influence to pacify the Mountain: in July 1860, as soon as he arrived in Syria, he sent the bishop together with Franco Efendi, one of his attachés, to the Kisrawan district to try to bring about a reconciliation between the peasants and the Khazin shaykhs who had been fighting since 1858.[45]

Tubiyya's role is difficult to assess. The flimsiness of the evidence against him is undeniable. Dufferin believed that the bishop had been cautious but that his influence was perceptible in every disturbance, even if "rather felt than seen." Khurshid Pasha could present only hearsay and "influence" as evidence. At the beginning of the disorders in Mount Lebanon, he had summoned the bishop. At that meeting, the bishop commented that the Christians in Druze territory were besieged and that concern for his co-religionists required that steps be taken to rescue them. Khurshid Pasha presented that comment as evidence; by saying it, Tubiyya had admitted that he had written circulars telling the Christians to leave the Druze districts. That seems to be the extent of the evidence which the bishop's critics could come up with.[46]

Tubiyya Awn professed his innocence, claiming that the charges against him could not be substantiated, a point Dufferin acknowledged. His extensive correspondence with his patriarch Boulus Mas'ad showed he wished to prevent, and later to stop, the bloodshed. For example, in a letter to Mas'ad written on May 23, 1860, the bishop worried that the Kisrawanis' intent to approach Druze areas would start a conflict, which would be "a sure road to destruction" and, to prevent that, he asked for permission to "stop this madness."[47] Even if one were to believe that Tubiyya helped stir up the Maronites and perhaps others in the early phases of the civil war, there was foresight in his warnings to the Christians. Whether or not he helped generate the situation that had led to these apprehensions, his fears that Christians would be massacred turned out to be true. Dufferin knew of at least one letter in which the bishop warned the Christians of Deir al-Qamar before the Druzes assaulted the town. The bishop indeed interfered in the affairs of the Mountain but, at least in this particular case, his interference turned out to be justified. In the letter, he confronted the war record of the Druze chiefs with their peaceful promises to the Christians; he warned the Christians that if they slept on "the cushions of security," they would undoubtedly see a repetition of the troubles of 1841 and 1845; and he prayed that God would open the eyes of the foolish Christians who would take no precautions against the threat of "destruction and perdition" from the Druzes. He did not spell out in writing what sort of precautions the Christians should take – that would have been most unwise on his part, as any call for military precautions would have made him vulnerable to the accusation that he was inciting his co-religionists to war. But given the bishop's mistrust of the Druzes, it was possible for his Maronite followers to assume that "precautions" included the use of arms. The bishop carried no weapons, of course, but many of the Maronite secular leaders and followers did. Their leaders must take the responsibility for how they interpreted the bishop's warnings, especially the *shuyukh al-shabab* who were ready, if not eager, to get into fights.[48]

That the Christians of Mount Lebanon were responsible for the civil war, as the Ottomans and the British claimed, was vehemently denied by Beclard, who clearly did not see eye to eye with the French consul general. Bentivoglio had described the Christians as aggressive at the outbreak of the war; he later toned his criticism down, but did not withdraw it. In September 1860, he wrote to Thouvenel that the Christians stirred up the French troops against the Druzes and the Muslims with "little chivalry," and that such behavior was completely characteristic of the attitude the Christians had shown all along.[49] Thouvenel was reported to have told Lord Cowley in January 1861 that "the Maronites were first excited to provoke the Druzes, and then the Druzes were stirred up to massacre the Maronites."[50] In sharp contrast, Beclard fell in line with La Valette's position. He protested that the Christians were completely innocent and placed the blame for the war on both the Ottoman authorities and the Druzes. To suit his argument, he simplified the past, ignoring the fact that the Druze also had had an administrative system, that the Shihabs had not always been Christians, and that at times even Bashir II had openly sided against Christians:

> There has been talk [here] of provocation [by the Christians]. What was their provocation allegedly directed against when the Mountain, stripped of its special Christian administrative system, was brought under the authority of the double *qaymaqams*? Can anyone also pretend that the massacres of 1842 and 1845 were caused by Christians? Should the Christians who have always been the victims of Druze fury be portrayed as agitators and so as the guilty party?[51]

Other commissioners also denied any Christian provocation. Among them Novikow said it was justified to talk of civil war only when the opposite sides of a conflict fought one another. But the Christians, far from fighting or provoking the Druzes, especially in Hasbaiya, Rashaiya, and Deir al-Qamar, had let themselves be massacred almost without resistance. The Christians had, it is true, subsequently assassinated Druzes in revenge, but even if they had and even if they were found guilty of "a few moral provocations," their reprisals against the Druzes had been isolated and in all did not amount to more than 150 dead, a mere trifle compared to what he put down at precisely 6,000 murders committed by the Druzes, of which 5,850 still remained unavenged.[52]

Time worked in favor of the claim that in Mount Lebanon the Christians had been innocent victims of Druze cruelty. It was formidably reinforced by the obvious and manifold signs of great Christian suffering for all to see when the deliberations of the commission took place: their terrible losses in lives in numbers still uncounted and undoubtedly regularly inflated, the dislocation of so many of them, sometimes more than once, the ubiquitous refugees, the wailings of family and relatives, the petitions from the clergy. All of this could only reinforce the image of the Christians as victims. That such was their fate in part because of their own provocation and in part on account of the cowardice of their co-religionists from the north was a point that the Druzes, the Ottomans, and the British kept bringing up. Recriminations from Christians and their supporters both in Syria and abroad almost but not quite buried the truth.

To the Ottomans, foreign intriguers were, like the Maronites – and often in connivance with the Maronites – responsible for the outbreak of the civil war. The machinations of French agents were a favorite Ottoman complaint. Wasfi Efendi blamed the French consul for being the driving force behind the Beirut committee. Khurshid Pasha complained that all but two of the Maronite agitators on that committee were European protégés. He also claimed that at the beginning of the war Maronite priests stirred up their parishioners by promising them that the French fleet would come to their assistance.

Ottoman officials singled out Russian agents who stirred up the Christians and undermined Ottoman rule in Syria. A petty example of Russian disrespect for an Ottoman general in Beirut in March 1861 led Abro Efendi to see no need for further comment to establish the part played by foreign authorities in the country's troubles. He wrote of "malevolent" efforts preventing the return of confidence in the country. So frustrated was he by accusations of Ottoman negligence and malevolence that he rejoiced at the news that two Druzes in French custody had escaped. He believed that the incident would make it difficult for Europeans again to reproach the Ottoman authorities for carelessness! He could not hide his distrust and dislike of Europeans, partly no doubt because he and his colleagues were so irritated by the presence of the detested French troops. In his opinion, they should be expelled. Regrettably, as he put it in the spring of 1861, there were far too many foreigners in Beirut.[53]

The Ottomans also claimed that foreign intervention had prevented the government from taking the measures necessary to prevent the escalation of war. In Mount Lebanon crimes went unpunished; it was also a refuge for criminals from other provinces. The Maronites and the Druzes, confident that they were backed by foreign powers, had opposed Ottoman authority. In those circumstances, what could the government have done? Injunctions, advice, punishment, and force had been of no use, as both factions ignored them. The local authorities had informed the central government that intervention had been urgently needed to prevent trouble, but the Porte, already under constant pressure from the Europeans, had been reduced to tolerating the insubordination of the Mountain rather than risk being accused of prejudice against the Christians. In the name of Christian freedom, the local authorities had been reduced to the role of spectators to events which they had neither the power nor the means to stop.[54]

In making this argument Fuad Pasha was in effect lobbying for direct Ottoman rule in Mount Lebanon. In doing so he stirred up the array of European concerns that lay behind all the commission's deliberations. Administrative reorganization of Mount Lebanon was the commission's central task and one of its most difficult. French, Ottoman, and British concerns *vis-à-vis* the future of Lebanon started by being mutually contradictory. The French government's first choice was a return of the Shihabs to power. It opposed direct Ottoman rule in Lebanon, preferring to stand by the 1842 Règlement (which it had previously opposed in its eagerness to advocate Shihabi rule), rather than see Mount Lebanon turned into one *pashalik* under the Ottoman administration. Commenting on the possibility of direct Ottoman rule, La Valette asked: "Is that why Europe intervened? ... The Turks who do not in the least regret the bloodshed in Syria would then have reasons to congratulate themselves that they made it flow." Beclard pushed for the unification of the two qaymaqamates in the hands of a Shihab prince and de Weckbecker supported his proposal.[55]

The British would not hear of a return of the Shihabs, and that was that. Dufferin was convinced that any effort to extend Maronite rule over either the Greek Orthodox or the Druzes was "cruel and impractical," that the independence of Lebanon was "incompatible with good government," and that an "intimate and supreme" control of Lebanon "alone would insure its tranquility." He advocated direct Ottoman rule in Lebanon, provided it was enlightened: he proposed a 17-point plan in which Syria would have a viceroy and an autonomous government not unlike the one in Egypt and, within Syria, an enlarged Lebanon consolidated into a single *pashalik* would be administered by a single individual, a Christian nominated by the central government. In this way, Dufferin argued, Christian jurisdiction could be extended, but the exclusive privileges of the Maronites would end, and the Orthodox minority would be protected. The officer to be appointed to rule Lebanon would be selected by the Porte and would govern at the central government's pleasure. A system of legal and municipal councils giving "each race and rite a due share in the administration of their local affairs" would also be established.[56]

The Ottoman government did not like Dufferin's plan, regardless of its entente with Britain, a natural ally, because it threatened to make Syria like Egypt, Ottoman in name but virtually independent under its own governors. As Ali Pasha put it to the Porte's ambassador to Great Britain, it advocated nothing less than a new practically independent principality under the direction of a European commission, and it aimed at separating Syria from Ottoman domination. There was no point in discussing its details, continued Ali Pasha; the plan was disastrous, and its principle unacceptable to the Porte. British rule in India had also led to bloodshed in the recent past, he remarked; yet no one had accused the British of negligence or incompetence or questioned its rule. Like the Ottomans, the British had done their duty by severely punishing the perpetrators of trouble. Had the Ottoman government failed to respond to the crisis as firmly as it had, then talk of substituting "a new state of things to the old" would have been understandable. Ali Pasha found the idea so preposterous that he was driven to comment that, after all, "we have never recognized the competence of the European commission in the organization of Syria proper." In the same vein, Fuad Pasha disapproved of outsiders trying to create in Ottoman lands a system somewhat similar to French rule in Algeria, British rule in India and Ireland, or Russian rule in the Caucausus, and he did not hide his opinions from Dufferin.[57]

The proposal was buried, proof, if any were needed, that the Ottomans had a decisive say in what Lebanon's future was to be. Discussions resumed and on March 20 the commission presented another draft, supported by all the commissioners except Beclard, and he would not alone be able to block it. In 47 articles it proposed establishing three separate qayma-qamates – Druze, Maronite, and Greek Orthodox – and a separate Greek Catholic administration for Zahleh, all of them under the Ottoman pasha in Sidon. By the end of April, however, French pressure in Europe had led the Austrian and Prussian commissioners to shift their position, and that caused a brief deadlock. On May 1, two more drafts were prepared. One of them in 16 articles outlined the reorganization of Lebanon under a single Christian governor.[58]

Ten days later, the commissioners all went to Istanbul to submit their proposals to an ambassadorial conference scheduled by Ali Pasha for May 30. There, discussions settled many issues before the conference even started. After pressing for the adoption of a modified version of Dufferin's plan which would place the Mountain under the pasha of Sidon with a Christian official overseeing the interests of his co-religionists, Bulwer agreed to go along with the rest of the European ambassadors in discussing the 16-article version.

The debate then centered on the choice of a governor for Mount Lebanon, with La Valette, supported by the Austrian and Prussian ambassadors, advocating a Maronite – preferably a Shihab – and Bulwer standing firm against it, supported by the Russian ambassador and, of course, the Ottoman government. Just before the opening of the conference, probably with the knowledge of La Valette, A.B. Lobanov-Rostovski, the Russian envoy to the Porte, proposed that the governor be Catholic and chosen by the Porte; Catholic did not exclude Maronite. When the conference began, however, Lobanov stood by La Valette when he advocated that the governor come from Lebanon, which the British and Ottomans vehemently opposed. Baron von Goltz, the Prussian minister, then suggested that the Porte be limited to selecting a Catholic for governor who could not be a Maronite. La Valette welcomed the compromise and proposed Da'ud Efendi, a high-ranking Armenian Catholic Ottoman official from Istanbul. He got his way, as he did on a separate status for Zahleh. La Valette was in a far stronger position than his subordinate Beclard, because of his ambassadorial rank, his distance from Lebanon, and his freedom from the interference of the likes of General Beaufort who, during his stay in Syria, had vigorously campaigned for the Shihabs and in doing so had, as Spagnolo put it, tied Beclard's hands while the commissioners met in Beirut.[59]

The "Règlement et Protocole relatifs à la réorganization du Mont Liban," approved on June 9, established the Mutasarrifiyya, the Lebanese administrative system that remained in place, with modification in 1864, until the First World War.[60] It made Mount Lebanon autonomous from the governorships of Beirut and Damascus, and administered by a non-local Christian governor or *mutasarrif*. The Règlement was purposely vague in saying that the governor had simply to be a "Christian," a vagueness that was intended to satisfy Russia that the Orthodox not be excluded and

France that Maronites could be elected. The governor was directly appointed by and responsible to the Porte for a renewable term which was first set for three years, as a trial period. In that period (extended to five years in 1864 when Da'ud Pasha's tenure came up for renewal) the governor could not be removed unless he could be shown to have failed in his duties by judicial inquiry. He had extensive powers, except over the courts. Criminal cases fell under the jurisdiction of the central authority and Lebanese commercial litigation under the Ottoman tribunal in Beirut. An administrative council was to assist the governor, and had to be consulted if Ottoman troops were to be called into active duty. The council had twelve members chosen from the six major sects of the Mountain: four Maronites, three Druzes, two Greek Orthodox, one Greek Catholic, one Shi'i, and one Sunni. Jews and Protestants were to be represented in the courts in cases involving their interests. The council members were to be elected for a term of six years by the village shaykhs, with new elections held for one-third of the councillorships in rotation every two years. Six adminstrative districts were to be created and governed by *mudirs* appointed by the governor. Shaykhs of *da'iras*, or communes of 500 inhabitants of the same sect, were to be elected, but in 1864 they were abolished. What lasted was that each village community elected its own shaykh, and the village shaykhs of each administrative district elected the council members from that district.[61] In mixed districts, shaykhs could exercise authority only over their co-religionists. The shaykhs acted as justices of the peace. Judiciary councils and a central 12-member court representing the major sects heard serious civil and criminal cases. A volunteer police force not to exceed in number 7 per 1,000 people was established, and the governor had the right to use it to disarm the population if he deemed it necessary.

The reading in Beirut of the firman establishing the Mutasarrifiyya took place in great pomp at the pine forest; it was presided over by Fuad Pasha and attended by some 10,000 spectators. "All the Ottoman dignitaries," wrote Spagnolo, "placed themselves at the center of the stage, leaving both the local and foreign guests well to either side. In the version of the document read out, no mention was made of the Powers ... In Ottoman eyes, the International Commission had only acted in an advisory capacity. Though the Ottomans felt obliged to accept its advice, they did so without recognizing any real abrogation of their sovereignty over Lebanon."[62]

A page had turned in the history of Lebanon and Syria; peace was there to stay.

CHAPTER 9

CIVIL WARS COMPARED

From 1861 to 1914, Lebanon was at peace, as it had been for most of its history, the one notable exception being the period between 1840 and 1860 and, in particular, the civil war of 1860. By 1861, peace reigned, Lebanon had been reorganized, and its factions again learned to live together in relative harmony, a harmony that lasted until the end of the Ottoman empire. During the First World War tensions surfaced, not caused by sectarianism but by the arrival of foreign armies, the suffering, destruction, and other effects of the war. Between 1920 and 1975, Lebanese communities also lived in relative harmony, aside from a period in 1958 when rivalries for power eventually produced sectarian tensions. Even when war broke out in 1975, it took years for it to generate sectarian hostilities on a large scale. In short, then, although both Lebanon's principal civil wars of the nineteenth and twentieth centuries eventually developed sectarian overtones, they did not begin as essentially sectarian.[1]

There are, of course, many differences between the nineteenth- and the twentieth-century conflicts. The territorial limits of modern Lebanon set up in the 1920s are different from those of the Double Qaymaqamate in the 1840s and 1850s or of the Mutasarrifiyya after 1861. In the nineteenth century, the conflict involved Druzes and Christians – mainly Maronites but also Greek Catholics and Greek Orthodox – and the massacres in Damascus involved Sunni Muslims and mainly Greek Orthodox Christians. In the twentieth, every community was drawn into the conflict in one way or another. The 1975 war also overshadowed its predecessor in brutality and duration, and in its destruction of Beirut, once an international capital.

Despite these differences, however, the two conflicts had one common essential ingredient that makes comparison useful. When they both did develop sectarian tensions, those tensions erupted into violence under a particular set of circumstances that revealed the special nature of the social and political structure of Lebanon and, more broadly, of the larger issue of conflicting loyalties. All heterogeneous societies have to ponder the question whether the policies of the central government and the pressures from the outside world will allow them to forge a lasting unity. What sort of unity should be aspired to? Can loyalty to an overarching nation-state coexist with, or win out over, loyalty to family, clan, tribe, or any ethnic, linguistic, racial, or religious identification? The case of Lebanon falls right in with these concerns.

Lebanon's future as a viable nation-state has now been called into question. As the historian Kamal Salibi points out in his insightful study of Lebanese identity, although all the countries surrounding Lebanon are artificial creations of the post-First World War settlement, at least until recently only Lebanon has been commonly described in those terms, partly because, at the time modern Lebanon was created, part of its population wanted to be separate, in contrast to people in other newly created neighboring states who had not formulated separatist ideologies and in fact considered them undesirable. Over 15 years of war also led many to question whether Lebanon was as viable a state as its neighbors.[2]

One way to look at the likelihood of Lebanon's unity or, for that matter, that of any other modern nation-state with peoples possessing diverse social identities, is by comparing the causes of the upheaval in the nineteenth century to the causes of the one in the twentieth century. What breaks the peace says something about the weaknesses in the Lebanese system, especially since, contrary to popular assumption, Lebanese history has as often as not been a peaceful one and the communities of the Middle East have not always been at, or on the verge of, war. When violence did break out it was a consequence each time of a loss of balance within the region and the upsetting of the status quo beyond it.

In Lebanese society, equilibrium rested on some three essential bases of coexistence. The first was a relative balance among communities, an acceptance of the position each held in society, and an observance of the limits that position put upon it. Those limits included acceptance of the recognized areas of concentration for the main communities that had been established in the eighteenth century and a commonality in culture and ways of living. Each group knew its place in the social hierarchy and stayed within its boundaries. Every religious group was used to intercommunal cooperation and coexistence, particularly in the towns where the Ottoman government and commercial transactions were centered and where Sunnis and Greek Orthodox were accustomed to dealing with one another. This was less so in the rural communities, especially among the Maronites and Druzes of Mount Lebanon, than in the trading cities; as a result they were more independent and less flexible than the city dwellers.

Despite that difference, however, all shared a common understanding of where they stood in society.

This standing was based on carefully delimited geographical, economic, and social positions; the basic social mores and values they all shared; and Ottoman practices and institutional developments, particularly the millet system, that allowed the Ottoman government to deal with the communities through their religious leaders. The millet system may not have been the elaborate construction historians once supposed, but it was a mechanism that allowed the Ottoman government to recognize that the communities existed and that some hierarchy had been established among them. To the extent that the system operated, it affirmed and enhanced mutual recognition, if not equality. As long as the status quo prevailed, social relations were harmonious.

In the twentieth century, the nature of state institutions continued to be a salient factor in the maintenance of social harmony. Institutional developments continued to promote intercommunal acceptance. In particular, Lebanon's political system – rooted in the constitution of 1926, revised in 1934, and in an unwritten agreement among the sects, known as the National Pact of 1943 – recognized confessional differences. According to this system, public offices and parliamentary seats were allocated to the various sects and communities on the basis of their numbers in the census of 1932. Eventually, because that census continued to be the basis of political representation in Lebanon long after it was outdated, the confessional system ceased to represent the society and became a straitjacket, but at the time of independence, it helped delineate the place and role of the major Lebanese communities and, in so doing, helped them define their relationships with one another. The relative harmony between the recognized Lebanese communities from the 1940s to the 1970s can be attributed in part to the confessional system. The civil war of 1958 was no exception: essentially it was a struggle of power between political factions rather than a sectarian war – for example many Maronites could be found siding against the Maronite Camille Chamoun.

Maintaining the balance of communities was another force promoting coexistence. The recognized place and role of the leading families of every community – a social hierarchy that depended on the ability of communal leaders to speak in the name of their followers and to deliver their constituencies and that ensured their status *vis-à-vis* other communities – maintained that balance. That leading families play a political role is essential in small political entities. The geographical and social structure of both Syria and Lebanon has a segmented character: defined by small-scale units, Lebanon's politics have always tended to be based on personal ties. Social and political equilibrium depended on the leading families of the various communities knowing one another and adhering to accepted and recognized rules. Through the centuries, acquaintance, recognition, and acceptance helped make coexistence possible. In the last years of the Ottoman empire, these personal ties were reinforced by official participation of the notables in mixed courts, municipalities, the parliaments of 1876 and 1908, and other forums produced by the Westernizing reforms of the nineteenth century.

In the twentieth century, too, the institutions of modern Lebanon have encouraged political alliances among leaders of different communities. In particular, parliamentary elections ensured intra- rather than intercommunal rivalries. Within every electoral district, a deputy to parliament is elected not only by members of his own religious community but by members of all religious communities in the district. Every electoral list has candidates of different religious communities running together against other lists of rival candidates from the same communities, guaranteeing political alliances that cut across communal lines.

Lebanon's republican form of government had encouraged the mutual recognition of established élites. The integration of society's upper echelons was encouraged during Lebanon's economic boom in the middle decades of the twentieth century. Originally most of the economically privileged class were Christians. With time, however, Sunnis and members of other communities joined the Christians in their prosperity. Observers stress the disunity in Lebanon's confessional political system and imbalanced economic growth, but as long as élites from all communities benefited from the system, the status quo was not threatened. Sunni leaders, who had originally objected to the separation of Lebanon from the rest of Syria in the 1920s, were won over to the idea of a separate Lebanon in the years that followed; today, they firmly believe in it. Time was beginning to broaden the base of Lebanon's élite and to work in favor of the cohesion of traditional leaders and privileged classes.

The existence of an institution standing above all the communities and their leading families was a third force promoting peaceful coexistence. Through a long process that had begun in the sixteenth century and had been consolidated by the eighteenth, one leading family imposed its will over all the others, and the leader of that family acted as arbiter among the others and as protector of their interests *vis-à-vis* the Ottoman authorities. The ruler's legitimacy depended, not on strictly religious or secular principles, but on his ability to transcend particular religious identities and interests in presiding over the affairs of state. Whatever his religious allegiance, he was expected to rise above the interests of his own community and to protect the general welfare. Between the late sixteenth and the late eighteenth century, these princes of the Mountain were sometimes Druze, sometimes Sunni, sometimes Maronite. That their religious affiliation was secondary is witnessed by the fact that they often weakened rival families of their own denomination by allying themselves with the leading families of other communities.

The same quasi-secular principle underlined the political system of Lebanon on the eve of the 1975 conflict. The president of independent Lebanon is also expected to rise above his community and to act as president of all Lebanese. It is no accident that the most tranquil periods of Lebanese history have been years in which the country was governed by presidents with a reputation for being "moderate" Christians. Charles Debbas – the first president and a Greek Orthodox – Bishara al-Khuri, Fuad Shihab, and Charles Hilu – all Maronites – were known as moderates who reached out to communities other than their own.

The most tranquil periods of modern Lebanese history have also been characterized by the alliance of the incumbent president with a powerful Sunni minister. The most notable example is the National Pact worked out by President Bishara al-Khuri and Prime Minister Riyad al-Sulh in 1943, which provided an institutional framework that recognized confessional differences.

If there were forces encouraging coexistence in Lebanese history, why did the internal equilibrium break down? The relative balance of communities was disrupted, both before the outbreak of 1860 and before the 1975 conflict. One cause of the disruption was demographic; shifts in populations upset the numerical equilibrium and the geographical concentration of communities. The Maronites in the nineteenth century and the Shi'is in the twentieth increased their population to the point of seriously upsetting the balance among the communities. In the eighteenth century, a Maronite population explosion led many among them to migrate to southern Lebanon, where the Druzes had previously lived unchallenged. In Lebanon, the last official census remains that of 1932, but birthrates and population movements, including the exodus by Shi'is from the rural districts of southern Lebanon to Beirut and other areas, leave no doubt that the country is undergoing a sizable demographic change, which involves both a growth of population and its concentration in Beirut. Particularly important has been the relative explosion of the Shi'i population, which has seriously undermined the demographic foundations on which Lebanon's government rests.

Demographic changes in themselves would not have been so threatening to the republic had they not been accompanied each time by major economic and social disruptions. In the nineteenth century the patterns of patronage disbursed were rearranged and religious categories strengthened. The growth of European influence in the Ottoman empire and the effects of the Industrial Revolution combined to benefit Christians and Jews at the expense of Muslims. All minorities had been comparatively well treated in the Ottoman empire, but now the Christians were given an advantage over the others. Already the largest group of non-Muslim subject peoples in the empire, they were now also protected as co-religionists by the various European powers in a way, and to a degree, that neither the weakening Ottoman government nor any one else was able to or willing to give to the traditionally privileged Sunnis. Druzes benefited from British paternalism, but not to the extent enjoyed by the Christian and perhaps Jewish minorities.

In the twentieth century, the Christians continued to enjoy economic ascendancy in Lebanon, especially after the French Mandate solidified Maronite supremacy. After independence, a prosperous class of Sunnis, Shi'is, and Druzes shared their privileged position; but in 1975 when war broke out, the uneven distribution of wealth that gave the upper hand to the Christians was the most visible outcome of the country's prosperity. Since the 1950s, Lebanon has been the financial and trading center of the Middle East; its rapid modernization left in its wake an increasingly radicalized and destitute population. This large and highly visible class of underprivileged people consisted chiefly of Lebanese Shi'is and Sunnis, Palestinians, and others who began to turn Beirut's outskirts into a poverty belt. They had no stake in maintaining the balance among Lebanese communities – in fact, had nothing to lose by its destruction – and could easily be manipulated by interest groups inside and outside the country that were bent on challenging the Lebanese system.

Uneven economic growth affected not only intersectarian, but intrasectarian, relations. Within every community and sect, the loss of social mobility undermined the popularity of traditional leaders. The polarizations of war do not necessarily reflect what was happening, but there is no doubt that the popularity and credibility of traditional leaders were diminishing. A major source of disruption in Lebanon today is precisely this erosion of the status of its leading families.

In the nineteenth century a whole set of international and regional factors also undermined their power. Some factors were economic: they include the integration of Mount Lebanon and the Syrian region into the Western-dominated economy and the consequent growth of the new, mostly Christian, urban-based trading and commercial classes. Other factors were more political in nature, such as the threat to the Ottoman regime in the

1830s by the Ottoman governor of Egypt, Muhammad Ali Pasha, who challenged his overlords by conquering the entire Syrian region. The changes in the balance of power between the weakened Ottoman government and the assertive European powers also had their effects on the leading families. Taken together, these developments undermined the power of the traditional feudal families of Mount Lebanon, especially the Druzes, and of the traditionally urban élites, particularly the Sunni notables.

In Mount Lebanon, although the Christian feudal families also lost power to the new merchant classes, a more general Christian political ascendancy was in the making, signaled in the late eighteenth century by the conversion of the Shihab princes of the province to Maronite Christianity and the reorganization of Mount Lebanon in the 1840s. Again in 1861, the civil war ended by giving Mount Lebanon a Christian ruler, who was advised by a representative council from the various sects of the Mountain but by convention could not himself be a native. This reunification under a Christian governor reflected the change in the political balance between Christians and Druzes.

In the twentieth century, internal, regional, and international developments again weakened the control over their constituencies of the type of leaders who rose to prominence in the later nineteenth century and created alternatives. The political system devised in the 1930s made room for the traditionally dominant communities and their leaders, but it was not flexible enough to accommodate new demographic, economic, and social forces that subsequently surfaced. In Lebanon the Shi'i population has outgrown the political role allocated to it. Refugee groups, such as the Palestinians, came in from outside Lebanon to disrupt a fragile balance of older communities which had left no place for newcomers.

The older established leaders have been challenged by alternative leaderships inside and outside the country. Nasserist and Ba'thist ideologies, Palestinian nationalism, populist Islamic movements, and Iranian fundamentalists have all weakened the hold of traditional Sunni and Shi'i leaders. Among the Maronites, no foreign ideologies have taken hold, but rival Maronite leaders have contested the power of the older established feudal families and have fragmented Maronite secular and religious leadership. The result is that the traditional Christian and Muslim notables have both been displaced by new, popularly based leaders of humble origins.

During the 15 years of war that began in 1975, these new leaders often were heads of militias. Only one of the traditional leading families preserved its full authority. The Druze leader Kamal Janbalat was able to present himself not only as someone from a high-ranking family and from the religious community that he stood for, but as an advocate of the more secular, semi-radical ideologies. Between the 1950s and the 1970s, he broadened the base of his appeal beyond his Druze followers to create the Progressive Socialist party, now led by his son. But with that exception, the old established leaders continued to appeal to ties, allegiances, and loyalties rather than to the mostly radical and populist ideologies favored by the new leadership.

The appeal of ideologies is still rudimentary. The most novel aspect of the new leaders often lies less in the ideological content of their messages than in the humbleness of their social origins. Still, they do represent a trend away from older styles of patronage-based élite politics, and, just as the Christians did in the nineteenth century, they draw their strength from outside Lebanon. While, in the nineteenth century, European backing gave Christians the upper hand, today the political balance seems to tip in favor of the popular leaders backed by Arab radical regimes or revolutionary Iran. These new leaders understandably have no more commitment to the balance that existed among the communities before the war than do the masses they attract; they have little reason to protect a political system too inflexible to make room for them, and they are not interested in making alliances with traditional politicians. This aggravates an already serious breakdown of communications among politicians.

Another major reason why internal equilibrium has broken down in Lebanon is the loss of neutrality by the supreme authority. In the 1830s, the last strong prince of the Mountain, Bashir II Shihab (1788–1840), sided with the Egyptian foreign invaders against the members of communities under his rule. His successor, the last Shihab prince, Bashir III (r. 1840-2) promoted the interests of the Ottoman central government, if only out of weakness. After him, the princedom of Mount Lebanon ended and was replaced between 1842 and 1860 by the double rule of a Maronite leader in the north of Mount Lebanon and a Druze leader in the south. Both were under the Ottoman provincial authority on the coast and unable to satisfy the needs of their populations, until finally the discontent boiled over in 1860. In 1861, a kind of neutral authority began to be reestablished under the Mutasarrifiyya.

In independent modern Lebanon, the presidency has never really been free of the political influence of the ruling clans. In times of crisis, its incumbent has therefore been unable to stand aloof, or at least to convince the other communities that that was what he was doing.

The differences between the regional and international situation in 1860 and in the 1970s largely account for the difference in the stakes of each conflict. Essentially, the conflict of 1860 was, and remained, a civil war. The conflict of 1975, although it had an internal Lebanese dimension, had also been a theater of war for all the hostile powers in the Middle East: a Syrian war, an Israeli war, a Palestinian war, an Arab–Israeli war, an Arab war, a great-power and super-power conflict. The internal dimension of that conflict on many occasions had been secondary to the foreign struggles being fought out on its territory. As evidence of that, one might note that sectarian hostilities appeared only after years of war and even then have been relatively limited.

That the stakes of the conflict were more local in 1860 than they were after 1975 accounts for the differences of magnitude, duration, and difficulties of eventual resolution. The number killed and injured in these wars is not certain, but the greater order of magnitude of the present conflict is undeniable. While the number of those killed in 1860 in Mount Lebanon did not exceed 11,000 and in Damascus 12,000, the number of victims for Lebanon's recent war may be over 100,000. At least double that number were wounded, and perhaps three or more times that figure were dislocated, often more than once. Without downplaying the enormity of the massacres of 1860 or the devastation they caused – it was the greatest upheaval in the history of Ottoman Syria – the recent conflict surpassed in destructiveness anything that preceded it, due in part to the availability and sophistication of modern weapons and, more generally, to modern technology, and to the greater number of hostile local, regional, and international parties involved. In both 1860 and 1975 and after, the internal equilibrium triggered conflict, but regional and international considerations determined its magnitude, if not its duration.

Similarities between the regional and international factors of the nineteenth- and twentieth-century conflicts are also striking. The Ottoman empire in the nineteenth century and its successor states in the twentieth became involved in the wars in Lebanon in a number of ways. They either allowed the fighting to go on; or they became a party to it; or they claimed to be helping to resolve it. The degree of involvement by the regional powers in the affairs of Lebanon was more pronounced in the recent conflict; nothing in the Ottoman period could, or did, equal the lavish training, financing, and arming of groups in Lebanon by its neighbors in recent times. Technology has made possible a level of interference undreamed of a century ago.

Another similarity between the nineteenth and twentieth centuries is that conflict has been tied to other conflicts outside its borders. In the nineteenth century, challenges to Ottoman supremacy were coming not only from within the empire, but also from without. The Ottoman regime was on the defensive, and its rule was being undermined. The rise of Christian and Jewish minorities and the rising influence of the colonial powers in the Middle East also undermined the traditionally privileged groups. Outbreaks in Aleppo, Mosul, Jedda, Damascus, Mount Lebanon, and elsewhere – of which the civil war of 1860 was only the most intense – can be attributed to the problems of an Ottoman regime trying to change its ways.

In the twentieth century, the sources of instability multiplied as the competing nation-states of the Middle East took on the Ottoman empire's role. The three most important sources of instability have been Arab–Israeli, inter-Arab, and inter-Muslim relations. Now, as in the nineteenth century, the potential for upheaval within an individual country and within the region is weakest when one regional center dominates.

A main theme of this book has been that the upsetting of a constantly renegotiated, finely tuned balance between the region's central state power and the forces of regional autonomy is largely responsible for political crisis. In the nineteenth century, Ottoman domination in Syria was seriously undermined by the Egyptian occupation in the 1830s. The Ottomans returned to Syria in 1840, but only with the help of the European powers. Challenged by a subject country, the Ottomans were restored only with outside support. The message was not lost on the local populations. In the twentieth century, the proliferation of regional centers in the Middle East has in itself been a source of great instability. Lebanon seems to fare poorest when no Arab power is clearly dominant. Lebanon learned the hard way to live with Nasser between 1958 and 1970. With the proliferation of centers of radicalism since then – Ba'thism, Palestinian nationalism, Islamic radicalism, and the rest – Lebanon has suffered far more. At this point, Lebanon's fate is so tied to regional rivalries that the price of peace in part may well be subservience to a strong neighbor.

If a small country like Lebanon seems to fare better when there is a dominant power in the region, the opposite applies for international equilibrium. In both the nineteenth and the twentieth centuries, a concert of great powers or superpowers has been critical for the promotion of peace. After 1860, peace came to Mount Lebanon because the Concert of Europe, in collaboration with the Ottoman government, created the settlement for Mount Lebanon that ushered in the period of stability between 1861 and the First World War. For most of the twentieth century, the superpowers were more polarized than the Great Powers ever were in the Middle East a century ago. Despite some attempts to work out a superpower entente in the region, none left its mark on it. The superpowers were also more involved in the Middle East than the Great Powers before them. There was no counterpart in the nineteenth century to the depth of superpower involvement in most of the twentieth. Even French commitment to the

Maronites in the nineteenth (and even twentieth) century was no match. In 1860, the Ottoman government along with the Concert of Europe settled the Lebanon situation because the Great Powers agreed on the protection of the Christians and because, despite their involvement with local groups, the European powers kept a certain distance. That distance has been lost in the last half-century. Superpower involvement in the Middle East for decades meant that their every move was tied to commitments to one or another of their Middle Eastern allies and that consequently no single power had credibility with the other parties in the region. No wonder that throughout a decade and a half of war an international agreement regarding Lebanon has not been possible. The end of the Cold War makes it more of an option now than at any other time since the outbreak of war in Lebanon; but it is a long way between an option and its actual realization.

What lessons can be drawn from the comparison between 1860 and the present for the resolution of conflict in Lebanon? One lesson is that the solution to Lebanon's problems, like the problems themselves, must involve a balance among its principal communities, a balance that requires the groups in power to make room for others. But with the recent mobilization and downward seepage of power to a variety of subordinate social classes, no nineteenth-century-style concordat struck between the élite leadership of different communities would be sufficient to restore harmony. Any cross-communal settlement, therefore, would require a strong democratic content. Another lesson is that the success of a settlement always involves the concurrence of regional and international powers. Without them, no war – and, hence, no peace – is feasible.

The civil war of 1860 is, then, important for understanding the present as well as the past and, more generally, for appreciating the challenges faced by other socially and culturally diverse modern nation-states. How it came about had much to do with a loss of balance between central state power and regional autonomy as well as between communities at the intra-regional or local level in the troubled decades of the nineteenth century. The deployment of military force by the Ottoman center certainly played a role in restoring order in the Syrian province. Yet the decades of peace that followed owed more to a regionally and internationally negotiated and guaranteed balance between center and region as well as communities within localities and regions. It was this that ushered in a lengthy phase of dialogue and coexistence in the history of Syria and Mount Lebanon.

APPENDIX

"Further Papers," Encl.4
in Moore–Russell, No. 28,
19 July 1860, pp. 62–3

Treaty of Peace between the Christians and Druses. [Translation of the treaty signed on 12 July 1860.]

We, the Undersigned, Kaimakam of the Christians, Deputies of the people, Emirs, and Mokattadjis, members of the Medjlis and Notables, have appeared, in obedience to the orders of his Excellency our Lord the Mushir of the Eyalet, before his Excellency's Kiahia and Lieutenant, his Excellency Wasfi Effendi, and after deliberation and discussion between us and the Kaimakam of the Druses and Deputies of the said nation, Emirs, Mokattadjis, members of the Medjlis and Notables, as to the duty of securing the means of repressing the dissensions that have arisen, of guarding the country, of restoring the tranquility and well-being of the people, in pursuance of the Mushirial orders, and of our love of country, have agreed as follows:

Seeing that from the commencement of this movement, whether on the part of the Government or on that of wise and orderly persons and lovers of peace, who know the value of order and tranquility, most active measures were taken to prevent its occurrence, and to preserve tranquility, and afterwards to quell it speedily, but owing to the efforts of designing and corrupt persons, especially those who have not the quality of compassion for children and infants, and to the folly of the turbulent, the agitation extended, no means remained of immediately quelling it and saving the shedding of blood, and restoring order, except by effecting a general pacification between the belligerents similar to the one concluded after the war of 1815, and that is upon the bases of "oblivion of the past."

Consequently, it has agreed and decided, after invoking the Divine assistance, to conclude peace upon the condition aforementioned; and that all that has passed from the beginning of the war to the present date is not liable to any claim or pretension on either side, neither at present nor in the future; that, after signing the Instruments of Peace, whoever should do anything calculated to occasion the recurrence of disorder will be punished by the authorities, and whoever takes part with him will be an accomplice in his crime and will be punished like him; that all functionaries should unite against whoever commences any such provocation, and give literal effect to the orders of the Government, in accordance with the established regulations: that the Kaimakams, Mokattadjis, and officers, should conform in their proceedings to the regulations and system of government of the Mountain, without any deviation therefrom, and readily execute the orders of the Government agreeable thereto, and should hasten to submit to the Governor whatever it is requisite they should submit to it, and exert themselves to bring about and to promote conciliation, goodwill, and union between the two nations, and the welfare and tranquility of all, and especially the speedy return of everyone to their homes in security, and put him in possession of his landed and immoveable property as formerly, without any trespass or injustice to anyone, and to give every possible assistance to all, in every respect, in pursuance with the Imperial will, under the auspices of his Excellency the Mushir, in case of need, and according to regulation, and that all should strenuously exert themselves to substitute harmony for strife, and restore general tranquility, &c.

Peace having been concluded upon these terms, with the agreement and consent of us all, this Instrument has been drawn up, and four copies written, two by each nation, in order that each nation should give one copy to the other; and two copies submitted by both nations to the Mushirial threshold, that they may be kept in the archives of the Government, to be adhered to and executed at present and for the future.

(Signed by the Kaimakam, Deputies, &c.)

NOTES

Introduction

1. Albert Hourani, "Revolution in the Arab Middle East," *Revolution in the Middle East*, pp.65-72; Hanna Batatu, *The Old Social Classes and the Revolutionary Movement of Iraq* (Princeton, 1978); *idem*, "Some Observations on the Social Roots of Syria's Ruling Military Group and the Causes of its Dominance," *Middle East Journal*, 35 (Summer 1981), pp.331-44; *idem*, "Political Power and Social Structure in Syria and Iraq," *Arab Society: Continuity and Change*, ed. Samih K. Farsoun (London, 1985), pp.34-47; *idem*, "The Egyptian, Syrian, and Iraqi Revolutions: Some Observations on their Underlying Causes and Social Character," Inaugural Lecture, Center for Contemporary Arab Studies, Georgetown University (Washington, DC, 1984); Walid Khalidi, "Political Trends in the Fertile Crescent," *The Middle East in Transition: Studies in Contemporary History*, ed. Walter Laqueur (New York: Praeger, 1958), pp.121-8. See also Bernard Lewis, "Islamic Concepts of Revolution," *Revolution in the Middle East and Other Case Studies*, ed. P.J. Vatikiotis, School of Oriental and African Studies: Studies on Modern Asia and Africa, No.9 (London, 1972), pp.30-40. Some of the ideas of this section are also found in Leila Fawaz, "Revolutions in the Arab World: Egypt, Syria, and Iraq," *World History Bulletin*, vol.7, no.1 (Fall-Winter 1989-90), pp.1-5.

2. Cornell Fleischer, *Bureaucrat and Intellectual in the Ottoman Empire: The Historian Mustafa Ali (1541-1600)* (Princeton: Princeton University Press, 1986), Part 2; Norman Itzowitz, *Ottoman Empire and Islamic Tradition* (Chicago, 1972); Halil Inalcik, *The Ottoman Empire: The Classical Age, 1300-1600*, tr. C. Imber and N. Itzowitz (New York, 1973); Albert Hourani, *A History of the Arab Peoples* (Cambridge, Mass.: Harvard University Press, 1991), Parts 3 and 4; Engin Akarlı, "Provincial Power Magnates in Ottoman Bilad al-Sham and Egypt, 1740-1840," *La vie sociale dans les provinces arabes à l'époque ottomane*, vol.3 (Zaghouan, Tunisia: Publications du Centre d'études et de recherches ottomanes, morisques, de documentation et d'information, 1988), pp.41-56. For a useful comparative statement and overview of recent scholarship see Suzanne Rudolph, "State Formation in Asia - Prolegomenon to a Comparative Study," in *Journal of Asian Studies*, 46, 4 (Nov 1987), pp.731-46.

3. For a comparative analysis see C.A. Bayly, "India and the West," *Asian Affairs*, vol. xix (old series vol.75), part 1 (February 1988), pp.3-29. On the provinces and regional successor states of the Ottoman empire, see the works of Abdul-Rahim Abu-Husayn, Engin Akarlı, Adnan Bakhit, Karl Barbir, Robert Ilbert, Afaf Lutfi Sayyid Marsot, Thomas Philipp, Abdul-Karim Rafeq, Kamal S. Salibi, Linda Schatkowski Schilcher, André Raymond, Abdeljelil Temimi, and others; on Iran, see John R. Perry, *Karim Khan Zand: A History of Iran, 1747-1779* (Chicago: University of Chicago Press, 1979); H.

Brydges, *The Dynasty of the Qajars* (1835); Said Arjomand, *The Shadow of God and the Hidden Imam: Religion, Political Order and Societal Change in Shi'ite Iran from the Beginning to 1980* (Chicago: University of Chicago Press, 1984); Juan Cole, *Roots of North Indian Shiism in Iran and Iraq: Religion and State in Awadh, 1722–1859* (Berkeley: University of California Press, 1988), and Nikki Keddie's works; on South Asia, see C.A. Bayly, *Indian Society and the Making of the British Empire* (New York: Cambridge University Press, 1988); Sugata Bose (ed.), *South Asia and World Capitalism* (Delhi: Oxford University Press, 1990). On social change, see Hanna Batatu, *The Old Social Classes and the Revolutionary Movements of Iraq* (Princeton: Princeton University Press, 1978); Joel Beinin and Zachary Lockman, *Workers on the Nile: Nationalism, Communism, Islam, and the Egyptian Working Class, 1882–1954* (Princeton: Princeton University Press, 1987); Ken Brown, *People of Sale: Tradition and Change in a Moroccan City 1830–1930* (Manchester, 1976); André Raymond, *Artisans et Commerçants au Caire* (1973); Peter Gran, *The Islamic Roots of Capitalism: Egypt, 1760–1840* (Austin: University of Texas Press, 1979); Judith Tucker, *Women in Nineteenth-Century Egypt* (New York: Cambridge University Press, 1985); Ken M. Cuno, *The Pasha's Peasants: Land Tenure, Society, and Economy in Lower Egypt, 1740–1858* (New York: Cambridge University Press, 1992); Abraham Marcus, *The Middle East on the Eve of Modernity: Aleppo in the Eighteenth Century* (New York: Columbia University Press, 1989); Bruce Masters, *The Origins of Western Economic Dominance in the Middle East: Mercantilism and the Islamic Economy in Aleppo, 1600–1750* (New York: New York University Press, 1988); C.A. Bayly, *Rulers, Townsmen and Bazaars: North Indian Society in the Age of British Expansion, 1770–1870* (New York: Cambridge University Press, 1983); Jean-Pierre Thieck, *Passion d'Orient*, ed. Gilles Kepel (Paris: Editions Karthala, 1992).

4. See, for instance, Lawrence Stone, "The Revival of Narrative: Reflections on a New Old History," *Past and Present*, no.85 (November 1979), pp.3–24. For a recent example of a marvelous use of the narrative, see Simon Schama, *Dead Certainties (Unwarranted Speculations)* (New York: Alfred A. Knopf, 1992).

5. See, for instance, Edward W. Said, *Orientalism* (1977); idem, *Culture and Imperialism* (London: Chatto and Windus, 1993).

6. See Ranajit Guha and Gayatri Chakravorty Spivak (eds.), *Selected Subaltern Studies* (New York: Oxford University Press, 1989). There is a voluminous and sophisticated literature on the history of "subaltern" social groups including peasants, workers, and women in South Asia that is not strictly part of the "subaltern school." See also Sugata Bose, "Peasant Labour and Colonial Capital," in *The New Cambridge History of India* (Cambridge: Cambridge University Press, 1993).

7. Gayatri Chakravorty Spivak, "Can the Subaltern Speak?" cited in Guha and Spivak (eds.), *Selected Subaltern Studies*, p.19.

8. On the importance of the state, see Peter Evans, Dietrich Rueschemeyer, and Theda Skocpol (eds.), *Bringing the State Back In* (Cambridge: Cambridge University Press, 1985).

9. William L. Ochsenwald, "The Jidda Massacre of 1858," *Middle Eastern Studies*, vol.13 (1977), pp.314–26; idem, *Religion, Society and the State in Arabia: The Hijaz under Ottoman Control, 1840–1908* (Columbus, Ohio: Ohio State University Press, 1984), pp.137–52; Bruce Masters, "The 1850 Events in Aleppo," *International Journal of Middle East Studies*, vol.22, no.1 (1990), pp.3–20; Moshe Ma'oz, *Ottoman Reform in Syria and in Palestine 1840–1861: The Impact of the Tanzimat on Politics and Society* (Oxford: Clarendon Press, 1968), pp.227–40.

NOTES

10. See, for instance, C.A. Bayly, "The Pre-History of 'Communalism'? Religious Conflict in India, 1700–1860," in *Modern Asian Studies*, vol.19, no.2 (April 1985), pp.177–203, and the growing literature on communalism in South Asian historiography which suggests interesting comparisons with Middle Eastern sectarianism.

1. Changing Worlds

1. W.B. Fisher, *The Middle East: A Physical, Social and Regional Geography* (London: Methuen, 1971), pp.420–1; Dominique Chevallier, *La société du Mont Liban à l'époque de la révolution industrielle en Europe* (Paris: Librairie Orientaliste Paul Geuthner, 1971), chapters 1 and 3; Salibi, *The Modern History of Lebanon*, pp.xi–xiii; idem, *A House of Many Mansions*, chapter 3; Hourani, *Syria and Lebanon*, chapter 1; Abdul-Karim Rafeq, *The Province of Damascus, 1723–1783* (Beirut, 1966); André Raymond (ed.), *La Syrie d'aujourd'hui* (Paris, 1980); Linda Schatkowski Schilcher, *Families in Politics: Damascene Factions and Estates in the 18th and 19th Centuries* (Stuttgart, 1985).

2. Fisher, *Middle East* (London: Methuen, 1971), pp.397, 420–1; Abdul-Karim Rafeq, *The Province of Damascus, 1723–1783* (Beirut: Khayats, 1966), pp.1–76; idem, *Buhuth fi'l-tarikh al-iqtisadi wa'l-ijtima'i li-bilad al-Sham fi'l-'asr al-hadith* (Damascus, 1974); Linda Schatkowski Schilcher, *Families in Politics*, chapter 1; Owen, *The Middle East*, p.29; Anne-Marie Bianquis, "Damas et la Ghouta," in *La Syrie d'aujourd'hui*, ed. André Raymond (Paris: Centre National de la Recherche Scientifique, 1980), pp.359–60; Bruce Masters *The Origins of Western Economic Dominance in the Middle East: Mercantilism and the Islamic Economy in Aleppo 1600–1750* (New York: New York University Press, 1988), pp.9–11.

3. Albert H. Hourani, "Religions," in the *Cambridge Encyclopaedia of the Middle East and North Africa*, ed. Trevor Mostyn and Albert Hourani (Cambridge: Cambridge University Press, 1988), pp.32–7; idem, *Minorities in the Arab World* (London: Oxford University Press, 1947), pp.3–6; Salibi, *Modern History of Lebanon*; idem, *A House of Many Mansions*, pp.5–6, chapters 4 and 5 and others, give a thorough account of the origins of the Maronites and others. See also Leila Fawaz, *Merchants and Migrants in Nineteenth-Century Beirut* (Cambridge, Mass.: Harvard University Press, 1983), pp.15–16.

4. Salibi, *A House of Many Mansions*, chapter 5 and others; Fuad I. Khuri, "The Alawis of Syria: Religious Ideology and Organization," *Syria: Society, Culture, and Polity*, eds. Richard Antoun and Donald Quataert (New York: State University of New York Press, 1991), pp.50ff; Fuad I. Khuri, *Imams and Emirs: State, Religion and Sects in Islam* (London: Saqi Press, 1990).

5. Rafeq, *Province of Damascus*, pp.1–76; Rafeq, *Buhuth*; Karl K. Barbir, *Ottoman Rule in Damascus: 1708–1758* (Princeton: Princeton University Press, 1980), pp.44, 65ff, and elsewhere.

6. Rafeq, *Province of Damascus*, pp.1–76; Barbir, *Ottoman Rule*, pp.108ff.

7. Albert Hourani has analyzed their relationships with the government and their urban population in an article which has become the classic reference on the subject: Hourani, "Ottoman Reform and the Politics of Notables," in *The Emergence of the Modern Middle East* (London: Macmillan, 1981), pp.36–66.

8. Ibid.

9. Barbir, *Ottoman Rule*, pp.56–64, 66–7; Rafeq, *Province of Damascus*, pp.85ff; Schilcher, *Families in Politics*, pp.27–35; Albert Hourani, "Ottoman Reform and the Politics of Notables," and "A Note on Revolutions in the Arab World," in *Emergence of the Modern*

Middle East, pp.36–74; Masters, *Origins of Western Economic Dominance*, pp.43ff; Albert Hourani, *History of the Arab Peoples* (Cambridge, Mass.: Harvard University Press, 1991), chapter 15.

10. Salibi, *House of Many Mansions*, pp.65–6. The best analysis of the nature of the Ma'n and Shihab rule over Lebanon is in *ibid.*, chapter 6.

11. For excellent descriptions of the Lebanese system, consult Iliya F. Harik, *Politics and Change in a Traditional Society, Lebanon 1711–1845* (Princeton: Princeton University Press, 1968); William R. Polk, *The Opening of South Lebanon, 1788–1840: A Study of the Impact of the West on the Middle East* (Cambridge, Mass.: Harvard University Press, 1963); Chevallier, *La société du Mont Liban*, chapter 6; Salibi, *Modern History of Lebanon*; Nasif al-Yaziji, "Risala tarikhiyya fi ahwal Lubnan fi 'ahdihi al-iqta'i'", *al-Masarra*, vol.22 (1936), nos. 5, 6, 8, and 9.

12. Harik, *Politics and Change*, pp.61ff; Chevallier, *La société du Mont Liban*, chapters 7, 10; Dominique Chevallier, "Aux origines des troubles agraires Libanais en 1858," *Annales: Economies, sociétés, civilisations*, XIV, no.1 (January–March 1959), pp.35–64; Dominique Chevallier, "Les cadres sociaux de l'économie agraire dans le Proche-Orient au début du XIXe siècle: le cas du Mont Liban," *Revue Historique*, ccxxxix (1968), pp.87–100; Yehoshua Porath, "The Peasant Revolt of 1858–61 in Kisrawan," *Asian and African Studies*, vol.2 (1966), pp.77–81; Alexander Schölch, "Was there a Feudal System in Ottoman Lebanon and Palestine?," *Palestine in the Late Ottoman Period*, ed. David Kushner (Jerusalem–Leiden: E.J. Brill, 1986), pp.130–45.

13. Mikha'il Mishaqa's memoirs "al-Jawab 'ala iqtirah al-ahbab" (Response to a Suggestion by Beloved Ones) were edited in an abridged text as *Muntakhabat min al-jawab 'ala iqtirah al-ahbab*, by Assad Rustom and Soubhi Abou Chacra, Ministère de l'Education Nationale et des Beaux-Arts, Direction des Antiquités, Textes et Documents, 2 (Beirut: Catholic Press, 1955). The full text of the original manuscript available at the Jaffet Library at the American University of Beirut has now been published as *Murder, Mayhem, Pillage, and Plunder: The History of the Lebanon in the 18th and 19th Centuries by Mikha'il Mishaqa*, tr. from the Arabic by Wheeler M. Thackston, Jr. (Albany, NY: State University of New York Press, 1988) (henceforth cited as "Mishaqa, *History of the Lebanon*). For this reference, see pp.4, 76, 88.

14. Harik, *Politics and Change*, chapters 2 and 3; Polk, *Opening of South Lebanon*, chapters 2–5; Chevallier, *La société du Mont Liban*, chapter 10.

15. Mishaqa, *History of the Lebanon*, pp.6–7; Salibi, *Modern History of Lebanon*, chapters 1 and 2.

16. Harik, *Politics and Change*, chapters 4 and 5.

17. Kamal S. Salibi, *Maronite Historians of Medieval Lebanon*, American University of Beirut, Faculty of Arts and Sciences Publication, Oriental Series, no.34 (Beirut: Catholic Press, 1959); Salibi, *Modern History of Lebanon*, pp.122ff; Harik, *Politics and Change*, chapters 5 and 6, and especially 7.

18. Salibi, *Modern History of Lebanon*, p.27.

19. Harik, *Politics and Change*, pp.208–22; Axel Havemann, *Rurale Bewegungen im Libanon-Gebirge des 19. Jahrhunderts. Ein Beitrag zur Problematik sozialer Veränderungen*, Islamkundliche Untersuchungen, vol.79 (Berlin: Klaus Schwarz Verlag, 1983).

20. Salibi, *Modern History of Lebanon*, chapter 2, gives a masterly account of the reign of Bashir II. This section relies heavily on that account.

21. Salibi, *House of Many Mansions*, pp.104–5; Dominique Chevallier, *La société du Mont*

Liban, chapter 14; *idem*, "Lyon et la Syrie en 1919: Les bases d'une intervention," *Revue Historique*, 224 (October–December 1960), pp.285–7; Boutros Labaki, *Introduction à l'histoire économique du Liban: soie et commerce extérieur en fin de période ottomane 1840–1914* (Beirut, 1984); Gaston Ducousso, *L'industrie de la soie en Syrie* (Paris: Librairie Maritime et Coloniale Challamel, 1918); Isma'il Haqqi, *Lubnan: Mabahith 'ilmiyya wa ijtima'iyya*, (Lebanon: Scientific and Social Studies), ed. Fuad Afram al-Bustani (Beirut: al-Matba'at al-Kathulikiyya, 1970), II, p.439; Kais Firro, "Silk and Agrarian Changes in Lebanon, 1860–1914," *International Journal of Middle East Studies*, vol.22 (1990), pp.151–69; Amir Haydar Ahmad al-Shihabi, *Lubnan fi 'ahd al-umara' al-Shihabiyyin* (Lebanon in the Period of the Shihab Emirs), ed. Fuad E. Boustany, new ed., 18 (Beirut, 1969), vols. 2 and 3; I.M. Smilianskaya, "Razlozhenie feodalnikh otoshenii v Sirii i Livane v Seredine XIX v" (The Disintegration of Feudal Relations in Syria and Lebanon in the Middle of the Nineteenth Century), tr. in *The Economic History of the Middle East, 1800–1914: A Book of Readings* (Chicago: University of Chicago Press, 1966), pp.234–47; Smilianskaya, *al-Harakat al-fallahiyya fi Lubnan*, tr. Adnan Jamus, ed. Salim Yusuf (Beirut: Dar al-Farabi, 1972); Roger Owen, *The Middle East in the World Economy, 1800–1914* (London, 1981), p.157.

22. Rafeq, *Province of Damascus*, pp.69–76; Rafeq, *Buhuth*; Owen, *Middle East*, pp.47, 51, 53ff; Bruce Masters, *The Origins of Western Economic Dominance in the Middle East: Mercantilism and the Islamic Economy in Aleppo 1600–1750* (New York: New York University Press, 1988); Jean-Paul Pascual, "La Syrie à l'époque ottomane (le XIXe siècle)," *La Syrie d'aujourd'hui*, pp.31–53.

23. Owen, *Middle East*, pp.86–7, 97–8; Schilcher, *Families in Politics*, pp.62–9; Charles Issawi, "Economic Change and Urbanization in the Middle East," in *Middle Eastern Cities: A Symposium on Contemporary Middle Eastern Urbanization*, ed. Ira M. Lapidus (Berkeley: University of California Press, 1969), pp.102–21; Iliya F. Harik, "The Impact of the Domestic Market on Rural–Urban Relations in the Middle East," in *Rural Politics and Social Change in the Middle East*, ed. Richard Antoun and Iliya Harik (Bloomington: Indiana University Press, 1972), pp.337–63; Charles Issawi, "British Trade and the Rise of Beirut," *International Journal of Middle East Studies*, 8 (1977), pp.91–101; *idem*, *The Fertile Crescent 1800–1914: A Documentary Economic History* (New York: Oxford University Press, 1988).

24. Kamal S. Salibi, "The 1860 Upheaval in Damascus as seen by al-Sayyid Muhammad Abu'l-Su'ud al-Hasibi, Notable and Later *Naqib Al-Ashraf* of the City," in *Beginnings of Modernization in the Middle East: The Nineteenth Century*, ed. William R. Polk and Richard L. Chambers, Publications of the Center for Middle Eastern Studies, no.1 (Chicago: University of Chicago Press, 1968), pp.190–1; Owen, *Middle East*, pp.98, 168, and elsewhere; Schilcher, *Families in Politics*, pp.62ff.

25. Schilcher, *Families in Politics*, pp.71–5; Rafeq, *Buhuth*; Owen, *Middle East*; Smilianskaya, "The Disintegration of Lebanese Feudal Relations."

26. Schilcher, *Families in Politics*, pp.82–6; Abdul-Karim Rafeq, "Land Tenure Problems and Their Social Impact in Syria around the Middle of the Nineteenth Century," in *Land Tenure and Social Transformation in the Middle East*, ed. Tarif Khalidi (Beirut: American University of Beirut, 1984), pp.371–96; Peter Sluglett and Marion Farouk-Sluglett, "The Application of the 1858 Land Code in Greater Syria: Some Preliminary Observations," *Land Tenures*, pp.409–21.

27. Salibi, *Modern History of Lebanon*, pp.44ff; Albert Hourani, "Lebanon: The Development of a Political Society," *Emergence of the Modern Middle East*, p.132.

28. Salibi, *House of Many Mansions*, p.69.

29. Chevallier, *La société du Mont Liban*, chapters 5 and 6; Salibi, *Modern History of Lebanon*, p.63. According to the findings of Chevallier, by around 1840 the Mountain had a population of at least 200,000 inhabitants, which represented an average of 250 per square mile of cultivable land, and a demographic threshold beyond which the Mountain could not adequately provide for its population. Of this total, the Christians formed about 78 percent, the Druzes 12 percent, and Shi'is and Sunnis the remainder in the territory that Bashir II had ruled. A further break-up of the population shows that the Christian qaymaqamate was about 91 percent Christians, 4 percent Druzes, and some 5 percent Shi'is and Sunnis; the Druze qaymaqamate was made of about 62 percent Christians, 32 percent Druzes, and 5 percent Shi'is and Sunnis.

30. Antun Dahir al-'Aqiqi, *Thawra wa fitna fi Lubnan* (Revolt and Revolution in Lebanon), ed. Yusif Ibrahim Yazbak (Beirut: Matba'at al-Ittihad, 1938), re-edited as *Lebanon in the Last Years of Feudalism, 1840–1868: A Contemporary Account by Antun Dahir al-'Aqiqi and Other Documents*, tr. with notes and commentary by Malcolm H. Kerr, American University of Beirut, Publications of the Faculty of Arts and Sciences, Oriental Studies series, no.33 (Beirut, 1959), p.18 (henceforth cited as Aqiqi, *Lebanon in the Last Years of Feudalism*).

2. Village and Town Life on the Eve of the Civil War

1. For the understanding of the general phenomena of local leadership and social relations in villages and small towns, consult the works of Samir Khalaf, Fuad Khuri, Michael Gilsenan, and those of Janet Abu-Lughod and Jacques Berque, and the thesis of Alixa Naff on Zahleh. To ensure that village life and traditions in Mount Lebanon are not forgotten, Anis Furayha described them in *Hadarat fi tarikh al-zawal: al-qaryat al-Lubnaniyya*, Oriental Studies series, no.28 (Beirut: American University of Beirut, 1957). Consult also the sources listed in Chevallier's preface to *La société du Mont Liban*, pp.xxxi–xxxiii.

2. Iskandar ibn Ya'qub Abkarius, *The Lebanon in Turmoil: Syria and the Powers in 1860: Book of the Marvels of the Time concerning the Massacres in the Arab Country*, tr. and annotated and provided with an introduction and conclusion by J.F. Scheltema (New Haven: Yale University Press, 1920), p.89 (henceforth cited as Abkarius, *Lebanon in Turmoil*); Alixa Naff, "A Social History of Zahle, the Principal Market Town in Nineteenth-Century Lebanon," Ph.D. diss., University of California, Los Angeles, 1972 (Ann Arbor, Mich.: University Microfilms, 1973). I have relied on Naff's very informative thesis for most of my information on that town. My discussions of Zahleh and Deir al-Qamar are reprinted (with minor revisions) from Leila Fawaz, "Zahle and Dayr al-Qamar: Two Market Towns of Mount Lebanon during the Civil War of 1860," in Nadim Shehadi and Dana Haffar Mills (eds.), *Lebanon: A History of Conflict and Consensus* (London: Centre for Lebanese Studies and I.B.Tauris and Co. Ltd., 1988), pp.49–63.

3. Naff, "Social History of Zahle," p.25, *passim*; Antoine Abdel Nour, *Introduction à l'histoire urbaine de la Syrie ottomane (XVIe–XVIIIe siècles)*, Publications de l'Université Libanaise, Section des Etudes Historiques, XXV (Beirut, 1982), pp.349–50; I.M. Smilianskaya, "The Disintegration of Feudal Relations in Syria and Lebanon in the Middle of the Nineteenth Century," tr. in *Economic History of the Middle East, 1800–1914: A Book*

of Readings, ed. Charles Issawi (Chicago: The University of Chicago Press, 1966), pp.227–47; Saba, "The Creation of the Lebanese Economy."

4. Naff, "Social History of Zahle," pp.52ff. Henri Guys, *Beyrouth et le Liban: Relation d'un séjour de plusieurs années dans ce pays* (Paris, 1850), II, p. 33, mentions 5,000 for what is probably the 1820s or 1830s. Charles Henry Churchill, *Mount Lebanon: A Ten Years' Residence from 1842 to 1860* (New York, 1973), II, p.217, estimated its population at 6,000 in the 1840s. Abkarius, *Lebanon in Turmoil*, gave Zahleh about 8,000 on p.88 and only 5,000 on p.94: the first estimate may refer to the later period in which Abkarius wrote (d.1885), and the second to the number of inhabitants around 1860. Cyril Graham, 18 July 1860, *Parliamentary Papers*, vol.69 (1860), "Further Papers Respecting Disturbances in Syria" (henceforth cited as "Further Papers"), p.42, referred to Zahleh as the largest town in Mount Lebanon with a population of 10,000. General Beaufort placed the population before the 1860 civil war at about 7,000 to 8,000: V., G4/1, Beaufort–Randon, 9 September 1860. The anonymous *Kitab al-ahzan fi tarikh waqi'at al-Sham Jabal Lubnan wama yalihima bi ma asaba al-Masihiyyin min al-Duruz wa'l-Islam fi 9 tammuz 1860*, p.29, mentions the figure 12,000. See also Chevallier, *La société du Mont Liban*, pp.61–2; Toufic Touma, *Paysans et institutions féodales chez les Druzes et les Maronites du Liban du XVIIe siècle à 1914*, Publications de l'Université libanaise, Section des Etudes Historiques, XXI (Beirut, 1972), I, p.221; Fawaz, "Zahle and Dayr al-Qamar."

5. All this section is based on Naff, "Social History of Zahle," chapters 2 and 3.

6. Naff, "Social History of Zahle," chapters 1 and 2; Churchill, *Druzes and Maronites*, p.107; Rev. J.L. Porter, *Five Years in Damascus* (London: John Murray, 1855), II, p.279; Jules Ferrette, quoted in Abkarius, *Lebanon in Turmoil*, p.90, n.117.

7. Naff, "Social History of Zahle," pp.99–109; John Lewis Burckhardt, *Travels in Syria and the Holy Land* (London: Macmillan, 1874), p.28.

8. Porter, *Five Years*, II, p.279.

9. Abkarius, *Lebanon in Turmoil*, pp.90–1; Naff, "Social History of Zahle," pp.54–5.

10. Salibi, *Modern History of Lebanon*, p.51; Naff, "Social History of Zahle," pp.269, 285; Husayn Ghadban Abu Shaqra (narrator) and Yusuf Khattar Abu Shaqra (writer), *al-Harakat fi Lubnan ila 'ahd al-mutasarrifiyya*, ed. 'Arif Abu Shaqra (Beirut: Matba'at al-Ittihad, 1952), p.120.

11. Salibi, *Modern History of Lebanon*, p.51; Abkarius, *Lebanon in Turmoil*, p.90; Naff, "History of Zahle," p.270.

12. 'Isa Iskandar al-Ma'luf, "Dayr al-Qamar ila 'ahd al-amir," extracts from an article in *al-Jinan*, repr. in *al-Mashriq* (April 1931), pp.302–4; Isma'il Haqqi, *Lubnan: Mabahith 'ilmiyya wa ijtima'iyya*, ed. Fuad Ifram al-Bustani (Beirut, 1970), pp.198, 359, 618; Mishaqa, *History of the Lebanon*, pp.14 and elsewhere; Abkarius, *Lebanon in Turmoil*, pp.53–4. As mentioned in chapter 1, under the Double Qaymaqamate Deir al-Qamar was the only town to have its own Druze and Christian *wakils*, distinct from those of the Manasif district, which protected it from the direct jurisdiction of the Abu Nakad shaykhs who lorded over the latter.

13. Baron I. Taylor, *La Syrie, la Palestine, et la Judée: Pélerinage à Jérusalem et aux Lieux Saints* (Paris: Le Maître, 1860), p.36.

14. al-Ma'luf, "Dayr al-Qamar ila 'ahd al-amir;" Abdel Nour, *Histoire urbaine*, p.361; Mishaqa, *History of the Lebanon*, pp.122–3.

15. Mishaqa, *History of the Lebanon*.

16. Abkarius, *Lebanon in Turmoil*, p.101; Taylor, *La Syrie*, p.36; Edouard Blondel, *Deux*

ans en Syrie et en Palestine (1838–1839) (Paris: P. Dufart, 1840), p.87; Roger Owen, *Middle East*, p.94; Saba, "Creation of the Lebanese Economy," p.9; Haqqi, *Lubnan*, p.442.

17. At the beginning of the century, according to Mishaqa, *History of the Lebanon*, it had 4,000 people; in 1832–33, Alphonse de Lamartine, *Voyage en Orient* (Paris: Hachette, 1875), p.220, reported 10,000–12,000 people, which seems too high. Guys, *Beyrouth et le Liban*, I, p.136, wrote that during the 1830s, Deir al-Qamar's population numbered 4,000 at most. I.M. Smilianskaya, *al-Harakat al-fallahiyya fi Lubnan*, tr. Adnan Jamus, ed. Salim Yusuf (Beirut, 1972), p.16, mentions that a Russian doctor named Ravalovich gave the population as 10,000 around 1840; more realistic estimates from the same period are probably Abkarius, *Lebanon in Turmoil*, p.98, who gives 7,000, and Charles H. Churchill, *The Druzes and the Maronites under Turkish Rule: From 1840 to 1860* (New York: Arno Press, 1973), p.104, who gives nearly 8,000. In 1860, Cyril Graham, "Further Papers," 18 July 1860, p.42, again mentioned the figure of 7,000. By 1859 it may have had as many as 10,000. See also Chevallier, *La société du Mont Liban*, pp.61–2.

18. F.O. 226/83, Rose–Stratford Canning, No.24, 30 April 1843; Churchill, *Druzes and Maronites*, p.104; V., G4/1, Beaufort–Randon, 9 September 1860; Henri Guys, *Beyrout et le Liban: Relation d'un séjour de plusieurs années dans ce pays* (Paris: Comptoir des Imprimeurs, 1850), p.36.

19. Mishaqa, *History of the Lebanon*, pp.95–105, and elsewhere.

20. *Ibid.*, pp.74–5, 85–8, and elsewhere.

21. *Ibid.*, pp.85–7.

22. *Ibid.*, pp.105ff.

23. *Ibid.*, pp.21, 43–5.

24. F.O. 226/83, Rose–Stratford Canning, No.24, 30 April 1843; Churchill, *Druzes and Maronites*, pp.105–17; Abkarius, *Lebanon in Turmoil*, p.99; I. de Testa, *Recueil des traités de la Porte Ottomane avec les puissances etrangères*, III, p.76, cited by Smilianskaya, *al-Harakat al-fallahiyya*, p.90.

25. Mishaqa, *History of the Lebanon*, pp.88–94.

26. *Ibid.*, pp.114–16.

27. F.O. 226/83, Rose–Stratford Canning, No.24, 30 April 1843; Salibi, *Modern History of Lebanon*, pp.49–52.

28. Chevallier, "Aux origines des troubles agraires libanais en 1858: aspects sociaux de la question d'Orient," *Annales: Economies, sociétés, civilisations*, XIV, no.1 (January–March 1959), pp.36–7; idem, *La société du Mont Liban*.

29. Chevallier, "Aux origines des troubles agraires libanais," pp.46–7; idem, "Que possedait un cheikh maronite en 1859? Un document de la famille al-Khazen," *Arabica*, vol.7 (1960), pp.72–84; Yehoshua Porath, "The Peasant Revolt of 1858–61 in Kisrawan," *Asian and African Studies*, vol.2 (1966), pp.79–81; Marwan R. Buheiry, "The Peasant Revolt of 1858 in Mount Lebanon: Rising Expectations, Economic Malaise, and the Incentive to Arm," in *The Formation and Perception of the Modern Arab World: Studies by Marwan R. Buheiry*, ed. Lawrence I. Conrad (Princeton: The Darwin Press, 1989), pp.499–511.

30. Harik, *Politics and Change*, p.208; Porath, pp.79–81; Chevallier, "Aspects sociaux de la question d'Orient," pp.43, 52–7; Churchill, in *Lebanon in the Last Years of Feudalism*, p.18; Paul Saba, "The Creation of the Lebanese Economy: Economic Growth in the Nineteenth and Early Twentieth Century," in Roger Owen (ed.), *Essays on the Crisis in Lebanon* (London: Ithaca Press, 1976), pp.1–22.

31. Salibi, *History of Lebanon*, chapter 5; Porath, "The Peasant Revolt of 1858–61 in Kisrawan."

32. Harik, *Politics and Change*, pp.120–1.

33. Abkarius, *The Lebanon in Turmoil*, p.63; Aqiqi, *Lebanon in the Last Years of Feudalism*, pp.55–7; Abu Shaqra, *al-Harakat fi Lubnan*, p.100; M.B.P, Awn–Mas'ad, 16 August 1959. Abkarius tells us the quarrel was between two children fighting over a chicken, Aqiqi that it was between two drivers over the collision of their pack animals, Abu Shaqra that a Druze man was transporting water on a donkey and the donkey accidentally hit a Christian child who fell, which precipitated the intervention of his relatives, Tubiyya Awn that a Druze hit a Christian child who reported it to his father, and the father accompanied by two other Christians sought revenge. See also Salibi, *Modern History of Lebanon*, pp.87–9; Cyril Graham, "Further Papers," p.40.

34. Churchill, *Druzes and Maronites*, pp.132–3; Abkarius, *The Lebanon in Turmoil*, p.67; Abu Shaqra, *al-Harakat fi Lubnan*, p.100.

35. In a letter to Patriarch Mas'ad, Tubiyya Awn wrote that for three days after the incident at Beit Meri, he tried to make peace between the Druzes and Christians and that he almost succeeded: M.P.B., Awn–Mas'ad, 16 August 1859. See also the call for peace by the Patriarch in M.P.B., Awn–Mas'ad, 16 August 1859; M.P.B., Awn–Mas'ad, 17 August 1859, mentions that the Druze and Maronite leaders met in Hammana to contain the crisis; M.P.B., Awn–Mas'ad, 31 August 1859, refers to a meeting between the Ottoman authorities and Druze and Maronite parties to discuss compensation for looted and burnt property.

36. Salibi, *Modern History of Lebanon*, pp.87–9.

37. Salibi, *Modern History of Lebanon*, p.89; Aqiqi, *Lebanon in the Last Years of Feudalism*, p.56; Churchill, *Druzes and Maronites*, pp.138–9. Abu Shaqra, *al-Harakat fi Lubnan*, p.99, mentions that Druze–Ottoman relations were good in 1860 because the Ottomans feared French designs in Lebanon.

38. Salibi, *Modern History of Lebanon*, p.90; Abkarius, *The Lebanon in Turmoil*, p.67.

3. Civil War in the Mountain

1. Churchill, *Druzes and Maronites*, p.176; Abkarius, *The Lebanon in Turmoil*, p.64.

2. Sources differ on the date of the attack on that monastery: March 9, according to Abkarius, *The Lebanon in Turmoil*, p.64; March 7 according to Scheltema who edited Abkarius' memoirs, quoting "the evidence pronounced at the alleged murderer's trial" (no source is given); the murder was discovered on March 19 according to the anonymous, "Tabrir al-Nasara mimma nusiba ilayhim fi hawadith sanat 1860," manuscript found and published by Father Louis Blaybil, *al-Mashriq*, vol.26 (1928), p.635; March 19, according to Beaufort d'Haupoul: V., G4/1, Beaufort–Randon, 9 September 1860; around mid-March, according to the French consul general in Beirut: A.E., CPC/B/12, Bentivoglio–Thouvenel, No.30, 30 June 1860; May 4, according to Churchill, *Druzes and Maronites*, p.140. See also Mishaqa, *The History of the Lebanon*, p.238; "Further Papers," "Memorial from the Christians of the Mixed Districts to Khorsheed Pasha, dated May 20, 1860," Encl. No.4 in No.1, Moore–Russell, 24 May 1860, 3. The Druze chronicler Abu Shaqra wrote that a monk from Damascus had ordered the killing of the father superior Athanasius Na'um because he hoped to replace him, and that Bashir Bey Nakad had been wrongly suspected of the killing and later exonerated: Abu Shaqra, *al-Harakat fi Lubnan*, p.102.

3. Churchill, *Druzes and Maronites*, p.176.
4. Churchill, *Druzes and Maronites*, pp.146, 151; Jessup, *Fifty-Three Years in Syria*, I, p.173; "Further Papers," Abela–Moore, Sidon, June 1, 1860, p.9.
5. A.E., MD/T/122, Annexe No.2, 45, 46, 47, et 48e séance, 1862, "Tableau Général des pertes des Chrétiens de Deir el Kamar d'après Yzzet-Effendi." The chart is actually broken into two with some similar information and some differences, partly explained by mistakes in hand copying (corrected in my text), partly by additions.
6. Another estimate of the houses lost is 705. However, if one adds up the houses on that list, the total is 652, in this case a clear-cut example of an adding mistake. Here, as with the other categories, I chose the more comprehensive figure – presumably the later one.
7. Churchill, *Druzes and Maronites*, p.176.
8. Churchill, *Druzes and Maronites*, p.140; Abkarius, *The Lebanon in Turmoil*, p.64, tells us that the murderer turned out to be a Druze from Kfar Qatra in the Manasif district, by the name of Muhy al-Din Abu Tin.
9. Aqiqi, *Lebanon in the Last Years of Feudalism*, p.57; A.E., CPC/B/12, Bentivoglio–Thouvenel, No.30, 30 June 1860.
10. Abkarius, *The Lebanon in Turmoil*, p.64.
11. V., G4/1, Beaufort–Randon, 9 September 1860. The quote is from A.E., CPC/B/12, Bentivoglio–Thouvenel, No.30, 30 June 1860.
12. *Ibid.*
13. A.E., CPC/B/12, Bentivoglio–Thouvenel, No.26, 23 June 1860; V., G4/1, Beaufort–Randon, 9 September 1860.
14. Abkarius, *The Lebanon in Turmoil*, p.64.
15. A.E., CPC/B/12, Bentivoglio–Thouvenel, No.30, 30 June 1860; "Further Papers," Moore–Bulwer, 18 May 1860, Encl.2 in No.1, Moore–Russell, 24 May 1860, 1; *ibid.*, "Memorial from the Christians of the Mixed Districts in Mount Lebanon to Khorsheed Pasha, dated May 20, 1860," Encl.4 in No.1, Moore–Russell, 24 May 1860, 2–3; *ibid.*, "The European Merchants at Beyrout to the Consular Body," 20 May, 1860, Encl.2 in No.3, Moore–Russell, 26 May 1860; M.P.B., Mas'ad–Awn, 18 May 1860; *ibid.*, Mas'ad–Bustani, 18 May 1860; *ibid.*, Hajj–Mas'ad, 23 May 1860; *ibid.*, Awn–Mas'ad, 23 May 1860.
16. "Further Papers," Moore–Bulwer, 31 May 1860, Encl.2 in No.5, p.6; A.E., CPC/B/12, Bentivoglio–Thouvenel, No.16, 31 May 1860; *ibid.*, Bentivoglio–Thouvenel, No.30, 30 June 1860; Churchill, *Druzes and Maronites*, p.141; Henri Harris Jessup, *Fifty-Three Years in Syria* (New York: Fleming H. Revell, 1910), I, pp.170–71; Salibi, *The Modern History of Lebanon*, p.90.
17. Abu Shaqra, *al-Harakat fi Lubnan*, pp.108–9; Anonymous, *Hasr al-litham 'an nakabat al-Sham*, first edition (Egypt, 1895), pp.192–3; A.E., CPC/B/12, Bentivoglio–Thouvenel, No.30, 30 June 1860; *ibid.*, Bentivoglio–Thouvenel, No.12, 3 June 1860; Abkarius, *The Lebanon in Turmoil*, pp.65–7; Aqiqi, *Lebanon in the Last Years of Feudalism*, p.58; Churchill, *Druzes and Maronites*, pp.143–5; Salibi, *The Modern History of Lebanon*, pp.90–1. According to Abd al-Karim Ghurayba, *Suriya fi'l-qarn al-tasi' 'ashar, 1840–1876* (Cairo, 1961–2), p.253, the author of *Hasr al-litham* is Nu'man ibn Abduh al-Qasatli: Fritz Steppat, "Some Arabic Manuscript Sources on the Syrian Crisis of 1860," *Les Arabes par leurs archives (XVIe–XXe siècles)*, ed. Jacques Berque and Dominique Chevallier (Paris: Centre National de la Recherche Scientifique, 1976), p.184.
18. M.P.B., Shahin–Awn, May 1860.

19. *Hasr al-litham*, pp.194–7; Abkarius, *The Lebanon in Turmoil*, p.67; A.E., CPC/B/12, Bentivoglio–Thouvenel, No.30, 30 June 1860. "Further Papers," Moore–Bulwer, 1 June 1860, Encl.6 in No.4, p.8.

20. Abkarius, *The Lebanon in Turmoil*, pp.67–8; Salibi, *The Modern History of Lebanon*, p.91.

21. A.E., CPC/B/12, Bentivoglio–Thouvenel, No.30, 30 June 1860.

22. Salibi, *The Modern History of Lebanon*, p.90; Churchill, *Druzes and Maronites*, pp.141–3; Aqiqi, *Lebanon in the Last Years of Feudalism*, p.57. According to Aqiqi, the troubles in the Arqub began after the Druzes had killed a priest who had been stirring up trouble.

23. Churchill, *Druzes and Maronites*, p.141.

24. Aqiqi, *Lebanon in the Last Years of Feudalism*, p.57; Churchill, *Druzes and Maronites*, pp.142–3; 'Isa Iskandar Ma'luf, *Tarikh madinat Zahla* (Zahla: Matba'at Zahla al-Fatat, 1911), pp.239–40; Anonymous, *Hasr al-litham 'an nakabat al-Sham* (Egypt, 1895), pp.139–40.

25. *Hasr al-litham*, p.139; Abkarius, *The Lebanon in Turmoil*, pp.91–2. Churchill, *Druzes and Maronites*, pp.141–2 and Naff, "A Social History of Zahle," p.362, mention that 3,000 Zahalni participated in the battle of Ain Dara. Aqiqi, *Lebanon in the Last Years of Feudalism*, p.60, wrote that in the first battle of Ain Dara, the men of Zahleh, totalling about 600 rifles, participated and that three days later, Zahalni and others participated in a second battle.

26. *Hasr al-litham*, p.140; Aqiqi, *Lebanon in the Last Years of Feudalism*, pp.57–8.

27. Abkarius, *The Lebanon in Turmoil*, pp.69–70.

28. Churchill, *Druzes and Maronites*, pp.87–8, 21–2, 2–27.

29. *Ibid.*, pp.177–8, 181–2, 187. On the divisions of the Zahalnis, see also Ma'luf, *Tarikh madinat Zahla*, pp.235–8.

30. *Ibid.*, p.81.

31. *Ibid.*, pp.137, 149.

32. *Ibid.*, pp.142–3.

33. Aqiqi, *Lebanon in the Last Years of Feudalism*, p.58; Churchill, *Druzes and Maronites*, p.187. The divisions among the Christians are also mentioned by Anonymous, *Nubdha mukhtasara fi fitan Suriya*, published as *Nubdha mukhtasara fi hawadith Lubnan wa'l-Sham (1840–62)*, by Louis Cheikho (Beirut: Imprimerie Catholique, 1927), pp.11, 13.

34. A.E., CPC/B/12, Bentivoglio–Thouvenel, No.15, 24 May 1860.

35. A.E., MD/T/123, Bentivoglio–Youssef Bey, No.6, 9 June 1860; *ibid.*, Bentivoglio–Youssef Bey, No.3, 13 June 1860.

36. Moore–Bulwer, 31 May 1860, Encl.2 in No.5, *Papers*, p.6.

37. Churchill, *Druzes and Maronites*, pp.149, 159; Aqiqi, *Lebanon in the Last Years of Feudalism*, p.56. Fath Allah ibn As'ad al-Jawish, "Athr Fath Allah aw mir'at al-madi," unpublished manuscript, Orient-Institut der Deutschen Morgenländischen Gesellschaft at Beirut, vol.2, p.298, tells us that his father As'ad, who resided in Deir al-Qamar, met with Bishop Tubiyya Awn in Beirut before the outbreak of hostilities in the Mountain, and that the bishop told him that Yusuf Karam was preparing 20,000 fighters, Abu Samra (of Bkassine) was arming 15,000, and that the people of Metn and of Zahleh would also unite their forces.

38. A.E., CPC/B/12, Bentivoglio–Thouvenel, No.30, 30 June 1860.

39. "Further Papers," Graham's report, 18 July 1860, 42; A.E., CPC/D/6, Lanusse–Thouvenel, No.86, 19 June 1860; Abkarius, *The Lebanon in Turmoil*, pp.64–5.

40. F.O. 195/601, Brant–Bulwer, No.15, 30 May 1860.

41. "Further Papers," Moore–Bulwer, 18 May 1860, Encl.2 in No.1; F.O. 195/601, Brant–Bulwer, No.15, 30 May 1860; Churchill, *Druzes and Maronites*, pp.146, 151.

42. Churchill, *Druzes and Maronites*, p.154.

43. Jessup, *Fifty-Three Years in Syria*, I, pp.169–70. See also Salibi, *The Modern History of Lebanon*, pp.91–2.

44. "Further Papers," Moore–Bulwer, 23 May 1860, Encl.3 in No.1, p.2; *Ibid.*, Moore–Bulwer, 1 June, 1860, Encl.6 in No.4, p.8; *ibid.*, "Memorial from the Christians of the Mixed Districts in Mount Lebanon to Khurshid Pasha, dated May 20 1860," Encl.4 in No.1, p.2; Salibi, *The Modern History of Lebanon*, pp.90ff; Abkarius, *The Lebanon in Turmoil*, pp.64ff; Churchill, *Druzes and Maronites*, pp.149 ff.; Aqiqi, *Lebanon in the Last Years of Feudalism*, pp.56ff.

45. "Further Papers," Moore–Bulwer, 1 June 1860, Encl.6 in No.4, p.8. See also Churchill, *Druzes and Maronites*, p.147; Salibi, *The Modern History of Lebanon*, p.93; A.E., CPC/B/12, Bentivoglio–Thouvenel, No.30, 30 June 1860.

46. F.O. 195/655, Moore–Bulwer, No.30, 3 June 1860; *ibid.*, Moore–Bulwer, No.29, 2 June 1860; A.E., CPC/B/12, Bentivoglio–Thouvenel, No.17, 3 June 1860; *ibid.*, Bentivoglio–Thouvenel, No.19, 8 June 1860; Churchill, *Druzes and Maronites*, pp.151–2; Salibi, *The Modern History of Lebanon*, p.95. The term "corn" (or wheat) is used in the texts cited.

47. *Hasr al-litham*, p.172; F.O., 195/655, Moore–Bulwer, No.31, 3 June 1860; *ibid.*, Moore–Bulwer, No.32, 6 June 1860; A.E., CPC/B/12, Bentivoglio–Thouvenel, No.18, 7 June 1860; *ibid.*, Bentivoglio–Thouvenel, No.19, 8 June 1860; *ibid.*, Bentivoglio–Thouvenel, No.29, 28 June 1860; "Further Papers," Graham's report, 18 July 1860, p.42. Note the French consul general wrote that although a few houses in the suburbs were burnt down, the town itself "almost did not suffer." Perhaps he was referring to the state of the town before the sack.

48. Churchill, *Druzes and Maronites*, pp.151–2.

49. *Ibid.*, p.153.

50. Salibi, *The Modern History of Lebanon*, pp.96ff; Churchill, *Druzes and Maronites*, p.140; "Further Papers," Graham–Dufferin, Beirut, 18 July 1860, Encl. in No.22, Dufferin–Russell, Paris, 5 August 1860; Abu Shaqra, *al-Harakat fi Lubnan*, p.119. *Hasr al-litham*, pp.148–9, traces the beginnings of Druze–Christian hostilities in Hasbaiya to May 19–21.

51. "Further Papers," Graham–Dufferin, 18 July 1860, in Dufferin–Russell, No.22, 5 August 1860, 41; *ibid.*, Moore–Russell, No.20, 14 July 1860, Postscript, 35; A.E., DPB/B/12, Bentivoglio–Thouvenel, No.27, 26 June 1860.

52. Aqiqi, *Lebanon in the Last Years of Feudalism*, p.57, mentioned a priest "who was instigating disturbances near the area of Jazzin." He was one of the early victims of the civil war, killed on the road sometime in the spring of 1860. Abu Shaqra, *al-Harakat fi Lubnan*, p.101, mentions that the inhabitants of Jezzine (and Deir al-Qamar) humiliated and cursed any Druze that crossed their town.

53. *Ibid.*, p.73.

54. Abkarius, *The Lebanon in Turmoil*, p.73, estimates the Druze forces at 1,500, and Churchill, *Druzes and Maronites*, p.156, at 2,000. See also Aqiqi, *Lebanon in the Last Years of Feudalism*, p.58; *Nubdha mukhtasara*, p.10; Abu Shaqra, *al-Harakat fi Lubnan*, pp.113–15.

55. Abkarius, *The Lebanon in Turmoil*, p.74.

56. *Ibid.*, p.73.

NOTES 243

57. Abu Shaqra, *al-Harakat fi Lubnan*, pp.113-15; A.E., CPC/B/12, Bentivogolio–Thouvenel, No.17, 7 June 1860; Abkarius, *The Lebanon in Turmoil*, p.74. See also A.E., CPC/B/12, Bentivoglio–Thouvenel, No.20, 9 June 1860; *ibid.*, Bentivoglio–Thouvenel, No.70, 30 June 1860.

58. Churchill, *Druzes and Maronites*, p.156. The Christians' exodus to the coast is mentioned in "Tanahhudat Suriya," p.18.

59. Mishaqa, *The History of the Lebanon*, p.241; "Further Papers," Abela–Moore, Encl. in No.9, Finn–Russell, 23 June 1860, p.17.

60. A.E., CPC/B/12, Bentivoglio–Thouvenel, No.18, 7 June 1860; Churchill, *Druzes and Maronites*, pp.156-7; A.E., CPC/B/12, Bentivoglio–Thouvenel, No.26, 23 June 1860; "Further Papers," "Extracts from Letters received at the American Consulate, from the Rev. Mr Ford and Mr Eddy, American Missionaries residing at Sidon," 3 June and 4 June 1860, Encl.12 in Moore–Russell, No.4, 7 June 1860, 12–13; F.O. 195/655.

61. A.E., CPC/B/12, Bentivoglio–Thouvenel, No.17, 3 June 1860; *ibid.*, Bentivoglio–Thouvenel, No.18, 7 June 1860; "Tanahuddat Suriya," p.21.

62. *Hasr al-litham*, p.152, dates the siege of the serai to June 4; Abkarius, *The Lebanon in Turmoil*, p.88, dates the massacre in the serai to June 11; Churchill, *Druzes and Maronites*, p.168, to June 10; Graham, "Further Papers," July 18 report, p.42, to June 6; the French consul general to June 11: A.E., CPC/B/12, Bentivoglio–Thouvenel, No.27, 26 June 1860.

63. F.O. 195/655, "Memorial from the Christians who escaped from Hasbaya dated 16 June 1860, presented to the Consul-General of Russia," in Moore–Bulwer, No.42, 27 June 1860; "Further Papers," Graham's report of 18 July 1860, 42; A.E., CPC/B/12, Bentivoglio–Thouvenel, No.27, 26 June 1860; A.E., CPC/D/6, Lanusse–Thouvenel, No.86, 19 June 1860; Churchill, *Druzes and Maronites*, pp.167, 170; Abkarius, *The Lebanon in Turmoil*, p.85. The Christians assembled in the serai on the invitation of Uthman Bey, according to local Christians, Graham, and Bentivoglio; on the invitation of their own elders, according to Churchill; because their spirit failed them, according to Abkarius.

64. "Further Papers," Graham's report, 18 July 1860, p.42; F.O. 195/655, "Memorial from the Christians who escaped from Hasbayya," in Moore–Bulwer, No.42, 27 June 1860. The numbers of those Nayifa Janbalat took under her protection vary from 120 to 200-plus women and children, to 400. Same sources as note 73.

65. Abkarius, *The Lebanon in Turmoil*, p.84; Churchill, *Druzes and Maronites*, p.162; Salibi, *The Modern History of Lebanon*, pp.98-9; "Further Papers," "The Christians of Rasheya and Surrounding Villages," statement of Michail Gabril, respecting the massacre at Rashaiya and its neighborhood, dated 29 June 1860, Encl.12 in No.13, Moore–Bulwer, 28 June 1860, p.26.

66. Salibi, *The Modern History of Lebanon*, p.99; F.O. 195/655, "Memorial from the Christians who escaped from Hasbayya," in Moore–Bulwer, No.42, 27 June 1860; A.E., CPC/B/12, Bentivoglio–Thouvenel, No.27, 26 June 1860.

67. Abkarius, *The Lebanon in Turmoil*, pp.83-4; Anonymous, "Tanahhudat Suriya" (The Sighs of Syria), manuscript, American University of Beirut, pp.19-20.

68. Churchill, *Druzes and Maronites*, pp.162-3; accepted by Salibi, *The Modern History of Lebanon*, p.94; "Further Papers," Graham's report of 18 July 1860, p.41.

69. Abkarius, *The Lebanon in Turmoil*, pp.84-5.

70. A.E., CPC/B/12, Bentivoglio–Thouvenel, No.22, 17 June 1860; Abu Shaqra, *al-Harakat fi Lubnan*, estimates that 23 Shihab emirs were killed.

71. Abkarius, *The Lebanon in Turmoil*, p.88.

72. Abkarius, *The Lebanon in Turmoil*, pp.87–8. See also Churchill, *Druzes and Maronites*, pp.170–2; "Further Papers," Graham's report of 18 July 1860, pp.41–2.

73. *Hasr al-litham*, p.158, mentions that in Hasbaiya and vicinity 734 Christians and 40 Druzes died; Abu Shaqra, *al-Harakat fi Lubnan*, p.119, wrote that 600 Christian men died in Hasbaiya, in addition to the 23 Shihab emirs. Over 800 died, according to those who survived the massacre; 970, according to the British consul in Damascus; some 1,100, according to Abkarius. The French consul general gave two estimates: a high one of 1,500 a few days after the massacre and, still later, a more tempered one of 975 including the Christians who had come to Hasbaiya from the Beqaa. The French consul in Damascus reported that over 900 people were killed in the serai: F.O. 195/655, "Memorial from the Christians who escaped from Hasbayya," in Moore–Bulwer, No.42, 27 June 1860; Brant–Bulwer, 30 June 1860, cited in Abkarius, p.88, n. 114; A.E., CPC/12, Bentivoglio–Thouvenel, No.22, 17 June 1860; *ibid.*, Bentivoglio–Thouvenel, No.27, 26 June 1860; *ibid.*, CPC/D/6, Lanusse–Thouvenel, No.86, 19 June 1860.

74. Graham's report of 18 July 1860, in "Further Papers," p.41.

75. Churchill, *Druzes and Maronites*, p.172; Abkarius, *The Lebanon in Turmoil*, p.88; Graham's report of July 18, 1860, in "Further Papers;" F.O. 195/655, "Memorial from the Christians who escaped from Hasbayya," in Moore–Bulwer, No.42, 27 June 1860.

76. "Further Papers," Graham's report of 18 July 1860, p.42; F.O. 195/655, "Memorial from the Christians who escaped from Hasbayya," in Moore–Bulwer, No.42, 27 June 1860; A.E., CPC/B12, Bentivoglio–Thouvenel, No.27, 26 June 1860.

77. "Tanahhudat Suriya," p.20; F.O. 195/655, "Translation of a Statement of Mr Gabril, Deputy of the Christians of Hasbeya addressed to the British Consulate General – on the Massacre at Rasheya and its Neighborhood – dated 29 June 1860," in Moore–Bulwer, No.46, 4 July 1860; A.E., CPC/B/12, Bentivoglio–Thouvenel, No.32, 4 July 1860.

78. F.O. 195/655, "Translation of a Statement of Mr Gabril ...;" A.E., CPC/B/12, Bentivoglio–Thouvenel, No.32, 4 July 1860; Mishaqa, *The History of the Lebanon*, p.243; Churchill, *Druzes and Maronites*, p.175; Salibi, *The Modern History of Lebanon*, p.101. While most sources mention one combined Druze attack on Rashaiya on June 11, the deputy of the Christians of Hasbaiya reported the Druzes had also attacked the town earlier, on a Tuesday – probably June 6. The losses at Rashaiya are mentioned in "Tanahhudat Suriya," p.20.

79. F.O. 194/601, Brant–Russell, No.5, 18 June 1860; Churchill, *Druzes and Maronites*, pp.176–7.

80. Abkarius, *The Lebanon in Turmoil*, pp.90–1.

81. How many of these skirmishes occurred is not clear, but the Melkite bishop of Zahleh – Basilios – and the bishop of the Greek Orthodox convent of Saidnaya Methodios reported that they were many. A.E., CPC/B/12, Bentivoglio–Thouvenel, No.28, 27 June 1860.

82. Salibi, *The Modern History of Lebanon*, p.102; Abkarius, *The Lebanon in Turmoil*, p.92ff; Mishaqa, *The History of the Lebanon*, pp.213–14; Aqiqi, *Lebanon in the Last Years of Feudalism*, pp.61–2; Churchill, *Druzes and Maronites*, pp.178ff; Naff, "A History of Zahle," p.363.

83. A.E., CPC/B/12, Bentivoglio–Thouvenel, No.24, 21 June 1860; *ibid.*, Bentivoglio–Thouvenel, No.28, 27 June 1860.

84. Seven thousand fighting men: Abkarius, *The Lebanon in Turmoil*, p.94, n.125; Naff, "A History of Zahle," p.364; both quoting Moore–Bulwer, 16 June 1860. Churchill,

Druzes and Maronites, p.186, estimated the entire Zahalni force at 4,000 and Abkarius, p.94, gave an unusually low estimate of 5,000 for the inhabitants of Zahleh, including strangers and allies. For estimates of the total population of Zahleh, see chapter 2.

85. Abu Shaqra, *al-Harakat fi Lubnan*, p.126.

86. Churchill, *Druzes and Maronites*, pp.182–3; Aqiqi, *Lebanon in the Last Years of Feudalism*, p.62; Abu Shaqra, *al-Harakat fi Lubnan*, p. 126; Naff, "A History of Zahle," p.364; Salibi, *The Modern History of Lebanon*, p.102.

87. Abu Shaqra, *al-Harakat fi Lubnan*, p.127.

88. *Ibid.*, pp.127–8. As to the numbers involved, Churchill, *Druzes and Maronites*, p.186, mentioned the Druzes and their allies were about double the number of Zahalni. By his estimate, this would amount to some 8,000 Druzes and allies, a figure far too high, given the entire Druze fighting force. "Further Papers," Brant–Bulwer, 26 June 1860, p.7, quoted a more realistic estimate of about 1,800 or 2,000 Druzes and probably 1,000 more of Kurds, Arabs (Bedouins), and Metwalis (Shi'is).

89. *Nubdha mukhtasara*, pp.15–16; Abkarius, *The Lebanon in Turmoil*, pp.95–7; Salibi, *The Modern History of Lebanon*, pp.103–4; Naff, "A History of Zahle," p.365. Abu Shaqra, *al-Harakat fi Lubnan*, p.127, referred to Khattar Imadi's preparations on the western flank, and p.128 to the neglected northern flank.

90. *Kitab al-ahzan*, p.28; Abu Shaqra, *al-Harakat fi Lubnan*, p.128; Abkarius, *The Lebanon in Turmoil*, p.98; Aqiqi, *Lebanon in the Last Years of Feudalism*, p.63; Churchill, *Druzes and Maronites*, pp.186–7; Salibi, *The Modern History of Lebanon*, pp.103–4; Naff, "A History of Zahle," pp.365–6.

91. "Further Papers," Brant–Bulwer, 26 June 1860, p.7, in No.5; Abkarius, *The Lebanon in Turmoil*, p.97 and n.131; Abu Shaqra, *al-Harakat fi Lubnan*, pp.129–30; Naff, "A History of Zahle," p.365; A.E., CPC/B/12, Bentivoglio–Thouvenel, No.24, 21 June 1860; V., G4/1, Beaufort–Randon, 9 September 1860.

92. A.E., CPC/B/12, Bentivoglio–Thouvenel, No.24, 21 June 1860; "Further Papers," Abela–Moore, 20 June 1860, in No.9, pp.5–18; *ibid.*, Finn–Russell, 2 July 1860 in No.10, p.18.

93. Abkarius, *The Lebanon in Turmoil*, p.98.

94. Kamal S. Salibi, "The 1860 Upheaval in Damascus as Seen by al-Sayyid Muhammad Abu'l Su'ud al-Hasibi, Notable and Later *Naqib al-Ashraf* of the City," in *Beginnings of Modernization in the Middle East: The Nineteenth Century*, ed. William R. Polk and Richard L. Chambers, Publications of the Center for Middle Eastern Studies, No.1 (Chicago: University of Chicago Press, 1968), pp.191–2; Muhammad Abu'l Su'ud al-Hasibi, "Lamahat min tarikh dimashq fi ahd al-Tanzimat," ed. Kamal S. Salibi, *al-Abhath*, vol.21, nos.2–4 (December 1968), p.125.

95. Salibi, "The 1860 Upheaval in Damascus," pp.191–5; al-Hasibi, "Lamahat," p.125.

96. F.O. 195/655, "Translation of a Letter from the Greek Bishop Malathios of Balbeck to Her British Majesty's Consul General in Syria (dated Gelbet [Jebbat] Bsharre, 19 July 1860)," in Moore–Bulwer, No.27, 14 August 1860; A.E., CPC/B/12, Bentivoglio–Thouvenel, No.28, 27 June 1860.

97. Abu Shaqra, *al-Harakat fi Lubnan*, p.130.

98. Mishaqa, *The History of the Lebanon*, pp.238–40.

99. Abkarius, *The Lebanon in Turmoil*, pp.112–13; F.O. 195/655, "Deposition of Shaker and Fathallah Djehami Haleby" in Moore–Bulwer, No.42, 27 June 1860; A.E., CPC/B/12, Bentivoglio–Thouvenel, No.29, 28 June 1860.

100. Abkarius, *The Lebanon in Turmoil*, pp.110–13; Jawish, "Athr Fath Allah," vol.2, p.299; A.E., CPC/B/12, Bentivoglio–Thouvenel, No.29, 28 June 1860; "Further Papers," Graham's report, 18 July 1860, p.43. V., G4/1, Beaufort–Randon, 9 September 1860.

101. Mishaqa, *The History of the Lebanon*, p.240; Abkarius, *The Lebanon in Turmoil*, pp.114–15; Aqiqi, *Lebanon in the Last Years of Feudalism*, p.59; F.O. 195/655, "Deposition of Shaker and Fathallah Djehami Haleby, 25 June 1860."

102. A.E., CPC/B/12, Bentivoglio–Thouvenel, No.29, 28 June 1860.

103. F.O. 195/655, "Deposition of Shaker and Fathallah Djehami Haleby."

104. *Nubdha mukhtasara*, pp.17–18; Abkarius, *The Lebanon in Turmoil*, pp.110–13; "Further Papers," Graham's Report, 18 July 1860, 43; F.O. 195/655, "Deposition of Shaker and Fathallah Djehami Haleby, 25 June 1860."

105. One problem with the date of the attack against Deir al-Qamar is that sources may have confused the day of the week and the date. For example, some sources make June 19 a Wednesday, while others make June 27 a Wednesday. A reconstruction of the calendar confirms that the 27th was indeed a Wednesday, so the 19th was a Tuesday. The reader must then decide whether it is more likely people remembered the day of the week or the date. Abu Shaqra, *al-Harakat fi Lubnan*, p.130, dated the beginning of the Druze attack against Deir al-Qamar to a Thursday, which would make it June 21. An eye-witness account received by the British consul general on June 25, dated the attack to Thursday, June 20: F.O. 195/655, "Deposition of Shaker and Fathallah Djehami Haleby." So did the French consul general, although that Thursday was actually June 21. Indeed, in the same letter where the French consul general referred to the 19th as a Wednesday, he then more correctly referred to the 22nd as a Friday: A.E., CPC/B/12, Bentivoglio–Thouvenel, No.29, 28 June 1860. In earlier correspondence, he had also correctly referred to June 17 as a Sunday: *ibid.*, Bentivoglio–Thouvenel, No.24, 21 June 1860. Cyril Graham mentioned June 21 as the date of the assault in one letter, but in another he wrote that on Wednesday, June 27, he left Beirut, to arrive at Deir al-Qamar the following morning, a Thursday, June 28, adding that the burning of the town had taken place just eight days earlier: F.O. 195/655, Graham, "Report on a Mission to the Druze Chiefs in Lebanon," 3 July 1860, in Moore–Bulwer, No.50, 14 July 1860. The *kavass* to the Prussian consulate at Beirut reported that he visited Deir al-Qamar on Wednesday, June 20 (correct in both day of the week and corresponding date), and that the massacre had occurred that day: "Further Papers," "Deposition of Hamoud Derian," Encl.9 in No.13, Moore–Russell, 5 July 1860, pp.23–5. The British vice-consul in Sidon reported the attack occurred on June 20: *ibid.*, Abela–Moore, 21 June 1860. See also *ibid.*, Graham's report of 18 July 1860, p.43; Mishaqa, *The History of the Lebanon*, p.240.

106. The French consul general mentioned 2,000 in a dispatch on June 28; other official French correspondence brought it down to 1,100 or 1,200. General Beaufort d'Haupoul, who headed the French expedition to Syria between August 1860 and June 1861, estimated some 1,700 died. Abkarius raised the figure to 2,100, and a French commentator to 2,730. Churchill wrote that the serai alone sheltered over 1,200 fugitives with their families. Graham wrote in July 1860: "Some say 900, some that 1,200 to 1,800 males actually perished in that one day." "Further Papers," "Deposition of Hamoud Derian;" *ibid.*, Graham's report of 18 July 1860, 44; A.E., DPB/B/12, Bentivoglio–Thouvenel, No.29, 28 June 1860; Churchill, *Druzes and Maronites*, pp.189–90; V., G.4/1, Beaufort–Randon, 9 Sept. 1860; Abkarius, *The Lebanon in Turmoil*, p.122 and n.174; "Tanahhudat Suriya," p.20.

107. F.O. 195/655, "Deposition of Shaker and Fathallah Djehami Haleby;" A.E., CPC/B/12, Bentivoglio–Thouvenel, No.29, 28 June 1860; Abkarius, *The Lebanon in Turmoil*, pp.116–17; Aqiqi, *Lebanon in the Last Years of Feudalism*, p.65; Abu Shaqra, *al-Harakat fi Lubnan*, p.131.

108. Abu Shaqra, *al-Harakat fi Lubnan*, p.131; "Further Papers," Graham's report of 18 July 1860, 43; Abkarius, *The Lebanon in Turmoil*, pp.117–18.

109. A.E., CPC/B/12, Bentivoglio–Thouvenel, No.29, 28 June 1860; F.O. 195/655, "Deposition of Shaker and Fathallah Djehami Haleby."

110. F.O. 195/655, "Deposition of Shaker and Fathallah Djehami Haleby"; Jessup, *Fifty-Three Years in Syria*, I, pp.188–9.

111. "Further Papers," "Deposition of Hamoud Derian"; *ibid.*, Graham's report of 18 June 1860, p.44; Mishaqa, *The History of the Lebanon*, p.240; F.O. 195/655, "Deposition of Shaker and Fathallah Djehami Haleby;" Abkarius, *The Lebanon in Turmoil*, p.130; Churchill, *Druzes and Maronites*, pp.190–1.

112. F.O. 195/655, "Deposition of Shaker and Fathallah Djehami Haleby;" A.E., CPC/B/12, Bentivoglio–Thouvenel, No.29, 28 June 1860.

113. Fawaz, *Merchants and Migrants*, chapters 4 and 5.

114. W.M. Thomson, *The Land and the Book*, new ed. (London: Nelson and Sons, 1913), pp.8, 15; J.A. Spencer, *The East: Sketches of Travels in Egypt and the Holy Land* (London: Murray, 1850), p.481; L.F. Caignart de Saulcy, *Carnets de voyage en Orient (1845–1869)*, intr., notes critiques, et appendices par Fernande Bassan (Paris: Presses Universitaires de France, 1955), p.90; Porter, *Five Years in Damascus*, I, pp.3–5.

115. U.S./3, Johnson–Williams, 2 June 1860; *ibid.*, Johnson–Cass, 8 June 1860; *ibid.*, Johnson–Cass, 9 June 1860; *ibid.*, Johnson–Morgan, 9 June 1860.

116. U.S./3, Johnson–Cass, 27 June 1860; F.O. 78/1557, Moore–Bulwer, No.41, 26 June 1860, in Moore–Russell, No.16, 27 June 1860; F.O. 195/677, Moore–Russell, No.11, 21 June 1861; *Nubdha mukhtasara*, pp.21–2.

117. F.O. 78/1557, Moore–Bulwer, No.41, 26 June 1860, in Moore–Russell, No.16, 27 June 1860.

118. U.S./3, Johnson–Cass, 23 June 1860.

119. F.O. 78/1557, Moore–Bulwer, No.41, 26 June 1860, in Moore–Russell, No.16, 27 June 1860; U.S./3, Johnson–Cass, 27 June 1860.

120. F.O. 78/1557, Moore–Bulwer, No.41, 26 June 1860, in Moore–Russell, No.16, 27 June 1860; *ibid.*, Moore–Bulwer, No.42, 27 June 1860; *ibid.*, Moore–Russell, No.19, 5 July 1860.

121. Moshe Ma'oz, *Ottoman Reform in Syria and Palestine: 1840–1861* (Oxford: Clarendon Press, 1968), p.230.

122. F.O. 78/1557, Finn–Russell, No.18, 2 July 1860; Ma'oz, *Ottoman Reform*, p.230.

123. F.O. 78/1557, Finn–Russell, No.19, 2 July 1860.

124. Ma'oz, *Ottoman Reform*, p.229.

125. Bruce Masters, "The 1850 Events in Aleppo: An Aftershock of Syria's Incorporation into the Capitalist World System," *International Journal of Middle East Studies*, vol.22, no.1 (February 1990), pp.3–20.

126. F.O. 78/1557, Skene–Russell, No.36, 28 June 1860.

127. F.O. 78/1557, Skene–Russell, No.36, 28 June 1860; *ibid.*, "Private communication from Damascus to Mr Webb," translated from German, Damascus, 25 June 1860, in Moore–Russell, No.19, 5 July 1860.

4. The Damascus "Incident"

1. Ibrahim Arbili, "al-Haditha aw hiya madhbahat sanat 1860 fi-Dimashq al-Sham," *al-Kalima*, vol.9, no.3 (March 1913), p.155; F.O. 195/601, Brant–Russell, No.4, 4 June 1860; *ibid.*, Brant–Bulwer, No.18, 13 June 1860 and other reports.
2. A.E., CPC/D/6, Lanusse–Thouvenel, 4 June 1860.
3. F.O. 195/601, Brant–Bulwer, 3 July 1860; A.E., CPC/D/6, Outrey–Touvenel, 28 July 1860; F.O. 195/601, Brant–Bulwer, No.19, 20 June 1860; *Kitab al-ahzan*, p.34; N. Elias Saad, "The Damascus Crisis of 1860 in the light of *Kitab al-Ahzan*: an unpublished eye witness account," M.A. thesis, American University of Beirut, 1974, p.31; Debbas memoirs.
4. Mishaqa, *The History of the Lebanon*, p.248. Arbili, "al-Haditha," p.156, repeats as his own Mishaqa's comment that the Christians could not even kill their own chickens but took them to the butcher to do the job.
5. A.E., CPC/D/6, Lanusse–Thouvenel, 4 June 1860. For an excellent coverage of Damascus' quarters, see Schilcher, *Families in Politics*, chapter 1.
6. Arbili, "al-Haditha," p.155; F.O. 195/601, Brant–Bulwer, No.18, 13 June 1860; *ibid.*, Brant–Russell No.5, 18 June 1860; *ibid.*, Brant–Bulwer, No.20, 26 June 1860; *ibid.*, "Report of Cyril Graham on the Condition of the Christians in the Districts of Hasbeya and Rasheya," in No.33 to Bulwer; F.O. 78/1520, Brant–Bulwer, No.12, 11 August 1860; F.O. 406/10, Robson's Memorandum in Dufferin–Chevallier, 189; Schilcher, *Families in Politics*, p.90, calculated that *Kitab al-ahzan* supposes some 7,000 refugees were in Damascus at the time of the riots. *Ibid.*, pp.90–1 contain a careful analysis of the Christian population of Damascus and its refugees at the time of the July riots.
7. Probably Mount Hermon (*Jabal al-sheikh*) which was covered with snow all the year round. I am grateful to Abdul-Karim Rafeq for this suggestion.
8. Mishaqa, *The History of the Lebanon*, p.248.
9. Arbili, "al-Haditha," pp.55–6; Mishaqa, *The History of the Lebanon*, p.249; F.O. 195/601, Brant–Russell, No.5, 18 June 1860; *Kitab al-ahzan*, pp.25–6; Saad, "The Damascus Crisis of 1860," p.27; Salibi, "The 1860 Upheaval in Damascus," p.192; Hasibi, *al-Abhath*, vol.21, nos.2–4 (December 1968), p.121.
10. F.O. 195/601, Brant–Bulwer, No.20, 26 June 1860.
11. Mishaqa, *The History of the Lebanon*, p.249; F.O. 195/601, Brant–Bulwer, No.20, 26 June 1860; *Kitab al-ahzan*, pp.25–6.
12. Debbas memoirs; A.E., CPC/D/6, Lanusse–Thouvenel, 2 July 1860; *ibid.*, Outrey–Thouvenel, 2 July 1860; *ibid.*, Outrey–Thouvenel, 28 July 1860; *Kitab al-ahzan*, pp.25–6; Saad, "The Damascus Crisis of 1860," p.27; Mishaqa, *The History of the Lebanon*, pp.248–9. Fritz Steppat, "Some Arabic Sources on the Syrian Crisis of 1860," in Berque and Chevallier (eds), *Les Arabes par leurs archives*, p.188, speculates that the anonymous authors of both *Kitab al-ahzan* and "Tanahhudat Suriya" belonged to the business community of Damascus.
13. See Lanusse reports in A.E., CPC/D/6; F.O. 195/601, Brant–Russell, No.5, 18 July 1860; *ibid.*, Brant–Bulwer, No.20, 26 June 1860.
14. Mishaqa, *The History of the Lebanon*, p.249; *Kitab al-ahzan*, p.34; Saad, "The Damascus Crisis of 1860," p.34; Salibi, "The 1860 Upheaval in Damascus," pp.191–3; Hasibi, "Lamahat," p.125; *Hasr al-litham*, p.224; "Tanahhudat Suriya," p.21; A.E., CPC/D/6, Outrey–Thouvenel, 28 July 1860.

15. A.E., CPC/D/6, Lanusse–Thouvenel, No.87, 2 July 1860; *ibid.*, Outrey–Thouvenel, 28 July 1860; *ibid.*, Lanusse–Thouvenel, 28 July 1860.

16. F.O. 195/601, Brant–Russell, No.5, 18 June 1860; *ibid.*, Brant–Bulwer, No.19, 10 June 1860; A.E., CPC/D/6, Lanusse–Thouvenel, No.87, 2 July 1860; Mishaqa, *The History of the Lebanon*, p.248; A.E., CPC/D/6, Outrey–Thouvenel, 28 July 1860.

17. F.O., 195/601, Brant–Bulwer, No.19, 20 June 1860; *ibid.*, "Private Communication from Damascus to Mr Webb," translated from German, Damascus, 25 June 1860, in Moore–Russell, No.19, 5 July 1860; *ibid.*, Brant–Russell, No.4, 4 June 1860; A.E., CPC/D/6, Lanusse–Thouvenel, No.88, 17 July 1860; Hasibi, "Lamahat," pp.76–7; Arbili, "al-Haditha," p.156; Anonymous, *Nubdha mukhtasara fi hawadith Lubnan wa al-Sham (1840–1862)*, ed. and reprinted from *al-Mashriq* by Louis Cheikho (Beirut: Imprimerie Catholique, 1927), p.25.

18. F.O., 195/601, Brant–Bulwer, No.19, 20 June 1860; *ibid.*, "Private Communication from Damascus to Mr Webb"; *ibid.*, Brant–Russell, No.4, 4 June 1860; A.E., CPC/D/6, Lanusse–Thouvenel, No.88, 17 July 1860.

19. F.O. 406/10, Robson's Memorandum in Dufferin–Russell, No.187, 23 September 1860; Mishaqa, *The Lebanon in Turmoil*, p.249; A.E., CPC/D/6, Outrey–Thouvenel, 28 July 1860; *Hasr al-litham*, p.224; *Kitab al-ahzan*, pp.37, 42–4; *Nubdha mukhtasara*, p.26; "Tanahhudat Suriya," p.22.

20. F.O. 406/10, Robson's Memorandum in Dufferin–Russell, No.187, 23 September 1860; F.O. 78/1557, Brant–Russell, 26 June 1860 (note that in this letter dated 26 June, Brant mentioned the festivities of the Bairam begun on that day); Abkarius, *The Lebanon in Turmoil*, p.129; A.E., CPC/D/6, Outrey–Thouvenel, 28 July 1860; *ibid.*, Lanusse–Thouvenel, No.87, 2 July 1860; *Hasr al-litham*.

21. Hasibi, "Lamahat," pp.124–5; F.O. 195/601, "Private Communication from Damascus to Mr Webb"; Mishaqa, *The History of the Lebanon*, pp.248–50; A.E., CPC/D/6, Lanusse–Thouvenel, No.87, 2 July 1860; *ibid.*, Outrey–Thouvenel, 28 July 1860; F.O. 406/10, Robson's Memorandum in Dufferin–Russell, No.187, 23 September 1860.

22. F.O. 406/10, Robson's Memorandum in Dufferin–Russell, No.187, 23 September 1860; Mishaqa, *The History of the Lebanon*, p.250.

23. A.E., CPC/D/6, Outrey–Thouvenel, 28 July 1860; F.O. 78/1519, "Copy of a Letter from a Turkish Muslim in Damascus (translated from the Turkish)," in Moore–Russell, No.27, 4 August 1860; *Kitab al-ahzan*, p.44; Hasibi, "Lamahat," p.126; *Nubdha mukhtasara*, p.26; Abkarius, *The Lebanon in Turmoil*, p.129; F.O. 406/10, Robson's Memorandum in Dufferin–Russell, No.187, 23 September 1860; Debbas memoirs. Hasibi mentioned that Frayj and Shami complained to Ahmad Pasha, Robson added Mitri Shalhub to the other two, and "Tanahhudat Suriyya," p.25, wrote that there was a rumor one of the Christian notables had objected to the government.

24. *Hasr al-litham*, p.228; *Nubdha mukhtasara*, p.26; F.O. 78/1519, "Copy of a Letter from a Turkish Muslim;" F.O. 406/10, Robson's Memorandum in Dufferin–Russell, No.187, 23 September 1860; *Kitab al-ahzan*, p.45; Debbas memoirs; Abkarius, *The Lebanon in Turmoil*, pp.129–30. The arrested boys were three, according to *Hasr al-litham*, two according to Robson and Debbas; no numbers are given in most sources.

25. *Hasr al-litham*, p.228; *Kitab al-ahzan*, pp.46–7; Hasibi in "Lamahat," p.194; Salibi, "The 1860 Upheaval in Damascus," pp.194–5; Saad, "The Damascus Crisis of 1860," p.38; "Tanahhudat Suriyya," p.25; Abd al-Razzaq al-Bitar, *Hilyat al-bashar fi tarikh al-qarn al-thalith ʿashar*, 3 vols. (Damascus, 1961–3), vol.1, p.260; Mishaqa, *The Lebanon in Turmoil*, p.250; F.O. 195/601, Brant–Bulwer, No.24, 11 July 1860.

26. F.O. 78/1519, "Copy of a Letter from a Turkish Muslim;" F.O. 406/10, Robson's Memorandum in Dufferin–Russell, No.187, 23 September 1860; *Hasr al-litham*, p.228; Abkarius, *The Lebanon in Turmoil*, p.130. On Halabi, see Salibi, "The 1860 Upheaval in Damascus," p.196, n.76; Schilcher, *Families in Politics*, p.94.

27. F.O. 406/10, Robson's Memorandum in Dufferin–Russell, No.187, 23 September 1860; F.O. 78/1519, "Copy of a Letter from a Turkish Muslim," wrote that people of the villages surrounding Damascus and the Arabs and Druzes came in crowds to the city after some hours and filled it; Abkarius, *The Lebanon in Turmoil*, p.131, wrote that Druzes from outside town joined the Muslim country-folk who were in the city; Debbas memoirs refer to villagers coming into town; Hasibi, "Lamahat," p.127, to more than a thousand Druzes coming in; Salibi, "The 1860 Upheaval in Damascus," p.195; Mishaqa, *The History of the Lebanon*, p.258, wrote that on the first day of the riots, the influx of Muslims and Druzes from the villages did not cease, and that the street was filled with people pouring in from the villages, bent on killing and looting; Churchill, *Druzes and Maronites*, p.212, mentioned the people of the suburbs came pouring in; A.E., CPC/D/6, Outrey–Thouvenel, 28 July 1860, mentioned the figure of 20,000; *Kitab al-ahzan*, p.52, estimated the crowd at 50,000. For clear explanations of the various quarters of Damascus, see N. Eliséeff, "Dimashk," *Encyclopaedia of Islam*, 2nd ed. (Leiden: Brill, 1965), II, pp.277–91; and Schilcher, *Families in Politics*, chapter 1.

28. Hasibi, "Lamahat," p.127; Salibi, "The 1860 Upheaval in Damascus," pp.194–5; F.O. 78/1519, "Copy of a Letter from a Turkish Muslim."

29. Hasibi, "Lamahat," pp.127–29; Abkarius, *The Lebanon in Turmoil*, p.130, including n.190; F.O. 406/10, Robson's Memorandum in Dufferin–Russell, No.187, 23 September 1860; Mishaqa, *The History of the Lebanon*, p.250.

30. Mishaqa, *The History of the Lebanon*, p.250; Hasibi, "Lamahat," p.128; *Hasr al-litham*, p.228, mentioned the Greek Orthodox church caught fire and the fire gave people the idea to burn things; A.E., CPC/D/6, Outrey–Thouvenel, 28 July 1860, mentioned roofs were burned in the bazaar; Churchill, *Druzes and Maronites*, p.211, wrote that a mat covering in the bazaar caught fire; Abkarius, *The Lebanon in Turmoil*, pp.130–1, wrote that two insurgents were killed, several others wounded, and the rest ran away until the troops were recalled to the citadel.

31. Abkarius, *The Lebanon in Turmoil*, pp.130–1, n.191; Mishaqa, *The History of the Lebanon*, p.251; A.E., CPC/D/6, Outrey–Thouvenel, 28 July 1860.

32. F.O. 78/1519, "Copy of a Letter from a Turkish Muslim."

33. F.O. 194/601, Brant–Russell, No.8, 16 July 1860; Hasibi, "Lamahat," p.128.

34. *Hasr al-litham*, p.229; Hasibi, "Lamahat," p.129; Salibi, "The 1860 Upheaval in Damascus," pp.195–6 and n.74; F.O. 195/601, Brant–Russell, No.8, 16 July 1860; *ibid.*, Robson's Memorandum in Dufferin–Russell, No.187, 23 September 1860; Mishaqa, *The History of the Lebanon*, p.250; A.E., CPC/D/6, Outrey–Thouvenel, 28 July 1860; *ibid.*, Lanusse–Thouvenel, No.88, 17 July 1860; F.O. 78/1519, "Copy of a Letter from a Turkish Muslim." Brant and Outrey tell us that Mustafa Bey al-Hawasili was a friend of Richard Wood, the British consul in Syria in the 1840s, under whose "patronage and kindness he [Hawasili] amassed money during the Crimean War."

35. F.O. 195/601, Brant–Russell, No.8, 16 July 1860; A.E., CPC/D/6 Outrey–Thouvenel, 28 July 1860; F.O. 78/1519, "Copy of a Letter from a Turkish Muslim."

36. 406/10, Robson's Memorandum in Dufferin–Russell, No.187, 23 September 1860; A.E., CPC/D/6, Outrey–Thouvenel, 28 July 1860; Mishaqa, *The Lebanon in Turmoil*,

p.250; F.O. 78/1519, "Copy of a Letter from a Turkish Muslim;" *A Journal of Desert and Syrian Wanderings in the Year 1860* (Dublin: Pattison Jolly, 1873), p.129; *Hasr al-litham*, pp.228–9; *Nubdha mukhtasara*, p.31; "Tanahhudat Suriya," p.27.

37. *Hasr al-litham*, p.229; "Tanahhudat Suriya," p.26ff; F.O. 406/10, Robson's Memorandum in Dufferin–Russell, No.187, 23 September 1860; F.O. 78/1519, "Copy of a Letter from a Turkish Muslim;" A.E., CPC/D/6, Le capitaine du vaisseau de La Roncière au ministre de la guerre, 11 July 1860.

38. Caesar E. Farah, "The Problem of the Ottoman Administration in the Lebanon 1840–1861," Ph.D. diss., Princeton University, 1957 (University Microfilms International, 1988), pp.220–2, makes the interesting connection between the Crimean war and the growth of Muslim resentment against Christians in Syria.

39. A.E., CPC/6, Outrey–Thouvenel, 28 July 1860.

40. *The Times*, 2 August 1860, p.12; F.O. 195/601, Brant–Moore, No.13, 10 July 1860 in Brant–Bulwer, No.24, 11 July 1860; A.E., CPC/D/6, Lanusse–Thouvenel, No.88, 17 July 1860; *ibid.*, Outrey–Thouvenel, 28 July 1860; F.O. 195/601, Brant–Russell, No.8, 16 July 1860; F.O. 78/1508, copy of a telegram, Bulwer–Russell, 16 July 1860, in Bulwer–Russell, No.404, 16 July 1860; "Further Papers," Moore–Bulwer, 11 July 1860, Encl.3 in No.16, Blunt–Russell, 17 July 1860, p.31; Abkarius, *The Lebanon in Turmoil*, pp.131–2, including n.196. Abkarius wrote that every servant and attendant at the Russian consulate was killed, but F.O. 406/10, Robson's Memorandum in Dufferin–Russell, No.187, 23 September 1860, mentioned the dragoman was killed and two servants escaped by hiding in the cellar. F.O. 78/1519, "Copy of a Letter from a Turkish Muslim," wrote that the French and English consulates were not burned because they were in the Muslim quarter, but other sources, including the French themselves, reported the French consulate was an early target of attack.

41. F.O. 195/601, Smylie Robson–Brant, 9 July 1860, in Brant–Moore, No.13, 10 July 1860.

42. Abkarius, *The Lebanon in Turmoil*, p.132, n.195; F.O. 195/601, Robson–Brant, 9 July 1860, in Brant–Moore, No.13, 10 July 1860; *ibid.*, Brant–Russell, No.8, 16 July 1860; Schilcher, *Families in Politics*, p.98. Although Mishaqa, *The Lebanon in History*, p.260, and Bulwer in F.O. 78/1508, copy of a telegram to Russell, in Bulwer–Russell, No.404, 16 July 1860, report that the English consulate alone had not been damaged, Scheltema points out that the Prussian and English consulates, outside the Christian quarter, were spared.

43. *The Times*, 2 August 1860, p.12; F.O. 195/601, Robson–Brant, 9 July 1860, in Brant–Moore, No.13, 10 July 1860; *ibid.*, Brant–Russell, No.8, 16 July 1860; *ibid.*, Brant–Bulwer, No.24, 11 July 1860; Schilcher, *Families in Politics*, p.92; *A Journal of Desert and Syrian Wanderings*, p.129, Abkarius, *The Lebanon in Turmoil*, p.132, n.196 mentions that Graham was Irish.

44. A.E., CPC/D/6, Outrey–Thouvenel, 28 July 1860; Mishaqa, *The History of the Lebanon*, p.250; F.O. 195/601, Brant–Moore, No.13, 10 July 1860, in Brant–Bulwer, No.24, 11 July 1860; *A Journal of Desert and Syrian Wanderings*, p.129.

45. F.O. 406/10, Robson's Memorandum in Dufferin–Russell, No.187, 23 September 1860; Abkarius, *The Lebanon in Turmoil*, pp.132–4; Mishaqa, *History of the Lebanon*, p.252; F.O. 78/1519, "Copy of a Letter from a Turkish Muslim."

46. F.O. 406/10, Robson's Memorandum in Dufferin–Russell, No.187, 23 September 1860; Mishaqa, *The History of the Lebanon*, pp.251–2 also report that on Wednesday,

Christians were rounded up and killed; F.O. 195/601, Brant–Bulwer, No.24, 11 July 1860.

47. F.O. 406/10, Robson's Memorandum in Dufferin–Russell, No.187, 23 September 1860; F.O. 78/1519, "Copy of a Letter from a Turkish Muslim."

48. Mishaqa, *The History of the Lebanon*, pp.255–60; Abkarius, *The Lebanon in Turmoil*, p.132, n. 196; *The Times*, 2 August 1860, p.12, citing M. Jules Ferrette in *The 'Banner of Ulster'*, 11 July.

49. Debbas memoirs.

50. F.O. 195/601, Brant–Moore, No.13, 10 July 1860, in Brant–Bulwer, No.24, 11 July 1860.

51. F.O. 195/601, Brant–Bulwer, No.24, 11 July 1860.

52. F.O. 78/1519, Graham–Moore, 26 July 1860, in Moore–Bulwer, No.54, 28 July 1860; F.O. 195/601, Brant–Bulwer, No.27, 24 July 1860; A.E., CPC/D/6, Lanusse–Thouvenel, No.88, 17 July 1860; *ibid.*, CPC/D/6, Outrey–Thouvenel, 28 July 1860.

53. Salibi, "The 1860 Upheaval in Damascus," p.196; Hasibi, "Lamahat," p.129; *Hasr al-litham*, pp.230–4; "Tanahhudat Suriya," pp.32ff; Mishaqa, *The History of the Lebanon*, pp.249–50; Abkarius, *The Lebanon in Turmoil*, p.134; Schilcher, *Families in Politics*, p.99; Arbili, "al Haditha," p.301, also praises Abd al-Qadir.

54. A.E., CPC/D/6, Outrey–Thouvenel, 28 July 1860; *Kitab al-ahzan*, pp.130–1, 210; Arbili, "al-Haditha," pp.226–8; Saad, "The Damascus Crisis of 1860," pp.51, 59–60; Mishaqa, *The History of the Lebanon*, pp.251, 30; Hasibi, "Lamahat," p.129; Salibi, "The 1860 Upheaval in Damascus," pp.195–7; Schilcher, *Families in Politics*, p.87. See also *Hasr al-litham*, p.235.

55. Salibi, "The 1860 Upheaval in Damascus," p.196; Hasibi, "Lamahat," p.129.

56. F.O. 78/1519, "Copy of a Letter from a Turkish Muslim." I have assumed the author of the letter is a man, although the letter is anonymous, a safe bet given the period.

57. F.O. 195/601, Brant–Moore, No.13, 10 July 1860, in Brant–Bulwer, No.24, 11 July 1860; Saad, "The Damascus Crisis of 1860," p.52; Hasibi, "Lamahat," pp.132–3; Salibi, "The 1860 Upheaval in Damascus," p.196.

58. Consult the works of Rafeq. For the events of Aleppo, see the exhaustive study of Masters, "The 1850 'Events' in Aleppo," pp.3–20.

5. International Response

1. An excellent study of this subject was written by Caesar E. Farah, "The Problem of the Ottoman Administration in the Lebanon 1840–1861," Ph.D. diss., Princeton University, 1957 (Ann Arbor, Mich.: University Microfilms International, 1988), p.292; Joseph Hajjar, *L'Europe et les destinées du Proche-Orient, II: Napoléon III et ses visées orientales 1848–1870*, vol.2 (Damascus: Tlas, 1988), p.980.

2. *The Lebanon in Turmoil*, p.143; also cited in Farah, "Ottoman Administration in Lebanon," p.292; *Souvenirs de Syrie*, p.200; Hariciye, Safvet Efendi–Canacuenos Bey, No.4301/117, 8 August 1860.

3. Hajjar, *Napoléon III*, vol.2, pp.980–1. For a summary of the careers of Mehmet Emin Ali Pasha (1815–71) and Mehmet Rushdi Pasha (1811–82), consult Ibrahim Alaettin Govsa, *Türk Meşhurları Ansiklopedisi* (Istanbul, n.d. [1945]), pp.34, 331.

4. Hajjar, *Napoléon III*, vol.2, pp.971, 980–1; A.E., CP/T/345, de la Valette–Thouvenel, Therapia, No.7, 13 June 1860; *ibid.*, No.13, 17 June 1860; *ibid.*, No.15, 4 July 1860; *ibid.*, No.29, 18 July 1860 and enclosure de la Valette–Bentivoglio, Therapia, No.56, 17 July 1860; *ibid.*, No.9, 20 June 1860. The textual translation of La Valette's "cela craque de tous côtés" is "everything is falling apart."

5. Hajjar, *Napoléon III*, vol.2, pp.971, 980–1.

6. Testa, *Recueil des traités de la Porte ottomane avec les puissances étrangères*, vol.6 (Paris, 1884), pp.92–3.

7. A.E., CP/T/345, enclosure of a letter from the sultan dated 16 July 1860, enclosed in Dépêche télégraphique, de la Valette, 17 July 1860; Hariciye, Safvet Efendi–Canacuenos Bey, No.4301/117, 8 August 1860: "les nouvelles exagérées et les appreciations malveillantes et erronées;" *ibid.*, Cabouly Efendi–Ambassadors of Turkey in Paris/London/Vienna, No.4488/46, 8 August 1860. For Ottoman concern over the coverage of the crisis in Europe, also see *ibid.*, Musurus Bey–Safvet Effendi, London, 12 July 1860; *ibid.*, Sadek–Callimaki, Vienna, 13 July 1860; *ibid.*, Musurus–Savfet Efendi, London, 19 July 1860; *ibid.*, Sadek, Vienna, 19 July 1860; *ibid.*, (Diran)–Safvet Efendi, Brussels, 18 August 1860; *ibid.*, Musurus–Safvet Efendi, London, No.1062, 27 August 1860; *ibid.*, Safvet Efendi–Musurus Bey, No.4602/80, 29 August 1860; *ibid.*, Rustem–Safvet Efendi, Turin, 23 August 1860; *ibid.*, Musurus–Safvet Efendi, London, No.1062, 27 August 1860; *ibid.*, Safvet Efendi–Musurus, No.466/86, 12 September 1860.

8. Hariciye, Sadek–Callimaki, Vienna, 13 July 1860; *ibid.*, (Diran)–Safvet Efendi, Brussels, 18 August 1860.

9. Hajjar, *Napoléon III*, vol.2, pp.970, 975; Edwards, *La Syrie*, pp.185, 204; A.E., CP/T/345, Telegram, de la Valette–Thouvenel, 7 July 1860; *ibid.*, de la Valette–Thouvenel, Therapia, No.9, 20 June 1860. F.O. 78/1510, Bulwer–Moore, No.17, 8 August 1860, in Bulwer–Russell, No.491, 8 August 1860, mentions that at the outset of the insurrection in Syria, a proposal was made to employ Egyptian troops in Syria. Farah, "The Problem of the Ottoman Administration in the Lebanon," p.292, tells us that Ottoman troops some 1,400 strong were sent to Syria on two war vessels, under the command of Qaputan Mustafa Pasha himself.

10. Govsa, *Türk Meşhurları Ansiklopedisi*, p.274. I am indebted to Feroz Ahmad for drawing my attention to this source and for translating the entry on Namık Pasha. See also Stanford J. Shaw and Ezel Kural Shaw, *History of the Ottoman Empire and Modern Turkey*, vol.II, *Reform, Revolution and Republic: The Rise of Modern Turkey 1808–1975* (Cambridge: Cambridge University Press, 1977), pp.48, 501; Ma'oz, *Ottoman Reform*, p.42. For an explanation of the office of *serasker* and its changing importance in the 1840s and 1850s, see *ibid.*, pp.40–2.

11. The best account of the riots in Jedda is found in William Ochsenwald, *Religion, Society and the State in Arabia: The Hijaz under Ottoman Control, 1840–1908* (Columbus, Ohio: Ohio State University Press, 1984), pp.137–52; *idem*, "The Jidda Massacre of 1858," *Middle Eastern Studies*, 13 (1977), pp.314–26. See also *idem*, "Muslim–European Conflict in the Hijaz: The Slave Trade Controversy, 1840–1895," *Middle Eastern Studies*, 16 (1980), pp.115–26.

12. A.E., CP/T/345, de la Valette–Thouvenel, Therapia, No.15, 4 July 1860, mentions that Bulwer campaigned for Umar Pasha and did not object as strongly as the French ambassador about Namık Pasha; F.O. 78/1508, Bulwer–Russell, No.412, 17 July 1860; F.O. 195/601, Brant–Bulwer, No.20, 26 June 1860. The Umar Pasha nominated

254 AN OCCASION FOR WAR

by Bulwer may be either Umer Lutfi Pasha (1806–71) or Umer Naili Pasha (1831–70); both are mentioned in Govsa, *Türk Meşhurları Ansiklopedisi*, p.301.

13. A.E., CP/T/345, de la Valette–Thouvenel, Therapia, No.9, 20 June 1860; *ibid.*, (de la Valette)–Thouvenel, 22 June 1860; *ibid.*, Telegram, de la Valette–Thouvenel, 8 July 1860; A.E., CP/T/346, de la Valette–Thouvenel, Therapia, No.37, 1 August 1860.

14. Hariciye, S.E. Safvet Efendi aux Représentants de la Porte à Londres, Paris, Vienne, Petersburg, Berlin, Turin, 25 July 1860, No.4462/43; *ibid.*, Abro Efendi, Beirut, 23 July 1860; A.E., CP/T/345, Extracts from a telegram from the Sublime Porte to its ambassador in Paris, 14 July 1860; *ibid.*, Telegram, de la Valette–Thouvenel, 8 July 1860; Hajjar, *Napoléon III*, vol.2, pp.975–6, 990; *Souvenirs de Syrie*, p.200; F.O. 78/1508, Bulwer–Russell, No.412, 17 July 1860; M. Tayyıb Gökbilgin, "1840'dan 1861'e kadar Cebel-i Lübnan Meselesi ve Drüziler" (The Mount Lebanon Problem and the Druzes, 1840–1861), *Belleten* (The Journal of the Turkish Historical Association), vol.10 (1946), p. 689; A. Haluk Ülman, *1860–1861 Suriye Buhranı: Osmanlı Diplomasisinden bir Örnek Olay* (The Syrian Crisis of 1860–1861 as a Case of Ottoman Diplomacy), (Ankara: Ankara University Political Science School Publication, 1966), p.38. Beaufort was told by Ottoman officials that the army of Syria with its reinforcements amounted to a maximum of 14,000 to 15,000 men in May 1861: V., G4/1, Beaufort–Randon, No.50, 5 May 1861; F.O. 195/660, Fraser – himself a military observer – was presented with a total of 23,000 which he rejected as unrealistic. Instead, deducting sick and other disabled soldiers, and allowing for "the usual incorrectness of Turkish returns," he opted for an estimate of some 16,000 to 17,000 troops in Syria – 4,000 of whom were in the mixed districts: F.O. 195/660, Fraser–Bulwer, No.10, 2 June 1861. These estimates are very close to those of 15,000 to 16,000 often quoted as the number of troops at Fuad Pasha's disposal.

15. "Fireman [*sic*] du sultan Abdul-Medjid à Fuad-pacha, en date du 8 au 18 juillet 1860 (dernière decade de zilhidje 1276)," in Testa, *Recueil*, vol.6, pp.190–1; F.O. 78/1519, copy of an English translation of the Imperial Firman enclosed in Moore–Bulwer, No.52, 21 July 1860, and in Moore–Russell, No.23, 21 July 1860.

16. On August 6, 1861, while still in Beirut, Fuad Pasha was appointed foreign minister for the fourth time, and on November 22 grand vizier. Before he died in February 1869, he was to serve as grand vizier again in 1863 and as acting grand vizier in the fall of 1867, and foreign minister for the fifth time in February 1867. He published several books, and he was awarded the title of Grand Cross of at least 27 various orders in Europe. For a summary of his career, consult Roderic H. Davison, "Fuad Pasha," *Encyclopaedia of Islam*, 2nd ed., pp.934–6; *idem*, *Reform in the Ottoman Empire: 1856–1876* (Princeton: Princeton University Press, 1963). See also *Lebanon in the Last Years of Feudalism*, p.70, n.1; Edwards, *La Syrie*, pp.185–8. Fuad Pasha was in Beirut on November 28, 1861, when a ship arrived with the sultan's firman appointing him grand vizier: F.O. 195/660, Fraser–Bulwer, No.78, 30 November 1861. He was back in Istanbul on December 21. A biography of Fuad Pasha is also available in İbnülemin Mahmut Kemal İnal, *Osmanlı Devrinde Son Sadrazamlar*, I, II (Istanbul, 1940–1), pp.149–95. See also A. Haluk Ülman, *1860–1861 Suriye Buhranı* (Ankara Universitesi Siyasal Bilgiler Fakültesi Yayınları), p.38, n.33.

17. Hajjar, *Napoléon III*, vol.2, p.991; Edwards, *La Syrie*, pp.184, 206–7; Farah, "Ottoman Administration in the Lebanon," p.294; A.E., CP/T/345, de la Valette–Thouvenel, Therapia, No.9, 20 June 1860; A.E., CP/T/346, Bentivoglio–de la Valette, 12 August 1860; Govsa, *Türk Meşhurları Ansiklopedisi*, p.331.

18. Hajjar, *Napoléon III*, vol.2, p.990.

19. Ülman, *1860–1861 Suriye Buhranı*, p.39, n.40, citing Abro Efendi, 17 July, from the ship *Taif*, Hariciye, karton 36, dosya 3; *Souvenirs de Syrie*, p.201; Farah, "Ottoman Administration in the Lebanon," p.293; A.E., CP/T/346, Fuad Pasha–Thouvenel, Beirut, (no day) September 1860.

20. Arrival in Beirut on July 17: V., G4/1, Beaufort–Randon, 9 September 1860; on July 18: Ülman, *1860–1861 Suriye Buhranı*, p.38, and n.35 citing Abro Efendi, 17 July, from the ship *Taif*: Hariciye, karton 36, dosya 3. The quotes are from the French text: "Proclamation de Fuad-pacha en date de Beirout le 19 juillet 1860 (30 zilhidje 1276)," in Testa, *Recueil*, vol.6, pp.91–2. The text is also available in F.O. 78/1519, copy, translation, Fuad Pasha's proclamation, in Moore–Bulwer, No.52, 21 July 1860, in Moore–Bulwer, No.23, 21 July 1860.

21. Edwards, *La Syrie*, pp.204–5.

22. Spagnolo, *France and Ottoman Lebanon*, p.30; Pierre de la Gorce, *Histoire du second empire*, 6th ed. vol.3, (Paris: Plon-Nourrit, 1903), p.313.

23. All my references from *Le Siècle* (Paris), July 1860; *The Times* (London), July–November 1860 (see Bibliography for issue dates).

24. Alice Edythe Mange, *The Near Eastern Policy of the Emperor Napoleon III* (Urbana: University of Illinois Press, 1940), pp.6–7; William E. Echard, *Napoleon III and the Concert of Europe* (Baton Rouge: Louisiana State University Press, 1983).

25. Mange, *Near Eastern Policy*, chapter 2; G.D. Clayton, *Britain and the Eastern Question: Missolonghi to Gallipoli* (London: Lion Library, 1974).

26. Echard, *Napoleon III*, pp.129–30.

27. Gorce, *Histoire du second empire*, III, pp.315–16.

28. Gorce, *Histoire du second empire*, III, pp.316–7, 323–6, passim; Mange, *Near Eastern Policy*, pp.82–4; Spagnolo, *France and Ottoman Lebanon*, pp.30–1; Farah, "Ottoman Administration in the Lebanon," pp.291–7; Echard, *Napoleon III*, p.130; Testa, *Receuil*, vol.6, pp.81–4.

29. Mange, *Near Eastern Policy*, p.85; Echard, *Napoleon III*, p.130; Spagnolo, *France and Ottoman Lebanon*, p.33; V., G4/1, "Ordres généraux du corps expéditionnaire de Syrie," No.2, "ordre général du 16 août 1860."

30. Echard, *Napoleon III*, pp.130–1; Spagnolo, *France and Ottoman Lebanon*, pp.33–4; Gorce, *Histoire du second empire*, chapter 19 on the expedition to China.

31. Marcel Emerit, "La crise syrienne et l'expansion économique française en 1860," *Revue Historique*, vol.ccvii (January–March 1952), pp.211–32. See also Schilcher, *Families in Politics*, p.92.

32. Echard, *Napoleon III*, pp.130ff and elsewhere. This section relies heavily on his findings.

33. Echard, *Napoleon III*, pp.123, 190, 131–2; Mange, *Near Eastern Policy*, pp.85–6; Gordon L. Iseminger, "The Anglo-French Alliance and the Occupation of Syria, 1860–1861," *North Dakota Quarterly*, vol.47, no.3 (Summer 1979), pp.4–10.

34. Echard, *Napoleon III*, pp.131–2; Mange, *Near Eastern Policy*, pp.85–8; Spagnolo, *France and Ottoman Lebanon*, p.34.

35. Mange, *Near Eastern Policy*, pp.87–8. The quote is found in *ibid.*, p.88, and is based on Russell, *Correspondence*, II, 266, Russell to Palmerston, 27 July 1860.

36. Echard, *Napoleon III*, pp.132–3; Mange, *Near Eastern Policy*, pp.86–7.

37. This section relies heavily on Mange, *Near Eastern Policy*, pp.88–9, and Echard,

Napoleon III, pp.132–4. See also Spagnolo, *France and Ottoman Lebanon*, p.34; Gorce, *Histoire du second empire*, vol.3, p.325.

38. Mange, *Near Eastern Policy*, p.94; Testa, *Recueil*, vol.6, pp.102–3.

39. Mange, *Near Eastern Policy*, pp.88–9. The text of the convention of 5 September 1860 and extracts from the protocols of 3 August 1860 are available in Testa, *Recueil*, vol.6, pp.42–6. The text of the protocol is enclosed in V., G4/1, Thouvenel–Hamelin, 4 August 1860.

40. *Souvenirs de Syrie*, p.228; Mange, pp.93–4, including n.121 on p.93. The composition of the expeditionary force can be found in V., G4/1, "Ordres généraux du corps expéditionnaire de Syrie," No.2, "ordre général du 16 août 1860."

41. V., G4/1, Thouvenel–Hamelin, 4 August 1860. The text is reproduced in Richard Edwards, *La Syrie 1840–1862* (Paris: Amyot, 1862), pp.198–9.

42. V., G4/1, Hamelin–Beaufort, Paris, 2 August 1860.

43. Edwards, *La Syrie*, pp.196–7; Spagnolo, p.35.

44. Baptistin Poujoulat, *La Vérité sur la Syrie et l'expédition française* (Paris: Gaume Frères et J. Duprey, 1861), preface xxi, and p.9.

45. Poujoulat, *La Vérité*, pp.2–3; Richard Edwards, *La Syrie 1840–1862*, p.196.

46. V., G4/6, Osmont–Randon, No.3, 2 August 1860; *ibid*., Osmont–Randon, No.5, 4 August 1860; F.O. 78/1519, Circular from Moore to British consuls in Syria, 30 July 1860, in Moore–Russell, No. 26, 1 August 1860. Osmont signed as colonel d'état major en Syrie; *Souvenirs de Syrie*, p.224, called him "le colonel de génie" or sapper.

47. V., G4/1, Osmont–Randon, No.3, 2 August 1860; *ibid*., No.4, 2 August 1860.

48. V., G4/1, Osmont–Randon, No.4, 2 August 1860.

49. Perthuis is known to us partly through an unpublished diary that the Comtesse de Perthuis, his mother, kept up and later annotated. It was put at my disposal by Fuad Debbas. Comtesse de Perthuis, "Carnet de voyage en Orient: 1853–1855, 1860–1862," 30 July 1860; *ibid*., 1 August 1860; V., G4/1, Osmont–Randon, No.4, 2 August 1860.

50. V., G4/1, Beaufort–Randon, No.2, B, 22 August 1860; *ibid*., Osmont–Randon, No.8, 16 August 1860; Perthuis, "Carnet de Voyage," 23 September; *Souvenirs de Syrie*, p.227.

51. *Souvenirs de Syrie*, p.227; Poujoulat, *La vérité*, preface xxi, and pp.9, 16–18.

52. V., G4/1, Osmont–Randon, No.3, 2 August 1860; Poujoulat, *La vérité*, p.17; Perthuis, "Carnet de Voyage," 16 August 1860.

53. V., G4/1, Osmont–Randon, No.3, 2 August 1860; *ibid*., Osmont–Randon, No.8, 16 August 1860; Poujoulat, *La vérité*, p.17; Perthuis, "Carnet de Voyage," 16 August 1860, and 18 August to 12 September 1860.

54. Perthuis, "Carnet de Voyage," 16 August 1860. In September 1860, she remained peeved at him for various social slights: *ibid*., 27 September.

55. *Souvenirs de Syrie*, p.228.

56. V., G4/1, "Ordres généraux du 7 août au 29 septembre 1860," No.1, "ordre général du 7 août 1860."

57. F.O. 78/1627, Fraser–Dufferin, 14 January 1861, in Dufferin–Bulwer, No.103, 17 January 1861.

58. A.E., CP/T/346, Bentivoglio–de la Valette, 12 August 1860.

59. A.E., CP/T/346, de la Valette–Thouvenel, No.40, Therapia, 8 August 1860; *ibid*., (unsigned), No.8, Constantinople, 31 August/12 September 1860; A.E., CP/T/347, Lavalle [*sic*]–Thouvenel, No.90, Therapia, 31 October 1860; A.E., CP/T/348, Lavalle [*sic*]–Thouvenel, Pera, 1 January 1861.

60. Perthuis, "Carnet de voyage," 18 August 1860; V., G4/1, "Ordres généraux du corps expéditionnaire de Syrie," No.3, "ordre général du 17 août 1860," signed by Beaufort.

61. Hariciye, Abro–Cabouly, 6 August 1860; V., G4/6, Osmont–Randon, No.5, 4 August 1860.

62. *Souvenirs de Syrie*, p.226; Poujoulat, *La vérité*, p.18.

63. V., G4/1, Beaufort–Randon, No.2, 22 August 1860; V., G4/5, Beaufort–Randon, No.3, 27 August 1860.

64. Examples of Beaufort planning to go to Damascus and Fuad Pasha returning to Beirut: V., G4/5, Beaufort–Randon, No.6, 12 September 1860; V., G4/1, Beaufort–Randon, 25 October 1860.

65. V., G4/1, Beaufort–Randon, 9 September 1860.

66. V., G4/5, Beaufort–Randon, No.6, 12 September 1860; *ibid.*, Beaufort–Randon, No.7, 21 September 1860.

67. V., G4/5, Beaufort–Randon, No.8, Beirut, 23 September 1860.

68. V., G4/5, Beaufort–Randon, Dayr al-Qamar, No.10, 27 September 1860; V., G4/1, Beaufort–Randon, Kab Elias, 6 October 1860; V., G4/1, Beaufort–Randon, Kab Elias, 20 October 1860.

69. V., G4/5, Beaufort–Randon, No.10, Dayr al-Qamar, 27 September 1860.

70. V., G4/1, Beaufort–Randon, No.17, Kab Elias, 20 October 1860.

71. V., G4/1, Beaufort–Randon, No.17, Kab Elias, 20 October 1860; V., G4/1, Beaufort–Randon, Beirut, 25 October 1860.

72. V., G/1, Beaufort–Randon, No.49, Beirut, 4 November 1860. The general seems to have made mistakes in counting his companies and where he sent them! In the same letter, on one page he mentioned that he had ordered four élite companies to leave Beirut for Baabda and on the next page, that "deux companies d'élite du 5e de ligne partent demain pour Babda où elles prendront leurs cantonnement d'hiver, avec elles celles du 13e de ligne." He referred to leaving 12 companies in Qabb Elias, but then accounts for 11 only. Perhaps the 12th was sent on to Zahleh.

73. V., G4/1, Beaufort–Randon, No.30, Beirut, 28 December 1860; V., G4/1, Beaufort–Randon, No.47, Beirut, 12 April 1861; V., G4/1, Beaufort–Randon, No.49, Beirut, 26 April 1861; V., G4/1, Beaufort–Randon, No.51, Beirut, 10 May 1861.

74. *Souvenirs de Syrie*, p.250; V., G4/1, Beaufort–Randon, Qabb Elias, 4 October 1860; *ibid.*, Beaufort–Randon, Qabb Elias, 20 October 1860. In that letter, he said that of all the Turkish officers with rank, Ahmad Pasha was the one he trusted most. The ill will and impotence of the Turks is also mentioned in V., G4/1, No.22, Beirut, 22 October 1860; V., G4/1, Beaufort–Randon, Beirut, 19 November 1860; V., G4/1, Beaufort–Randon, No.32, Beirut, 12 January 1861; V., G4/1, Beaufort–Randon, No.39, Beirut, 25 February 1861; V., G4/1, Beaufort–Randon, No.44, Beirut, 24 March 1861.

75. V., G4/1, Beaufort–Randon, No.22, 22 October 1860: "dois appeler sérieusement son attention." V., G4/1, "Résumé d'une conversation [du Lt.Col. Chanzy] avec M. Novikoff Commissaire russe (12 janvier 1861)," V., G4/1, Beaufort–Randon, No.34, 27 January 1861; V., G4/1, Beaufort–Randon, No.36, Beirut, 10 February 1861; V., G4/1, Beaufort–Randon, No.49, Beirut, 26 April 1861. General Auguste-Alexandre Ducrot, *La Vie militaire du Général Ducrot d'après sa correspondance (1839–1871)*, published by his children (Paris: E. Plon, Nourrit et Cie, 1895), vol.1, p.406, writes that soldiers complained that Beaufort neglected his troops to take care of politics. *Ibid.*, p.416, cites Osmont criticizing Beaufort, and pp.412, 417, 419, include other criticisms of the general.

76. V., G4/1, Beaufort–Randon, No.49, 26 April 1861; V., G4/1, Beaufort–Randon, No.50, 5 May 1860; V., G4/1, Beaufort–Randon, No.51, 10 May 1861.

77. V., G4/1, Beaufort–Randon, 6 October 1860; V., G4/1, Beaufort–Randon, No.34, Beirut, 26 January 1860; V., G4/5, Beaufort–Randon, No.7, 21 September 1860; V., G4/1, Beaufort–Randon, Qabb Elias, 20 October 1860; V., G4/1, Beaufort–Randon, 19 November 1860. Fuad Pasha delaying return from Damascus to impede the work of the commission: V., G4/1, Beaufort–Randon, No.48, Beirut, 19 April 1861. Turkish agents touring the Mountain to undo Beaufort's recent visit there: V., G4/1, Beaufort–Randon, No.50, Beirut, 5 May 1861.

78. V., G4/5, Beaufort–Randon, No.7, 21 September 1860; V., G4/1, Beaufort–Randon, No.21, 19 November 1860; V., G4/1, Beaufort–Randon, No.50, 5 May 1860; V., G4/1, "Ordres généraux du corps expéditionnaire de Syrie," No.53, "ordre général du 1 juin 1861."

79. Perthuis, "*Carnet de voyage*," 16 August 1860.

80. A.E., CP/T/346, Fuad Pasha–Thouvenel, (no day) September 1860.

81. F.O. 195/1625, Dufferin–Bulwer, No.6, 8 September 1860; *ibid.*, Dufferin–Bulwer, No.9, 13 September 1860; V., G4/6, Osmont–Randon, No.7, 8 August 1860.

82. V., G4/2, d'Arricau–Beaufort, 3 June 1861.

83. Hariciye, (Le chargé d'affaire), légation à Berlin–Sefvet Efendi, Berlin, 14 August 1860.

84. Gökbilgin, "1840'dan 1861'e kadar Cebel-i Lübnan Meselesi ve Drüziler," p.699; V., G4/1, Beaufort–Randon, No.28, 16 December 1860; V., G4/1, Beaufort–Randon, Beirut, No.50, 5 May 1861; Hariciye, Abro Efendi–Cabouly, 19 March 1861.

85. V., G4/1, "Ordres généraux du corps expéditionnaire de Syrie," No.31, "ordre général du 2 octobre 1860;" V., G4/1, Osmont–Randon, No.4, 2 August 1860; *ibid.*, Beaufort–Randon, No.17, 20 October 1860; *ibid.*, Beaufort–Randon, No.21, 19 November 1860; *ibid.*, Beaufort–Randon, No.22, 22 October 1860; *ibid.*, Beaufort–Randon, No.49, 26 April 1861; V., G4/2, d'Arricau–Beaufort, 2 June 1861; V., G4/1, Beaufort–Randon, No.28, 16 December 1860; *ibid.*, Beaufort–Randon, No.50, 5 May 1860. Ottoman displeasure at French presence is clear from Fuad Pasha's various comments to Dufferin, Beaufort, and others. See, for example, V., G4/1, Fuad Pasha–Beaufort, 17 March 1861, in Beaufort–Randon, No.44, 24 March 1861; *ibid.*, "Traduction d'un avis adressé par le Patriarche des Grecs catholiques aux prêtres et aux religieux de son patriarchat," 2 May 1861, in Beaufort–Randon, No.52, 19 May 1861. Ottoman displeasure at the French expedition is also documented in the correspondence of Abro Efendi. See for example Hariciye, Abro Efendi–Cabouli Efendi, Beirut, 6 August 1860.

86. V., G4/1, Beaufort–Randon, No.34, Beirut, 27 January 1861; V., G4/1, Beaufort–Randon, No.36, Beirut, 10 February 1861; V., G4/1, Beaufort–Randon, No.41, Beirut, 10 March 1861; V., G4/1, d'Arricau–Beaufort, Bayt al-Din, 11 March 1861, in Beaufort–Randon, No.43, Beirut, 15 March 1861.

87. V., G4/1, Beaufort–Randon, No.46, Beirut, 29 March 1861. Fuad Pasha for direct Ottoman rule in Mount Lebanon: V., G4/1, Beaufort–Randon, No.46, Beirut, 29 March 1861; V., G4/1, Beaufort–Randon, No.50, Beirut, 5 May 1861 where several incidents are mentioned in detail; V., G4/1, Beaufort–Randon, No.51, Beirut, 10 May 1861 where several incidents in Mount Lebanon are mentioned and Damascus is described as, essentially, unsafe; V., G4/1, Beaufort–Randon, No.53, Beirut, 24 May 1861. Situation in the country gets worse every day: V., G4/2, d'Arricau–Beaufort, Bayt al-Din, 1 June 1861.

88. V., G4/1, Fuad–Beaufort, 17 March 1861, in Beaufort–Randon, Beirut, No.44, 24 March 1861; V., G4/1, Beaufort–Randon, No.46, Beirut, 29 March 1861.

89. V., G4/1, Beaufort–Randon, No.47, Beirut, 12 April 1861; V., G4/1, Beaufort–Randon, No.48, Beirut, 19 April 1861, and its enclosure no.1, Fuad–Beaufort, Damascus, 16 April 1861, enclosure 1; V., G4/1, Beaufort–Randon, No.49, Beirut, 26 April 1861; V., G4/1, Beaufort–Randon, No.50, Beirut, 5 May 1861.

90. Mange, *Near Eastern Policy*, p.95.

91. *Ibid.*, pp.94–8.

92. V., G4/1, Beaufort–Randon, Beirut, No.46, 7 April 1861; V., G4/1, Beaufort–Randon, d'Arricau – not mentioned, 1 June 1861; F.O. 195/660, Fraser–Bulwer, No.15, 11 June 1861.

93. *Souvenirs de Syrie*, p.296; V., G4/1, Beaufort–Randon, No.50, Beirut, 5 May 1861.

94. V., G4/2, Outrey–Beaufort, 6 June 1861.

95. *Souvenirs de Syrie*, p.301.

96. V., G4/1, Beaufort–Randon, Beirut, No.55, 7 June 1861. See also Ernest Louet, *Expédition de Syrie, Beyrouth, Le Liban, Jérusalem 1860–1861* (Paris: Amyot, 1862), pp.387–8.

97. *Souvenirs de Syrie*, pp.298–9. The evacuation of Syria by the French troops was completed on June 10: F.O. 195/660, Fraser–Bulwer No.15, 11 June 1861.

6. Retribution and the Restoration of Order in Damascus

1. F.O. 78/1519, Graham–Moore, 26 July 1860, in Moore–Bulwer, No.54, 28 July 1860; *Hasr al-litham*, p.229. See also A.E., CPC/D/6, Lanusse–Thouvenel, No.88, 17 July 1860.

2. Schilcher, *Families in Politics*, pp.89–91, has carefully examined population estimates for Damascus and concluded that before the riots and the influx of refugees, Christians of the inner quarter of the city under attack (i.e. not counting Christians in the Maidan and other suburbs) constituted some 8,000 to 10,000. She estimates conservatively that among them, some 2,000 died during the riots, plus a few foreigners and an unknown but small number of refugees. I would tend to agree with her conclusions, except for the refugee estimate which could easily have run into the hundreds. Mishaqa, *The History of the Lebanon*, p.248, estimated the number of Muslims and troops in Damascus at no more than 30,000, not counting the Muslims in the surrounding villages who accounted for more than 100,000 and the Christian men of all sects who amounted to 3,000. This estimate is much lower than that of Lanusse who, just before the riots, estimated at 25,000 the numbers of Christians and Jews who lived in Damascus: A.E., CPC/D/6, Lanusse–Thouvenel, No.87, 2 July 1860. Other estimates are available in Abkarius, *The Lebanon in Turmoil*, pp.136–7, n.204; *Hasr al-litham*, pp.230, 235. F.O. 78/1520, Brant–Bulwer, No.12, 11 August 1860, wrote: "It has been ascertained with tolerable accuracy that about 3,500 Christian natives of Damascus were massacred and about 2,000 strangers who had taken refuge in the Town for safety." Brant later that month gave higher figures, perhaps because he included people who died after the massacres, and partly perhaps because as time went on, estimates became more exaggerated: in F.O. 195/601, Brant–Bulwer, No.40, 30 August 1860, Brant thus mentioned that probably 10,000 died from "wounds and sufferings, by loss of parents and relations, and of property." The low estimate of 500

Christians dead was quoted after the first day of riots by the Greek vice-consul at Damascus, and reported to the British admiralty by a captain on a British ship anchored at Beirut: "Further Papers," Paynter–Martin, 11 July 1860, Encl.1 in No.15, Pennell–Hammond, 26 July 1860. It was quoted again on July 18 by Colonel O'Reilly who was attached to Fuad Pasha's mission in Syria: F.O. 78/1509, Bulwer–Russell, No.464, 30 July 1860, and Great Britain, *Parliamentary Papers*, vol.68, 1860, State Papers-Syria, p.56, O'Reilly–Bulwer, 18 July 1860, Encl. in No.73, Bulwer–Russell, 1 August 1860. "Further Papers," Paynter–Martin, 13 July 1860, Encl.2 in No.21, Paget–Hammond, 3 August 1860, reported that the number of dead Christians was variously estimated to be from 600 to 1,500; and then added a later account that an English resident in Damascus estimated the dead at 2,000. By August 1, Bulwer reported that Lanusse estimated those killed at Damascus at 8,000, Colonel O'Reilly at 500, and Brant at 5,000. He added: "But the fact is, no one yet can pretend to give a correct figure of this kind:" F.O. 78/1510, Bulwer–Russell, No.476, 1 August 1860, and Encl. At the end of July, Outrey wrote that it was impossible to be precise about the number of victims and "perhaps it will never be possible to do so" because after the massacres of Rashaiya and Hasbaiya, Damascus had received a great number of refugees from these towns and surrounding villages. Nonetheless, he went on, it was believed that the dead and disappeared could not be estimated at less than 6–7,000: A.E., CPC/D/6, Outrey–Thouvenel, 28 July 1860. By August 10, Moore reported that Brant was now certain that more than 5,000 Christians had died in Damascus, and that Lanusse raised the estimate to 8,000: F.O. 78/1519, Moore–Russell, No.31, 10 August 1860. That Lanusse believed about 8,000 had died is confirmed in A.E., CPC/D/6, Lanusse–Thouvenel, No.88, 17 July 1860. By August 30, Brant had raised the figure to probably 10,000: F.O. 78/1520, Brant–Bulwer, No.40, 30 August 1860. F.O. 78/1519, Moore–Russell, No.26, 1 August 1860 and *Parliamentary Papers*, vol.68 (1860), State Papers-Syria, p.67, No.85, Moore–Russell, 1 August 1860, reported that Graham estimated those killed in Damascus at 4,000 to 5,000, the French and Prussian consuls to 6,000. In September 1860, Dufferin wrote that the lowest estimate of the number of Christians killed at Damascus alone was 5,000: F.O. 195/1625, Dufferin–Bulwer, No.3, 8 September 1860. The historian M. Tayyıb Gökbilgin, "1840'dan 1861'e kadar Cebel-i Lübnan Meselesi ve Drüziler," *Belleten*, vol.10 (1946), p.692, mentions that four or five hundred people died in the massacre in Damascus.

3. F.O. 406/10, Robson's Memorandum in Dufferin–Russell, No.187, 23 September 1860; F.O. 78/1519, "Copy of a Letter from a Turkish Muslim in Damascus (translated from the Turkish)," in Moore–Russell, No.27, 4 August 1860; A.E., CPC/D/6, Outrey–Thouvenel, 28 July 1860, mentioned that not one house, of about 3,000, was standing. "Further Papers," Paynter–Martin, 13 July 1860, Encl.2 in No.21, Paget–Hammond, 3 August 1860, reported that estimated loss of property amounted to about £1.2 million sterling.

4. F.O. 195/601, Brant–Bulwer, No.27, July 1860; F.O. 78/1519, Moore–Russell, No.26, 1 August 1860; *ibid.*, Moore–Bulwer, No.54, 28 July 1860 and Encl.; Graham–Moore, 26 July 1860; *ibid.*, Graham–Moore, 30 July 1860; F.O. 78/1520, Brant–Russell, No.10, 28 July 1860; *ibid.*, Brant–Bulwer, 4 August 1860.

5. F.O. 78/1519, Moore–Russell, No.31, 10 August 1860; F.O. 78/1520, Brant–Russell, No.10, 28 July 1860; Debbas memoirs; A.E., CPC/D/6, Outrey–Thouvenel, 30 July 1860; Churchill, *The Druzes and the Maronites*, p.216; A.E., CPC/D/6, Outrey–Thouvenel, 28 July 1860; A.E., CP/T/346, Bentivoglio–Thouvenel, 12 August 1860.

6. F.O. 78/1519, Graham–Moore, 30 July 1860, in Moore–Russell, No.26, 1 August 1860; F.O. 78/1557, Brant–Russell, 26 June 1860; F.O. 78/1520, Brant–Russell, No.10, 28 July 1860; F.O. 195/601, Brant–Bulwer, No.27, 27 July 1860; A.E., CPC/D/6, Outrey–Thouvenel, 28 July 1860; F.O. 195/601, Brant–Bulwer, No.8, 16 July 1860; F.O. 78/1519, Moore–Russell, No.33, 16 August 1860 and Encl.; *ibid.*, Moore–Russell, 16 August 1860; *ibid.*, Moore–Bulwer, No.64, 3 September 1860; *ibid.*, Moore–Russell, No.49, 7 November 1860.

7. F.O. 78/1520, Brant–Russell, No.10, 28 July 1860; F.O. 195/601, Brant–Bulwer, No.25, 18 July 1860; *ibid.*, Brant–Bulwer, No.27, 27 July 1860. Mu'ammar (Muhammer) Pasha is referred to by Brant as "our new Valee" in *ibid.*, Brant–Russell, No.9, 16 July 1860; see also *ibid.*, Brant–Bulwer, No.26, 23 July 1860; F.O. 78/1519, Graham–Moore, 26 July 1860 in Moore–Bulwer, No.54, 28 July 1860. Khalid Pasha is referred to as Ferik of the troops and second in command at Damascus, formerly in Ibrahim Pasha's army, in F.O. 195/601, Brant–Bulwer, No.40, 30 August 1860; he is described as in charge of the Damascus police in *ibid.*, Brant–Bulwer, No.26, 23 July 1860; and as commanding the troops dispatched to Damascus in *ibid.*, Brant–Bulwer, No.25, 18 July 1860. On Khalid Pasha, see also A.E., CPC/D/6, Outrey–Thouvenel, 28 July 1860; *ibid.*, Outrey–Thouvenel, 30 July 1860. Brant, Wrench spell the new *vali*'s name Muhammer Pasha, and it appears that way in the published British correspondence. F.O. 78/1520, Wrench–Russell, No.38, 28 November 1860, mentioned him as the former *vali* who left Damascus on November 24. He was replaced temporarily by Rayyis Shukri Pasha, but the new *vali* of Damascus, Emin Mukliss Pasha, was expected to arrive soon.

8. A.E., CPC/D/6, Outrey–Thouvenel, 28 July 1860; F.O. 78/1626, 7e séance du 30 octobre 1860.

9. F.O. 195/601, Brant–Russell, No.8, 16 July 1860; *ibid.*, Brant–Bulwer, No.26, 18 July 1860; A.E., CPC/D/6, Outrey–Thouvenel, 19 July 1860.

10. A.E., CPC/D/6, Outrey–Thouvenel, 19 July 1860; *ibid.*, 28 July 1860.

11. F.O. 195/601, Brant–Bulwer, No.25, 18 July 1860, tells us that this first caravan had 50 people, but this seems to be a slip for 500; A.E., CPC/D/6, Outrey–Thouvenel, 28 July 1860, wrote that the first expedition had 500 to 600 Christians in it, and this is an estimate more in line with other reports on the size of caravans of refugees reaching Beirut. Dimitri Debbas in his memoirs wrote that the first caravan, of which he was a member, was made up of 840 people. Debbas, who wrote his memoirs years after the events of 1860, also remembered this first caravan to have left on the first Monday eight days after the "incident:" i.e., July 16, if he is counting from the first day of the riots; and Brant, in the dispatch of July 18 mentioned above, wrote that the first caravan left on July 17.

12. A.E., CPC/D/6, Outrey–Thouvenel, 30 July 1860; F.O. 78/1519, Moore–Russell, No.26, 1 August 1860.

13. Fawaz, *Merchants and Migrants*, chapter 5. Some of the information on Dimitri Debbas' description of the riots of July 1860 is available there as well, in a more condensed form.

14. F.O. 195/601, Brant–Bulwer, No.25, 18 July 1860; A.E., CPC/D/6, Lanusse–Thouvenel, No.88, 17 July 1860.

15. F.O. 195/601, Brant–Bulwer, No.26, 23 July 1860; *ibid.*, Brant–Bulwer, No.27, 24 July 1860; *ibid.*, Brant–Bulwer, No.25, 18 July 1860.

16. F.O. 195/601, Brant–Bulwer, No.25, 18 July 1860; *ibid.*, Brant–Bulwer, No.26, 23

July 1860; F.O. 78/1520, Wrench–Russell, No.38, 28 November 1860. Wrench mentions that 2,000 troops arrived under Khalid Pasha and that more troops were expected and required. Moore reported on July 11 that some 3,000 troops arrived in Beirut on July 10, 1,600 of which were going on to Damascus under Khalid Pasha: "Further Papers," Moore–Bulwer, 11 July 1860, Encl.1 in No.20, Moore–Russell, 13 July 1860. *Ibid.*, Paynter–Martin, 11 July 1860, Encl.2 in No.15, Pennell–Hammond, 26 July 1860, reported that 1,400 out of the 3,000 troops were to be sent to Damascus; *ibid.*, No.24, Brant–Russell, 16 July 1860, mentioned that 1,800 troops had left Beirut for Damascus. In addition, about 800 troops came in from the Hawran under Mustafa Pasha, and about 500 from Baalbek under Emin Pasha.

17. A.E., CPC/D/6, Lanusse–Thouvenel, No.88, 17 July 1860; F.O. 78/1519, Moore–Russell, No.25, 28 July 1860, and enclosures; A.E., CP/T/346, de la Valette–Thouvenel, No.40, 8 August 1860.

18. F.O. 78/1519, Graham–Moore, 30 July 1860, in Moore–Russell, No.26, 1 August 1860; *ibid.*, Moore–Bulwer, No.52, 21 July 1860, in Moore–Russell, No.23, 21 July 1860; *ibid.*, Graham–Moore, 26 July 1860, in Moore–Bulwer, No.54, 28 July 1860; F.O. 195/601, Brant–Bulwer, No.26, 23 July 1860; *ibid.*, Brant–Bulwer, No.27, 24 July 1860; A.E., CPC/D/6, Outrey–Thouvenel, 28 July 1860; F.O. 78/1520, Brant–Russell, No.10, 28 July 1860.

19. F.O. 78/1519, Graham–Moore, 26 July 1860, in Moore–Bulwer, No.54, 28 July 1860; *ibid.*, Graham–Moore, 30 July 1860, in Moore–Russell, No.26, 1 August 1860.

20. F.O. 78/1519, Graham–Moore, 26 July 1860, in Moore–Bulwer, No.54, 28 July 1860; *ibid.*, Graham–Moore, 30 July 1860, in Moore–Russell, No.26, 1 August 1860; F.O. 195/601, Brant–Bulwer, No.40, 30 August 1860; A.E., CPC/D/6, Outrey–Thouvenel, 28 July 1860.

21. F.O. 78/1519, Graham–Moore, 26 July 1860, in Moore–Bulwer, No.54, 28 July 1860; *ibid.*, Graham–Moore, 30 July 1860, in Moore–Russell, No.26, 1 August 1860; F.O. 195/601, Brant–Bulwer, No.26, 23 July 1860; A.E., CPC/D/6, Outrey–Thouvenel, p.s., 31 July 1860, in his letter of 30 July 1860.

22. Haricye, Abro–Cabouly, Beirut, 24 July 1860; F.O. 78/1519, Graham–Moore, 26 July 1860, in Moore–Bulwer, No.54, 28 July 1860; F.O. 78/1520, Brant–Bulwer, No.29, 31 July 1860; A.E., CPC/D/6, Outrey–Thouvenel, 30 July 1860; F.O. 78/1519, Moore–Russell, 1 August 1860.

23. Haricye, (Diran)–Savfet, Brussels, 18 August 1860; F.O. 78/1519, Moore–Russell, No.28, 6 August 1860; see also Encl. Fuad (Pasha)–Moore, confidential report from Damascus, 4 August 1860; A.E., CPC/D/6, Outrey–Thouvenel, 30 July 1860.

24. Haricye, (Sermac)–Safvet, Berlin, 14 August 1860; *ibid.*, Abro–Cabouly, 6 August 1860; F.O. 78/1519, Moore–Russell, No.28, 6 August 1860; V., G4/1, Osmont–Randon, No.8, 16 August 1860.

25. A.E., CPC/D/6, Outrey–Thouvenel, 30 July 1860.

26. Haricye, Abro Efendi, Beirut, 23 July 1860.

27. A.E., CPC/D/6, Outrey–Thouvenel, 30 July 1860; Haricye, Abro–Cabouly, 6 August 1860.

28. F.O. 195/1625, unsigned, Damascus, 8 September 1860, enclosure in Dufferin–Bulwer, No.3, 8 September 1860; A.E., CPC/D/6 Outrey–Thouvenel, p.s., 31 July 1860, in his letter of 30 July 1860; F.O. 78/1520, Brant–Bulwer, No.12, 11 August 1860; Hariciye, Abro–Cabouli, 6 August 1860.

29. CPC/D/6, Outrey-Thouvenel, 30 July 1860.

30. Hariciye, Abro–Cabouly, Beirut, 6 August 1860; F.O. 195/1625, unsigned, Damascus, 8 September 1860; F.O. 78/1519, Fuad (Pasha)–Moore, confidential report from Damascus, 4 August 1860, in Moore–Russell, No.28, 6 August 1860; F.O. 78/1520, Brant–Bulwer, 4 August 1860; F.O. 78/1519, Moore–Russell, No.31, 10 August 1860, mentioned that the arrests had reached between 700 and 800; F.O. 78/1520, Brant–Bulwer, No.31, 9 August 1850, mentioned that 750 were under arrest; V., G4/1, Osmont–Randon, No.8, 16 August 1860, that more than 700 people had been arrested in Damascus.

31. F.O. 78/1520, Brant–Bulwer, 4 August 1860; F.O. 78/1519, Fuad (Pasha)–Moore, confidential report from Damascus, 4 August 1860, in Moore–Russell, No.28, 6 August 1860.

32. Hariciye, Musurus-Safvet, No.1065, London, 7 September 1860; F.O. 195/1625, unsigned, Damascus, 8 September 1860, enclosure in Dufferin–Bulwer, No.3, 8 September 1860, mentioned 56 were hanged and shot. Beaufort confirms that 167 people had been executed in Damascus on 20 August: V., G4/1, Beaufort–Randon, No.2, 22 August 1860. Dufferin was not as well informed when he reported on 3 September that only 56 people had actually been executed out of the total population of Damascus: perhaps he was thinking only of those hanged or was unaware of those shot: F.O. 195/1625, Dufferin–Bulwer, No.3, 8 September 1860; Dufferin repeated that only 56 Damascenes were punished in F.O. 78/1627, Dufferin–Bulwer, No.92, 30 December 1860. Details of the executions are given in a report by a medical officer in the Turkish service; this officer mentioned that 57 people had been hanged while other reports say 56: W. Rogers's memo enclosed in F.O. 78/1629, Dufferin–Russell, No.99, 21 April 1861. Fuad Pasha sent a communication to Brant that 57 criminals had been hanged and 110 shot: F.O. 78/1520, Brant–Bulwer, No.36, 20 August 1860. I chose to go by the estimates of those in charge, as they would be most accurate.

33. W. Rogers's memo enclosed in F.O. 78/1629, Dufferin–Russell, No.99, 21 April 1861; F.O. 78/1520, Brant–Bulwer, No.36, 20 August 1860. The Green Maidan (*al-maydan al-akhdar*) is mentioned in Ibn Tulun, *I'lam al-wara*, ed. M. Dahman (Damascus, 1964), p. 6. The text mentions that Sultan Salim's Mosque was next to the Green Maidan, but that mosque is in Salihiya. To confuse the name of Sultan Süleyman's Mosque for Salim's Mosque was not uncommon.

34. F.O. 195/1625, unsigned, Damascus 8 September 1860, enclosure in Dufferin–Bulwer, No.3, 8 September 1860; F.O. 78/1520, Brant–Bulwer, No.12, 11 August 1860; *ibid.*, Brant–Bulwer, No.20, 20 September 1860; V., G4/1, Beaufort–Randon, No.2, 22 August 1860; F.O. 78/1625, 4e séance du 15 octobre 1860; F.O. 78/1519, Moore–Bulwer, No.63, 29 August 1860; F.O. 78/1628, part I (Jan. 27–Feb. 24, 1861): "Listes des personnes condamnées à mort et des personnes qui ont été envoyées à Constantinople et jetées au bagne pour leur participation aux événements de Damas."

35. F.O. 78/1628, part I (Jan. 27–Feb. 24, 1861): "Listes des personnes condamnées."

36. I am extremely grateful to Abdul-Karim Rafeq for his help in identifying the quarters and suburbs of Damascus.

37. Abdul-Karim Rafeq, "New Light on the 1860 Riots in Ottoman Damascus," *Die Welt des Islams*, vol.28 (1988), pp.412–30. See also *idem*, "The Social and Economic Structure of Bab-al-Muṣalla (al-Midan), Damascus, 1825–75," *Arab Civilization: Challenges and Responses: Studies in Honor of Constantine K. Zurayk*, ed. George N. Atiyeh and Ibrahim M. Oweiss (New York: State University of New York Press, 1988), pp.272–311.

38. Hariciye, Abro–Cabouly, 6 August 1860; F.O. 78/1519, Moore–Bulwer, No.67, 5

September 1860; *ibid.*, Fuad (Pasha)–Moore, confidential report from Damascus, 4 August 1860, in Moore–Russell, No.28, 6 August 1860; F.O. 78/1625, 4e séance du 15 octobre 1869; *ibid.*, Dufferin–Bulwer, No.33, 26 October 1860.

39. F.O. 78/1520, Brant–Bulwer, No.48, 25 September 1860; *ibid.*, Brant–Russell, No.31, 8 October 1860.

40. F.O. 78/1520, Brant–Bulwer, No.48, 25 September 1860; F.O. 78/1625, 4e séance du 15 octobre 1860; F.O. 78/1520, Brant–Russell, No.31, 8 October 1860; *ibid.*, Wrench–Russell, No.35, 20 October 1860; F.O. 78/1520, Brant–Bulwer, No.40, 30 August 1860; *ibid.*, Brant–Bulwer, No.31, 9 August 1860.

41. F.O. 78/1625, 4e séance du 15 octobre 1860; F.O. 78/1520, Wrench–Russell, No.35, 20 October 1860; F.O. 78/1626, 8e séance du 2 novembre 1860; V., G4/1, Beaufort–Randon, 25 October 1860. For a list of the *majlis* and ex-officio members, consult Schilcher, *Families in Politics*, pp.54–5, 100–1, and the rest of chapter 4.

42. A.E., CPC/D/6, Lanusse–Thouvenel, 4 June 1860; *ibid.*, Lanusse–Thouvenel, 19 June 1860; *ibid.*, Lanusse–Thouvenel, No.87, 2 July 1860; *ibid.*, Outrey–Thouvenel, 28 July 1860; F.O. 195/601, "Private Communication from Damascus to Mr. Webb," translation from German, Damascus, 25 June 1860, in Moore–Russell, No.19, 5 July 1860; *ibid.*, Brant–Bulwer, 3 July 1860; *ibid.*, Brant–Bulwer, No.40, 30 August 1860.

43. F.O. 195/601, Brant–Bulwer, 3 July 1860; *ibid.*, Brant–Russell, No.8, 16 July 1860.

44. Mishaqa, *The History of the Lebanon*, p. 209; A.E., CPC/D/6, Lanusse–Thouvenel, 19 June 1860; *ibid.*, Lanusse–Thouvenel, No.87, 2 July 1860; F.O. 195/601, Brant–Bulwer, 3 July 1860.

45. A.E., CPC/D/6, Lanusse–Thouvenel, No.87, 2 July 1860; F.O., 195/601. Brant–Bulwer, 3 July 1860. See also Schilcher, *Families in Politics*, pp.93–4.

46. F.O. 78/1509, Bulwer–Russell, No.447, Therapia, 25 July 1860.

47. F.O. 195/601, Brant–Bulwer, 3 July 1860.

48. F.O. 78/1519, "Copy of a Letter from a Turkish Muslim;" F.O. 195/601, Brant–Bulwer, No.40, 30 August 1860.

49. Mishaqa, *The History of the Lebanon*, p.217; *Kitab al-ahzan*, pp.42–3; Debbas memoirs; Hasibi, "Lamahat," pp.76–7; "The Damascus crisis of 1860," pp.35–6.

50. Gökbilgin, "1840'dan 1861'e kadar Cebel-i Lübnan Meselesi ve Drüziler," p.693; F.O. 195/601, "Private Communication from Damascus to Mr. Webb;" *ibid.*, Brant–Bulwer, No.40, 30 August 1860.

51. F.O. 195/601, Brant–Bulwer, No.40, 30 August 1860.

52. F.O. 78/1519, Moore–Russell, No.29, 6 August 1860.

53. A.E., CPC/D/6, Lanusse–Thouvenel, 4 June 1860; F.O. 195/601, Brant–Russell, No.8, 16 July 1860; *ibid.*, Brant–Russell, No.19, 20 June 1860.

54. A.E., CPC/D/6, Outrey–Thouvenel, 28 July 1860; F.O. 195/601, Brant–Bulwer, No.25, 18 July 1860; *ibid.*, Brant–Bulwer, No.26, 23 July 1860; Abkarius, *The Lebanon in Turmoil*, p.129, and footnote 189 for Scheltema's explanation; F.O. 78/1519, "Copy of a Letter from a Turkish Muslim."

55. F.O. 195/601, Brant–Russell, No.8, 16 July 1860; *ibid.*, Brant–Bulwer, No.40, 30 August 1860.

56. F.O. 195/601, Brant–Russell, No.5, 18 June 1860; *ibid.*, Brant–Bulwer, No.19, 20 June 1860; *ibid.*, Brant–Bulwer, No.20, 26 June 1860.

57. İsmail Hami Danişmend, *İzahlı Osmanlı Tarihi Kronolojisi* (Istanbul, 1961), vol.4, pp.191–3.

NOTES

58. F.O. 78/1510, O'Reilly–Bulwer, 18 July 1860, in Bulwer–Russell, No.477, 1 August 1860; F.O. 78/1509, Bulwer–Russell, No.464, 30 July 1860; F.O. 78/1519, Moore–Bulwer, No.52, 21 July 1860, in Moore–Russell, No.23, 21 July 1860; Hariciye, Abro Efendi, Beirut, 23 July 1860.

59. F.O. 78/1625, Dufferin–Bulwer, No.4, 8 September 1860.

60. Danişmend, *İzahlı Osmanlı Tarihi Kronolojisi*, pp.191–3; F.O. 78/1520, Bulwer–Russell, No.476, 1 August 1860.

61. F.O. 78/1519, Moore–Russell, No.31, 10 August 1860; *ibid.*, Moore–Russell, 16 August 1860; F.O. 78/1520, Brant–Bulwer, No.34, 16 August 1860; *ibid.*, Brant–Bulwer, No.40, 30 August 1860.

62. F.O. 78/1519, Moore–Russell, No.67, 5 September 1860; *ibid.*, Dufferin–Bulwer, No.2, (blank) September 1860; F.O. 78/1519, Moore–Russell, 16 August 1860; Danişmend, *İzahlı Osmanlı Tarihi Kronolojisi*, p.193, writes that with reference to Ahmad Pasha's condemnation, Fuad Pasha said: "While I never cut a chicken or shot a bird in my life, look what God made me do!"

63. F.O. 78/1620, Dufferin–Bulwer, No.4, 8 September 1860; F.O. 78/1625, enclosure of 8 September 1860 in Dufferin–Bulwer, No.3, 8 September 1860.

64. Danişmend, *İzahlı Osmanlı Tarihi Kronolojisi*, p.193; F.O. 78/1625, Dufferin–Bulwer, No.3, 8 September 1860; F.O. 78/1519, Moore–Bulwer, No.70, 11 September 1860 in Moore–Russell, No.43, 14 September 1860; F.O. 78/1520, Brant–Russell, Dufferin–Russell, No.99, 21 April 1861.

65. F.O. 78/1629, Memorandum enclosed in Dufferin–Russell, No.99, 21 April 1861; V., G4/5, Beaufort–Randon, No.6, 12 September 1860; Bitar, *Hilyat al-bashar*, vol.3, pp.260ff; Danişmend, *İzahlı Osmanlı Tarihi Kronolojisi*, pp.191–3.

66. F.O. 78/1519, Moore–Bulwer, No.52, 21 July 1860, in Moore–Russell, No.23, 21 July 1860; F.O. 78/1626, 9e séance du 10 novembre 1860; F.O. 78/1525, enclosure of 8 September in Dufferin–Bulwer, No.3, 8 September 1860: names of two of the three officers of Deir al-Qamar and Beit al-Din.

67. F.O. 78/1519, Moore–Russell, No.24, 26 July 1860; *ibid.*, Moore–Bulwer, No.52, 21 July 1860, in Moore–Russell, No.23, 21 July 1860: Khurshid to Latakia; F.O. 78/1625, Tribunal appointed to try Khurshid Pasha, in Dufferin–Bulwer, No.11, 21 September 1860; F.O. 78/1628, Part 2, "Minute on the Judgment Proposed ... " in Dufferin–Bulwer, No.122, 24 February 1861; F.O. 78/1627, "Sentence of Khurshid Pasha," No.1, in Dufferin–Russell, No.90, 30 December 1860.

68. F.O. 78/1628, Part 2, "Minute on the Judgment Proposed, 4e séance du 15 octobre 1860;" 78/1627, "Sentence of Tahir Pasha," No.2, in Dufferin–Russell, No.90, 30 December 1860; "Sentence on Suliman Nuri Bek (Colonel)," No.3, in *ibid.*; "Sentence of Wasfi Efendi and Ahmed Efendi," No.4, in *ibid*; F.O. 78/1626, 9e séance du 10 novembre 1860.

69. F.O. 78/1520, Brant–Russell, No.31, 8 October 1860.

70. F.O. 78/1520, Wrench–Bulwer, No.58, 5 November 1860, in Wrench–Russell, No.36, 5 November 1860; F.O. 7/1625, 4e séance du 15 octobre 1860; F.O. 78/1520, Wrench–Bulwer, No.61, 29 November 1860; *ibid.*, Wrench–Bulwer, No.62, 12 December 1860.

71. F.O. 78/1625, unsigned, Damascus, 8 September 1860, in Dufferin–Bulwer, No.3, 8 September 1860.

72. V., G4/1, Beaufort–Randon, No.2, 22 August 1860; F.O. 78/1520, Brant–Russell,

No.15, 25 August 1860; F.O. 78/1625, unsigned enclosure, 8 September 1860, in Dufferin–Bulwer, 8 September 1860; F.O. 78/1626, 7e séance du 30 october 1860.

73. F.O. 195/660, Fraser–Bulwer, No.59, 10 October 1860.

74. F.O. 78/1520, Brant–Bulwer, No.35, 16 August 1860; *ibid.*, Brant–Russell, No.15, 25 August 1860; *ibid.*, Wrench–Bulwer, No.61, 29 November 1860; *ibid.*, Wrench–Bulwer, No.62, 12 December 1860; *ibid.*, Brant–Russell, No.31, 8 October 1860; F.O. 78/1625, unsigned enclosure, 8 September 1860, in Dufferin–Bulwer, 8 September 1860; F.O. 195/660, Fraser–Bulwer, No.59, 10 October 1861; F.O. 78/1520, Brant–Russell, No.20, 20 September 1860.

75. F.O. 78/1626, séance du 21 novembre 1860; F.O. 78/1520, Wrench–Bulwer, No.62, 12 December 1860; V., G4/1, Beaufort–Randon, No.28, 16 December 1860.

76. A.E., CP/T/348, Outrey–de la Valette, Pera, 9 January 1861, in de la Valette–Thouvenel, No.6, Pera, 9 January 1861; F.O. 78/1629, Fraser–Dufferin, No.26, 19 April 1861.

77. F.O. 195/660, Fraser–Bulwer, No.59, 10 October 1861.

78. F.O. 78/1626, 7e séance du 30 octobre 1860; *ibid.*, "Note des sommes distribuées aux chrétiens victimes des derniers événements," in Dufferin–Bulwer, No.41, 3 November 1860; F.O. 78/1620, Brant–Russell, No.30, 5 October 1860; V., G4/1, Beaufort–Randon, No.39, 25 February 1861; F.O. 78/1625, Dufferin–Bulwer, No.33, 26 October 1860.

79. F.O. 78/1510, Fuad Pasha–Moore, 4 August 1860, in Moore–Russell, No.28, 6 August 1860; F.O. 78/1626, 7e séance du 30 octobre 1860; F.O. 78/1520, Brant–Russell, No.20, 20 September 1860; F.O. 78/1626, 8e séance du 2 novembre 1860.

80. F.O. 78/1626, 7e séance du 30 octobre 1860; F.O. 78/1520, Wrench–Bulwer, No.62, 12 December 1860.

81. F.O. 78/1626, 8e séance du 2 novembre 1860.

82. F.O. 78/1520, Brant–Bulwer, No.48, 25 September 1860; *ibid.*, Brant–Russell, No.30, 5 October 1860.

83. F.O. 78/1626, séance du 17 novembre 1860.

84. F.O. 195/660, Fraser–Bulwer, No.35, 27 July 1861.

85. *Ibid.*

86. F.O. 195/660, "Extract from a Despatch from Mr Consul Rogers to Colonel Fraser," and enclosure, Damascus, 23 July 1861. Although Rogers wrote that the entire losses of the Christians amounted to about 300,000 purses, the enclosure spelled out the figure of 400,000 purses or *kişe*s (i.e. 200 million piastres, as 1 purse equaled 500 piastres).

87. F.O. 195/660, Fraser–Bulwer, No.35, 27 July 1861.

88. F.O. 78/1625, enclosure of 8 September 1860 in Dufferin–Bulwer, No.3, 8 September 1860.

89. F.O. 195/659 (April–May 1861), "Arrête de l'impôt extraordinaire et secours imposé sur les habitants de l'Eyalet de Damas;" F.O. 78/1586, Rogers–Russell, No.14, 10 June 1861. See also the more general "Proclamation" in *ibid.*

90. F.O. 195/659 (April–May 1861), "Arrête de l'impôt extraordinaire." Except for the total for the district of Iki Kabouli which is quoted as 48 purses, the same figures are available in *ibid.*, tables enclosed in Dufferin–Bulwer, No.201, 11 May 1861. See also F.O. 78/1586, "Proposition for the Levy of a Sufficient Sum to Compensate the Christians for their Losses;" *ibid.*, "Abstract of the Decision for the Indemnity of the Christians of Damascus." Ma'arrat al-Nu'man should be with Aleppo.

91. F.O. 78/1520, Brant–Bulwer, No.12, 11 August 1860; F.O. 78/1626, séance du 17 novembre 1860; F.O. 78/1626, 8e séance du 2 novembre 1860. That 35 million piastres equaled £291,000 is in F.O. 78/1626, Dufferin–Bulwer, No.71, 29 November 1860. That they equal 7 million francs is in *ibid.*, séance du 21 novembre 1861.

92. F.O. 78/1626, séance du 21 novembre 1860.

93. F.O. 78/1520, Brant–Bulwer, No.12, 11 August 1860; F.O. 78/1626, séance du 17 novembre 1860; *ibid.*, 8e séance du 2 novembre 1860; *ibid.*, Dufferin–Bulwer, No.71, 29 November 1860.

94. F.O. 78/1626, séance du 17 novembre 1860; F.O. 78/1626, 8e séance du 2 novembre 1860.

95. F.O. 78/1626, Dufferin–Bulwer, No.71, 29 November 1860; F.O. 78/1627, Dufferin–Russell, No.41, 19 December 1860.

96. F.O. 195/660, Fraser–Bulwer, No.66, 4 November 1861. F.O. 78/1586, "Proposition for the Levy of a Sufficient Sum to Compensate the Christians for their Losses," article 2, mentioned that the population of Damascus exceeded 30,000 men.

97. F.O. 195/660, Fraser–Bulwer, No.66, 4 November 1861; *ibid.*, Fraser–Bulwer, No.5, 24 May 1861. See also F.O. 78/1627, Dufferin–Russell, No.41, 19 December 1860. In his letter of November 4, Fraser complained that the Druzes of Mount Lebanon had suffered losses nearly seven times greater than the Muslims of Damascus, although the latter were "universally" acknowledged to be the more guilty of the two. While some 30,000 Damascene Muslims had furnished no more than 12.5 million piastres, some 7,000 Lebanese Druzes had been deprived of their property to the amount of 20 million piastres notwithstanding the fact they had delivered up the booty they had taken during the civil war.

98. Schilcher, *Families in Politics*, p.83; F.O. 195/601, Brant–Bulwer, No.25, 18 July 1860.

99. F.O. 78/1630, Part 2, Fraser–Dufferin, 2 May 1861, in Dufferin–Russell, No.108, 5 May 1861; F.O. 195/659, Fraser–Dufferin, No.36, 17 May 1861; F.O. 78/1520, Brant–Russell, No.31, 8 October 1860.

100. F.O. 78/1586, Rogers–Bulwer, No.27, 24 June 1861; F.O. 195/660, Fraser–Bulwer, No.45, 17 August 1861; *ibid.*, Fraser–Bulwer, No.20, 25 June 1860.

101. F.O. 195/660, Fraser–Bulwer, No.54, 2 October 1861.

102. F.O. 78/1586, Rogers–Russell, No.14, 10 June 1861; *ibid.*, Rogers–Bulwer, No.27, 24 June 1861; *ibid.*, "List of Mohammedans who conducted themselves with Perfect Rectitude during the outbreak at Damascus in 1860," Rogers, 12 June 1860; F.O. 195/660, Fraser–Bulwer, No.22, 25 June 1861, and enclosed Memorandum.

103. F.O. 78/1586, Rogers–Bulwer, No.27, 24 June 1861; F.O. 78/1626, 8e séance du 2 novembre 1860.

104. F.O. 78/1586, Rogers–Bulwer, No.27, 24 June 1861; F.O. 78/1626, 8e séance du 2 novembre 1860.

105. F.O. 78/1586, Rogers–Bulwer, No.27, 24 June 1861.

106. F.O. 195/660, Fraser–Bulwer, No.23, Aintat, 29 June 1861; F.O. 78/1586, Rogers–Bulwer, No.27, 24 June 1861.

107. F.O. 195/660, Fraser–Bulwer, No.23, Aintat, 29 June 1861.

108. F.O. 195/660, Fraser–Bulwer, No.23, Aintat, 29 June 1861.

109. Debbas memoirs; Fawaz, *Migrants and Merchants*, p.98.

110. F.O. 78/1586, Rogers–Bulwer, No.55, 26 December 1861; F.O. 78/1520, Wrench–Bulwer, No.62, 12 December 1860.

111. *Ibid.*

112. F.O. 195/660, Fraser–Bulwer, No.23, 29 June 1861; *ibid.*, Fraser–Bulwer, No.59, 10 October 1861; *ibid.*, Fraser–Bulwer, No.35, 27 July 1860; F.O. 78/1586, Rogers–Bulwer, No.55, 26 December 1861.

7. Reconstruction and the Restoration of Order in Mount Lebanon

1. V., G4/1, Beaufort–Randon, No.2, 22 August 1860; *ibid.*, Beaufort–Randon, No.17, 20 October 1860. The figure of 200 villages burned comes from F.O. 78/1626, "Substance of an Interpellation addressed by Lord Dufferin to Fuad Pasha at the 8th Sitting of the Syrian Commission November 10, 1860," in Dufferin–Bulwer, No.46, 14 November 1860; V., G4/1, Beaufort–Randon, No.44, 24 March 1861.

2. V., G4/1, Beaufort–Randon, No.44, 24 March 1861; *ibid.*, Du Preuil–Beaufort, 5 April 1861. See also V., Beaufort–Randon, No.32, 12 January 1861; F.O. 78/1629, Fraser–Dufferin, No.22, 4 April 1861.

3. V., G4/1, Beaufort–Randon, No.44, 24 March 1861; V., G4/1, Beaufort–Randon, No.32, 12 January 1861. F.O. 78/1629, Fraser–Dufferin, No.22, 4 April 1861, mentioned that no more than half a dozen men and 100 women and children were in Hasbaiya.

4. V., G4/1, Beaufort–Randon, 11 October 1860; *ibid.*, Beaufort–Randon, No.17, 20 October 1860; *ibid.*, Beaufort–Randon, No.44, 24 March 1861.

5. V., G4/1, Portalis–Beaufort, 29 September 1860; *ibid.*, Beaufort–Randon, 4 October 1860; *ibid.*, Beaufort–Randon, No.51, 10 May 1861; *ibid.*, "Extrait d'une lettre du 18 janvier écrite par le colonel commandant des troupes françaises à Beteddin;" M.P.B., Bustani–Mas'ad, 19 August 1860, refers to Druze attacks on Christians despite the presence of French troops in Beirut.

6. V., G4/1, Osmont–Randon, No.8, 16 August 1860; V., G4/6, Osmont–Randon, No.7, 8 August 1860; V., G4/2, Aubrey–Beaufort, 3 June 1861; *ibid.*, Beaufort–Randon, No.51, 10 May 1861; *ibid.*, Ahmed Pasha–Beaufort, 17 April 1861; *ibid.*, d'Arricau–Beaufort, No.187, 15 April 1861.

7. V., G4/1, Beaufort–Randon, No.39, 25 February 1861; *ibid.*, "Extrait d'une lettre écrite de Damas le 21 janvier, par le commandant Cerez en mission dans cette ville;" *ibid.*, Beaufort–Randon, No.44, 24 March 1861.

8. V., G4/1, Beaufort–Randon, No.39, 25 February 1861.

9. F.O. 78/1629, Fraser–Dufferin, No.22, 4 April 1861; V., G4/5, Beaufort–Randon, No.10, 27 September 1860; V, G4/2, d'Arricau–Beaufort, No.219, 4 May 1861; *ibid.*, d'Arricau–Beaufort, No.183, 13 April 1861, and enclosure, the petition from the inhabitants of the village; V., G4/1, Beaufort–Randon, No.48, 19 April 1861, and enclosure: "Pétition des chrétiens de Deir el Kamar;" V., G4/2, d'Arricau–Beaufort, No.187, 15 April 1861; V., G4/1, Beaufort–Randon, No.55, 7 June, 1861.

10. V., G4/1, No.48, 19 April 1861; V., G4/2, d'Arricau–Beaufort, No.187, 15 April 1861; V., G4/1, Beaufort–Randon, No.48, 19 April 1861; V., G4/2, d'Arricau–Beaufort, No.219, 4 May 1861; *ibid.*, d'Arricau–Chanzy, 20 May 1861; V, G4/1, Beaufort–Randon, No.41, 10 March 1861; *ibid.*, Beaufort–Randon, No.48, 19 April 1861.

11. V., G4/1, Portalis–Beaufort, 29 September 1860. It probably was Antoine Fortune Portalis. For more information on the family, consult Boutros Labaki, *Introduction à*

l'histoire économique du Liban: soie et commerce extérieur en fin de période Ottomane (1840–1914), Publications de l'Université Libanaise, Section des études économiques, IV (Araya, Lebanon: Imprimerie Catholique, 1984).

12. V., G4/1, Beaufort–Randon, 6 October 1860; *ibid.*, Beaufort–Randon, 4 October 1860; V., G4/1, A. Portalis (probably Antoine Fortune)–Beaufort, 29 September 1860.

13. V., G4/1, Fuad Pasha–Beaufort, 17 March 1861, in Beaufort–Randon, No.44, 24 March 1861; V., G4/2, Ahmed Pasha–Beaufort, 17 April 1861.

14. V., G4/1, Beaufort–Randon, No.50, 5 May 1861; *ibid.*, Beaufort–Randon, No.51, 10 May 1861; V., G4/2, d'Arricau–Beaufort, No.187, 15 April 1861; V., G4/1, Beaufort–Randon, No.48, 19 April 1861.

15. V., G4/1, Beaufort–Randon, 11 October 1860; V., G4/2, d'Arricau–Beaufort, No.183, 13 April 1861; V., G4/1, Beaufort–Randon, No.48, 19 April 1861, and enclosure: "Pétition des chrétiens de Deir el Kamar."

16. V., G4/2, d'Arricau–Beaufort, No.219, 4 May 1861; V., G4/1, Beaufort–Randon, 6 October 1860; *ibid.*, Beaufort–Randon, No.17, 20 October 1860; *ibid.*, Beaufort–Randon, No.20, 9 October 1860; V., G4/2, d'Arricau–Beaufort, 3 June 1861; F.O. 78/1626, 7e séance du 30 octobre 1860.

17. F.O. 78/1626, 7e séance du 30 octobre 1860.

18. V., G4/1, Beaufort–Randon, No.20, 9 October 1860; *ibid.*, Beaufort–Randon, No.25, 2 December 1860; *ibid.*, Beaufort–Randon, 6 October 1860; *ibid.*, Beaufort–Randon, No.46, 7 April 1861; F.O. 78/1626, 7e séance du 30 octobre 1860.

19. Aqiqi, *Lebanon in the Last Years of Feudalism*, p.71; V., G4/1, Beaufort–Randon, No.35, 12 January, 1861.

20. F.O. 78/1626, 7e séance du 30 octobre 1860; V., G4/2, d'Arricau–Beaufort, 1 June 1861; *ibid.*, d'Arricau–Beaufort, 2 June 1861; V., G4/1, Beaufort–Randon, 11 October 1860; *ibid.*, Beaufort–Randon, 6 October 1860.

21. F.O. 78/1626, 7e séance du 30 octobre 1860; V., G4/1, Beaufort–Randon, No.44, 24 March 1861.

22. V., G4/1, Beaufort–Randon, No.20, 9 October 1860; V., G4/5, d'Arricau–Beaufort, No.70, 22 October 1860.

23. V., G4/1, Beaufort–Randon, No.28, 16 December 1860; *ibid.*, Beaufort–Randon, 6 October 1860; *ibid.*, Beaufort–Randon, No.46, 7 April 1861; F.O. 78/1626, 7e séance du 30 octobre 1860.

24. V., G4/1, Du Preuil–Beaufort, 5 April 1861, in Beaufort–Randon, No.46, 7 April 1861.

25. V., G4/1, Beaufort–Randon, No.46, 29 March 1861; *ibid.*, Beaufort–Randon, No.49, 26 April 1861; *ibid.*, Beaufort–Randon, No.44, 24 March 1861.

26. V., G4/1, Beaufort–Randon, No.55, 7 June 1861; F.O. 195/660, Fraser–Bulwer, No.12, 7 June 1861.

27. V., G4/1, No.44, 24 March 1861; *ibid.*, Encl., Fuad Pasha–Beaufort, 17 March 1861; V., G4/2, d'Arricau–Beaufort, No.219, 4 May 1861; *ibid.*, d'Arricau–Beaufort, 1 June 1861.

28. V., G4/1, Beaufort–Randon, No.50, 5 May 1861; *ibid.*, "Traduction d'un avis adressé par le Patriarche des Grecs catholiques aux prêtres et aux religieux de son patriarchat, le 2 mai, 1861;" *ibid.*, "Ordre de Fuad Pasha affiché dans les villes, inseré dans le journal arabe de Beyrouth et lu dans toutes les réunions publiques (mai 1861)," in Beaufort–Randon, No.52, 19 May, 1861. The government would by no means allow

"le bout du nez de l'un de ses sujets soit endommagé avant d'avoir fait verser la dernière goutte du sang de ses employés."

29. V., G4/1, Beaufort–Randon, No.21, 19 November 1860; *ibid.*, Beaufort–Randon, No.25, 2 December 1860.

30. Aqiqi, *Lebanon in the Last Years of Feudalism*, p.71.

31. V., G4/1, Beaufort–Randon, No.20, 9 October 1860; *ibid.*, Beaufort–Randon, No.21, 19 November 1860; *ibid.*, Beaufort–Randon, No.46, 7 April 1861.

32. V., G4/1, Beaufort–Randon, No.20, 9 October 1860; *ibid.*, Beaufort–Randon, No.21, 19 November 1860; *ibid.*, Beaufort–Randon, No.46, 7 April 1861.

33. V., G4/5, Beaufort–Randon, No.10, 27 September 1860; V., G4/1, "Extrait d'une lettre du capitaine membre du comité de reconstruction à Deir el Kamar (22 janvier);" *ibid.*, d'Arricau–Beaufort, No.41, 9 October 1860; *ibid.*, d'Arricau–Beaufort, No.50, 11 October 1860; *ibid.*, d'Arricau–Beaufort, 23 October 1860; *ibid.*, d'Arricau–Beaufort, No.80, 25 October 1860; V., G4/1, Beaufort–Randon, No.32, 12 January 1861; *ibid.*, Beaufort–Randon, No.52, 19 May 1861; Aqiqi, *Lebanon in the Last Years of Feudalism*, p.71.

34. V., G4/5, d'Arricau–Beaufort, No.50, 11 October 1860; V., G4/1, Beaufort–Randon, 4 October 1860; V., G4/2, d'Arricau–Beaufort, 3 June 1861.

35. V., G4/1, Beaufort–Randon, No.49, 26 April 1861.

36. V., G4/1, Beaufort–Randon, No.48, 19 April 1861; *ibid.*, Beaufort–Randon, 4 October 1860; *ibid.*, Beaufort–Randon, 11 October 1860; F.O. 78/1626, 7e séance du 30 octobre 1860. Druze complaints of Christians cutting wood in the Metn district: F.O. 195/660, No.6, 28 May 1861.

37. V., G4/2, d'Arricau–Beaufort, 1 June 1861.

38. V., G4/5, Beaufort–Randon, No.10, 27 September 1860; F.O. 78/1629, Fraser–Dufferin, No.22, 4 April 1861.

39. V., G4/2, letter to d'Arricau, 2 June 1861; *ibid.*, d'Arricau–Beaufort, 1 June 1861; V., G4/1, d'Arricau–Beaufort, 11 March, 1861, in Beaufort–Randon, No.43, 15 March 1861; F.O. 195/660, Fraser–Bulwer, No.10, 2 June 1861.

40. V., G4/2, d'Arricau, 1 June, 1861; *ibid.*, Outrey–Beaufort, 6 June 1861; V., G4/1, Beaufort–Randon, No.55, 7 June 1861. F.O. 195/660, Fraser–Bulwer, No.10, 2 June 1861.

41. V., G4/1, Beaufort–Randon, No.2, 22 August 1860; V., G4/5, Beaufort–Randon, No.3, 27 August 1860; V., G4/1, Beaufort–Randon, No.55, 7 June 1861.

42. V., G4/2, d'Arricau–Beaufort, 1 June 1861.

43. V., G4/1, Portalis–Beaufort, 24 August 1860; V., G4/1, Beaufort–Randon, No.17, 20 October 1860; *ibid.*, Beaufort–Randon, No.49, 26 April 1861.

44. V., G4/1, Beaufort–Randon, No.49, 26 April 1861; V., G4/5, d'Arricau–Beaufort, No.70, 22 October 1860; V., G4/2, d'Arricau–Beaufort, No.192, 18 April 1861, enclosures: "Statistique de la population de Deir el Kamar, à la date du 1er avril, 1861," "Statistique de la population de Deir el Kamar, à la date du 6 avril, 1861," "Statistique de la population de Deir el Kamar, à la date du 11 avril, 1861." In his dispatch No.19 of 26 April 1861, Beaufort wrote that the population of Deir al-Qamar was close to 1,400, and in V., G4/1, Beaufort–Randon, No.52, 19 May 1861, he repeated that the population had earlier reached 1,400. However, I have preferred to quote the detailed statistics provided by d'Arricau where the highest total for April is 1,343.

45. V., G4/1, d'Arricau–Beaufort, No.221, 6 May 1861, and enclosure: "Statistique de la population de Deir el Kamar, à la date du 6 mai, 1861"; *ibid.*, d'Arricau–Beaufort, No.227, 13 May 1861, and enclosure: "Statistique de la population de Deir el Kamar,

à la date du 12 mai, 1861"; *ibid.*, d'Arricau–Beaufort, No.231, 16 May 1861, and enclosure: "Statistique de la population de Deir el Kamar, à la date du 16 mai, 1861." V., G4/1, "Statistique de la population de Deir el Kamar, à la date du 20 mai, 1861;" and "Statistique de la population de Deir el Kamar, à la date du 26 mai, 1861."

46. F.O. 195/660, Fraser–Bulwer, No.10, 2 June 1861.

47. *Ibid.*; V., G4/1, Beaufort–Randon, No.55, 7 June 1861. On the likelihood that "the last inhabitant" of Deir al-Qamar would leave it when the French troops do, see also V., G4/2, d'Arricau–Beaufort, 3 June 1861.

48. V., G4/1, Osmont–Randon, No.8, 16 August 1860; V., G4/1, Beaufort–Randon, 11 October 1860; *ibid.*, Beaufort–Randon, No.49, 26 April 1861; *ibid.*, Beaufort–Randon, No.50, 5 May 1861

49. In August 1860, Colonel Osmont, who helped supervise the arrival of the French troops in Syria, reported that most of the Ottoman troops were in Damascus with Fuad Pasha. In February, 1861, Halim Pasha, commanding officer of the army in Syria, told Maxime Outrey, French consul in Damascus who became consul general in Beirut in 1862, and Major Cerez of the general staff of the French expeditionary force, that the Turkish troops guarding Damascus and its suburbs amounted to 6,000. Beaufort commented that all the information at his disposal showed this number to be exaggerated, but it is hard to know how informed he was about Damascus from which he was kept away by the Ottomans, or how impartial he was, given his desire to play a more forceful role in the Syrian interior and to present French forces as an indispensable supplement to inadequate Ottoman ones. F.O. 195/660, Fraser–Bulwer, No.10, 2 June 1861; V., G4/1, Osmont–Randon, No.2, 22 August 1860; *ibid.*, "Résumé de conversations qui ont eu lieu à Damas entre Halim Pasha commandant l'armée d'Arabistan, M. Outrey consul de France, et le Commandant Cerez attaché a l'Etat Major du General Beaufort," Encl. in Beaufort–Randon, No.39, 25 February 1861; *ibid.*, Beaufort–Randon, No.44, 24 March 1861; *ibid.*, Beaufort–Randon, 6 October 1860; V., G4/1, Cauberty, "Renseignements recueillis le 12 mai, 1861;" *ibid.*, "Renseignements politiques," 14 mai, 1861; *ibid.*, Cauberty, "Renseignements recueillis le 19 mai, 1861."

50. Even by the admission of trained army officers: V., G4/6, Osmont–Randon, No.7, 8 August 1861.

51. V., G4/1, Beaufort–Randon, No.36, 10 February 1861.

52. *Ibid.*; V., G4/1, Beaufort–Randon, 9 September 1860.

53. V., G4/6, Beaufort–Randon, No.29, 23 September 1860; V., G4/1, "Extrait d'une lettre de Damas le 21 janvier, par le commandant Cerez en mission dans cette ville"; V., G4/1, Osmont–Randon, No.8, 16 August 1860; V., G4/5, Beaufort–Randon, No.6, 12 September 1860; *ibid.*, Beaufort–Randon, No.7, 21 September 1860; *ibid.*, Beaufort–Randon, No.17, 20 October 1860; *ibid.*, Beaufort–Randon, No.39, 25 February 1861; *ibid.*, Beaufort–Randon, No.46, 29 March 1861; *ibid.*, Beaufort–Randon, No.50, 5 May 1861. The estimate of the number of armed Druzes is by Cerez.

54. V., G4/1, Beaufort–Randon, No.32, 12 January 1861.

55. V., G4/5, Beaufort–Randon, No.6, 12 September 1860; *ibid.*, Beaufort–Randon, No.7, 21 September 1860; V., G4/5, Beaufort–Randon, No.8, 23 September 1861; summary of all the important Druze families and leaders in V., G4/1 Beaufort–Randon, No.38, 15 February 1861; V., G4/1, Beaufort–Randon, No.19, 4 October 1861, says that 11 Druze chiefs had been arrested and in prison at Beirut since September 21.

56. V., G4/1, "Extrait d'une lettre du capitaine Moch membre du comité chargé des

travaux de reconstruction de reinstallation des chrétiens à Deir el Kamar (Deir el Kamar 19 janvier)."

57. V., G4/1, Beaufort–Randon, No.41, 10 March 1861; *ibid.*, Beaufort–Randon, No.43, 15 March 1861; *ibid.*, Beaufort–Randon, No.44, 24 March 1861; F.O. 78/1629, Dufferin–Bulwer, No.141, 23 March 1861. The figures quoted in my text come from: F.O. 78/1630, "26e séance. Annexe N.3. Traduction. Tableau des Druzes condamnés à la déportation et à la détention. 1861." The list has 249 entries, but there is a mistake in the numbering, which jumps from 100 to 102, so in reality there are 248 names on it. Also, the table of sentences repeats "id" for the same sentence on three occasions – nos. 146, 158, 166 – and that should be ignored for a correct count. Note that Dufferin's report of 23 March gives slightly different figures, perhaps reflecting small differences between the sentences and their executions: 16 of the prisoners condemned to deportation were left behind, on account of sickness, while the remaining 155 were sent into exile. Another 55 were sentenced to one year's detention, 10 or 20 to two years, 6 to thirteen years, and 9 to nine years.

58. F.O. 78/1630, "26e séance. Annexe N.3. Traduction. Tableau des Druzes condamnés à la déportation et à la détention. 1861."

59. *Ibid.*

60. *Ibid.*

61. F.O. 78/1628, Part 2, "Minutes on the judgment proposed to be passed on the Turkish Officials and Druze Chiefs by the Extraordinary Tribunal of Beirut," in Dufferin–Bulwer, No.122, 24 February 1861.

62. V., G4/1, Beaufort–Randon, No.32, 12 January 1861.

63. F.O. 78/1626, 9e séance du 10 novembre 1860.

64. F.O. 78/1629, Dufferin–Bulwer, No.141, 23 March, 1861. The report does not mention Abd al-Malik's first name, but from other reports it is safe for me to assume it is Yusuf who is being discussed in it.

65. V., G4/1, "Extrait d'une lettre du capitaine Moch."

66. V., G4/1, Beaufort–Randon, No.49, 26 April 1861; F.O. 78/1629, Dufferin–Bulwer, No.141, 23 March 1861.

67. V., G4/1, Beaufort–Randon, No.39, 25 February 1861; *ibid.*, Beaufort–Randon, No.41, 10 March 1861; *ibid.*, Beaufort–Randon, No.46, 7 April 1861. Another example of probable European intervention in the carrying out of sentences: Ali Janbalat's sentence of exile was commuted to one of local detention, by a letter from the grand vizier to Fuad Pasha: F.O. 195/660, No.56, 2 October 1861.

68. F.O. 78/1626, Dufferin–Bulwer, No.54, 17 November 1860; V., G4/1, Fuad Pasha–Beaufort, 17 March 1861, in Beaufort–Randon, No.44, 24 March, 1861; F.O. 78/1630, Part 2, Dufferin–Bulwer, No.195, 10 May 1861. As late as October 1861, no execution of Druzes involved in 1860 had taken place: F.O. 195/660, Fraser–Bulwer, No.61, 17 October 1861; *ibid.*, Fraser–Bulwer, No.75, November 29 1861.

69. F.O. 78/1630, Part 2, Dufferin–Bulwer, No.195, 10 May 1861; *ibid.*, Dufferin–Bulwer, No.196, 10 May 1861.

70. F.O. 195/660, Fraser–Bulwer, No.17, 15 June 1861.

71. F.O. 195/660, Fraser–Bulwer, No.23, 29 June 1861.

72. F.O. 195/660, Fraser–Bulwer, No.17, 15 June 1861. Fraser does not say outright that he gave financial support to the family, but it is clear from several of his references. Here, for example, he wrote that he had repeatedly "alleviated" the plight of Janbalat's widow.

NOTES 273

73. F.O. 195/660, Fraser–Bulwer, No.23, 29 June 1861; *ibid.*, Fraser–Bulwer, No.29, 13 July 1861.

74. F.O. 195/660, Fraser–Bulwer, No.42, 10 August 1861; *ibid.*, Fraser–Bulwer, No.66, 4 November 1861.

75. F.O. 78/1630, Part 1, Moore–Dufferin, 26 April, 1861, in Dufferin–Bulwer, No.170, 26 April 1861.

76. V., G4/1, Beaufort–Randon, No.17, 20 October 1861; *ibid.*, Beaufort–Randon, No.46, 7 April 1861; F.O. 78/1629, Dufferin–Bulwer, No.147, 29 March 1861.

77. F.O. 78/1629, Dufferin–Bulwer, No.162, 20 April 1861; F.O. 78/1630, Part 1, Pincoffs–Dufferin, 23 April 1861, in Dufferin–Bulwer, No.163, 24 April 1861; *ibid.*, Dufferin–Russell, No.104, 1 May 1861; F.O. 78/1630, Part 2, Pincoffs–Dufferin, 10 May 1861, in Dufferin–Russell, No.111, 10 May 1861; *ibid.*, Dufferin–Bulwer, No.193, 10 May 1861.

78. F.O. 78/1629, Dufferin–Bulwer, No.162, 20 April 1861; F.O. 78/1630, Part 1, Dufferin–Bulwer, No.163, 24 April 1861; F.O. 78/1630, Part 2, Dufferin–Bulwer, No.193, 10 May 1861, and enclosure by E.T. Rogers, 6 May 1861; *ibid.*, Pincoffs–Dufferin, 10 May 1861, in Dufferin–Russell, No.111, 10 May 1861.

79. F.O. 78/1630, Part 2, Dufferin–Russell, No.115, 11 May 1861; *ibid.*, Dufferin–Bulwer, No.195, 10 May 1861; V., G4/1, Beaufort–Randon, No.52, 19 May 1861.

80. V., G4/1, Beaufort–Randon, No.52, 19 May 1861; Salibi, *Modern History of Lebanon*, p.109.

81. F.O. 78/1628, Part 2, Dufferin–Bulwer, No.122, 24 February 1861.

82. F.O. 78/1626, Dufferin–Bulwer, No.59, 20 November 1860.

83. F.O. 78/1628, Part 2, "Minutes on the judgment proposed to be passed on the Turkish Officials and Druze Chiefs by the Extraordinary Tribunal of Beirut," in Dufferin–Bulwer, No.122, 24 February 1861.

84. *Ibid.*

85. F.O. 78/1628, Part 2, Dufferin–Bulwer, No.132, 7 March 1861.

86. F.O. 78/1630, Part 2, Dufferin–Bulwer, No.193, 10 May 1861.

8. The Peace Settlement

1. "Further Papers," Paynter–Martin, 13 July 1860, Encl.2 in No.21, Paget–Hammond, 3 August 1860, p.38; Aqiqi, *Lebanon in the Last Years of Feudalism*, p.69.

2. "Further Papers," Paynter–Martin, 13 July 1860, Encl.2 in No.21, Paget–Hammond, 3 August 1860, p.38; *ibid.*, Translation, "Treaty of Peace between the Christians and Druses," Encl.4 in No.28, Moore–Russell, 19 July 1860, pp.62–3.

3. F.O. 78/1520, Brant–Bulwer, No.29, 31 July 1860; *ibid.*, Brant–Bulwer, No.40, 30 August 1860.

4. F.O. 78/1626, Dufferin–Bulwer, No.38, 31 October 1860.

5. F.O. 78/1520, Brant–Bulwer, No.31, 9 August 1860; V., G4/5, Beaufort-Randon, No.3, 27 August 1860; *ibid.*, Beaufort–Randon, No.7, 21 September 1860, and other correspondence; F.O. 78/1510, Bulwer–Brant, 8 August 1860, in Bulwer–Russell, No.491, 8 August 1860.

6. F.O. 78/1624, Draft, (to) Dufferin, No.1, Foreign Office, 30 July 1860; *The Dictionary of National Biography*, Supplement January 1901–December 1911, Vol. I (London:

Oxford University Press), pp.171–6; P.R.O.N.I., D&A/320, Reel 1; *ibid.*, Reel 2, Vol. VIII, William Fraser–Dufferin, Edinburgh, 5 April 1858. References to Dufferin's elegant public speaking in P.R.O.N.I., MD&A/22, Reel 4, Vol. XI, Duke of Argyll–Dufferin, 22 May 1860; *ibid.*, Morley–Dufferin (May 1860).

7. P.R.O.N.I., MD&A/22/Reel 5, Vol. XII, Graham–Dufferin, 26 August 1860; P.R.O.N.I., D/1071H/C, Cowley–Dufferin, Paris, 21 December 1860; P.R.O.N.I., D&A/320/Reel 1, Dufferin–Fraser, 25 September 1860.

8. F.O. 78/1624, Draft, (to) Dufferin, No.1, Foreign Office, 30 July 1860; P.R.O.N.I., MD&A/22/Reel 5, Vol. XII, James Graham–Dufferin, London, 15 August 1860.

9. P.R.O.N.I., D&A/320/Reel 1, Dufferin–Fraser, 16 January 1861; *ibid.*, Dufferin–Fraser, 15 January 1861; *ibid.*, Dufferin–Fraser, 17 January 1861.

10. P.R.O.N.I., MD&A/22/Reel 1, vol. VIII, Richardson–Dufferin, London, (April?) 1857; *ibid.*, vol. VII, Richardson–Dufferin, (July?) 1857. That Dufferin was an illiberal and unjust landlord is the complaint of 45 of his former tenants in P.R.O.N.I., D&A/320/Reel 2, Gladstone Papers, "Memorial Sent to The Right Hon. W.E. Gladstone M.P., by Former Tenants of Lord Dufferin's Ards Estate," 11 February 1881.

11. P.R.O.N.I., D&A/320/Reel 1, Dufferin–Fraser, 12 November 1860; F.O. 78/1519, Moore–Bulwer, No.65, 3 September 1860; *ibid.*, Moore–Bulwer, No.67, 5 September 1860; V., G4/5, Beaufort–Randon, No.6, 12 September 1860; P.R.O.N.I., D&A/320/Reel 1, Dufferin–Fraser, 15 January 1860; *ibid.*, Dufferin–Fraser, 17 January 1861.

12. A.E., CP/T/346, (Thouvenel)–de la Valette, No.68, 17 August 1860; *ibid.*, "Projet d'instruction pour le commissaire de S(a) M(ajesté) en Syrie;" F.O. 78/1624, Draft, (to) Dufferin, No.1, Foreign Office, 30 July 1860.

13. P.R.O.N.I., MD&A/22/Reel 5, Vol. XII, Graham–Dufferin, 6 August 1860; *ibid.*, Ducie–Dufferin, 7 August 1860; *ibid.*, Graham–Dufferin, 26 August 1860. Graham's letter which was considered for publication in the press is not included in the Dufferin papers. From a comparison of the Dufferin papers and the Foreign Office ones, I am certain that it is the letter published in "Further Papers," Graham–Dufferin, 18 July 1860, Encl. in No.22, Dufferin–Russell, 5 August 1860: Ducie commented on 7 August that he had received Dufferin's letter of 5 August and with it Graham's letter. He added that Lord Wodehouse begged him, from Lord John Russell, to give up the idea of publishing the letter in *The Times*, as they proposed instead to publish Graham's letter, or rather an extract of it.

14. F.O. 78/1519, Moore–Bulwer, No.65, 3 September 1860; F.O. 195/1625, Dufferin–Bulwer, No.1, 3 September 1860; *ibid.*, Dufferin–Bulwer, No.9, 13 September 1860; F.O. 78/1519, Moore–Bulwer, No.67, 5 September 1860; *ibid.*, Moore–Russell, No.44, 14 September 1860; *Documents diplomatiques et consulaires relatifs à l'histoire du Liban: et des Pays du Proche-Orient du XVIIe siècle à nos jours*, ed. Adel Ismail, Documents recueillis sous l'égide de l'émir Maurice Chehab (Beirut: Editions des œuvres politiques et historiques, 1978), 1e partie: les sources françaises, vol. 10: consulat général de France à Beyrouth (1853–1861), p.251, Bentivoglio–Thouvenel, No.57, 3 septembre 1860.

15. F.O. 78/1625, Dufferin–Bulwer, No.17, 28 September 1860, in Dufferin–Russell, No.12, 29 September 1860; F.O. 78/1630, Part 2, Dufferin–Russell, 11 May 1861; *ibid.*, Dufferin–Bulwer, No.199, 11 May 1861; *ibid.*, Dufferin–Hammond, 11 May 1861, and enclosure: Dufferin–Burnaby, 10 May 1861; F.O. 195/660, Fraser–Bulwer, No.23, 29 June 1861; *ibid.*, Fraser–Bulwer, No.28, 13 July 1861; F.O. 195/660, Fraser–Bulwer, No.69, 13 November 1861; F.O. 78/1625, 42e séance du 9 decembre 1861; *ibid.*, Fraser–Bulwer,

No.30, 13 July 1861; *ibid.*, Hariciye, (Bulwer)–Ali Pasha, Constantinople, 2 July 1861; *ibid.*, (Ali Pasha?)–Bulwer, No.5224/60, 10 July 1861. Churchill, p.258, wrote that the commission met until 5 March 1861: in fact, they met far longer than that. Consult also Spagnolo, *France and Ottoman Lebanon*, pp.36ff; Gökbilgin, "1840'dan 1861'e kadar Cebel-i Lübnan Meselesi ve Drüziler," p.696.

16. A.E., CP/T/348, La Valette–Thouvenel, No.1, 1 January 1861.

17. P.R.O.N.I., D/1071H/C, De Rehfues–Dufferin, 26 November 1860: De Rehfues stated that he would dispense with his escort of French troops to prevent doubts about his neutrality; F.O. 78/1628, Dufferin–Bulwer, No.122, 24 February 1861, in which Dufferin expresses his regret that the French and Prussian commissioners subscribed to the death sentence against 11 guilty Druze shaykhs; F.O. 78/1629, Dufferin–Russell, No.91, 4 April 1861, in which Dufferin explains that in regard to the sentencing of Turkish and Druze prisoners, de Rehfues was far more in concert with Beclard than any other of the commissioners; Churchill, *The Druzes and the Maronites*, p.278; the Prussian commissioner sided, for example, with his French colleague in favor of French troops in Damascus: F.O. 78/1625, 2e séance du 9 octobre 1860; F.O. 78/1519, Moore–Russell, No.44, 14 September 1860.

18. F.O. 78/1630, Part 2, Dufferin–Bulwer, No.183, 2 May 1861.

19. F.O. 195/660, Fraser–Bulwer, No.23, 29 June 1861.

20. F.O. 78/1625, 2e séance du 9 octobre 1860; *ibid.*, 3e séance du 11 octobre 1860; Gökbilgin, p.696.

21. F.O. 78/1625, 3e séance du 11 octobre 1860; *ibid.*, 4e séance du 15 octobre 1860.

22. F.O. 78/1625, Annexe No.1 au Protocol de la 3e séance du 11 octobre 1860; *ibid.*, 4e séance du 15 octobre 1860; F.O. 78/1626, 7e séance du 30 octobre 1860.

23. F.O. 78/1627, 16e séance du 29 decembre 1860, Beclard's comments.

24. F.O. 78/1520, Brant–Bulwer, No.48, 25 September 1860; F.O. 78/1627, Dufferin–Russell, No.41, 19 December 1860; F.O. 78/1628, Annexe No.3, 22e séance du 27 février 1861.

25. F.O. 78/1628, séance du 27 février 1861; A.E., CP/T/345, de la Valette–Thouvenel, No.49, 22 June 1860. De la Valette made an additional comment which is puzzling: he explained the Ottoman tendency to let matters deteriorate in Mount Lebanon by their wish to then blame anarchy on the political arrangement of 1845. In 1842, the Ottomans had ended the Shihab emirate which the French favored, and put the Mountain under more direct Ottoman rule, so that the success of that system was to Ottoman advantage. Perhaps de la Valette assumes here that the Ottomans resented the qualifications added in 1845 to the 1842 arrangement, which enabled the minorities in each qaymaqamate to express their grievances. In reality, the 1845 arrangement was the creation of Shakib Efendi, who as Ottoman foreign minister initiated these revisions and discussed them at length with communal leaders and representatives of the Great Powers. His role in bringing them about is acknowledged in the fact that they are known as the Shakib Efendi regulations. I am grateful to Engin Akarlı for his insights on this matter.

For other instances of the French blaming the Turks for the civil war see *ibid.*, de la Valette–Thouvenel, No.7, 13 June 1860; *ibid.*, de la Valette–Thouvenel, No.13, 17 June 1860; *ibid.*, de la Valette–Thouvenel, 20 June 1860; *ibid.*, (probably Thouvenel)–de la Valette, 22 June 1860; Beclard's comments in F.O. 78/1628, séance du 29 janvier 1861. The quotation from Abd al-Qadir's conversation with Moore is found in F.O. 78/1586,

"Memorandum of Conversations with the Emir Abd-El-Kader," in Moore–Russell, No.19, 8 August 1860.

26. A.E., CPC/D/7, Hecquart–Drouyn de Lhuis, Damascus, 18 October 1862.

27. F.O. 78/1626, "Substance of an Interpellation addressed by Lord Dufferin to Fuad Pasha at the 8th Sitting of the Syrian Commission, 10 November 1860," in Dufferin–Bulwer, No.46, 13 November 1860; F.O. 78/1519, Moore–Bulwer, No.26, 31 May 1860; *ibid.*, Moore–Bulwer, No.52, 21 July 1860, in Moore–Russell, No.23, 21 July 1860; F.O. 78/1520, Brant–Bulwer, No.40, 30 August 1860.

28. F.O. 78/1510, Bulwer–Moore, No.17, 8 August 1860, in Bulwer–Russell, No.491, 8 August 1860.

29. F.O. 78/1626, Dufferin–Bulwer, No.40, 3 November 1860. The same opinion is found in F.O. 78/1627, Dufferin–Russell, No.41, 19 December 1860.

30. Gökbilgin, pp.690–2.

31. Hariciye, (Abro)–Cabouli, Beirut, 7 March 1861.

32. F.O. 78/1628, Annexe No.3, 22e séance du 27 février 1861; F.O. 78/1625, Annexe No.1, Protocole de la 3e séance du 11 octobre 1860; A.E., CP/T/345, de la Valette–Thouvenel, No.13, Therapia, 17 June 1860; F.O. 78/1628, séance du 29 janvier 1861; F.O. 78/1627, séance du 29 decembre 1860.

33. A.E., CP/T/345, "Traduction d'une dépêche du gouvernement général de Beyrouth," in de la Valette–Thouvenel, No.9, Therapia, 20 June 1860; F.O. 78/1557, Translation, Khurshid Pasha to the Grand Vizier, dated 13 Zil-Kadeh 76 (Dhu'l Qa'da), in Bulwer–Russell, No.366, 2 July 1860; F.O. 78/1628, Annexe No.3, 22e séance du 27 février 1861. The administrative reorganization of Syria during the Tanzimat period is discussed in Ma'oz, *Ottoman Reform in Syria and Palestine*, pp.31–2.

34. A.E., CP/T/345, de la Valette–Thouvenel, No.29, 18 July 1860 and Encl., de la Valette–Bentivoglio, No.56, 17 July 1860; *ibid.*, de la Valette–Thouvenel, No.7, 13 June 1860; *ibid.*, de la Valette–Thouvenel, No.9, 20 June 1860; *ibid.*, de la Valette–Thouvenel, No.13, 17 June 1860; F.O. 78/1519, Moore–Bulwer, No.26, 31 May 1860; F.O. 78/1510, Bulwer–Brant, 8 August 1860.

35. F.O. 78/1557, Translation, Khurshid Pasha to the Grand Vizier; F.O. 78/1519, Moore–Bulwer, No.20, 20 May 1860; Hariciye, (Abro)–Cabouly, Beirut, 7 March 1861.

36. F.O. 78/1628, séance du 27 février 1861; *ibid.*, séance du 29 janvier 1861; F.O. 78/1628, Part 2, "Minute on the Judgment proposed to be passed on the Turkish Officials and Druze Chiefs, by the Extraordinary Tribunal of Beirut," in Dufferin–Bulwer, No.122, 24 February 1861; F.O. 78/1627, Dufferin–Russell, No.41, 19 December 1860.

37. F.O. 78/1628, séance du 27 février 1861; *ibid.*, séance du 29 janvier 1861.

38. F.O. 78/1519, Moore–Bulwer, No.26, 31 May 1860; F.O. 78/1557, Bulwer–Russell, No.366, 2 July 1860; A.E., CP/T/345, de la Valette–Thouvenel, No.7, Therapia, 13 June 1860.

39. A.E., CP/T/345, from Khurshid Pasha, "Traduction d'une dépêche du gouvernement général de Beyrouth," in de la Valette–Thouvenel, No.9, Therapia, 20 June 1860; F.O. 78/1628, Annexe No.3, 22e séance du 27 février 1861.

40. Salibi, *The Modern History of Lebanon*, p.89; A.E., CP/T/345, from Khurshid Pasha, "Traduction d'une dépêche du gouvernement général de Beyrouth;" F.O. 78/1557, translation, Khurshid Pasha to the Grand Vizier. Both the French and British translations of Khurshid Pasha's text used the term "national committee." The spelling of the names of the committee's members varied slightly: in the French text, they were

NOTES

Mansour Mat, Naoum Keifani, Esad Sabit, Jacoub Saleit, Nicola Naqqach, Habib Gochou, Mansour Ade, and Eioub Tarabolomi. In the English text, they were Mansour Teian, Naoum Keifane, Jakoub Sabit or Sabih (probably Tabit), Nicola Nakkash, Habib Kashoua, Mansour Ada, Essaad Sabit, Eyoub Tarabulousi (probably Mansour Edde, Ayyoub Traboulsi, Mansour Tyan, Naoum Kayfani, Yakoub Tabit).

41. F.O. 78/1519, Moore–Bulwer, No.26, 31 May 1860; *ibid.*, Moore–Bulwer, No.20, 20 May 1860; A.E., CP/T/345, from Khurshid Pasha, "Traduction d'une dépêche du gouvernement général de Beyrouth;" F.O. 78/1557, translation, Khurshid Pasha to the Grand Vizier.

42. F.O. 78/1519, Moore–Bulwer, No.26, 31 May 1860; *ibid.*, Moore–Bulwer, No.20, 20 May 1860; A.E., CP/T/345, de la Valette–Thouvenel, No.9, Therapia, 20 June 1860.

43. F.O. 78/1520, Brant–Bulwer, No.40, 30 August 1860; F.O. 195/660, Fraser–Bulwer, No.66, 4 November 1861; F.O. 78/1625, Dufferin–Russell, No.41, 19 December 1860; F.O. 78/1628, séance du 29 janvier 1861; F.O. 78/1628, Part 2, Dufferin–Bulwer, No.122, 24 February 1861, and Encl.: "Minute on the Judgment proposed to be passed on the Turkish Officials and Druze Chiefs, by the Extraordinary Tribunal of Beirut."

44. F.O. 78/1627, Dufferin–Bulwer, No.105, 18 January 1861; F.O. 78/1625, Dufferin–Russell, No.41, 19 December 1860; F.O. 78/1629, Dufferin–Bulwer, No.148, 29 March 1861; F.O. 195/660, Fraser–Bulwer, No.10, 2 June 1861.

45. F.O. 78/1519, No.54, 28 July 1860 in Moore–Russell, No.25, 28 July 1860.

46. F.O. 78/1627, Dufferin–Bulwer, No.105, 18 January 1861; F.O. 78/1625, Dufferin–Russell, No.41, 19 December 1860; F.O. 78/1557, translation, Khurshid Pasha to the Grand Vizier.

47. M.P.B., Awn–Mas'ad, 23 May 1860, and other correspondence. For a defense of the bishop and an explanation of the Maronite clergy's positions, consult an anonymous witness account written by someone close to the bishop: *Tabrir al-Nasara mimma nusiba ilayhim fi hawadith sanat 1860* (The exoneration of Christians from what was attributed to them in the events of 1860), manuscript found in the Maronite monastery Dar Sayyidat Luwayza and published by Father Louis Bulaybil, *al-Mashriq*, vol. 26 (1928), pp.631–44. Consult also a secondary source: Antoine Lubbos, *Tawajjuhat al-iklirios al-Maruni fi Jabal Lubnan (1842–1867): watha'iq Bkirki* (The positions of the Maronite Clergy in Mount Lebanon [1842–1867]: the Bkerke Archives) (Beirut, 1991).

48. F.O. 78/1628, translation of a "Letter from Bishop Tobia of Beirut to the Chief People of Deir el Kamar dated 20 May 1860," in Dufferin–Bulwer, 7 March 1860.

49. *Documents diplomatiques et consulaires*, p.254, Bentivoglio–Thouvenel, No.57, 3 September 1860.

50. F.O. 78/1627, Dufferin–Bulwer, No.100, 13 January 1861, in Dufferin–Russell, No.50, 10 January 1861.

51. F.O. 78/1628, séance du 29 janvier 1861.

52. F.O. 78/1628, séance du 29 janvier 1861; *ibid.*, séance du 27 février 1861. In F.O. 78/1628, Part 2, Dufferin–Bulwer, No.122, 24 February 1861, Dufferin suggests that Novikow changed his position when he reported that the day before Novikow had accused the Christians of having begun the attack upon the Druzes "along the whole boundary of the mixed Districts." Dufferin added that Novikow usually believed with "implicit faith" Christian evidence and was influenced by stories of Druze atrocities. Dufferin reported Novikow's alleged change of position because he was probably pleased

that Novikow had made a point he himself kept making. However, an examination of Novikow's arguments at the commission's meeting of 27 February quoted above shows that, in fact, he continued to excuse the Christians and that he dismissed or played down their aggressiveness.

53. F.O. 78/1519, Moore–Bulwer, No.20, 20 May 1860; A.E., CP/T/345, de la Valette–Thouvenel, No.9, Therapia, 20 June 1860; F.O. 78/1557, translation, Khurshid Pasha to the Grand Vizier; Hariciye, (Abro)–Cabouly, Beirut, 7 March 1861; *ibid.*, Abro–Cabouly, Beirut, 19 March 1861; *ibid.*, Abro–Cabouly, Beirut, 24 March 1861.

54. F.O. 78/1628, Annexe No.3, 22e séance du 27 février 1861.

55. A.E., CP/T/346, [Thouvenel]–La Valette, No.63, 2 April 1861; A.E., CP/T/348, La Valette–Thouvenel, No.1, 1 January 1861; F.O. 78/1627, Dufferin–Bulwer, No.100, 13 January 1861, in Dufferin–Russell, No.50, 10 January 1861. For a concise and excellent coverage of the commission's discussions about the future organization of Mount Lebanon, see Spagnolo, *France and Ottoman Lebanon*, pp.36–47.

56. F.O. 78/1627, Dufferin–Bulwer, No.100, in Dufferin–Russell, No.50, 10 January 1861; *ibid.*, Dufferin–Bulwer, No.94, 1 January 1861; Spagnolo, *France and Ottoman Lebanon*, p.37.

57. F.O. 78/1629, Dufferin–Bulwer, No.136, 14 March 1861; A.E., CP/T/348, 'Ali Pasha–Musurus Pasha, No.4925/115, 22 January 1861, in Outrey–Thouvenel, Constantinople, 23 January 1861; Gökbilgin, p.700. See also Ülman, *1860–1861 Suriye Buhranı*, section V.

58. Spagnolo, *France and Ottoman Lebanon*, p.38; Gökbilgin, pp.701–2; F.O. 78/1629, Dufferin–Bulwer, No.139, 23 March 1861, and Encl. No.1: "Projet de Réorganization de la Montagne," and Encl. No.2; F.O. 78/1630, Part I, Dufferin–Bulwer, No.169, 25 April 1861; *ibid.*, [Meade]–Hammond, 26 April 1861; F.O. 78/1630, Part 2, Dufferin–Bulwer, No.178, 30 April 1861; *ibid.*, Dufferin–Russell, No.107, 5 May 1860.

59. This entire section about the discussions in Istanbul relies heavily on Spagnolo, *France and Ottoman Lebanon*, pp.39–41.

60. *Ibid.*, "Règlement fondamental relatif à l'administration du Mont-Liban en date du 30 Zilkadeh 1277 H; 9 juin 1861," *Documents diplomatiques et consulaires*, vol.11, pp.102–11; Spagnolo, *France and Ottoman Lebanon*, pp.41–4; Gökbilgin, p.702. For an excellent study of the Mutasarrifiyya period, read Engin Deniz Akarlı, *The Long Peace: Ottoman Lebanon, 1861–1920* (London: I.B.Tauris, 1993).

61. For more information on the administrative council, consult Akarlı, *The Long Peace*, chapter 4, and *idem*, "The Administrative Council of Mount Lebanon," *Lebanon: A History of Conflict and Consensus*, pp.79–100.

62. Spagnolo, *France and Ottoman Lebanon*, p.46.

9. Civil Wars Compared

1. The comparison between 1860 and the war since 1975 was published as "Understanding Lebanon," *The American Scholar*, vol.54, no.3, (Summer 1985), pp.377–84.

2. Kamal Salibi, *A House of Many Mansions: The History of Lebanon Reconsidered* (Berkeley: University of California Press, 1988), pp.31–2.

BIBLIOGRAPHY

Government Documents

Documents diplomatiques et consulaires relatifs à l'histoire du Liban et des Pays du Proche-Orient du XVIIe siècle à nos jours. Ed. Adel Ismail. Beirut: Editions des œuvres politiques et historiques, 1978. Part 1: Sources françaises. vol.10: consulat général de France à Beyrouth (1853–1861); vol.11: consulat général de France à Beyrouth (1861–1864).

France. Ministère de la Défense, Archives militaires, Vincennes. Expédition de Syrie 1860–1861. Numéro des cartons ou registres: G4/1 et G4/2 (correspondance générale 1860–1861); G4/3 (journal des opérations, etc.); G4/4 (correspondance d'intérêt secondaire); G4/5 and G4/6 (correspondance générale supplément).

France. Archives du Ministère des Affaires Etrangères, Paris. Series: Correspondance politique de l'origine à 1871, Turquie. Consulat Divers. Correspondance des consuls. Beyrouth. Vols.11 (1856–1859), 12 (Janvier–Septembre 1860), 13 (Octobre 1860–Décembre 1861), 14 (Janvier 1862–Juillet 1863), 15 (Août 1863–Septembre 1864), 16 (Octobre 1864–Juillet 1865), 17 (Août 1865–Décembre 1866), 18 (1867–68).

France. Archives du Ministère des Affaires Etrangères, Paris. Series: Correspondance politique de l'origine à 1871, Turquie. Consulat Divers, Correspondance des consuls. Damas. Vols.4 (1856–Septembre 1857), 5 (Octobre 1857–Décembre 1859), 6 (1860–1861), 7 (Janvier 1862–Juin 1863), 8 (Juillet 1863–Juin 1865), 9 (Juillet 1865–Décembre 1867).

France. Archives du Ministère des Affaires Etrangères, Paris. Series: Correspondance Politique de l'origine à 1871, Turquie. Consulat Divers, Correspondance des consuls. Alep. Vols.3 (1857–1863), 4 (1862–1869).

France. Archives du Ministère des Affaires Etrangères, Paris. Series: Correspondance politique de l'origine à 1871, Turquie. Consulat Divers, Correspondance des consuls. Jérusalem. Vols.6 (1858–1859), 7 (1860–1862).

France. Ministère des Affaires Etrangères, Paris. Archives des Postes. Ambassade Turquie. Correspondance avec les échelles. Beyrouth 1860–1861. Unbound letters. Armée Corps d'expédition en Syrie, 31 août 1860–7 juin 1861. Documents sur la Syrie et sur le Liban 1860–1861. M. Schefer, Mission en Syrie, septembre 1860–octobre 1861, Gouvernement du Liban, Projet.

France. Archives du Ministère des Affaires Etrangères, Paris. Mémoires et documents, Turquie 1840–63. Syrie et Liban. Vols.122 (1840–63), 123 (1860–81).

France. Ministère des Affaires Etrangères, Paris. Correspondance politique. Turquie. Vols.346 and 347 (1860), 348 (Janvier–Mars 1861), 349 (Avril–Mai 1861), 350 (Juin–Juillet 1861), 351 (Août–Septembre 1861), 352 (Novembre–Décembre 1861).

France. Archives du Ministère des Affaires Etrangères, Paris. Correspondance consulaire et commerciale. Damas. vol.4 (1856–1859).

France. Les Archives du Ministère des Affaires Etrangères, Paris. Correspondance consulaire et commerciale. Beyrouth. vol.7 (1854–1863).

Noradounghian, Gabriel Effendi. *Recueil d'actes internationaux de l'empire ottoman.* vol.2 (1789–1856). vol.3 (1856–1878). Paris: Cotillon, 1900–1902.

Testa, Baron I. de. *Recueil des Traités de la Porte ottomane avec les puissances étrangères.* vol.6. Paris: Muzard, 1884.

United Kingdom. Accounts and Papers. vol.61 (1856), p.353; vol.67 (1861), p.499; vol.69 (1860), Session 24 January–23 August 1860: State Papers, China, Japan, Syria, Papers and Reports (May–July 1860): "Papers Relating to the Disturbances in Syria," June 1860; "Further Papers Relating to the Disturbances in Syria," June 1860. In continuation of "Papers Presented to Parliament July 23, 1860;" vol.68 (1861), Session 5 February–6 August 1861: State Papers, Syria.

United Kingdom. Hansards Parliamentary Debates, 3rd Series. Vols.159 (7 June–20 July 1860), 160 (23 July–28 August 1860), 161 (5 February–18 March 1861).

United Kingdom. Public Record Office, Foreign Office Archives, London. Series F.O. 195. Vols.601 (1858–1860); 647 (1858–1860); 648 (1858–1860); 655 (1860); 656 (September–November 1860); 657 (November–December 1860); 658 (January–March, 1861); 659 (April–May, 1861); 660 (May–December 1861); 677 (January–December 1861), 700 (1861).

United Kingdom. Public Record Office, Foreign Office Archives. London. Series F.O. 78. Vols.1450 (January–December 1859); 1508 (from Bulwer, 1–23 July, 1860); 1509 (from Bulwer, 24–31 July, 1860); 1510 (from Bulwer, August 1860); 1519 (from Moore, January–December 1860), 1520 (consuls, January–December 1860); 1537 (consuls, January–December 1860), 1538 (consuls, January–December 1860), 1539 (consuls, 1860), 1557 (1860); 1586 (consuls, 1861); 1624 (June 1860–June 1861); 1625 (July–October 1860); 1626 (November–December 1860); 1627 (14–24 December, 1860); 1628 (January–March, 1861); 1629 (15 March–21 April, 1861); 1630, part 1 (28 April–4 June, 1861); and part 2 (May 1861); 1727 (October 1862–January 1863).

United Kingdom. Public Record Office, Foreign Office Archives. London. Series F.O. 406. vol.10 (Correspondence 1860–1861).

United Kingdom. Public Record Office, Foreign Office Archives. London. Series F.O. 226. Vols.152 (1861), 155 (1861).

United Kingdom. Public Record Office. Foreign Office Archives. London. Confidential Papers. F.O. 881. vol.983 (January–July 1861).

United Kingdom. Public Record Office of Northern Ireland. Belfast. Dufferin and Ava Related Papers in the British Library. mic. 320, as summarized in: Description Reels 1 and 2. Contemporary Biography, Letters to C. Griffin, 1870.

United Kingdom. Public Record Office of Northern Ireland. Belfast. Correspondence of the first Marquess of Dufferin and Ava, mic. 22, as summarized in Description Reels 1, 4 and 5. vol.11, Correspondence of the Duke of Argyll with Dufferin, 22 May 1860.

United Kingdom. Public Record Office of Northern Ireland. Belfast. Dufferin Papers, Syrian Papers D/1071H/C. Cowley-Dufferin, 1860.

United States. National Archives. United States Consuls, Washington, DC Series: Dispatches from the US Consuls in Beirut, 1836–1906, T367. vol.3 (30 January 1857–31 December 1860). vol.4 (15 February 1861–31 December 1863).

Other Primary Sources

Abkarius, Iskandar ibn Ya'qub. "Kitab nawadir fi malahim Jabal Lubnan" (Massacres rarely equaled in Mount Lebanon). MS 956.9 A 15, Jafet Library, American University, Beirut.
— *The Lebanon in Turmoil: Syria and the Powers in 1860*. Tr. J.F. Scheltema. New Haven: Yale University Press, 1920.
Abu Shaqra, Husayn Ghadban (narrator), and Yusuf Khattar Abu Shaqra (writer), *al-Harakat fi Lubnan ila 'ahd al-mutasarrifiyya* (The troubles in Lebanon until the period of the Mutasarrifiyya), ed., 'Arif Abu Shaqra. Beirut: Matba'at al-Ittihad, 1952.
Anonymous [possibly Nu'man ibn 'Abduh al-Qasatli]. *Hasr al-litham 'an nakabat al-Sham* (Unveiling the Calamities of Damascus) Cairo, 1895.
Anonymous. "Kitab al-ahzan fi tarikh waqi'at al-Sham wa Jabal Lubnan wa'ma yalihi ma bi ma asaba al-Masihiyin min al-Duruz wa'l Islam fi 9 tammuz 1860." MS 956.9 K 62kA, Jafet Library, American University, Beirut.
Anonymous [possibly Father Yusuf Farahyan]. "Nubdha mukhtasara fi fitan Suriya," published as *Nubdha mukhtasara fi hawadith Lubnan wa'l-Sham (1840–1862)*, ed. Louis Cheikho. In *al-Mashriq*, vol.24, no.11 (1926), pp.801–24, 915–38. Also published separately as *Nubdha mukhtasara fi hawadith Lubnan wa'l-Sham (1840–1862)*. Beirut: Imprimerie Catholique, 1927. Ms. in the Armenian Catholic monastery of Bzummar, Lebanon, according to Fritz Steppat, "Some Arabic Manuscript Sources on the Syrian Crisis of 1860," *Les Arabes par leurs archives*, eds. Jacques Berque and Dominique Chevallier (Paris: Centre National de la Recherche Scientifique, 1976), p.184.
Anonymous. *Souvenirs de Syrie (Expédition Française de 1860) par un témoin oculaire*. Paris: Plon-Nourrit, 1903.
Anonymous. "Tabrir al-Nasara mimma nusiba ilayhim fi hawadith sanat 1860" (The exoneration of Christians from what was attributed to them in the events of 1860), ed. Louis Bulaybil, *al-Mashriq*, vol.26 (1928), pp.631–44. Ms. in Maronite monastery Dar Sayyidat Luwayza in Lebanon, according to Fritz Steppat, "Some Arabic Manuscript Sources on the Syrian Crisis of 1860," *Les Arabes par leurs archives*, eds. Jacques Berque and Dominique Chevallier (Paris: Centre National de la Recherche Scientifique, 1976), p.184.
Anonymous. "Tanahhudat Suriya" (The sighs of Syria). Ms. 790, catalogued as MS 956.9 T16, Jafet Library, American University, Beirut, originally in the library of Isa Iskandar Ma'luf.
al-'Aqiqi, Antun Dahir. *Thawra wa fitna fi Lubnan: Safha majhula min tarikh al-jabal min 1841 ila 1873* (Revolt and Revolution in Lebanon: an unknown page of the history of the Mountain from 1841 until 1873), ed., Yusuf Ibrahim Yazbak. Beirut: Matba'at al-Ittihad, 1938.
Arbili, Ibrahim. "al-Haditha aw hiya madhbahat sanat 1860 fi Dimashq al-Sham," *al-Kalima*, vol.9, no.3 (March 1913), pp.151–16; no.4 (April 1913), pp.219–28; no.5 (May 1913), pp.296–301; no.6 (June 1913), pp.352–65; no.7 (July 1913), pp.406–19.
Bakhkhash, Na'um. *Akhbar Halab*. Ed. Yusuf Qushaqji. 2 vols. Aleppo: Mataba'at al-Ihsan, 1985–7.
al-Bitar, Abd al-Razzaq. *Hilyat al-bashar fi tarikh al-qarn al-thalith 'ashar*, ed. Muhammad Bahja al-Bitar. 3 vols. Damascus, 1961–3. vol.1.
Churchill, Charles H. *The Druzes and the Maronites under Turkish Rule from 1840 to 1860*. New York: Arno Press, 1973.

— *Mount Lebanon: A Ten Years' Residence from 1842 to 1852 Describing the Manners, Customs and Religion of Its Inhabitants.* 3 vols. London: Saunders & Otley, 1853.

Debbas, Dimitri. "Mudhakkirat." Ms. in the private library of Fuad Debbas in Paris, France.

Ducrot, Général Auguste-Alexandre. *La Vie Militaire du Général Ducrot d'après sa correspondance (1839–1871).* Published by his children. 2 vols. Paris: E. Plon, Nourrit et Cie, 1895.

Haqqi, Isma'il. *Lubnan: Mabahith 'ilmiyya wa ijtima'iyya*, ed. Fuad Afram al-Bustani. 2 vols. Beirut: al-Matba'at al-Kathulikiyya, 1969–70.

al-Hasibi, Muhammad Abu'l Su'ud. "Lamahat min tarikh Dimashq fi 'ahd al-Tanzimat," ed. Kamal S. Salibi, *al-Abhath*, vol.21, no.1 (March 1968), pp.57–78; nos. 2–4 (December 1968), pp.117–53; vol.22, nos.1–2, pp.51–69.

al-Hattuni, Mansur Tannus. *Nubdha tarikhiyya fi'l-muqata'a al-Kisrawaniyya*, ed. Yusuf Ibrahim Yazbak. 2nd ed. Beirut, 1956.

al-Jawish, Fath Allah ibn As'ad. "Athar Fath Allah aw mir'at al-madi." Orient-Institut der Deutschen Morgenländischen Gesellschaft manuscript collection, Beirut, Lebanon.

Jessup, Henri Harris. *Fifty-Three Years in Syria*. 2 vols. New York: Fleming H. Revell, 1910.

Jobin, (Abbé) Jean-Baptiste, ed. *La Syrie en 1860 et 1861: Lettres et documents formant une histoire complète et suivie des massacres du Liban et de Damas, des secours envoyés aux chrétiens et de l'expédition française.* Lille: J. Lefort, 1880.

Kerr, Malcolm H., ed. and trans. *Lebanon in the Last Years of Feudalism, 1840–1868: A Contemporary Account by Antun Dahir al-'Aqiqi and Other Documents.* Beirut: American University of Beirut, 1959.

Lebanon. Bkerke. Archives du Patriarchat Maronite. Tiroir du Patriarche Boulos Mas'ad, Documents de l'an 1859.

Lenormant, François. *Une Persécution des Christianisme en 1860. Les Derniers Evénements de Syrie.* Paris: Ch. Douniol, E. Dentu, 1860.

— *Histoire des massacres de Syrie en 1860.* Paris: L. Hachette, 1861.

Mishaqa, Mikha'il. *Kitab mashhad al-a'yan bi-hawadith Suriya wa Lubnan*, ed. Milham Khalis Abduh and Andrawus Hanna Shakhashiri. Cairo, 1908.

— *Murder, Mayhem, Pillage and Plunder: The History of the Lebanon in the 18th and 19th Centuries*, tr. Wheeler M. Thackston, Jr. Albany, NY: State University of New York Press, 1988.

Perthuis, Comtesse de. "Carnet de Voyage en Orient, 1853–1855, 1860–1862." Ms. in the private library of Fuad Debbas in Paris, France.

Porter, J.L. *Five Years in Damascus*. 2 vols. London: Murray, 1855.

Qasatli, Nu'man ibn 'Abduh. *al-Rawda al-ghanna' fi Dimashq al-fayha*. Beirut: Dar al-Ra'id al-'Arabi, 1982.

al-Qayati, Shaykh Muhammad Abd al-Jawad. *Nafhat al-Sham fi rihlat al-Sham*. Beirut: Dar al-Ra'id al-'Arabi, 1981.

Rochemonteix, Le Père Camille de, S.J. *Le Liban et l'expédition française en Syrie 1860–1861, documents inédits du général A. Ducrot*. Paris: A. Picard, 1921.

Saint-Marc, Girardin. *La Syrie en 1861. Conditions des chrétiens en Orient.* Paris: Didier et Cie, 1862.

al-Shidyaq, Shaykh Tannus. *Kitab akhbar al-a'yan fi Jabal Lubnan*, ed. Fouad E. Boustany. Publications de l'Université libanaise, Section des études historiques, 19. 2 vols. Beirut: Imprimerie Catholique, 1970.

al-Shihabi, Amir Haydar Ahmad. *Lubnan fi 'ahd al-umara' al-Shihabiyyin*, ed. Asad Rustum

and Fouad E. Boustany. 3 vols. Publications de l'Université libanaise, Section des études historiques, 17. Beirut, n.p. 1969. Vols.2-3.
Syria, Damascus. *Markaz al-watha'iq al-tarihiyya.* Shari'a Court Registers. "Sijillat al-mahkamat al-shar'iyya," vols.536, 555.
Syria, Damascus. Greek Orthodox Patriarchate. Registers of the old Greek Orthodox families of Damascus in 1885. "Sijill 'a'ilat al-Ta'ifa fi'l al-Sham sanat 1885."
Jordan, University of Amman. Markaz al-abhath wa'l-makhtutat (Center for Documents and Manuscripts). Microfilms collected from Hariciye (Foreign Ministry) archives in Istanbul.
United States. Records of the Congregationalist Syrian Mission, Houghton Library, Harvard University, Cambridge, Mass, A.B.C. 16.8.1. vols.6-8 (1860-71).

Newspapers

Le Siècle (Paris), 18 July 1860, 19 July 1860; 20 July 1860; 21 July 1860; 22 July 1860; 23 July 1860; 25 July 1860; 26 July 1860; 27 July 1860; 28 July 1860; 29 July 1860; 30 July 1860; 31 July 1860.
The Times (London), 6 July 1860; 9 July 1860, 10 July 1860; 11 July 1860; 12 July 1860; 13 July 1860; 14 July 1860; 15 July 1860; 22 July 1860; 17 July 1860; 18 July 1860; 20 July 1860; 21 July 1860; 23 July 1860; 24 July 1860; 27 July 1860; 29 July 1860; 30 July 1860; 31 July 1860; 1 August 1860; 2 August 1860; 4 August 1860; 5 August 1860; 12 August 1860; 14 August 1860; 17 August 1860; 18 August 1860; 19 August 1860; 25 August 1860; 31 August 1860; 2 September 1860; 6 September 1860; 30 September 1860; 7 October 1860; 14 October 1860; 18 November 1860.

Secondary Works

Abdel Nour, Antoine. *Introduction à l'histoire urbaine de la Syrie Ottomane (XVIe–XVIIIe siècle).* Publications de l'Université libanaise, Section des études historiques, 25. Beirut: Imprimerie Catholique, 1982.
Abou Nohra, Joseph, "L'évolution du système politique libanais dans le contexte des conflicts régionaux et locaux." *Lebanon, A History of Conflict and Consensus,* ed. Nadim Shehadi and Dana Haffar Mills. London: Centre for Lebanese Studies in association with I. B. Tauris, 1988, pp.31–48.
Abraham, Anthony J. *Lebanon at Mid-Century: Maronite–Druze Relations in Lebanon 1840–1860: A Prelude to Arab Nationalism.* Washington DC: University Press of America, 1981.
Abu-Husayn, Abdul-Rahim. "The Iltizam of Mansur Furaykh: A Case Study of *Iltizam* in Sixteenth-Century Syria." *Land Tenure and Social Transformation in the Middle East,* ed. Tarif Khalidi. Beirut: American University of Beirut Press, 1984, pp.249–56.
— *Provincial Leadership in Syria, 1575–1650.* Beirut: American University of Beirut, 1985.
Abu-Izzedin, Nejla M. *The Druzes: A New Study of Their History, Faith and Society.* Leiden: E.J. Brill, 1993.
Abu-Manneh, Butrus. "The Establishment and Dismantling of the Province of Syria." *Problems of the Modern Middle East in Historical Perspective: Essays in Honour of Albert Hourani,* ed. John Spagnolo. Reading: Ithaca Press, 1992, pp.8–26.
Ajami, Fuad. *The Vanished Imam: Musa al-Sadr and the Shia of Lebanon.* Ithaca, N.Y.: Cornell University Press, 1986.
Akarlı, Engin Deniz. "Judiciary Organization in Ottoman Lebanon as a Mechanism of

Social Consolidation 1861–1918." *Revue d'Histoire Maghrébine*, 1983, pp.59–72.
— "Taxation in Ottoman Lebanon, 1861–1915." *al-Abhath*, 35 (1987), pp.29–51.
— "The Administrative Council of Mount Lebanon." *Lebanon: A History of Conflict and Consensus*, ed. Nadim Shehadi and Dana Haffar Mills. London: The Centre for Lebanese Studies in association with I.B.Tauris, 1988, pp.79–100.
— "Provincial Power Magnates in Ottoman Bilad al-Sham and Egypt, 1740–1840." *La vie sociale dans les provinces arabes à l'époque ottomane*, ed. Abdeljelil Temimi. Zaghouan: Centre d'études et de recherches ottomanes, morisques, de documentation et d'information, 1988. vol.3, pp.41–56.
— *The Long Peace: Ottoman Lebanon, 1861–1920* (London: I.B.Tauris, 1993).
Alamuddin, Najib, *Turmoil: The Druzes, Lebanon and the Arab–Israeli Conflict*. London: Quartet Books, 1993.
Anderson, Matthew Smith. *The Eastern Question 1744–1923, A Study in International Relations*. New York: Macmillan, 1966.
Antoun, Richard, and Iliya Harik, eds. *Rural Politics and Social Change in the Middle East*. Bloomington: Indiana University Press, 1972.
Aviau de Piolant, Vicomtesse d'. *Au pays des Maronites*. Paris: H. Oudin, 1882.
Awit, Michel. *Les Maronites: Que sont-ils? Que veulent-ils?* Bekerke, Lebanon, 1989.
Baaklini, Abdu. *Legislative and Political Development: Lebanon, 1842–1972*. Durham, NC: Duke University Press, 1970.
al-Baʻlabakki, Mikhaʼil Musa Alluf. *Tarikh Baʻlabakk*. 2nd ed. Beirut: al-Matbaʻat al-adabiyya, 1904.
Barbir, Karl K. *Ottoman Rule in Damascus: 1708–1758*. Princeton, NJ: Princeton University Press, 1980.
Bardet, A. *La Syrie et la France*. Paris: E. Dentu, 1861.
Baron, Salo Wittmayer. "The Jews and the Syrian Massacres of 1860." In *Proceedings of the American Academy for Jewish Research*, vol.4 (1932–3), pp.3–31.
Baudicour, Louis de. *La France en Syrie*. Paris: E. Dentu, 1860.
— *La France au Liban*. Paris: E. Dentu, 1879.
Baz, Salim. *Pièces diplomatiques relatives aux événements de 1860 au Liban*. Beirut: Librarie Antoine, 1974.
Bertou, J. de. "La réorganisation du Liban." *Le Correspondant*, 53 (June 1861), pp.380–4.
Betts, Robert Brenton. *The Druze*. New Haven, Conn.: Yale University Press, 1988.
— "The Indigenous Arabic-Speaking Christian Communities of Greater Syria and Mesopotamia." Ph.D. diss., The Johns Hopkins University, 1968. Ann Arbor: University Microfilms International, 1968.
Beydoun, Ahmad. "Les civils, leurs communautés et l'Etat dans la guerre comme système social au Liban," *Social Compass*, vol.35, no. 4 (1988), pp.585–606.
— *Identités confessionnelles et temps social chez les historiens libanais contemporains*. Publications de l'Université libanaise, Section des études philosophiques et sociales, 15. Araya, Lebanon: Imprimerie Catholique, 1984.
Beyhum, Nabil. "Espaces urbain, espaces politiques: ville, état et communautés à Beyrouth vers 1975. Eléments pour une problématique." *Lebanon, A History of Conflict and Consensus*, ed. Nadim Shehadi and Dana Haffar Mills. London: Centre for Lebanese Studies in association with I.B.Tauris, 1988, pp.274–304.
— ed. *Reconstruire Beyrouth: Les paris sur le possible*. Collection Etudes sur le monde arabe, no.5. Lyons: Maison de l'Orient Méditerranéen, 1991.
Bianquis, Anne-Marie. "Damas et la Ghouta." *La Syrie d'aujourd'hui*, ed. André Raymond. Paris: Centre National de la Recherche Scientifique, 1980, pp.359–84.

Binder, Leonard, ed. *Politics in Lebanon.* New York: Wiley, 1966.
Blaisdell, Donald C. *European Financial Control in the Ottoman Empire.* New York: Columbia University Press, 1929.
Bourget. "Les événements de 1860 au Liban et l'intervention française," *Revue des Troupes coloniale,* vol.3, no.9 (January 1938), pp.7–42.
Buheiry, Marwan. "The Peasant Revolt of 1858 in Mount Lebanon: Rising Expectations, Economic Malaise and the Incentive to Arm." *Land Tenure and Social Transformation in the Middle East,* ed. Tarif Khalidi. Beirut: American University of Beirut, 1984, pp.291–302.
— and Leila Ghantus, eds. *The Splendor of Lebanon: Eighteenth-Century and Nineteenth-Century Artists and Travellers.* New York: Caravan Books, 1978.
Burke, Edmund III. "Changing Patterns of Peasant Protest in the Middle East 1750–1950." *Peasants and Politics in the Modern Middle East,* ed. John Waterbury and Farhad Kazemi. Miami: Florida International University Press, 1991, pp.24–37.
— "Rural Collective Action and the Emergence of Modern Lebanon: A Comparative Historical Perspective." *Lebanon: A History of Conflict and Consensus,* ed. Nadim Shehadi and Dana Haffar Mills. London: Centre for Lebanese Studies in association with I.B.Tauris, 1988, pp.14–30.
Buse, G. "As Regards the Echo the 1860 Massacres in Syria and Lebanon Had in the United Principalities." *Analele Universitatii Bucaresti Istorie,* vol.15 (1966), pp.197–200.
Cerbella, Gino. "L'Azione dell'emiro Abd El-Qader contro i drusi, massacratori, nel 1860, dei Cristiani di Damasco." *Africa,* March 1973, pp.51–64.
Charles-Roux, François. *France et Chrétiens d'Orient.* Paris, 1939.
Chevallier, Dominique. "Aspects Sociaux de la Question d'Orient: Aux origines des troubles agraires libanais en 1858." *Annales: Économies, Sociétés, Civilisations,* vol.14, no.1 (January–March 1959), pp.35–64.
— "Les cadres sociaux de l'économie agraire dans le Proche Orient au debut du XIXe siècle: le cas du Mont Liban." *Revue Historique,* 239 (January–March 1968), pp.87–100.
— "Que Possédait un Cheikh Maronite en 1859? Un document de la famille al Khazen." *Arabica,* vol.7 (1960), pp.72–84.
— "Signes de Beyrouth en 1834." *Bulletin d'Etudes Orientales,* vol.25 (1972), pp.211–28.
— *La société du Mont Liban à l'époque de la révolution industrielle en Europe.* Paris: Librairie Orientaliste Paul Geuthner, 1971.
— "Western Development and the Eastern Crisis in the Mid Nineteenth Century: Syria, Confronted with the European Economy." *The Beginnings of Modernization in the Middle East,* ed. William R. Polk and Richard L. Chambers. Chicago: University of Chicago Press, 1968, pp.205–22.
Choueiri, Youssef M. *Arab History and the Nation-State: A Study in Modern Arab Historiography, 1820–1980.* New York: Routledge, 1989.
— "Ottoman Reform and Lebanese Patriotism." *Lebanon, A History of Conflict and Consensus,* ed. Nadim Shehadi and Dana Haffar Mills. London: Centre for Lebanese Studies in association with I.B.Tauris, 1988, pp.64–78.
Cobban, Helena. *The Making of Modern Lebanon.* London: Hutchinson, 1985.
Conrad, Lawrence I. *The Formation and Perception of the Modern Arab World: Studies by Marwan R. Buheiry.* Princeton, NJ: The Darwin Press, 1989.
Corm, Georges. *Géopolitique du conflit Libanais.* Paris: La Découverte, 1987.
— "Myths and Realities of the Lebanese Conflict." *Lebanon, A History of Conflict and Consensus,* ed. Nadim Shehadi and Dana Haffar Mills. London: Centre for Lebanese Studies in association with I.B.Tauris, 1988, pp.258–74.

D'Aloux, Gustave. "Le Liban et Davoud Pacha." *Revue des Deux Mondes*, vol.58 (1865), pp.139–68; vol.63 (1866), pp.5–49.
Davie, May. "Les familles grecques orthodoxes de la ville de Beyrouth à travers les cahiers du *Badal askariyyat* (1876–1895)." *Annales d'histoire et d'archéologie*, vol.5 (1986), p.44.
— "Histoire démographique des Grecs Orthodoxes de Beyrouth (1870-1939)." Mémoire de maîtrise. Université Saint-Joseph, Beirut, 1987.
Davison, Roderic H. "Turkish Attitudes Concerning Christian–Muslim Equality in the 19th Century." *American Historical Review*, vol.59, no.4, (1953–4) pp.844–62.
— *Reform in the Ottoman Empire: 1856–1876*. Princeton: Princeton University Press, 1963.
Deguilhem, Randi. "Les documents du waqf et la recherche actuelle du Moyen Orient." *Actes du VIème congrès du CIEPO (Comité International d'Etudes Pré-Ottomanes et Ottomanes) tenu à Cambridge, Angleterre, juillet 1984*, ed. Abdeljelil Temimi. Zaghouan, Tunisia: Centres d'Etudes et de Recherches ottomanes, morisques, de documentation et d'information, 1987, pp. 95–102.
— "La réorganisation du waqf dans les provinces Syriennes Ottomanes." *Arab Historical Review for Ottoman Studies*, no.5–6 (February 1992), pp.31–8.
Devereux, Robert. *The First Ottoman Constitutional Period*. Baltimore, Md.: The Johns Hopkins Press, 1963.
Driault, Edouard. *La Question d'Orient depuis son origine jusqu'à la paix de Sèvres 1920*. Paris: Felix Alcan, 1921.
Dubar, Claude, and Salim Nasr. *Les classes sociales au Liban*. Paris: Fondation nationale des sciences politiques, 1974.
al-Duwayhi, Butrus. *Tarikh al-ta'ifa al-Maruniyya*. Beirut, 1890.
Edwards, Richard. *La Syrie, 1840–1862; histoire, politique, administration, population, religions et mœurs, événements de 1860 d'après des actes officiels et des documents authentiques*. Paris: Amyot, 1862.
Elisséeff, N. "Dimashk." *Encyclopaedia of Islam*. 2nd ed., vol.2. Leiden: Brill, 1965, pp.277–91.
Emerit, Marcel. "La Crise syrienne et l'expansion économique française en 1860." *Revue Historique*, vol.207 (1952), pp.212–32.
Entelis, John P. *Pluralism and Party Transformation in Lebanon: al-Kata'ib 1936–1970*. Leiden: E.J. Brill, 1974.
Farah, Caesar E. "The Lebanese Insurgence of 1840 and the Powers." *Journal of Asian History*, vol.1 (1967), pp.105–32.
— "Necip Pasha and the British in Syria 1841–1842." *Archivium Ottomanicum*, vol.2 (1970), pp.115–53.
— "The Problem of the Ottoman Administration in the Lebanon 1840–1861." Ph.D. diss., Princeton University, 1957. Ann Arbor: University Microfilms International, 1958.
— "Protestantism and British Diplomacy in Syria." *International Journal of Middle East Studies*, vol.7 (1976), pp.321–44.
— "The Quadruple Alliance and Proposed Ottoman Reforms in Syria 1839–1841." *International Journal of Turkish Studies*, vol.2 (1981), pp.101–30.
— "The Road to Intervention: Fiscal Politics in Ottoman Lebanon." *Papers on Lebanon*, 13. Oxford: Centre for Lebanese Studies, 1992.
Fawaz, Leila Tarazi. *Merchants and Migrants in Nineteenth-Century Beirut*. Cambridge, Mass.: Harvard University Press, 1983.
— "Understanding Lebanon." *American Scholar*, vol.54, no.3 (Summer 1985), pp.377–84.

— "Women and Conflict in Lebanon." *Problems of the Modern Middle East in Historical Perspective: Essays in Honour of Albert Hourani*, ed. John Spagnolo. Reading: Ithaca Press, 1992, pp.63–77.
— "Zahle and Dayr al-Qamar: Two Market Towns of Mount Lebanon during the Civil War of 1860." *Lebanon: A History of Conflict and Consensus*, ed. Nadim Shehadi and Dana Haffar Mills. London: Centre for Lebanese Studies in association with I.B.Tauris, 1988, pp.49–63.
Firro, Kais M. *A History of the Druzes*. Leiden: E.J. Brill, 1992.
Furayha, Anis. *Hadarat fi tarikh al-zawal: al-qaryat al-Lubnaniyya*. Publications of the American University of Beirut, Oriental Studies series, no.28. Junieh, Lebanon, 1957.
— *Isma' ya Rida!* 3rd ed. Beirut: Naufal, 1977.
Gilsenan, Michael. "A Modern Feudality? Land and Labor in North Lebanon, 1858–1950." *Land Tenure and Social Transformation in the Middle East*, ed. Tarif Khalidi. Beirut: American University of Beirut, 1984, pp.449–64.
— "Law, Arbitrariness and the Power of the Lords of North Lebanon." *History and Anthropology*, vol.1, no.2 (1985), pp.381–98.
— "From Village to Towns? Notes on a Site in Time of War." *Middle Eastern Cities in Comparative Perspective*, ed. Kenneth Brown, Michel Jole, Peter Sluglett, Sami Zubaida. Franco–British Symposium, London, 10–14 May 1984. London: Ithaca Press, 1986, pp.213–23.
Gökbilgin, Tayyib M. "1840'dan 1861'e kadar Cebel-i Lübnan Meselesi ve Drüziler" (The Lebanese question and the Druze from 1840 to 1861), *Belleten*, vol.10 (1946), pp.641–703.
Haddad, Robert M. *Syrian Christians in Muslim Society: An Interpretation*. Princeton, NJ: Princeton University Press, 1970.
Hajjar, Joseph. *L'Europe et les destinées du Proche-Orient I: Mohammed Ali d'Egypte et ses ambitions Syro-Ottomanes 1815–1848*. Damascus: Tlass, 1988.
— *L'Europe et les destinées du Proche-Orient. II: Napoléon et ses visées orientales 1848–1870*, 3 vols. Damascus: Tlass, 1988.
Hanf, Theodor. *Coexistence in Wartime Lebanon: Decline of a State and Rise of a Nation*. London: I.B.Tauris, 1993.
Harik, Iliya F. "The Impact of the Domestic Market on Rural–Urban Relations in the Middle East." *Rural Politics and Social Change in the Middle East*, ed. Richard Antoun and Iliya Harik. Bloomington: Indiana University Press, 1972, pp.337–63.
— *Politics and Change in a Traditional Society: Lebanon, 1711–1845*. Princeton NJ: Princeton University Press, 1968.
Hatoum, N. "L'Opinion française et la question de Syrie (1860–1861)." Thèse, Faculté des Lettres de l'Université de Paris, 1945.
Havemann, Axel. *Rurale Bewegungen im Libanon-Gebirge des 19. Jahrhunderts. Ein Beitrag zur Problematik sozialer Veränderungen*. Islamkundliche Untersuchungen, vol.79. Berlin: Klaus Schwarz Verlag, 1983.
Hitti, Philip. "The Impact of the West on Syria and Lebanon in the 19th Century." *Cahiers d'histoire mondiale*, vol.2, no.3 (1955), pp.608–33.
Hokayem, Antoine. "Les Tanzimat et leurs répercussions sur le Liban: rapports dialectiques entre tolerance et intolérance dans l'Empire ottoman au XIXème siècle." *Cultural Tolerance*, ed. Maurad Wahba. Cairo: Anglo-Egyptian Bookshop, 1982, pp.39–52.
Hopwood, Derek. *The Russian Presence in Syria and Palestine, 1843–1914: Church and Politics in the Near East*. Oxford: Clarendon Press, 1969.

Hourani, Albert H. "Lebanon: The Development of a Political Society." A. Hourani, *The Emergence of the Modern Middle East.* London: Macmillan, 1981, pp.124–41.
— "Lebanon From Feudalism to State." *Middle East Studies,* vol.2 (1960), pp.256–63.
— *Minorities in the Arab World.* London: Oxford University Press, 1947.
— "Ottoman Reform and the Politics of the Notables." *The Beginnings of Modernization in the Middle East,* ed. William R. Polk and Richard L. Chambers. Chicago: University of Chicago Press, 1968, pp.41–68.
— "Political Society in Lebanon: A Historical Introduction." *Papers on Lebanon,* 1. Oxford: Centre for Lebanese Studies, 1985.
— *Syria and Lebanon: A Political Essay.* London: Oxford University Press, 1946.
— and Nadim Shehadi, eds. *The Lebanese in the World: A Century of Emigration.* London: Centre for Lebanese Studies in association with I.B.Tauris, 1992.
Ismail, Adel. *Renversement et déclin du feudalisme libanais 1840–1860.* Beirut: Harb Bijjani, 1958.
Issawi, Charles, ed. *The Economic History of the Middle East.* Chicago: University of Chicago Press, 1966.
— "Lebanese Agriculture in the 1850s: A British Consular Report." *American Journal of Agricultural Studies,* vol.1 (1973), pp.66–88.
— *The Fertile Crescent 1800–1914: A Documentary Economic History.* New York: Oxford University Press, 1988.
Joseph, Rick. "The Material Origins of the Lebanese Conflict of 1860." B.Litt. thesis. Oxford University, 1977.
Joumblatt, Kamal. *I Speak for Lebanon,* tr. Michael Pallis, as recorded by Philippe Lapousterle. London: Zed Press, 1982.
Khair, Antoine A. *Le Moutacarrifat du Mont-Liban.* Publications de l'Université libanaise, Section des études juridiques, politiques et administratives, 2. Beirut: Imprimerie Catholique, 1973.
Khalaf, Samir. "Communal Conflict in 19th-Century Lebanon." *Christians and Jews in the Ottoman Empire: The Functioning of a Plural Society,* ed. Benjamin Braude and Bernard Lewis. New York: Holmes and Meier, 1982.
— *Persistence and Change in 19th-Century Lebanon: A Sociological Essay.* Beirut: American University of Beirut Press, 1979.
Khalidi, Walid. *Conflict and Violence in Lebanon: Confrontation in the Middle East.* Harvard Studies in International Affairs, 38. Cambridge, Mass.: Center for International Affairs, Harvard University, 1979.
Khalifa, Isam K. *Abhath fi tarikh Lubnan al-mu'asir.* Beirut, 1985.
Khater, Ahmad F., and Antoine F. Khater. "Assaf: A Peasant of Mount Lebanon." *Struggle and Survival in the Modern Middle East,* ed. Edmund Burke III. Berkeley: University of California Press, 1993, pp.31–43.
Khoury, Philip S. *Urban Notables and Arab Nationalism: The Politics of Damascus 1860–1920.* Cambridge, Eng.: Cambridge University Press, 1983.
Khuri, Fuad I. *Imams and Emirs: State, Religion and Sects in Islam.* London: Saqi Books, 1990.
— "Rural–Urban Migration in Lebanon: Motivation and Adjustments." *Cultural Resources in Lebanon.* Beirut: Librairie du Liban, 1969, pp.135–46.
— "The Social Dynamics of the 1975–77 War in Lebanon." *Armed Forces and Society,* vol.7, no.3 (1981), pp.383–408.
— *From Village to Suburb: Order and Change in Greater Beirut.* Chicago: University of Chicago Press, 1975.

Khuri, Sami. *Une histoire du Liban à travers les archives des Jésuites 1816–1845*. Beirut: Dar el-Machreq, 1985.
— *Une histoire du Liban à travers les archives des Jésuites 1846–1862*. Beirut: Dar el-Machreq, 1992.
Labaki, Boutros. "La filature de la soie dans le sundjak du Mont Liban: une expérience de croissance industrielle dépendante 1810–1914." *Arabica*, vol.29 (1982), pp.80–90.
— *Introduction à l'histoire économique du Liban: soie et commerce extérieur en fin de période ottomane 1840–1914*. Beirut: Université libanaise, 1984.
— "Sériculture et commerce extérieur: Deux aspects de l'impact européen sur l'économie du Liban et de son environnement arabe en fin de période Ottomane (1840–1914)." Thèse de doctorat de 3e cycle, Ecole Pratique des Hautes Etudes, Paris, 1974.
Latror, André. *La Vie rurale en Syrie et au Liban, études d'économie sociale*. Beirut: Imprimerie Catholique, 1936.
Lewis, Norman N. "The Frontier of Settlement in Syria 1800-1950." *International Affairs*, vol.31 (1955), pp.48–60.
— *Nomads and Settlers in Syria and Jordan*. New York: Cambridge University Press, 1987.
Louet, Ernest. *Expédition de Syrie, Beyrouth, le Liban, Jérusalem 1860–1861*. Paris: Amyot, 1862.
Lubbos, Antoine. *Tawajjuhat al-iklirios al-Maruni fi Jabal Lubnan (1842-1867): watha'iq Bkirki*. (The positions of the Maronite clergy in Mount Lebanon [1842-1867]: the Bkerke Archives.) Beirut, 1991.
al-Ma'luf, Isa Iskandar. *Tarikh madinat Zahla*. Zahleh: Matba'at Zahla al-Fatat, 1911.
— "Dayr al-Qamar 'ala 'ahd al-amir." Extracts from an article in *al-Jinan*, reprinted in *al-Mashriq*, April 1931, pp.302–4.
Mange, Alye Edythe. *The Near Eastern Policy of the Emperor Napoleon III*. Urbana: University of Illinois Press, 1940.
Ma'oz, Moshe. "Communal Conflicts in Ottoman Syria during the Reform Era: The Role of Political and Economic Factors." *Christians and Jews in the Ottoman Empire: The Functioning of a Plural Society*, ed. Benjamin Braude and Bernard Lewis. New York: Holmes and Meier, 1982, pp.91–105.
— "The Impact of Modernization on Syrian Politics and Society during the Early Tanzimat Period." *Beginnings of Modernization in the Near East*, ed. William R. Polk and Richard L. Chambers. Chicago: University of Chicago Press, 1968, pp.333–49.
— *Ottoman Reform in Syria and in Palestine 1840–1861: The Impact of the Tanzimat on Politics and Society*. Oxford: Clarendon Press, 1968.
Massad, Paul, and Nassib Wehaiba al-Khazin. *Documents inédits*. vol.2, fasc. 6. Achkouth, Lebanon, n.d.
Masters, Bruce. *The Origins of Western Economic Dominance in the Middle East: Mercantilism and the Islamic Economy in Aleppo, 1600–1750*. New York: New York University Press, 1988.
— "The Sultan's Entrepreneurs: the *Avrupa Tüccarıs* and the *Hayriye Tüccarıs* in Syria," *International Journal of Middle East Studies*, vol.24, no.4 (November 1992), pp.579–97.
— "Power and Society in Aleppo in the 18th and 19th Centuries." *Revue du Monde musulman et de la Méditerranée*, vol.62 (1992), pp.151–8.
— "The 1850 'Events' in Aleppo: An Aftershock of Syria's Incorporation in the Capitalist World System." *International Journal of Middle East Studies*, vol.22, no.1 (February 1990), pp.3–20.
— "Trading Diasporas and 'Nations': The Formulation of National Identities in Ottoman Aleppo." *International History Review*, vol.9, no.3 (August 1987), pp.345–67.

Messarra, Antoine N. *The Challenge of Coexistence.* Oxford: Center for Lebanese Studies, 1988.
Monglave, Eugène de. "Expédition de Syrie." *Revue de l'Orient,* vol.12 (1860), pp.375–84, 446–8.
Moosa, Matti. *The Maronites in History.* Syracuse, NY: Syracuse University Press, 1986.
Naff, Alixa. "A Social History of Zahle, the Principal Market Town in Nineteenth-Century Lebanon." Ph.D. diss., University of California, Los Angeles, 1972. Ann Arbor: University Microfilms International, 1973.
Norton, Augustus Richard. *Amal and the Shi'a: Struggle for the Soul of Lebanon.* Austin: University of Texas Press, 1987.
Ochsenwald, William. "The Financial Basis of Ottoman Rule in the Hejaz 1840–1877." *Nationalism in a Non-National State,* ed. William W. Haddad and William Ochsenwald. Columbus: Ohio State University Press, 1977, pp.129–49.
— "The Jidda Massacre of 1858." *Middle Eastern Studies,* vol.13 (1977), pp.314–26.
Ortayli, Ilhan. "Ideological Structure of Syria and Lebanon in the 19th Century and Ottoman Counter Measures." *Revue d'Histoire Maghrébine,* 1985, pp.149–55.
Owen, Roger. *The Middle East in the World Economy.* London: Methuen, 1981.
— "The Silk Reeling Industry of Mount Lebanon 1840–1914: A Study of the Possibilities and Limitations of Factory Production in the Periphery." In *The Ottoman Empire and the World Economy,* ed. Huri Islamoglu-Inan. London: Cambridge University Press, 1987, pp.271-83.
Pascual, Jean-Paul. "La Syrie à l'époque Ottomane (le XIXe siècle)." *La Syrie d'aujourd'hui,* ed. André Raymond. Paris: Centre National de la Recherche Scientifique, 1980, pp.31–53.
Philipp, Thomas. *The Syrians in Egypt 1775–1975.* Berliner Islamstudien, vol.3. Stuttgart: Franz Steiner Verlag, 1985.
— ed. *The Syrian Land in the 18th and 19th Century: The Common and the Specific in the Historical Experience.* Berliner Islamstudien, vol.5. Stuttgart: Franz Steiner Verlag, 1992.
Polk, William R. *The Opening of South Lebanon, 1788–1840: A Study of the Impact of the West on the Middle East.* Cambridge, Mass.: Harvard University Press, 1963.
Porath, Yehoshua. "The Peasant Revolt of 1858–61 in Kisrawan." *Asian and African Studies,* vol.2 (1966), pp.77–157.
Poujade, M. Eugène. *Le Liban et la Syrie 1845–1860.* Paris: A. Bourdilliat, 1860.
Poujoulat, Baptistin. *La vérité sur la Syrie et l'expédition française.* Paris: Gaume Frères et J. Duprey, 1861.
Puryear, Vernon John. *International Economics and Diplomacy in the Near East: A Study of British Commercial Policy in the Levant, 1834–1853.* Stanford, Calif.: Stanford University Press, 1935.
Rafeq, Abdul-Karim. *Buhuth fi al-tarikh al-iqtisadi wa'l-ijtima'i li-bilad al-Sham fi'l-'asr al-hadith.* Damascus, 1974.
— "The Impact of Europe on a Traditional Economy: The Case of Damascus, 1840–1870." *Economies et sociétés dans l'Empire ottoman (fin du XVIIIe–début du XXe siècle): Actes du colloque de Strasbourg (1er–5e juillet 1980),* ed. Jean-Louis Bacqué-Grammont and Paul Dumont. Paris: Centre National de la Recherche Scientifique, 1983, pp.419–32.
— "Land Tenure Problems and Their Social Impact in Syria around the Middle of the Nineteenth Century." *Land Tenure and Social Transformation in the Middle East,* ed. Tarif Khalidi. Beirut: American University of Beirut Press, 1984, pp.371–96.
— "The Law Court Registers and Their Importance for a Socio-Economic and Urban Study of Ottoman Syria." *L'Espace social de la ville arabe,* ed. Dominique Chevallier. Paris: G.P. Maisonneuve et Larousse, 1979, pp.51–8.

— "New Light on the 1860 Riots in Ottoman Damascus." *Die Welt des Islams*, vol.28 (1988), pp.412–30.
— *The Province of Damascus, 1723–1783*. Beirut: Khayats, 1966.
— "The Social and Economic Structure of Bab al-Midan, Damascus, 1825–1875." *Arab Civilization, Challenges, and Responses*, Studies in Honor of Constantine K. Zurayk, ed. George N. Atiyeh and Ibrahim M. Oweiss. Albany: State University of New York Press, 1988, pp.272–311.
Raymond, André, ed., *La Syrie d'aujourd'hui*. Paris: Editions du Centre National de la Recherche, 1980.
Reilly, James A. "Shari'a Court Registers and Land Tenure around 19th-Century Damascus." *Middle East Studies Association Bulletin*, vol.21 (1987), pp.155–69.
— "Status Groups and Property Holding in the Damascus Hinterland, 1828–1880." *International Journal of Middle East Studies*, vol.21 (1989), pp.517–39.
Rondot, Pierre. *Les Institutions politiques du Liban: Des communautés traditionnelles à l'état moderne*. Paris: Institut d'études de l'Orient contemporain, 1947.
— "L'intervention internationale de 1860 au Liban," *Etudes*, November 1960, pp.203–12.
Saab, Ann Pottinger. "English and Irish Reactions to the Massacres in Lebanon and Syria, 1860." *Muslim World*, vol.74, no.1 (January 1984), pp.12–25.
Saad, Elias N. "The Damascus Crisis of 1860 in the Light of *Kitab al-Ahzan*, an Unpublished Eye Witness Account." M.A. thesis, American University of Beirut, 1974.
Saba, Paul. "The Creation of the Lebanese Economy: Economic Growth in the 19th and 20th Centuries." *Essays on the Crisis in Lebanon*, ed. Roger Owen. London: Ithaca Press, 1976, pp.1–22.
— "The Development and Decline of the Lebanese Silk Industry." B.Litt. thesis. Oxford University, 1977.
Salam, Nawaf, "Les communautés religieuses au Liban." *Social Compass*, vol.35, no.4 (1988), pp.455–64.
Salamé, Ghassan. "Lebanon's Injured Identities: Who Represents Whom during a Civil War?" *Papers on Lebanon*, 2. Oxford: Center for Lebanese Studies, 1986.
Salibi, Kamal S. "The 1860 Upheaval in Damascus as Seen by al-Sayyid Muhammad Abu'l-Su'ud al-Hasibi, Notable and Later Nagib al-Ashraf of the City." *Beginnings of Modernization in the Middle East: The Nineteenth Century*, ed. William R. Polk and Richard L. Chambers. Publications of the Center for Middle Eastern Studies, No. 1. Chicago: University of Chicago Press, 1968, pp.185–202.
— *A House of Many Mansions: The History of Lebanon Reconsidered*. Los Angeles: University of California Press, 1988.
— *Maronite Historians of Medieval Lebanon*. American University of Beirut, Faculty of Arts and Sciences Publication, Oriental Studies series, no.34. Beirut: Catholic Press, 1959.
— *Modern History of Lebanon*. London: Weidenfeld and Nicolson, 1965.
Saliby-Yehia, Hoda. "Pouvoir étatique et dynamique développement: l'expérience de deux états successeurs de l'Empire Ottoman, la Syrie (1876–1963) et le Liban (1876–1964)." Thèse de doctorat en histoire, Université de Paris I, 1992.
Schilcher, Linda Schatkowski. *Families in Politics: Damascene Factions and Estates in the 18th and 19th Centuries*. Stuttgart: Franz Steiner Verlag, 1985.
— "The Hauran Conflicts of the 1860s: A Chapter in the Rural History of Modern Syria." *International Journal of Middle East Studies*, vol.13 (1981), pp.159–79.
Schlict, Alfred. *Frankreich und die syrischen Christen 1799–1861: Minoritäten und Europäischer Imperialismus im Vorderen Orient*. Berlin: Klaus Schwarz Verlag, 1981.

— "The Role of Foreign Powers in the History of Lebanon and Syria From 1799 to 1861." *Journal of Asian History*, vol.14 (1980), pp.97–126.

Schölch, Alexander. "Was There a Feudal System in Ottoman Lebanon and Palestine?" *Palestine in the Late Ottoman Period: Political, Social and Economic Transformation*, ed. David Kushner. Jerusalem: Yad Izhak Ben-Zvi, 1986, pp.130–45.

Schopoff, A. *Les Réformes et la protection des Chrétiens en Turquie, 1673–1904, Bérats, Protocols, Traités, Capitulations, Conventions, Arrangements, Memorandums, etc.* Paris: Plon-Nourrit, 1904.

Seikaly, Samir M. "Land Tenure in 17th-Century Palestine: The Evidence from *al-Fatawa al-Khayriyya*." *Land Tenure and Social Transformation in the Middle East*, ed. Tarif Khalidi. Beirut: American University of Beirut Press, 1984, pp.397–408.

Shehadi, Nadim, and Dana H. Mills, eds. *Lebanon: A History of Conflict and Consensus*. London: I.B.Tauris, 1988.

Sirriyeh, Hussein. "Lebanon: The Impending Crisis, 1840–1975." *Arab Affairs*, vol.9 (1989), pp.70–93.

Sluglett, Peter, and Marion Farouk-Sluglett. "The Application of the 1858 Land Code in Greater Syria: Some Preliminary Observations." *Land Tenure and Social Transformation in the Middle East*, ed. Tarif Khalidi. Beirut: American University of Beirut Press, 1984, pp.409–21.

Smilianskaya, I.M. "The Disintegration of Feudal Relations in Syria and Lebanon in the Middle of the Nineteenth Century." *The Economic History of the Middle East, 1800–1914*, ed. Charles Issawi. Chicago: University of Chicago Press, 1966, pp.227–47.

— *al-Harakat al-fallahiyya fi Lubnan*, tr. 'Adnan Jamus, ed. Salim Yusuf. Beirut: Dar al-Farabi, 1972.

Spagnolo, John P. "Constitutional Change in Mount Lebanon, 1861–1864." *Middle East Studies*, January 1971, pp.25–48.

— "The Definition of a Style of Imperialism: The Internal Politics of the French Educational Investment in Ottoman Beirut." *French Historical Studies*, 1974, pp.563–84.

— *France and Ottoman Lebanon, 1861–1914*. London: Ithaca Press for the Middle East Center, 1977.

— "Mount Lebanon, France and Daud Pasha; A Study of Some Aspects of Political Habituation." *International Journal of Middle East Studies*, vol.7 (1971), pp.148–67.

Steppat, Fritz, "Some Arabic Manuscript Sources on the Syrian Crisis of 1860." *Les Arabes par leurs archives*, ed. Jacques Berque and Dominique Chevallier. Paris: Centre National de la Recherche Scientifique, 1976, pp.183–91.

Suleiman, Michael W. *Political Parties in Lebanon: The Challenge of a Fragmented Political Culture*. Ithaca, N.Y.: Cornell University Press, 1967.

Temperley, Harold W.V. *England and the Near East: The Crimea*. London: Archon Books, 1964.

Thobie, Jacques. *Intérêts et impérialisme français dans l'Empire ottoman 1859–1914*. Paris: Imprimerie Nationale, 1977.

Thompson, Elizabeth. "Ottoman Political Reform in the Provinces: The Damascus Advisory Council in 1844–45," *International Journal of Middle East Studies*, vol.25, no.3 (August 1993), pp.457–75.

Tibawi, Abdul Latif. *British Interests in Palestine, 1800–1901*. Oxford: Clarendon Press, 1961.

— "Russian Cultural Penetration of Syria and Palestine in the 19th Century." *Royal Central Asian Journal*, vol.53 (1966), pp.166–82.

Touma, Toufic. *Paysans et institutions féodales chez les Druses et les Maronites du Liban du XVIIe siècle à 1914.* 2 vols. Publications de l'Université libanaise, Section des études historiques, 20. Beirut: Imprimerie Catholique, 1971–2.

Ülman, A. Haluk. *1860–1861 Suriye Buhranı: Osmanlı Diplomasisinden bir Örnek Olay.* Ankara, n.d.

Van Leewen, Richard. "Monastic Estates and Agricultural Transformation in Mount Lebanon in the 18th Century." *International Journal of Middle East Studies,* vol.23, no.4 (November 1991), pp.601–17.

— "Notables and Clergy in Mount Lebanon: The Khazin Sheiks and the Maronite Church (1736–1840)." Ph.D. diss., University of Amsterdam Institute for Near Eastern and Islamic Studies, 1992.

Verney, Noel, and George Dambmann. *Les Puissances étrangères dans le Levant en Syrie et en Palestine.* Paris: Guillaumin, 1900.

Vogüé, Marie-Eugène-Melchior, Vicomte de. *Les Evénements de Syrie.* Paris: Charles Douniol, 1860.

Weightman, George H. "Systems of Social Stratification in Three North Lebanese Towns." *Asian Studies,* vol.4, no.3 (December 1966), pp.491–9.

al-Yaziji, Nasif. "Risala tarikhiyya fi ahwal Lubnan fi 'ahdihi al-iqta'i," *al-Masarra,* vol.22 (1936), nos.5, 6, 8, and 9.

Zakkar, Suhayl. *Bilad al-Sham fi'l-qarn al-tasi' 'ashar: riwaya tarikhiyya mu'asira li-hawadith 'am 1860 wa muqqidmatuha fi Suriya wa Lubnan.* Damascus: Dar Hasan, 1982.

Reference Works

Bibliography of AUB Faculty Publications, 1866–1966, ed. Suha Tamim. Beirut: American University of Beirut Press, 1966.

Daghir, Yusuf As'ad. *al-Usul al-'arabiyya lil-dirasat al-Lubnaniyya: Dalil bibliyghrafi* (Arabic sources on Lebanese studies: a bibliographical guide). Beirut, 1972.

Dictionary of National Biography, Supplement January 1901–December 1911, vol.1. London: Oxford University Press.

Khairallah, Shireen. "Bibliography of Periodical Literature on the Near and Middle East." *Middle East Journal,* 1947.

Saliba, Maurice. *Index Libanicus: An Analytical Survey of Publications in European Languages on Lebanon.* Antelias, Lebanon: 1979.

INDEX

Abbasid dynasty, 9, 11
Abd al-Majid I, Sultan, 101
Abd al-Malik, Yusuf, 180, 181, 185; retrial of, 184
Abd al-Malik family, 17, 18, 54, 184
Abd al-Qadir, 80, 82, 83, 84, 87, 89, 91, 92, 93, 94, 97, 98, 99, 110, 134, 136, 138, 144, 159, 180, 203
Abdallah Pasha, 20, 40
Abdul Salam Bey, 150
al-Abid, Umar Agha, 98
Abi-Ikr, Ghalib, 41–2
Abkarius, Iskandar ibn Ya'qub, 36, 41, 46, 50, 52, 55, 62, 68, 70, 72, 73, 84, 98, 101
Abro Efendi, 106, 143, 148, 151, 175, 199, 200, 205, 207, 213
Abu Basil, Antun Basha, 87
Abu'l-Lama, Bashir Ahmad, 44
Abu'l-Lama, Haydar, 28
Abu'l-Lama family, 17, 54, 66
Abu Nakad family, 16–17, 29, 40, 51, 54, 55, 58, 181, 184
Abu Samra, 59, 60
Abu Shaqra, 46, 66, 67, 69, 72
agriculture, 8, 11, 17, 33, 173; specialization in, 24
Ahmad, Kenj, 62
Ahmad Pasha, 58, 61, 78, 82, 83, 84, 88, 96, 99, 103, 124, 133, 135, 137, 144, 146, 147, 148, 149, 165, 166, 167, 168, 188, 206; animosity with Damascus notables, 145; death sentence against, 150, 151, 205; execution of, 150; popularity of, in Damascus, 144; sentencing of, 149; trial of, 149
Ahmad Pasha, governor of Sidon, 151
Ain Dara: first battle of, 53, 64, 66; second battle of, 52
Ain Meassir, massacre at, 183
Ain Sofar, 165, 179
Akif Agha, 84

Alawi community, 12
Aleppo, 13, 14, 99; clashes in, 77, 100
Algerian troops, 136; helping Christians, 97, 152, 159
Ali, cult of, 11, 12
Ali Pasha, 101, 104, 106, 215, 216
Ali Wasfi Efendi, 151
'ammiyyah rising, 20
Anglo-American Relief Committee, 135
Anglo-Ottoman convention (1838), 23
Anti-Lebanon, 8, 9, 12
al-Aqiqi, Antun Dahir, 52, 72, 172
Arbili, Ibrahim, 98
Arbili, Yusuf, 98
arrack, distilling of, 33
d'Arricau, Colonel, 124, 129, 176
Arslan, Ahmad, 28, 29
Arslan, Muhammad, 189
Arslan family, 17, 54
al-Aryan, Shibli, 27, 36
Aryan family, 63
al-Ashya, Hajj Hasan, 160
al-Atrash, Isma'il, 55, 56, 61, 63, 64, 67, 185, 189, 190
al-Attar, Salim, 98
Austria, 21, 103, 108, 109, 111, 112, 113, 199, 200, 216; consulate, 82, 90, 91
Austrian relief committee, 201
Azar family, 17
al-Azm, Abdallah, 99, 143
al-Azm, Ali, 143
Azm family, 15, 26

Baabda, 29, 50, 51, 56, 125; attack on, 53, 184
Baalbek, 13, 15, 34, 36, 49, 64, 68, 79, 137, 157, 165, 175, 179; destruction of, 69
al-Badawi, Muhammad Rashid, 142
al-Bahnasi, Hasan, 87
Bahout, Habib, 71
al-Bakri, Hajj, 97

294

INDEX

Barozzi, Dr, 101
Bashir II, 16, 17, 19, 20–1, 24, 36, 37, 38, 39, 40, 41, 42, 44, 53, 64, 189, 212, 225; deposed, 26
Bashir III, 26, 225; deposed, 27
Batrun, 12, 13, 15
Bayazid, Muhammad Id, 160
Baydar, Hanna, 40
Beaufort, 114–19, 120, 121, 122, 123, 124, 125, 126, 127, 130, 131, 150, 166, 167, 170, 171, 172, 174, 175, 180, 181, 188, 194, 196, 216; departure of, 127
Beclard, Commissioner, 158, 187, 195, 198, 199, 208, 212, 214, 215, 216
Bedouins, 66, 67, 76, 100
Beirut, 49, 54, 63, 69, 70, 73, 74, 75, 78, 108, 116, 118, 120, 122, 124, 125, 131, 135, 138, 140, 148, 151, 162, 169, 175, 176, 180, 181, 184, 193, 194, 195, 199, 211, 217; destruction of, 218
Beirut Committee, 70, 71, 209, 213
Beirut–Damascus road, 55, 66, 116, 117, 123, 140, 165, 168, 179
Beit al-Din, 42, 70, 72, 73, 124, 125, 151, 164, 165, 166, 173, 176, 178, 190
Beit Meri, 45–6, 50, 51, 54
Belgium, 102; consulate, 90
Bentivoglio, Count, 75, 101–2, 109, 116, 117, 118, 120, 189, 207, 212
Beqaa valley, 8, 9, 13, 21, 24, 33, 34, 36, 49, 64, 79, 123, 124, 125, 138, 168, 169, 175
Bird, Mr, 71, 73
al-Bitar, Abd al-Razzaq, 150
Bkassine, 59; sacked, 60
Boulus Mas'ad, Patriarch, 45, 211
Brant, James, 78, 79, 80, 81, 83, 90, 91, 92, 95, 97, 104, 134, 137, 138, 139, 143, 144, 145, 146, 147, 148, 154, 156, 157, 194, 207, 210
British consul, 49, 51, 54, 56, 57, 69, 75, 77, 78, 80, 136, 146, 156, 186, 199 see also United Kingdom
Bsharreh, 12, 13, 15, 53, 60
Bulwer, Sir Henry Lytton, 102, 104, 105, 145, 149, 191, 194, 204, 207
Burckhardt, John, 35
burial of dead, 32, 173, 174
Butros, Bishop, 210

Canaris, Mr, 201
capitulations system, 23

caravans, 34, 136; plundering of, 25; trade, 9, 22, 24, 25 (dislocation of, 100)
Catholics: Greek, 10, 13, 30, 34, 35, 36, 39, 68, 75, 80, 89, 100, 175, 215, 217, 218; Roman, 109, 111
censuses, 28
center–region dynamic, 5
Cerez, Commandant, 173
Chalcedon, Council of, 10
Chamoun, Camille, 220
Chanzy, Lieutenant-colonel, 122, 123, 131
al-Chawish, Butrus, 38
Christianity, 11, 12; conversion to, 16; sects of, 10
Christians, 11, 13, 18, 20, 22, 23, 24, 26, 27, 28, 29, 39, 48, 50, 51, 53, 54, 55, 57, 61, 66, 67, 70, 82, 96, 104, 111, 118, 119, 120, 126, 128, 131, 139, 151, 167, 171, 172, 174, 180, 184, 189, 190, 194, 200, 207, 210, 216, 218, 222, 223, 224, 226; as clerks, 18, 83, 84, 87; attacks by, 49; attacks on, 35, 48, 56, 75, 77, 85, 92, 93, 100, 102, 112, 134, 137, 140, 142, 148, 168, 181, 191, 205, 208; attempt to poison, in Damascus, 133; Damascus quarter (clearing of, 153, 163; rebuilding of, 153, 154; ruined, 132; guarding of, 145–6, 147); disarming of, 21, 70, 71, 72; discrimination against, 205; divisions among, 53; exodus from Beirut, 193; exodus from Damascus, 97, 136; extension of jurisdiction, 215; fleeing of, 46, 164, 211; helped by Muslims, 157; in Beirut, panic among, 193; in Ottoman empire, 114; killing of, 51, 52, 55, 57, 60, 62, 67, 72, 77, 78, 88, 90, 92, 93, 104, 108, 109, 112, 137, 159, 166, 183, 189, 198, 202, 213; living conditions of, 113; notables, 135; of Damascus, 25, 80, 129 (estimated losses, 156; reparations for, 162; threat to, 144 see also Christians, Damascus quarter); panic in Beirut, 76; privileged position of, 100, 221, 223; relations with Druzes, 42, 70, 191, 193, 207, 212, 203; remaining in Hasbaiya, 164; reparations for, 155, 156–63, 187; resentment against, 40, 58, 81; resettlement of, 177; return to villages, 176; robbery of, 165; sheltered in Damascus, 96, 97, 99 (in citadel, 153); shops looted, 92; survival of, 133; taken

as hostages, 185; talk of emigration, 153, 176, 177; villages, 123 (attacked, 59, 63, 68)
churches: burning of, 87, 137; looting of, 89
Churchill, Charles Henry, 41, 45, 52, 58, 73
civil wars, comparison of, 218–28
consulates *see* France, European, United Kingdom etc
convents: burning of, 91, 137; destruction of, 132
Costi, Abdu, 90
cotton industry, 25, 38
Cowley, Lord, 109, 111, 212
Crusades, 9, 119

Dahdah family, 17, 18
Dahir family, 17
Dahr al-Ahmar, 63
Dahr al-Baidar, incident at, 52
Damascus, 9, 13, 14, 77, 120, 122, 123, 138, 169, 170, 180, 202; consuls misjudge situation, 207; defended against Wahhabis, 20; economy of, 25, 158; filled with refugees, 80; fortification of citadel, 83; garrison reinforced, 179; massacre at, 78–100, 103, 107, 121, 132, 144, 193, 202, 218, 226 (instigators of, 140–1, 142, 160; alleged role of Ahmad Pasha, 146; lack of witnesses to, 143; origins of, 149; taxation of instigators, 156); post-riot problems, 163; restoration of order in, 132–63; sectarian tensions in, 100; street patrols introduced, 152; taxation of population, 156–63; under Ottoman control, 179
Damascus governorate, 9, 14, 15, 21, 34, 61, 62, 103, 144, 145, 149
Danish Efendi, 106
Da'ud Pasha, 216, 217
de la Valette, Charles Jean *see* La Valette
death sentence, 17, 140, 159; for Ahmad Pasha, 150, 205; for Christian accused of killing Muslim, 75, 76; for Druze chiefs, 182; for instigators of massacres, 142 (commuted, 186, 189); for Ottoman troops, 151; possible for Khurshid Pasha, 151; obstructed by Europeans, 185 *see also* executions
deaths, statistics for, 57, 132, 226
Debbas, Charles, 222
Debbas, Dimitri, 94, 96, 97, 98, 99, 133, 134, 136, 145, 162

decentralization, trend towards, 2
Deir al-Qamar, 16, 17, 24, 29, 36, 37–42, 46, 47, 49, 53, 70, 71, 75, 76, 101, 105, 123, 124, 125, 150, 164, 165, 166, 168, 169, 170, 171, 173, 175, 176, 184, 189, 190, 191; as haven from government, 40; attack on, 56, 58, 70, 180, 211; garrisons at, 205; massacre at, 69, 72–3, 97, 99, 181, 182, 183, 203, 204, 210; population of, 177–8; prosperity of, 38; rebuilding of, 173, 174; refugees from, 154; revolt in, 21; sacking of, 57, 72; second attack on, 69
Digby, Jane, 160
disarming, 217: of Christians, 21, 70, 71, 72; of Druzes, 114; of Muslims, 27
Double Qaymaqamate, 27, 28, 30, 33, 37, 44, 46, 212, 214, 218 *see also qaymaqam* system
Druzes, 12, 13, 15, 16, 18, 20, 21, 23, 24, 28, 29, 30, 39, 40, 41, 42, 45, 48, 50, 51, 52, 53, 54, 56, 57, 59, 60, 61, 62, 63, 64, 65, 67, 69, 70, 71, 72, 73, 77, 78, 82, 83, 85, 89, 95, 108, 120, 123, 124, 125, 126, 129, 131, 133, 134, 136, 144, 146, 150, 151, 159, 163, 164, 165, 166, 167, 170, 171, 172, 177, 180, 181, 185, 208, 210, 214, 217, 218, 219, 222, 225; abuse of, 176; attacks on, 42, 167, 168, 208; confiscation of grain, 175; disarming of, 114; excesses of, 210; fear of French, 177; humiliation of, 187; killing of, 48, 49, 52, 55, 57, 62, 67, 166, 167, 168; leadership sapped, 19; levies imposed on, 169, 187; peace with Christians, 70, 193; peace with Maronites, 102, 112; property confiscated, 187; relations with Christians, 36, 40, 191, 203, 207; relations with Maronites, 21, 22, 27, 45–6, 105, 106, 212; trials of, 184; under British protection, 186, 196; villages looted, 165
Ducrot, Général Auguste-Alexandre, 131
Dufferin, 127, 142, 149, 150, 151, 154, 157, 158, 180, 185, 186, 187, 188, 189, 190, 191, 194, 195, 200, 203, 204, 207, 210, 211, 214, 215; protection of Druzes, 197; support of Fuad Pasha, 197
Dutch consul, 90

"Eastern Question," 108, 112

INDEX

Echard, William, 111
Egypt, 3, 8, 10, 12, 20, 21, 28, 39, 111, 215; occupation by, 44, 54, 74, 85, 100, 227 (Druze rebellion against, 55, 63)
Emerit, Marcel, 110
emigration, 19, 135
emirate system, end of, 26
"ethnic" civil wars, background to, 5
European commission, 142, 143, 151, 153, 154, 155, 156, 157, 170, 185, 199, 200, 201, 203, 208, 217
European consulates, 42, 48, 80, 101, 136; in Damascus, attacked, 91
European consuls, 50, 56, 74, 83, 89, 138, 143, 144, 207; call for protection of, 69
European powers, 6, 102, 105, 106, 107, 108, 125, 142, 147, 149, 163, 167, 185, 193, 195; encroachment in Middle East, 3; involvement in Lebanon, 227; possibility of military intervention, 113; relation with Ottoman empire, 15, 18, 22, 223; trade with, 25
European relief committee, 174
European residents, 25, 135, 139, 155; killing of, 104; mistrusted, 79; panic of, in Damascus, 90
executions: of massacre instigators, 139, 140; of Ottoman troops, 171, 197; of Yusuf Shihab, 20
exile: of Druzes, 182; of instigators of massacres, 141, 142; of Yusuf Abd al-Malik, 185; sentences, 183

Fakhr al-Din II, 15, 16
families, feudal, undermined, 224
feudalism, 16
forced labor, 20
France, 22, 23, 28, 54, 60, 101, 102, 105, 108, 109, 111, 113, 134, 139, 144, 145, 147, 152, 163, 166, 168, 170, 171, 172, 175, 176, 179, 180, 185, 187, 198, 199, 202, 213, 214, 215, 216, 217; and Maronites, 196; consulate, 91, 109, 112, 117, 134, 135 (sacking of, 112 see also French consul); mandate, 130, 223; relations with Ottoman empire, 128, 173, 203, 204; role in Syria, 113, 115, 119, 196; troops in Syria, 110, 112, 118, 120, 123, 128, 129, 167, 173, 177, 180, 212 (landed at Sidon, 108); troops leave Mount Lebanon, 131
Franco Nasri Efendi, 106, 211

Fraser, Major, 159, 160, 171, 179, 186, 195, 196
Frayj, Hanna, 84
Frazer, Mr, 90
French consul, 49, 50, 52, 53, 55, 56, 57, 59, 65, 68, 71, 72, 75, 76, 78, 79, 80, 82, 89, 104, 116, 122, 126, 189, 198, 207, 212 see also France
Fuad Pasha, 101, 104, 107, 112, 114, 116, 117, 119, 120, 121, 122, 123, 126, 127, 129, 131, 133, 135, 136, 138, 142, 143, 146, 147, 148, 149, 150, 151, 152, 153, 154, 155, 156, 157, 158, 159, 160, 161, 162, 167, 169, 170, 171, 172–3, 175, 177, 179, 180, 181, 184, 185, 186, 187, 194, 196, 197, 200, 201, 204, 205, 206, 207, 208, 211, 217; antipathy towards Beaufort, 128; appointed envoy to Syria, 105; arrival in Damascus, 139; role in Syria, 195

Gessler, Colonel, 152
al-Ghabbatieh, 59
Ghandur Bey, 167
al-Ghazzi, Umar, 143
Gökbilgin, T.M., 146
Goltz, Baron von, 216
Gorshakov, Prince Alexander, 109
Graham, Cyril, 59, 72, 97, 132, 133, 138, 195, 198
Graham, James, 196
Graham, William, murder of, 140
grain: distribution of, 201; rations rejected by Christians, 174; riots, 6
Greek consulate, 82, 90, 201
Greek Orthodox community, 10, 13, 15, 28, 30, 34, 36, 53, 75, 79, 80, 92, 108, 153, 175, 214, 217, 218, 219, 222

Hadeth, 51; attack on, 184
hajj see Mecca
Hakim, caliph, 12
al-Halabi, Abdallah, 85, 92, 95, 96, 99, 143; arrest of, 142
Halil Agha, 61
Halim Pasha, 138, 181
Hamad, Asad, 181
Hamada, Ali, 62, 189, 190
Hamada family, 15, 17, 73, 74
Hamdan, Jamal al-Din, 184
al-Hamdan, Wakid, 61
Hamelin, Admiral, 114, 119

Hamid Bey, 151
Hamilton-Temple-Blackwood, Frederick Temple, Lord Dufferin *see* Dufferin
Hammana, destruction of, 164
Hamza, Abd al-Qadir, 143
Hamza, As'ad Efendi, 98
Hamza, Mahmud Efendi, 81, 98
Hanidi, Hazim, 61
Hannawi, Abu Ali, 61
Harfush family, 36, 64
Hasan Bey, 106, 120, 151
Hasan, al-Sayyid, 80
Hasbaiya, 58, 59, 61, 62, 157, 166, 180, 181, 183, 189; garrisons at, 205; massacre at, 62–3, 79, 81, 82, 97, 99, 148, 164, 182, 190, 203, 204, 210; refugees from, 154
Hashim Agha, 133, 134
al-Hasibi, Ahmad, 80, 82, 85, 87, 98, 99, 133, 143
al-Hasibi, Muhammad Abu'l Su'ud, 68, 80
Hasr al-litham, 97, 132
d'Hautpoul, Charles de Beaufort *see* Beaufort
Havis Agha, 150
al-Hawasili, Mustafa Bey, 84, 88, 91, 142
Hawran, 8, 9, 20, 33, 34, 62, 63, 78, 80, 123, 129, 138, 146, 165, 177, 180, 181, 184, 185, 186
Hazmiyeh, 205, 206
highwaymen, 165
Hilu, Charles, 222
honor, upholding of, 32
Hourani, Albert, 14
housing, 171, 173, 201; rebuilding of, 173; shortage of, in Damascus, 153
Hubaysh family, 16, 17, 18, 44
Husni Bey, 68

Ibrahim Agha, 50
Ibrahim Pasha, 20, 21, 114
Imad, Ali, 52
Imad, Asad, 184
Imad, Khattar, 52, 66, 184
Imad, Qasim, 60, 73
Imad family, 17, 18
al-Imadi, Abdallah Efendi, 95, 98
indemnity plan, objections to, 161
indemnities *see* reparations
instigators: identification of, 201; punishment of, 178; classified in three band, 202 *see also* leniency *and* massacres
international response to civil war, 101–31

iqta' system, 16, 43
Iran, 22
Iraq, 22
Islam, 224; conversion to, 9, 139 (forced, 92, 137, 152); spread of, 11
Isma'il, Hajj, 160
Isma'il Hami Danişmend, 150
Isma'il Pasha, 75, 76, 116, 123, 129, 172

Jabal Sheikh, 124, 165
Jabri, Uthman, 98
Jamil Bey, 107
Janbalat, Bashir, 19, 38
Janbalat, Kamal, 224
Janbalat, Nayifa, 61, 63
Janbalat, Sa'id, 30, 58, 59, 60, 61, 69, 73, 74, 169, 170, 171, 181, 183, 186, 189, 191; imprisonment of, 188; property confiscated, 187; death of, 197; question of role in massacres, 190; tuberculosis of, 188
Janbalat, Salim, 184, 187
"Janbalat" faction, 18, 19
Janbalat family, 17, 18, 28, 53, 54, 58, 123, 186
al-Jazzar Pasha, Ahmad, 19, 20, 40
Jbail, 12, 13, 15
Jedda, massacre at, 105
Jehenne, Rear Admiral, 110, 117
Jessup, Henri Harris, 55
Jesuits, 34
Jews, 13, 20, 22, 23, 25, 26, 37, 40, 77, 100, 135, 156, 159, 217, 223, 226; voluntary contribution to reparations, 159
Jezzine, 46, 49, 59, 60, 123, 176, 183, 184, 189, 190; killings in, 182

al-Kabir, Ali Bey, 3
al-Kal'ani, 61
Karam, Yusuf, 53, 65, 67, 174
Kayfani, Na'um, 209
Kfar Biraan, looting of, 77
Kfar Nabrakh, 164
Khalid Pasha, 135, 137, 140, 147, 152, 181
Khalwat al-Baiada, 61
Khatir, Abdallah Abu, 65
Khayr, Abduh Efendi, 95
Khazin family, 16, 17, 18, 19, 23, 43, 44, 45, 211
al-Khuri, Bishara, 222
Khurshid Pasha, 45, 50, 56, 73, 75, 151, 204, 205, 206, 207, 209, 211, 213

INDEX

Kisrawan, 34, 43–5, 49, 50, 51, 52, 53, 56, 67, 125, 129, 211; rebellion in, 20
Kitab al-ahzan, 67, 68, 80, 81, 98
al-Kudari, Mahmud, 98
Kurds, 69, 85, 88, 93, 100, 137

La Gorce, Pierre de, 109
La Valette, 101, 102, 105, 120, 121, 194, 203, 207, 209, 212, 214, 216
land: ownership patterns of, 16, 158; restoration of confiscated, 186
Lannes, Napoleon Auguste, 109
Lanusse, Chief Secretary, 78, 81, 82, 88, 134, 135, 137, 138, 144, 145, 147
Latif, Marun, 174
Lebanon: control of, difficulties of, 179–80; creation of, 219; demographic change in, 222; equilibrium of coexistence, 219; independence of, 214; modern institutions of, 221; population figures, 177; reorganization of, 216; structure of, 220
leniency towards instigators, 184, 208
livestock, stealing of, 165, 166
Lobanov-Rostovski, A.B., 216
looting, 47, 48, 50, 67, 69, 72, 73, 88, 89, 92, 93, 102, 128, 145, 146, 165, 167, 181, 182; recovery of property, 139, 154, 155, 172, 201
Ludolf, Count, 199

Ma'n family, 15, 16, 17, 23, 24, 37, 39
al-Mahayni, Salim Agha Shurbaji, 85, 88, 98
Mahmud II, Sultan, 103, 106
al-Maidan quarter of Damascus, 134
male children, adulation of, 32
al-Ma'luf, Isa Iskandar, 37
Maronite Christians, 10, 11, 12, 17, 18, 23, 30, 39, 43, 44, 45, 48, 49, 52, 53, 56, 60, 65, 75, 108, 109, 111, 130, 175, 176, 180, 196, 208, 209, 210, 212, 213, 214, 215, 216, 217, 218, 219, 220, 222, 223, 224, 228; migration of, 13, 222; reconciliation with Druzes, 21, 102, 112; relations with Druzes, 22, 27, 45–6, 105, 106, 204, 212; rising of, 20; role of clergy, 6
Maronite Young Men's League, 46, 56
Martin, Vice-Admiral, 110
mattresses: distribution of, 171; requisitioning of, 154
Mecca, pilgrimage to, 9, 14, 147

Medawwar, Ibrahim, 95
Mehmet Namık Pasha, 103–5
Messageries Maritimes, 115, 117
Metn, 21, 34, 45, 49, 50, 51, 54, 56, 65, 66, 67, 164, 181, 184; rebellion in, 20
Metternich, Prince von, 28
Mishaqa, Ibrahim, 70
Mishaqa, Jibra'il, 69
Mishaqa, Mikha'il, 38, 39, 40, 39, 64, 73, 79, 80, 81, 82, 88, 98; escape of, 93–4
Mishaqa, Rufa'il, 69, 70
Mishaqa family, 38, 39
Misk family, 91
missionaries, 56; American, 71, 90, 185; Catholic, 18; European, 34; Presbyterian, 35, 55, 79
monasteries, attacks on, 47, 92
money-lending, 23, 26, 37, 38, 159
Moore, Noel, 75, 76, 142, 146, 147, 199, 200, 201, 203, 204, 209
mosques, building of, 77
Mount Lebanon, 8, 9, 12, 13, 16, 20, 22, 24, 170, 219; and Ottoman administration, 15, 27, 28; as Maronite haven, 11; as refuge for criminals, 214; autonomy of, 17, 33; bandits on, 205; blockaded by Egypt, 21; class formation in, 3; devastation of, 164; French interest in, 122, 126, 127; French troops in, 123, 125; Fuad Pasha in, 172; lack of leadership, 192; land ownership in, 158; proposed direct Ottoman rule, 129, 214; proposed division of, 200; raising of reparations, 170; reconstruction of, 164–92; relief measures for, 169; reorganization of, 224; tension in, 40, 46
Mu'ammar Pasha, 103, 135, 136, 137, 138
al-Mubayyad, Yusuf, 59–60
mudabbir, position of, 18
Muhammad Ali Bey, 148, 150
Muhammad Ali Pasha, 3, 10, 20, 28, 224
Muhammad Sa'id Bey, 88
Muhammad Suwaydan Agha, 203
mulberry cultivation, 43
multazim see tax farmers
*muqata'ji*s, 16, 17, 19, 24, 30, 32, 193
Muslim notables, 14, 26, 81, 82, 84, 95, 96, 122, 134, 145, 156; arrests of, 142; disarming of, 27; trials of, 143
Muslims, 11, 13, 74, 75, 78, 79, 81, 93, 100, 104, 108, 117, 118, 129, 133, 134, 138,

139, 144, 153, 156, 157, 159, 165, 166, 223; and reparations, 154; hostility to Christians, 146; killing of, 87
Mustafa Pasha, 121, 151, 185
Mustafa Shukri Efendi, 70, 71
Mutasarrifiyya, institution of, 7, 216, 217, 218, 225
Muzhir family, 17

Najeau, Father, 134
Nakad, Bashir Miri, 73, 184, 186
Nakad, Khattar, 71
Nakad family, 70, 74
Napoleon III, 108, 109, 110, 111, 112, 113, 115, 129, 130
narrative, revival of, 4
Nassif, Dahir, 168
Nasuh Pasha, 143
National Pact (1943), 220, 222
Na'um, Athanasius, 47, 48
al-Nawafli, 61
Nestorians, 10
Ni'ma, Abdallah, 60
Nimr, Muhammad Agha, 80
notables *see* Muslims *and* Christians
Novikow, E.P., 199, 201, 208, 212
Nuri Bey, 65
al-Nuri, Sa'id Agha, 98

Osman Bey, 148, 150
Osmont, Colonel, 116, 117, 124, 139
Ottoman administration, 9, 13, 15, 20, 27, 28, 29, 34, 42, 56, 59, 68, 69, 70, 71, 73, 102, 107, 129, 136, 138, 142, 152, 160, 163, 167, 170, 175, 181, 185, 187, 190, 191, 194, 198, 202, 213, 214, 215, 217, 219, 220, 225; alleged responsibility for massacres, 203, 205; troops, 50, 58, 60, 62, 63, 64, 65, 69, 74, 82, 97, 103, 116, 122, 124, 146, 171, 179, 180, 190, 198, 205, 208, 217, 228 (efficiency questioned, 147; land in Beirut, 130; mistreatment by, 172; punishment of, 143; sent to Syria, 105)
Ottoman empire, 3, 10, 14, 21, 44, 48, 51, 74, 89, 100, 101, 103, 105, 110, 113, 114, 118, 120, 125, 133, 134, 155, 172, 177, 193, 206, 209, 221, 227; decline of, 22; economic troubles of, 169; Europeans within, 23; in Syria, 21; judged unfit to rule, 204; occupation of, 2; rebellion against, 40; regional concerns of, 7; relations with Europeans, 144; relations with France, 119, 121, 173; status of minorities, 6; weakening of central power, 5
Ottoman Land Code (1858), 26
Outrey, Maxime, 79, 82, 89, 97, 98, 126, 130, 134, 135, 136, 138, 149, 158

Palestinians, 223, 224
Palmerston, Lord, 111, 112
Paynter, Captain, 193
Persigny, Victor Fialin, 111, 112
Perthuis, Countess de, 118, 121
Perthuis, Edmond de, 117, 118, 119, 201
Perthuis, Louise de, 118, 127
Pestalozza, Dr, 188
police force, established in Mount Lebanon, 48
Porter, J.L., 35–6
Poujoulat, Baptistin, 115, 117, 122
Progressive Socialist Party, 225
Protestant church, 11, 36, 217
Prussia, 21, 108, 109, 111, 112, 113, 142, 152, 199, 200, 202, 216; consulate, 90, 91

*qabaday*s, 34, 35, 37, 41
Qabb Elias, 124–5, 179; French troops at, 125
Qadro, Faris Agha, 68
Qasim Husayn al-Din, 181
Qatana, Muhammad, 80
qaymaqam system, 27, 28, 29, 35, 37, 181, 189, 193 *see also* Double Qaymaqamate
"Qaysi" faction, 18

Rafeq, Abdul-Karim, 142
Rashaiya, 36, 63, 157, 179, 180; garrisons at, 205; massacre at, 63–4, 79, 81, 82, 97, 99, 148, 164, 182, 203, 204, 210; refugees from, 154
Raslan, Muhammad Qasim, 184
Ra'uf Bey, 107, 122
al-Rayyis, Jiryus, 62
refugees, 74, 75, 170, 173; Christian, 134 (in Damascus, 79, 133); in Beirut, 76, 136, 198; Muslim, 165; relief for, 135, 152, 154, 168, 169; resettlement of, 175
Règlement Shakib Effendi, 30
Rehfues, Commissioner de, 142, 158, 199, 208
relief, for refugees *see* refugees

INDEX

reparations, 169, 173, 174, 176, 186, 201
resettlement policy, 184
Reshid Pasha, Mustafa, 106
revenge, 167, 213
Riza Pasha, 101
Robson, Smylie, 79, 90, 91, 133, 138, 159
Rogers, E.T., 188
Rose, Colonel, 39, 41, 42
Rushdi Pasha, 101
Russell, Lord John, 112, 196
Russia, 21, 23, 28, 102, 108, 109, 111, 112, 113, 144, 148, 199, 202, 215, 216, 217; blamed for troubles, 101, 213
Russian consul, 90, 135
Rüstü Pasha, Şirvanizade Mehmet, 106, 153

Saʿad al-Din, 58, 62
Sabit, Asad, 209
Saʿid, Ali, 184
Said, Edward, 3
Salibi, Kamal, 219
Salih, Shaykh, 96
Salih Zaki Bey, 87, 88
al-Samman, Abd al-Karim, 84
al-Sawtari, Muhammad, 94
sectarianism, 4, 5, 6, 19, 22, 24, 26, 27, 45, 81, 100, 160
Selim Pasha, death of, 145
Shahin, Taniyus, 44, 50, 54, 56, 65
Shakib Efendi, 30
Shakir Pasha, 151
Shalhub, Mitri, 84
Shami, Antun, 84
Shams, Salim, 58
al-Shamʿuni, Zakkhur, 41
al-Shantiri, Yusuf, 65
Shaqra, Husayn, 36
Shawish, Khalil, 72-3
Shawqat Efendi, 106
shaykh al-shabab, 33, 37, 44, 50, 212
Shehadi, Khalil, 89
Shiʿi Muslims, 6, 11, 12, 13, 15, 17, 30, 36, 60, 61, 64, 66, 68, 77, 137, 217, 222, 223, 224; "Sevener," 12; "Twelver," 12
Shibli, Muhy al-Din, 184, 186
Shihab dynasty, 15, 16, 17, 18, 23, 26, 27, 28, 37, 38, 39, 46, 50, 54, 58, 61, 62, 63, 64, 74, 80, 120, 209, 211, 212, 214, 216; members killed, 62
Shihab, Emir Ali, 63
Shihab, Emir Haydar, 17

Shihab, Fuad, 222
Shihab, Saʿad al-Din, 189, 191
Shihab, Yusuf, 19; execution of, 20
Shuf, 12, 13, 17, 23, 34, 48, 52, 53, 54, 60, 67, 71, 73; Ottoman control of, 15
Shurbaji, Abdallah, 94, 95
Sidon, 13, 74, 75, 151, 215, 216; massacre at, 205
silk farming, 34, 47, 50, 55, 166, 176, 178
silk trade, 17, 18, 22, 23, 24, 37, 38, 39, 43, 110, 162, 174, 185
Souvenirs de Syrie, 130
starvation, 171
Suez Canal, 110, 111
Süleyman I, Sultan, 2
Süleyman Nuri Bey, 151
Süleyman Pasha, 3, 20
al-Sulh, Riyad, 222
Sunni Muslims, 6, 11, 13, 15, 17, 20, 23, 30, 60, 68, 75, 137, 217, 218, 219, 221, 222, 223
Syria, 13, 20, 21, 24, 34, 35, 40, 76, 79, 163, 187, 202, 210, 215, 221; and silk trade, 24; as "French territory," 115; as crossroad, 9; Catholic interest in, 18; conquered by Ibrahim Pasha, 20; Egyptian occupation, 26; reconquered by Ottomans, 26; reorganization of, 206; structure of, 220; treasury of, depleted, 169

Tahir Pasha, 69, 70, 71, 105, 106, 151, 189, 190, 191
Talhuq, Hasan, 181
Talhuq, Husayn, 183, 188
Talhuq family, 17, 18, 51, 54, 184
Tami, Ali, 168
Tanzimat reforms, 2, 22, 26, 100, 102, 206
Tassif Pasha, 105
Tawil, Hasan Agha, 62
tax farmers, 14, 15, 16, 34
taxation, 14, 21, 22, 28, 29, 43, 44, 170; collection of, 158; disbursement of funds, problem of, 161; of Damascus population, 156-63; of land, 16; of Mount Lebanon, 20
textile industry, in Damascus, 25
Thouvenel, Edouard-Antoine, 65, 109, 110, 111, 112, 113, 114, 127, 130, 212
al-Tinawi, Abd Agha, 80
Tiyan, Mansur, 209

town life, nature of, 31–46
Tripoli, 13
Tubiyya Awn, 46, 49, 56, 57, 176, 209, 210, 211, 212
Tyre, 74, 75

Umar Pasha, 27, 77, 104, 171, 176, 178, 187
al-Umari, Abd al-Hadi, 143
Umayyad dynasty, 9, 11
Umayyad Mosque, 83, 85, 89, 90, 146; alleged Christian plot against, 137
United Kingdom, 22, 23, 28, 30, 42, 103, 105, 108, 109, 112, 113, 130, 151, 159, 163, 180, 187, 188, 195, 197, 198, 202, 204, 207, 210, 213, 214, 215; consulate, 42, 90, 91, 104, 122, 134 (*see also* British consul); warships present, 60, 63
United States of America (USA), 39; consulate, 90
Uthman Bey, 58, 59, 61, 62

Vatican, 18
village life, nature of, 31–46

Wadi Shahrut, 51
Wadi Taym, 12, 15, 21, 49, 56, 58, 61, 62
wakil system, 29, 30
Wasfi Efendi, 209, 213

water, supplies of, 8, 9, 31, 33, 116, 174; cutting of, 55
weapons, imported by Maronites, 210
Weckbecker, Commissioner de, 199, 200, 201, 208, 214
West, impact of, 2
women: abduction of, 89, 99, 139; assaults on, 171; escape from Damascus, 96; rape of, 171; suffering of, 166; treatment of, 72, 137, 184; work of, 31

"Yazbaki" faction, 18, 19, 191
Yazigi, Esber, 95
Yazigi, Hasan Agha, 69
"Yemeni" faction, 18
Yorgaki, Mr, 82
Yusuf, Marun, 165
Yusuf Agha, 58

Zabadani, village, 79
Zahleh, 33–7, 51, 52, 53, 64, 65, 151, 173, 175, 182, 184, 191, 215; defeat of, 67, 69, 72, 81, 103, 189 (celebrated in Damascus, 68, 81, 83); entrenchment of, 66; fighting in, 66, 79, 82, 101; killings at, 183; proposed separate status for, 216; rebuilding of, 174
Zayd al-Din, 189